THE RUNNING KIND

THE RUNNING KIND
LISTENING TO MERLE HAGGARD

DAVID CANTWELL

UNIVERSITY OF TEXAS PRESS ❦ AUSTIN

Originally published in 2013 as *Merle Haggard: The Running Kind*

First edition © 2013 by David Cantwell
Revised edition copyright © 2022 by David Cantwell
All rights reserved
Printed in the United States of America

♾ The paper used in this book meets the minimum requirements of ANSI/NISO Z39.48-1992 (R1997) (Permanence of Paper).

Library of Congress Cataloging-in-Publication Data

Names: Cantwell, David, author. | Cantwell, David. Merle Haggard.
Title: The running kind : listening to Merle Haggard / David Cantwell.
Other titles: American music series.
Description: Revised edition. | Austin : University of Texas Press,
    2022. | Series: American music series | "Originally published in
    2013 as Merle Haggard: the running kind"—Title page verso. |
    Includes bibliographical references and index.
Identifiers: LCCN 2021038715
ISBN 978-1-4773-2236-9 (cloth)
ISBN 978-1-4773-2568-1 (PDF)
ISBN 978-1-4773-2569-8 (ePub)
Subjects: LCSH: Haggard, Merle. | Haggard, Merle—Criticism
    and interpretation. | Country music—History and criticism. |
    Country musicians—United States—Biography.
Classification: LCC ML420.H115 C36 2022 |
    DDC 782.421642092 [B]—dc23
LC record available at https://lccn.loc.gov/2021038715

doi:10.7560/322369

His wild kind has been among us always, since the beginning: a young

man with his temptations, a hero without wings.

OWEN WISTER

Everything in a life depends on how that life accepts its limits...

JAMES BALDWIN

CONTENTS

THE RUNNING KIND

INTRODUCTION

"SILVER WINGS"

KANSAS CITY, MISSOURI, SEPTEMBER 14, 2001

O n the Friday after terrorist attacks murdered thousands, crashed four airliners, and reduced New York City's Twin Towers to rubble, Merle Haggard played a concert in Kansas City, Missouri. The instant he took the stage, he was pelted with requests—demands, really—that quickly coalesced into an impatient chant.

> *Fight! N! Side!*
> *Fight! N! Side!*
> *Fight! N! Side!*

It went on and on like that, the fans yelling at the singer, for what seemed like forever. For his part, Merle had the look of a man who knew full well what it was going to be like this night but who was irritated and disappointed all the same when he found out he was right again. He sighed.

For just a second there, the Hag appeared not like a star at all, but like the old man he was, vulnerable and a little frail: at sixty-four, he was only half a decade or so beyond having had his arteries scraped clean by angioplasty. He looked small, too: Merle stood five feet seven but needed cowboy boots to do it. Most of all that evening, he looked world-weary and a little put out by all these people screaming at him, as if they really imagined they could order him around. Hadn't they been paying attention to the words they'd been singing along with all these years? Not even his own mama had been able to tell Merle Haggard what to do.

Haggard shook his head slowly from side to side. And like so much else in his career, the gesture might have been interpreted in a number of ways. Was he telling the audience that he planned to play what he damned well pleased, no matter how aggressive their requests? Was he expressing disbelief at the audience's enthusiasm for him, or disgust at his fans' insistence on a fightin' side he seemed, just then, unable or unwilling to muster? Was he merely shaking loose the cobwebs of one more day spent staring out the window of his tour bus? Or was he maybe wishing he'd never stepped off it, longing instead to be back on board a Silver Eagle that was so small and known and comfortable that it felt like home sweet home but that felt like a prison cell, as well, and for the same reasons?

Merle didn't speak. He just leaned into the mike and started to sing:

> *Silver wings, shining in the sunlight*
> *Roaring engines, headed somewhere in flight*
> *They're taking you away and leaving me lonely*
> *Silver wings, slowly fading out of sight*

It was a song he'd written a very long time ago, back in the late sixties when it seemed every song Merle Haggard wrote became an instant country classic—and this in an era when country records routinely shimmered with pop appeal and when not a few pop hits exploited a twang and fresh-air charm swiped from their country cousins. The song was "Silver Wings," and in 1969 it had played B-side to his "Workin' Man Blues" single, the hit that had provided him with something of a nom de plume in those final moments before another hit, "Okie from Muskogee," became his new signature song and new identity. "Okie from Muskogee" and its follow-up release, "The Fightin' Side of Me," had freed Haggard forever from mere country stardom, while also chaining him tightly to an image he had to fight to live down. Except, that is, whenever he made a point of living up to it, in the process foiling yet again the expectations of anyone who'd have preferred he live it down. The only person who got to be the boss of Merle Haggard was Merle Haggard.

Haggard didn't leave the stage that night without performing "The

Fightin' Side of Me," of course. But he did it only when he was ready and in the manner he wanted. This show's version of "Fightin' Side" didn't threaten a "boot in yer ass," in the "just-out-lookin'-for-a-fight" style of "Courtesy of the Red, White and Blue (The Angry American)," the still-to-come Toby Keith hit that would soon serve as a "Fightin' Side" for a new century. Merle's "Fightin' Side," this night, was much more in the way of a heavy sigh and a rolling up of the sleeves in order to tackle dirty but necessary work. And members of that evening's audience (though not without a few to-be-expected exceptions) sang along in the same sober fashion Merle went out of his way to model. "We've been getting a lot of requests for this one this week," he introduced the song. "We hadn't had to play it for a very long time." Another heavy sigh, and then: "Fortunately."

"This country doesn't need to be incited with 'Fightin' Side of Me,'" he explained to me a few weeks later when I asked him about what I'd seen. "It needs to know that we're together, but it sure doesn't need to be incited."

On record all those years ago, Merle had sung the haunted lines of "Silver Wings" with an aching lilt, backed by a doom-saying piano figure that sounded anguished and felt hopeless. Even so, thanks to the song's relaxed melody and the record's shimmering string arrangement, Merle had created a "Silver Wings" back then that felt openhearted and generous. That "Silver Wings" offered heartache at its just-loveliest. Tonight, though, Merle's pretty images—metal wings shining in sunlight all too reminiscent of that Tuesday's impossibly bright and blue sky—sounded hideous. He sang the familiar words in a voice choked and dazed, like he might be about to throw up. The boisterous crowd, which had been spoiling for a fight only a moment before, was shamed silent, turned reverent in a breath. All that rage was pushed aside to reveal the tears and still-bleeding wound beneath.

He closed his show that night, as he so often had, with "Okie from Muskogee." The crowd sang along with every word but sounded especially fierce and determined on the line "We still wave Old Glory down at the courthouse" and on that word "proud."

"I'm proud to be an Okie from Muskogee."

Since he first sang those words in 1969, Merle Haggard had enjoyed artistic and professional triumphs few can match. He'd charted more than one hundred country hits, including thirty-eight chart-toppers and seventy-one top tens. He'd acted in films and on television, entertained presidents, and soberly appraised his nation from the cover of *Time*. He'd released dozens of studio albums and another half dozen or more live ones, performed upward of ten thousand concerts, been inducted into the Country Music Hall of Fame, and seen his songs performed by everyone from Dean Martin to Lynyrd Skynyrd to Elvis Costello, from Tammy Wynette and Willie Nelson to the Grateful Dead and Bob Dylan. In 2011 he was even feted, alongside Paul McCartney and Oprah Winfrey, as a Kennedy Center honoree. So you couldn't blame the man for taking a lot of pride in what he'd accomplished. As he crowed in one song from the heady years just after "Okie from Muskogee" sent him down the road to becoming not only a star but an icon and even, momentarily, an American idol: "Lord! Lord! I've done it all!"

So what? Half a century on, Merle Haggard is best known, still, for one phrase, for one irresistible musical hook (love it or leave it, but try not to sing along!), for one politically charged, era-defining, and, as it played out, era-transcending declaration. He wrote hundreds of other songs, and dozens of those were stone country classics, but today, when people beyond his core audience recognize the name Merle Haggard at all, it's overwhelmingly for that one damned song. The Hag did it all, but he's famous ("infamous," some would charge) for a single, ideologically loaded shotgun blast of what, from here in the twenty-first century, we recognize as an early heartland rehearsal of identity politics, one early return of fire in what became termed the Culture War: "I'm proud to be an Okie from Muskogee."

In its first draft, the Culture War was called the Generation Gap, and that's where I come in. I bought my very first 45 rpm record, "War," by Edwin Starr, in the summer of 1970, but the truth is I settled for "War" only because the store was out of my first choice, "The Fightin' Side of Me," by Merle Haggard. I was just nine, so if I sensed any political tension between my favorites it was inchoate: I wanted both records because I thought both records sounded cool. I still do. The political contradictions became apparent to me soon enough, though. I grew up in a hard-toiling blue-collar household, the rock-and-soul son of a country-music-favoring father, himself a union man who worked his ass off for a plumbing and heating company. My dad's kitchen-table talk—about the hippies, "the Blacks," the Vietnam War, welfare, and, always, the struggle to keep a roof over our heads and food on the table—was echoed in any number of Merle Haggard lyrics. I've been thinking about the ideas Haggard sang about ever since, seconding an argument here and rejecting others there but singing along with his indelible melodies either way. I'm not alone: as much as any American musical artist, and certainly as much as any country artist, Haggard, in his music, intersected with the great issues of his times—those surrounding class and race, war and peace, and, most of all, freedom.

This book is the attempt of this critic and more-or-less lifelong Merle Haggard fan at writing a monograph on the man's music—on the songs he wrote and, a key but too-often-elided distinction, the records he made. What it is *not* is a biography. Haggard deserves a doorstop along the lines of what RJ Smith has written for James Brown or what Gary Giddins is doing for Bing Crosby (to choose artists of comparable significance to Haggard), but that's not the intent here. Of course, the basic plot points of Haggard's life get covered here. I was fortunate to interview Haggard a few times over the years and will quote some from our conversations, but for the biographical details I've relied almost exclusively on the many times Haggard went on record, at length, about his life. Most notably I've relied on his two autobiographies, the stylish *Sing Me Back Home* (from 1981, written with Peggy Russell) and the gussied-up transcription *House of Memories* (1999, with Tom Carter), plus a couple of dozen lengthy magazine profiles and countless interviews, reviews, and previews in daily and weekly periodicals stretching across fifty years.

I'm much less interested in recounting Haggard's life story for its own sake (that is, in trivia) than in engaging the character Haggard and his audience created through the decades. What I hope to offer is strong-minded criticism—close listening, in historical and social contexts—of one of the singular careers in American popular music. Haggard released a staggering eighty-plus albums (a total that nearly doubles if you count best-of sets and other off-brand anthologies), so what follows isn't comprehensive—some of my own favorite Haggard tracks don't get so much as a mention. I am going to focus primarily on the first half of his career, roughly the middle 1960s through the middle 1980s, when Haggard created the bulk of his best music. I particularly want to look at that period in the late sixties and early seventies when his music mattered most widely and intensely—and helped to invent the America we live in today. Let's call that Merle's Muskogee Moment, those years when Haggard's work intersected with both the headlines and the pop charts, thanks mostly to his era-defining hit "Okie from Muskogee."

Yet Merle Haggard, his music and legacy, can't be reduced to a song.

Haggard became an adopted son of the "Okie"-saluting—and largely bourgeois—"silent majority." But he was born to the working class and nearly always wrote and sang about grown-up joys and troubles from that perspective. His songs were about working hard at jobs you hated but still coming up short on the rent. He wrote about being transformed by love and about being crushed by it, about feeling trapped by circumstances and looking to make a break. He sang, imperfectly, about American racism when his country contemporaries didn't dare. He regularly sang one version or another of "ain't no woman gonna change the way I think," but notably that stance almost always left his characters depressed and alone. His patriotism was passionate and, at times, devolved to a nationalism that conflated mere symbols of freedom for the thing itself, but his attitudes both softened and strengthened in his final years.

He was deemed a "conservative," of course, repeatedly, and that was not wrong. But his body of work should also be heard as a type of what critic Ellen Willis terms cultural radicalism, a "celebration of freedom and pleasure and its resistance to compulsive, alienated work." His rebellions understood, and were even respectful of, everyday blue-collar conformities but were not tamed by them. At the same time, his defiance was typically subsumed into a type critic Raymond Williams identifies as the "exile." He "may support the principles of dissenting causes, but…cannot join them. He is too wary of being caught and compromised. What he has primarily to defend is his own living pattern, his own mind, and almost any relationship is a potential threat to this." Except when it wasn't. Haggard was dynamic and contradictory, moment to moment and across the decades.

Still, in the public's mind, Merle Haggard *is* the Okie from Muskogee, a perception as prevalent among fans as detractors. So our first order of business is a reminder that the man known as the "Okie from Muskogee" was neither. Merle Haggard was not, as his image-defining anthem concludes, "from Muskogee, Oklahoma, U-S-A." Strictly speaking, he wasn't even an Okie, not in the loaded-up-the-truck-and-moved-to-Californy sense seared into our collective imaginations by John Steinbeck's 1939 *The Grapes of Wrath* and John Ford's film version of the novel released the following year; by the Farm Security Administration (FSA) photography of Dorothea Lange, Walker Evans, and Ben Shahn; and by the *Dust Bowl Ballads* of Woody Guthrie.

Merle Haggard missed the migration so indelibly documented, and mythologized, by those earlier artists. His story skips the Exodus and begins in the Promised Land, which in his people's version of the American Dream meant the San Joaquin Valley, county of Kern, in a little town (at the time not much more than a glorified Hooverville) called Oildale, situated just on the outskirts of the city of Bakersfield, California, U-S-A.

Historians have noted that the movement of white southerners during the last century to the industrial cities of the North and to the corporate farms and oil fields of the West shares revealing parallels with the experiences of European immigrants to America. Both groups were viewed as unwelcome, not-quite-white outsiders. As both consequence of and contribution to that perception, they settled in tight-knit communities—in a Little Italy, say, or a Little Oklahoma—where the old country's foodways, entertainment preferences, religious practices, and other customs to some degree persisted, providing continuity and comfort to displaced people, and where substantial quantities of emotional energy, not to mention one's paycheck, remained devoted to the places and people left behind. Route 66 stands in the Dust Bowlers' imagination as something akin to the place held by Ellis Island in European immigrant lore. Crowded labor camps were these migrants' tenement slums. "Okie" was their Mick or Polack, wop or kike.

In the logic of this comparison, Merle Haggard wasn't an immigrant himself but first-generation, a child of immigrants. And like fellow first-generation songwriters George and Ira Gershwin and Yip Harburg (whose parents were Russian Jews), or like Jerome Kern and Sammy Cahn (the sons of German and Austrian Jews, respectively), Merle was born in the Promised Land to parents whose identity would forever be bound up with the Old Country.

Put another way, Haggard wasn't a latter-day Tom Joad, yanked from the silver screen and dropped into America from the last reel of Ford's *The Grapes of Wrath*. He was John Ford—the artist son of immigrants (Irish, in the director's case)—who had heard his ancestors' stories of struggle and discrimination all his life, was even on the receiving end of some of that contempt, but who ultimately could only imagine the thrill and terror of creating a new life in a new land that, to him, wasn't new at all but just... home. And who then turned his imaginings into art.

I like this way of thinking about Haggard because it places him in the company he deserves—not only with fellow legends of country music, but right alongside any and all contributors to our Great American Songbook.

To my ears Haggard's vocal peers include Bessie Smith and Frank Sinatra, George Jones and Aretha Franklin. He stands among songwriting greats such as Irving Berlin and Hank Williams, Chuck Berry, Bob Dylan, and Holland, Dozier, Holland—and shoulder-to-shoulder with great American artists, period.

This perspective can aid us, too, in trying to unravel "Okie from Muskogee," in terms of both the button-busting pride the song affirms in its bear hug of a particular identity and the deep ambivalence it betrays toward that identity. The song points straightforwardly to what Haggard felt he shared with his parents as a birthright, but it also underscores the great distance he felt, inevitably, from their experience, separated from it as he was by so many years and miles, not to mention by the twists and turns of his very different life. When first uttered in 1969, "I'm proud to be an Okie from Muskogee" was itself evidence of that distance, of just how far Haggard had come. After all, in the years after his parents transplanted to the San Joaquin Valley—that is, in the place and time he would grow up in the 1940s and 1950s—if you'd called Merle an "Okie," this future working-class hero likely wouldn't have taken it as some folksy honorific. He likely wouldn't have taken it at all and might've even offered to kick your teeth in for a witty rejoinder.

CHAPTER 1

"HUNGRY EYES," 1969

"A canvas-covered cabin in a crowded labor camp stand out in this memory I revive..."

That's how Merle begins his greatest record, but before he can even get his thoughts together, he's being pricked by the sharpened-knife's edge of James Burton's acoustic guitar—*A canvas* (stab) *covered cabin* (stab) *stand out*...Those stabs, and the way Merle's voice flinches ever so slightly in response, are our first signals that this particular backward glance will not be in the least "nostalgic." That's a label routinely used to describe country music, and Haggard's music specifically, sometimes even with good reason. But while "Hungry Eyes" begins with a memory revived, what follows— basically, a laying out of the material conditions that kill people's spirits and that, more slowly, kill people—is not the Good Old Days.

What Merle has in mind is painful even to recall, let alone reveal. In a country that still loves to blame poverty on the moral failures of the poor themselves, experiences like his are supposed to be shameful. Merle's too-proper, almost genteel "in this memory I revive," then, serves him as a shield. It keeps at arm's length a past the singer isn't at all sure he's prepared to face. And he has to be careful, must maintain a distance (though a *safe* distance isn't really an option), because he already knows what he's going to find. He remembers his daddy praying for a change that didn't come, and "the loss of courage as [his parents'] age began to show," and all of it reflected in his mother's "hungry eyes."

Merle's song depicts an American tragedy like something out of Arthur Miller: a father's prayers for a better way of life, ultimately futile; a mother's strong faith, whittled away; the conviction that a change must be on the way, and then...no change of any size. As a child, Haggard tells us in the song, he was "just too young to realize that another class of people put us somewhere just below." The way Merle drops down to that "realize" and drags it out...*ree-uh-liiize*...the way he makes the word bristle and ball its fists...*real lies*...it all makes plain that while Okie kids may have been innocent, they'd get taught a lesson soon enough.

Across the years this matriarch's eyes still haunt, and Haggard meets her gaze. He wills himself not to blink and dares us to do the same. At each chorus he has the melody leap tenderly when he says the word "Mama," when he sings the name "Daddy." They hungered, not for luxuries, but only for "things [they] really needed." Yet their lives were such that the most basic human needs—a roof over your head, food in your gut, and would a little respect be too much to ask?—had been elevated to luxuries, could only be *conceived* as luxuries. Merle pictures all of this, plain as day, and shudders, once again a defensive little boy: *It wasn't 'cause my daddy didn't try.* The music around him sounds hungry and exposed, too, barely clothed for most of the record by acoustic guitar and brushes that nag at a drumhead.

Halfway through, though, a string arrangement rises up, luxurious and evoking every fine thing his parents deserved, every meager thing they needed and couldn't afford. Now, here, Haggard has those strings glitter and shimmer all around him, just for show and just because he can. And because they sound like tears.

"Hungry Eyes" didn't so much as dent the pop charts, but on country radio it climbed to #1 in May 1969. Its all-too-apt B-side was "California Blues." He's headed, Haggard tells us in his version of the old Jimmie Rodgers song, to a place "where they sleep out ev-er-ee night." To hear Haggard sing "California Blues" with "Hungry Eyes" still echoing in your ears makes it hard to miss his point. Folks out West don't bed down under California stars just because the weather is pleasant. They sleep outside because they don't have houses. A "canvas-covered cabin," after all, is just a fancy name for a tent.

A half decade earlier, soul master Sam Cooke had conjured an image similar to the one "Hungry Eyes" recalls with such caution. "I was born by the river in a little tent," Cooke sings in "A Change Is Gonna Come," not merely reviving a memory but marching forward from it with a confidence bred of gospel community and shared struggle. *I know that a change is gonna come.*

"Hungry Eyes" cries a reply, but from his dead-or-dying end of the 1960s, Merle Haggard doesn't sound confident; he sounds alone. He's seen people who prayed for a better life, too, he insists, people with faith just as strong. *But I don't recall a change of any size.* He sure as hell recalls the unanswered prayers, though, and he'll never forget those eyes.

CHAPTER 2

THE ROOTS OF HIS RAISING

In 1938 the agricultural economist Paul Taylor (aka Dorothea Lange's husband) delivered an address to the Commonwealth Club of California entitled "What Shall We Do with Them?" "Them" were the Okies, and Taylor had bad news for his well-heeled and already-alarmed San Francisco audience: "Between the middle of 1935 and the end of 1937" and "by automobile alone," at least 221,000 "them" had entered the state of California. This total, we now know, included four members of the Haggard family. It was in the middle of 1935 that James and Flossie Haggard loaded their two kids into a 1926 Chevy and motored west on Route 66. And it was in 1937, in California, that Flossie gave birth to the family's third child, a boy, whom she and James named Merle Ronald.

Save for a couple of years' residence in Nashville during the close of the 1970s, California is where Jim and Flossie's youngest lived his entire life. He was, however, awarded the status of "Honorary Okie" in 1969. We can hear the public presentation of the honor on the album he released later that year, *Okie from Muskogee: Recorded "Live" in Muskogee, Oklahoma.* The mayor of Muskogee, milking the biggest chamber of commerce moment he'd ever have, awards Haggard the key to the city and declares the thirty-two-year-old singer an official Okie. "I've been called one all my life," the Hag laughs. "I might as well put the pin on." Then, to great cheers: "I'm proud of it!"

"I wasn't actually born here in Muskogee," Merle explains a bit later, by way of introducing the song that made the award possible. "But...I think most all of my dad's folks were born between here and Checotah somewhere." He'd never visited before, but "Muskogee was a word and a town that I've heard about since I was knee-high."

Both of Merle's parents, as well as his two older siblings, Lowell and Lillian, were from the general Muskogee vicinity. The four of them left northeast Oklahoma and lit out for California on July 15, 1935, at "about eleven o'clock in the morning." We know the date and hour of their departure thanks to an interview Merle's mother did with *American Heritage* in 1977 (she was about to turn seventy-five), part of a feature on Dust Bowl refugees and their escape hatch of choice, "Route 66: Ghost Road of the Okies." Flossie Haggard's account is iconic, as if it had been ripped straight from John Steinbeck's typewriter. Flossie remembered that the Haggards "headed for California on Route 66," at that point still unpaved for long stretches, "as many friends and neighbors had already done." The family's "1926 model Chevrolet which Jim had overhauled" was crammed with much of what they owned, and it pulled a two-wheel trailer piled high with the rest:

> We had all our groceries with us—home sugar-cured bacon in a lard can, potatoes, canned vegetables, and fruit. We camped at night and I cooked bread in a Dutch oven....My sister Flora and family had gone to California a year before, so she sent us forty dollars to pay our expenses. I know now it took a lot of nerve to start so poorly equipped, but the Good Lord was with us and we made it in four days.

In a 2003 interview with music writer Dave Hoekstra, Merle remembered his father telling him that the trip actually took seven days, not four, but whatever its length, the journey wasn't without harrowing moments. In the breath-robbing heat of an Arizona summer, the Chevy broke down. And then their water ran out:

> Just when I thought we weren't going to make it, I saw this boy coming down the highway on a bicycle. He was going all the way from Kentucky to Fresno. He shared a quart of water with us and helped us fix the car. Everybody'd been treating us like trash, and I told this boy, "I'm glad to see there's still some decent folks left in this world."

Worsening their troubles, Flossie was ailing. So when a filling station attendant suggested they wait for nightfall before making their way across the Mojave Desert, they took his advice and briefly camped just across the Colorado River from Needles, California. When at last they reached the lush San Joaquin Valley, Flossie recalled:

> We found many of our friends living in shacks made of cardboard or anything that could make a shelter from the sun, and provide a place to call home. They were working people, they did anything they could find to do, mostly picking fruit until cotton-picking time. Many lived principally on cull fruits that the growers rejected and which could be gotten without cost.

This, too, is all very Joads-ian. Take a picture and it would fit nicely into an exhibit of Dorothea Lange photos. Give it a melody and you'd have a Woody Guthrie song. Better yet, you'd have a song Merle recorded in 1968 called "California Cottonfields."

"Cottonfields" opens with a deep, foreboding nylon-string guitar lick, courtesy of Nashville Cat Jerry Reed. That kickoff has always reminded me a bit of thunder rumbling in the distance: Could be a storm's on the way, it says. But only on the way, and only maybe, so warnings are shoved quickly aside in favor of James Burton's Dobro, which dances about with a sprightly, aspiring spring in its step. Merle sets the scene: A poor family's patriarch dreams of getting out from under his "run-down, mortgaged Oklahoma farm," then finally saves and scrapes together the Do-Re-Mi to do it. He loads his family and a few belongings into an old Model A while kin, friends, and other neighbors drop by either to pick the bones ("Some folks came to say farewell and see what all we had to sell") or to wish them luck ("Some just came to shake my daddy's hand"), and then the man and his family are off, California-bound.

"California was his dream of paradise," Merle explains. Here's why: "For he had seen pictures in magazines that told him so." Merle's voice catches just a bit at that, choking up in bitter sympathy. At each chorus, the melody launches Hag's baritone with an almost anthemic lift, then yanks his voice back to dusty, dissatisfied earth. That's because Haggard knows, now, what the song's father didn't know, then; he knows that the truth of that dream wasn't going to be a paradise at all but "labor camps...filled with worried men with broken dreams." He knows California would likely offer the man, at best, only backbreaking work at crap wages. And that some rich man's cotton fields would be "as close to wealth as Daddy ever came."

The Haggards settled just outside of Bakersfield in an area called Oildale. This was "a collection of company camps and small settlements—Oil Center, Standard Camp, Riverview" that, according to memoirist and historian Gerald Haslam, were separated from Bakersfield proper by "dairies and farms, the Kern River and a certain frame of mind." Haslam, an Oildale native and Merle's grade-school classmate, writes that most folks there "didn't give a hoot for genteel aspirations." Citing the Oildale community's "supposed bigotry," Haslam notes, too, that the town "developed a reputation for roughness and racism."

The Haggards were lucky as hell compared to many other new Oildale residents. When they arrived in the summer of 1935, Jim and Flossie got work, almost immediately, at a small dairy, milking and tending forty Holsteins. This good fortune helped the Haggards avoid the prospect of what Steinbeck once described with grim irony as "Starvation under the Orange Trees." Nor did Merle's parents do time as what Steinbeck elsewhere termed "The Harvest Gypsies." Merle's future rival/friend Buck Owens called them "fruit tramps," those migrant laborers who moved up and down the state picking plums and lettuce, working the California apple orchards and cotton fields. The dairy gig lasted only a couple of months, but fortune again smiled on the new Californians. At a time when migrant workers were typically paid twenty cents an hour or less (and frequently had to strike to get it), Jim Haggard got on as a carpenter, for twice that amount, with the Santa Fe Railroad.

Jim and Flossie and the kids didn't have to reside for long in one of the state's many crowded labor camps, either. The Haggards succeeded in getting a refrigerated train car to live in. Flossie recalled that its owner was looking for "someone to cut windows and doors to make it livable.... She offered us nine months rent to do this work." Haggard family lore, per Merle's second autobiography, *House of Memories*, has it that this woman was reluctant to set the Haggards loose on converting the reefer: "I've never heard of an Okie who'd work," she sneered. "I've never heard of one who wouldn't," Jim snapped back.

"We moved in on September 15, 1935," Flossie continued. "It was a difficult task, cutting through several inches of steel, wood and insulation, after working a full day's work at a job. But when we finished it was a comfortable place to live." Flossie kept a garden and canned what she could. These were difficult times for the Haggards, but they only had to look to family and friends, their extant dreams of paradise dashed by wage slavery in oil fields or cotton patches, to know for certain things could be far worse. "I can see Mom and Dad with shoulders low, both of them working a double row," Merle sings in another of his Okie ballads, "Tulare Dust," but reality was different. While James Haggard had spent more than his share of time in the cotton fields of Oklahoma, the Haggards avoided that fate in California. "My husband could pick 500 pounds of cotton a day," Flossie said in 1977, "but fortunately he never had to."

"California Cottonfields" has been among my favorite Haggard tracks since I first heard it as a college undergraduate in the early 1980s. It spoke of unrealized aspirations I understood all too well having watched the men in my own family work and dream and grow old, of blue-collar dreams that begin as sure things, grow ever more elusive, then fade to one more dead end, eight more hours of shoveling dirt or laying tar, and it reminded me, yet again, of what I hoped to avoid by going to college in the first place. The words to "California Cottonfields" made my heart swell and break while its rhythms swung with subtle ferocity—a potent combination. It's a testament to the intimate emotional presence of Merle's vocals and to his savvy in selecting material—and to my own youthful faith in "authenticity"—that it never occurred to me, then, that this great Merle Haggard song might not have been written by Merle Haggard. Already I knew his songs included some memorably dramatic embellishments: Haggard "turned twenty-one in prison" all right, as "Mama Tried" begins, but he wasn't "doing life without parole." Still, I figured it was just common knowledge that Merle's songs were autobiographical.

"Cottonfields" blends seamlessly with Haggard's Okie image, and it particularly echoes "Hungry Eyes." Both songs begin with what we're told is personal history, a past buried for a time but now willfully unearthed. "Cottonfields" opens with "My drifting memory goes back to the spring of '43 ...," and "Hungry Eyes" with one of the great first lines in all of country music, "A canvas-covered cabin in a crowded labor camp stand out in this memory I revive." The father in "Cottonfields" hopes for a change of luck, but the narrator/son shakes his head at the very idea: "The only change that I recall is when his dark hair turned to silver-grey." The narrator/son in "Hungry Eyes" remembers his dad praying for better times, too, but God appears unmoved by these pleas, so the story's the same in the end: "I don't recall a change of any size. Just a little loss of courage as [his] age began to show."

A few years later, I bothered to check the writing credits (a good habit to learn) and found, to my initial disbelief, that "Cottonfields" wasn't written by Haggard but cowritten by Dallas Frazier and Earl Montgomery. In the 1960s and 1970s, Dallas Frazier was one of the most successful songwriters going, penning a string of indelible country, pop, and rock hits as diverse as "There Goes My Everything," "All I Have to Offer You (Is Me)," "Beneath Still Waters," "Alley Oop," "Mohair Sam," and "Elvira," among quite a few others. In 1943, though, Frazier was just another Cali-bound Okie, a three-year-old kid out of Spiro, Oklahoma. When Dallas and his parents arrived in the San Joaquin that year, his folks went straight to the fields. "My dad and mother worked in orchards and what have you," he explained to me. "I think they pulled the olives and picked up potatoes, too, but mostly they picked cotton....My first job was picking cotton. I was six. We lived in labor camps.

"Like the one Merle sings about," he volunteered. "Canvas-covered cabins, you know. They would build a hardwood floor, just out of boards, and then they would stretch a little canvas frame over it." Which isn't to say that "California Cottonfields," with its opening images of an abandoned plow, left-behind canned goods, and a loaded-down jalopy, is simply a musical snapshot borrowed from the Frazier family album.

"Imagination always gets into songs," Frazier reckoned. "There might be a root of truth, and there's things in that particular song that is true. I think my dad did have a Model A first time we drove out [to California]. But I don't remember it all, either. I was too small, just a kid. So, it's dramatized. I tell you what, though, my dad didn't have a farm to sell [unlike the father in "Cottonfields"]. My dad was born poor and he died poor. And he was poor all in between."

In an early chapter of *The Grapes of Wrath*, Steinbeck likens his westward-bound Okie clan to a "land turtle"—slow-moving but patient.

Haggard's parents, by contrast, seem to have had a bit of the jackrabbit in them. They spent the twenties springing about the country, settling here and moving there. Up in Chicago, Jim got on at a stove factory in 1925, then was hired by Hill and Hubble, a steel company that relocated his family several times over the next couple years—first to Indiana, then to Pennsylvania, then Ohio. What's more, when Merle's parents and siblings came to California in 1935, they were actually making a return trip. They'd lived in California a few months in 1929, moving there for Flossie's health (her doctor recommended a warmer climate) and in search of a better way of life. On the road and in the big city, the Haggards necessarily acquired a worldliness that belies the naïve and ignorant Okies of stereotype.

And the Haggards want you to know it. They sympathize with the migrant masses but take pains to distinguish themselves from them, and they aren't alone. Capitalist economies create winners and losers by their very nature, a truth that's easier to ignore when times are flush, but that was impossible to avoid during the Great Depression, especially for working-class folks only just scraping by before the Crash. One angle people work to secure their shaky status in desperate times is to shove for position, in whatever puny ways they can, up the class ladder, insisting loudly upon what we might call their essential human dignity: *I've never heard of an Okie who* wouldn't *work*. A simultaneous tactic is to smash the fingers of those clinging to rungs just below, buying whole into assumptions that deny the dignity of others even while asserting your own comparative worth: *Everybody'd been treating us like trash*. Flossie's irritation is simple enough to decipher. Her family didn't deserve such treatment, because her family was decent. Trash was other people. Always is.

An all-American working-class attitude, that—as hopeful as it is defensive. Merle's mother stressed during her *American Heritage* interview that welfare was one place the Haggards never were. Merle's older sister, Lillian, underscores a similar point in a series of remembrances collected in Merle's first autobiography, *Sing Me Back Home*. "There's something else I've always wanted to clear up," she writes. "We were not papershack poor. My father was a farmer and a rancher in Oklahoma when he met my mother." Likewise, Merle emphasizes that "unlike most of the Okies, Mama and Daddy were making it on a forty-acre farm they had leased.... The farm was producing at an average rate," he says, "and Daddy had himself a good team of work horses, a wagon, some farm equipment and a '31 Model-A Ford."

Make no mistake: the Haggards' life in Oklahoma was a difficult one. But they weren't going hungry, either. The first acres they'd leased upon returning from California had been sold out from under them. They'd had to start over, again, but now they had a few cows for milk. They raised some hogs and grew a little cotton; they had a new car; they were getting by. The Haggard family was certainly doing better than most of their neighbors, many of whom were even then pulling up stakes to motor west. And they couldn't have helped but understand that the lesson of each departure was that it takes only a bad break or two for everything to unravel, for "getting by" to descend to "scraping by" and, finally, "good-bye." In the Haggards' case, Bad Break #1 was a drought in 1934 that devastated their crop. Bad Break #2 was a fire that destroyed their barn and its contents later that year.

Okie legend aside, the so-called Dust Bowl refugees mostly weren't chased out of Oklahoma—or any of the other "Okie" mother countries (Missouri, Kansas, Arkansas, and Texas)—by the Dust Bowl itself. In *American Exodus*, James Gregory notes that of the hundreds of thousands of southwestern migrants to California, only about sixteen thousand hailed from the Dust Bowl proper. So forget dust storms. The Okies confronted a perfect storm of misery and dislocation—technological transformations piled on meteorological and economic crises, often exacerbated by personal devastations like the fire at the Haggard place, all stacking up, trouble upon trouble, to send people packing. Overproduction of wheat and cotton lowered prices for those cash crops after World War I, contributing to depression in the early 1920s. In the thirties, many landowners who were paid to keep acres out of production used the money to buy tractors and other equipment, further reducing the need for farm labor and speeding the end of a sharecropping system that even in the best of times provided workers little more than subsistence living. "Then came the drought and the grasshoppers," Paul Taylor writes in "What Shall We Do with Them?" "Whole sections of the rural population already loosened by the accumulating forces of successive depressions were finally dislodged by a catastrophe of nature." That was why, Taylor explains, even as the droughts ended in the late thirties, "the tide of refugees flowing westward scarcely slacken[ed]."

After their barn and feed went up in smoke, the Haggards moved a few miles away, to Checotah, but only temporarily. "Mr. Haggard ran a service station through the winter and spring of 1935," Flossie recalled. By summer, they were gone.

The Great Depression drove tens of thousands of Okie families to leave their homes, but Americans had been flocking to California for several decades by the time the Haggards headed west for good. That line in "California Cottonfields," the one about paradise-promising magazine photos, points to one of the reasons. California had long been ballyhooed in popular culture, not to mention by the state's various chambers of commerce, as a land of unlimited opportunity and abundance, a place where the daring and ambitious could strike it rich quick or at least achieve, taking what no doubt would be only a slightly longer view, the Jeffersonian ideal of small-farm ownership. Slick magazine spreads promoted a cornucopia of natural riches and a Mediterranean-like climate, while handbills from wealthy California farmers' associations, circulated far and wide, promised plentiful employment at high wages. If you wanted to achieve the American Dream, California was the place to be.

The state's in-house marketing department was Hollywood. Think, for instance, of King Vidor's wonderful 1928 silent comedy, *Show People*, where Marion Davies plays a small-town Georgia girl who journeys west to become a movie star...and becomes one! Or of 1934's *It's a Gift*, in which W. C. Fields's character relocates to sunny Southern California to live the sweet life running an orange grove only to get rich instead via a sweet real estate deal.

It's a Gift opens with a Victrola needle dropping on a 78 rpm platter of Al Jolson's "California, Here I Come." California's the place, Jolson shouts to the world on that 1924 hit, "where bowers of flowers bloom in the spring" and where "each morning at dawning birdies sing at everything." Jolson's picture isn't in a magazine, but it nonetheless paints California as a "Big Rock Candy Mountain" come to life—and only a few days' drive away. "A garden of Eden" as Woody Guthrie phrased the expectation, "a paradise to live in or to see." Long before the Depression, Americans, the Haggards included, were jumping at the chance to go to California.

But the Okies didn't jump in the thirties; they were pushed. The difference between earlier generations of California newcomers and the ones who arrived during the diaspora of the Great Depression—the difference between the Haggards of 1929 and the Haggards of 1935—is the difference between "Where do I want to go?" and "Where in the world *can* I go?" It's the difference between the eager optimism of Jolson's "California, Here I Come" ("Open up that Golden Gate!") and the desperation of, say, Woody Guthrie's Dust Bowl–era adaptation of "Goin' Down the Road Feelin' Bad" ("I'm looking for a job at honest pay.... My children need three square meals a day"). The immediate prods for heading west naturally varied from family to specific family—"baked out" or "tractored out," "burned up" or "blown away," a bad case of ramblin' fever, or just plain busted. But as Guthrie sang in another of his songs from that time, the out-of-options result was all too often the same: "So Long, It's Been Good to Know Yuh."

When Merle's parents left Oklahoma in 1935, they were but drops in a flood of white working-class families who at that moment were being swept out of the Southwest and toward work in the oil, fruit, and cotton fields of the Pacific Coast. They hungered for Something Better but would have settled for Things They Really Needed. Frequently they got neither, because "another class of people put [them] somewhere just below."

More than *just*, actually. The California establishment has always worked overtime to ensure that its cheap immigrant laborers of the moment—the Chinese in the nineteenth century, Mexicans in the 1920s and '30s, and straight on through to today—were put in their place and that they damn well stayed there. True to form, then, Californians well up the class chain perceived the influx of so many southwestern refugees not so much as a flood but as a plague or infestation. James Gregory and fellow historian Peter La Chapelle each note that Golden State newspapers and magazines, including *California*, the official publication of the state's chamber of commerce, frequently reported on these new arrivals as if they weren't humans at all but dumb and dangerous animals, as rats or roaches, an "ever oncoming horde of undesirables" that "swarmed" and "smothered" the state. The newcomers were called ignorant and lazy, freeloaders, scum. The *Los Angeles Times* regularly referred to the migrants as "white trash." Everywhere they were portrayed as shiftless indigents who bred incessantly, were prone to crime, were so naturally filthy as to pose a public health risk, and just more or less threatened the decline of Western civilization as a whole. Up and down California's Central Valley, signs read: "No Okies."

"It's a complex situation to be called an Okie," Merle explained in 2000 to journalist RJ Smith. "You could tell what [the speakers] meant by the tone of their voice, as to whether or not it was the same as the N-word." As Merle recalled, with characteristic understatement, for a short film honoring his 1994 induction into the Country Music Hall of Fame: "They called my father Okie. Wasn't sometimes all that friendly when they said it."

"Yes, there was a lot of prejudice," Dallas Frazier remembered. "You were white trash from Oklahoma, was all. You were despised. California, the native Californian, felt they had been invaded. Being in those camps was at the bottom of the barrel as far as life goes. It was."

When we think of art and artists inspired by the Dust Bowl, Haggard is right there on the short list today with Steinbeck and Ford, Lange and Guthrie. But Merle didn't want to hear that.

During the sensation that was "Okie from Muskogee," and coming on the heels of common-man Haggard hits like "Hungry Eyes" and "Workin' Man Blues," some reporters, figuring they'd put two and two together, asked Merle what he thought of Woody Guthrie, himself proud to be an Okie from Okemah. At the time Haggard claimed he didn't know who Woody was. Well, why would he? Guthrie never sold many records, was barely known, even in Oklahoma, and was long gone from California by the time Merle would have been paying attention. Then again, Haggard was a history buff with a well-developed specialty in the tight connections between Okie and Cali music cultures...

But Merle's seemingly studious lack of interest in Guthrie aside, the Haggard clan surely could be expected to recognize their family legend mirrored back to them in the black-and-white images of Hollywood movies and FSA photos, would recognize their lives in the parched voices of popular front–era song and story, particularly *The Grapes of Wrath*. That's what Kris Kristofferson thought. In 1971, when he was among the very few country songwriters keeping up with Haggard's sky-high songwriting standards, Kristofferson told journalist Paul Hemphill that the way for Merle to quell the liberal criticism brought on by "Muskogee" and its even more strident follow-up, "The Fightin' Side of Me," would be to record an album-length tribute to *The Grapes of Wrath*. "That'd bring 'em back to roost," Kristofferson figured. It would also have furthered the connection people were making between Haggard and Guthrie, who in 1940, with "Tom Joad," had done something similar to Kristofferson's suggestion.

Kristofferson's idea might have seemed like a no-brainer, but it was never going to happen. In his liner notes to *Untamed Hawk*, the first of three Haggard box sets released by Bear Family Records, Dale Vinicur informs us that "Merle and his family have always taken issue with the Steinbeck *Grapes of Wrath* characterization of the California migrants as a hopeless and pathetic population." Trash Is Other People.

"Most of [the Okies] weren't tramps," Haggard told Vinicur. "They were just people that were relocating. Proud people that were being transplanted because of a drought. The thing that [Steinbeck] did not capture, the thing he left out, was the ingredient called pride. He had these people making some sort of forced migration like the Cherokees out of Tennessee. And it wasn't that way. They came out here with pride in their eyes."

This appraisal is revealing. Pride, after all, would seem to be just about all that poverty-stricken outlaw Tom Joad has—and he has it in abundance. At the very least, Steinbeck's Joad family is no more lacking in pride than the parents Merle creates in "Hungry Eyes," who remain hungry while losing courage with the passing years. In any event, forced relocation, whether via the Trail of Tears or Route 66, hardly precludes one from proclaiming, as did Merle in the title of a 1969 hit, "I Take a Lot of Pride in What I Am." Perhaps Merle is confusing Steinbeck's *The Grapes of Wrath*, as depicted in Ford's 1940 film, with the portrayal of poverty-stricken Georgians in Erskine Caldwell's genuinely hopeless and pathetic *Tobacco Road* (1932)— the film version of which Ford directed in 1941. Or maybe for some readers Steinbeck's work has become conflated, however bizarrely, with that era's whole cruel climate of antipathy for, and abuse of, the very people presented so sympathetically by Steinbeck and Haggard alike.

"That's not our story," Haggard told *Rolling Stone*'s Jason Fine in 2009. "We didn't yield to the Depression."

Dallas Frazier's song "California Cottonfields" is like a movie, full of wide shots and narrative sweep, akin to *The Grapes of Wrath*. Merle Haggard's "Hungry Eyes" is a photograph, and a close-up at that. That's typical— Haggard songs tend to be stingy with story, preferring instead the meditative expression of one sort or other of anxious emotion. The recording Merle and his Strangers made of "Hungry Eyes"—cut late in 1968, topping the country charts early the next year—is a musical adjunct to, and the artistic equal of, *Migrant Mother*, the photograph that Dorothea Lange took of

Florence Thompson in 1936. The women in both works, Lange's migrant mother and Haggard's "Mama," document an internal war between pride and inferiority, dignity and shame.

Merle wasn't raised by his parents in a canvas-covered cabin, let alone in a shelter, so-called, as tenuous and inhumane as the propped-up, open-air half-a-hut where Lange photographed Thompson and her children. But he grew up in a repurposed train car, which is disgrace and honor enough. And his aunt and uncle did indeed live in a labor camp tent home where Merle stayed often following his father's death. It was there that Merle learned that "Mama never had the luxuries she wanted," even in the Promised Land, even though all she wanted was what she really needed.

What could be more shameful? And I don't mean for the Haggards. *They came out here with pride in their eyes*, but those eyes, like Florence Thompson's, remained hungry for their basic needs, nonetheless. In America.

Dallas Frazier had a minor country hit at the tail end of 1969 with his own recording of "California Cottonfields." It debuted on *Billboard*'s Hot Country Singles chart just as "Okie from Muskogee" was itself poised to take the top spot. Haggard had cut his own "Cottonfields" back in the spring, and though it wouldn't be released for a couple of years (on 1971's *Someday We'll Look Back*), it complemented perfectly the rich, artistic Okie universe he was busy developing at the time. Besides "Okie from Muskogee," there were "Tulare Dust," "The Legend of Bonnie and Clyde," "They're Tearing the Labor Camps Down," and, of course, "Hungry Eyes," all Haggard originals and all cut within the several months that bookended the arrival of "Muskogee" on the charts. During an only slightly broader period, Merle also recorded several Okie-alluding numbers by other writers: pride of place goes to Frazier's "California Cottonfields," but there were also Red Lane's "One Row at a Time," Jimmie Rodgers's pre–Dust Bowl "California Blues," Bob Wills's "Cotton Patch Blues," and even the Hank Mills–penned country-pop standard "Little Ole Wine Drinker Me." Haggard, playing a heartsick sot in some Windy City tavern, kicks that one off by slurring, "I'm praying for rain in California, so the grapes can grow and they can make more wine."

Taken together, these recordings—call them his Kern County Suite— are a striking portrait of the San Joaquin's Depression-era immigrants, both post- and (less so) premigration, as close as country music is likely to come to producing its own Yoknapatawpha County. The details that Merle voices in these songs, and the characters he gives voice to—"I'm going to California where they sleep out every night," "Everything we had was sold or left behind," "Where's a hungry man gonna live at in this town," "a canvas-covered cabin in a crowded labor camp," "Oh, I miss Oklahoma but I'll stay if I must"—snap the listener to with a shock of recognition, an illusion of the real that's only trebled in power by the back-sore ache in Merle's sunburnt baritone. And never mind that even in the songs he wrote himself, Merle fictionalizes as needed the actual details of his life, and of his family's, for reasons thematic or musical or both. As Norman Hamlet, legend of the pedal steel guitar and a longtime member of Haggard's band the Strangers, once summarized: "A lot of people think the songs [Merle's] done are experiences he's had. Some of them are not necessarily personal experiences, but experiences of seeing other people in the same situation." And turning what he saw into art.

Not to put too fine a point on it, but…when Merle sings in his presumably autobiographical "Tulare Dust" that "I can see Mom and Dad with shoulders low, both of them pickin' on a double row," he is making it up; his autobiographies make plain he never saw his parents pick cotton, let alone worked the fields at their side. He's making it up, too, when he tells us in that song's following verse that he arrived in the Golden State with his parents in the winter of 1942, as he is in the next verse when he declares, "I miss Oklahoma," a place he never lived. That iconic "canvas-covered cabin" in "Hungry Eyes" was not where Merle grew up or where his "father raised a family…with two hardworking hands"—though it was where Merle's beloved great-uncle and great-aunt, Escar and Willie Harp, resided for a time and where he visited often. In "Okie from Muskogee" it would have been more accurate, autobiographically speaking, for Merle to have written "I'm proud to be a California-born-and-bred son of an Okie from the Checotah area." But it wouldn't have sung as well.

I stress the creative licenses taken here, risk even belaboring them, not to insinuate any dishonesty or deception on Haggard's part. Rather, my aim is to disabuse us of the perception that Merle Haggard was ever a purely, or even a primarily, autobiographical songwriter and music maker. His work is deeply personal, damn near straight down the line—he sang of what he knew, and what he knew best was how he *felt*—but we want to be leery of drawing a straight line from the sincere and personal feelings of Merle's often autobiographically inspired lyrics to the precise life details that people tend to assume when his songs are regularly referred to as "autobiographical." We want to avoid, in other words, that most dead-end of critical formulas, authenticity.

As he presents his earliest years in both *Sing Me Back Home* and *House of Memories*, Merle Haggard's story doesn't bring to mind the film version of the Okie-themed *The Grapes of Wrath* so much as it recalls another John Ford classic, 1941's *How Green Was My Valley*. This comparison casts Haggard in the role of the Roddy McDowall character—baby of the family, small and sickly (young Merle suffered from the fungal infection known locally as valley fever), but also a handsome, whip-smart charmer, doted upon by parents and older siblings. The narrator in Haggard's autobiographies, as in Ford's *Valley*, is a grown man, deeply nostalgic, reviving tough and cherished memories of the working-class roots of his raising, and both stories conclude with the death of the father.

Jim Haggard died in 1946, when Merle was nine. Back east, his dad had been a part-time musician—he knew his way around a variety of string instruments but was particularly fond of the fiddle—playing at dances and in bars and with his friends. But he gave up that part of his life when he married in 1919. Flossie, wanting a reliable husband and steady provider, insisted on it, especially after their first children were born, Lillian in 1921 and Lowell the year after.

Hag's memories of his father, at least the ones he was willing to share publicly, tended to the generic, even the cliché: Merle going for drives with his father or going fishing; Merle on eager lookout for his father to come home from work each afternoon; Jim taking his son to pick out a puppy. These were "those nine precious years," as he called them, when Merle had a father by his side. Afterward came that scary, directionless decade when, Merle writes, "something went out of the world that I was never able to replace."

That's how Merle prefaces his blow-by-blow recounting of the story he identified as the defining trauma of his life, a series of images that lie "still like crumpled paper inside [his] mind." Racing home from church ahead of his mother one Wednesday evening, Merle finds his father sitting still and silent in a darkened living room, weeping. Jim manages to choke out the word "stroke." There's a frantic scramble to a Bakersfield hospital and, over the next few days, Jim's seeming recovery. Next comes a four-hour road trip in Lowell's '39 Chevy to see a specialist in Los Angeles, Merle's memories of the trip punctuated by the father turning in his seat periodically to smile and tap the son's knee. In L.A. Flossie serves her husband and sons lunch on the ground while they kill time waiting for Jim's appointment. "Some…city slicker might have seen us in the park and thought we were just another family of red-neck Okies having our baloney and crackers, and in a way we were."

Inside the hospital Jim is directed to take a seat in a wheelchair. Just then, an artery bursts, and his father's face turns blue. Jim Haggard collapses, crashes, into the chair and is rushed down the hall and away. "I stood there and I saw it, but I don't—or I *can't*—remember any of it."

Two more brain hemorrhages were yet to come, and a second stroke. Merle recalls the next few days as a blur. He is at his aunt Flora's house, and then, suddenly, Lowell is there, too. Merle remembers Lowell, a grown man at this point, in his early twenties, taking him in his arms, rocking back and forth and crying. "Merle, we ain't got no Daddy…"

Merle dealt with his childhood directly in "Born with the Blues," a song he wrote and recorded late in his career as a duet with George Jones for their 2006 album *Kickin' Out the Footlights…Again*. Jones lays out the first verse, but the story is all Haggard's: "Dad was my hero / God called him away / Mama was lonely / And I was afraid." There's a certain poignancy to that, especially in the context of his typically fetching (if a tad familiar) melody, and if you care at all about his life story, Merle's turn at his lyric is also affecting: "Raised in a boxcar / and born with the blues" is a nicely compressed bit of bio. On the other hand, to swipe a metaphor from Meyer Abrams, "Born with the Blues" is all mirror and no lamp.

More illuminating, and more representative of the way Haggard's art tended to work, is a song that, in 1976, became Merle's twenty-third #1 country hit, "The Roots of My Raising." If you didn't know any better, you might fairly conclude that the song's story is pulled from the details of the singer's life. That's certainly the impression encouraged by the *Roots of My Raising* album cover, which shows Merle standing alongside a new Cadillac parked in front of a dilapidated homestead, a city slicker come-a-callin' in the country. That's what the song's about, too, a man going home to see his father.

Again, though, as on so many of his most successful recordings, "The Roots of My Raising" has the feel of autobiography but was written by someone else—in this case, Merle's longtime friend Leonard Sipes, aka country singer Tommy Collins. An Okie latecomer who relocated from the Oklahoma City area to Bakersfield in 1952, Collins wrote "The Roots of My Raising" with his own Oklahoma childhood in mind. "I wanted to capture something of those precious, simple days when you didn't have to lock your house" is how Collins explained it to journalist Tom Roland. "You didn't worry about people stealing. You picked people up on the road and gave them a ride without the fear of having a gun pulled on you; if a neighbor's barn burned down, or his house, the other neighbors got together and built him another one. It was a great life."

Collins paints a pretty picture here, but his memories seem too perfect to ring entirely true. No way do they correspond to the Haggards' Oklahoma experience: if neighbors had been able, or willing, to replace their barn when it burned in 1934, Jim and Flossie might never have abandoned Oklahoma in 1935. In any event, Collins left most of these rose-colored memories out of his song. If he hadn't, Merle, whose tendency toward musical nostalgia rarely ran to anything quite so idealized, probably wouldn't have been drawn to record "Roots" in the first place.

The record begins with a swinging little guitar that conjures up earlier times by mimicking the sound of some old Lefty Frizzell record, but it is quickly replaced by Norman Hamlet conjuring a pedal steel guitar that sounds timeless or, better yet, outside time's limits, like a dream....Merle is returning to some old Oklahoma home place. Upon arrival he spies his silver-haired daddy sleeping in a chair—and smiling, for in his hand the father is holding a photo of his dear-departed wife, the singer's mother. Merle has journeyed a great distance to be here—he's passed from highway to blacktop to gravel road—but finding his dad at peace is apparently all he needed to see, so he gets back in his Caddy and drives away....Maybe home, to California?

Obviously, this isn't Merle's story, not entirely. But it's close enough for country. When he recorded Tommy Collins's song in 1976, Haggard's own father was long dead, gone for over thirty years, while it was his mother who was still alive. Haggard was still able to pose with Flossie five years later for the cover of a gospel album he dedicated to her, *Songs for the Mama That Tried*. Thanks to that gospel set and, more so, to songs like "Mama

Tried" and "[Mama's] Hungry Eyes," Merle acquired a strong association with that venerable country tradition, the mother song. The truth, though, is that fathers show up in his songs at least as often. There are the fathers in Frazier's "California Cottonfields" and his own song "Daddy Frank." There's his "I Wonder If They Ever Think of Me," where a Vietnam POW remembers his old man telling him, "You'll come back a better man." There's the father of nine kids in "Workin' Man Blues" who dreams of chucking his responsibilities and catching the next train straight to...Anywhere But Here. There's his 1996 version of Iris DeMent's "No Time to Cry" and the plainspoken pain of its opening line, "My father died a year ago today." There's the on-the-road-again dad who "Got a Letter from My Kid Today," and then there's that line from "I Take a Lot of Pride in What I Am," which sure *feels* like it came from his real life: "I keep thumbing through the phone books and looking for my daddy's name in every town." In the Haggard catalogue there are fathers almost anywhere you look. Desperate dads, pushover dads, single dads and absent dads, dads who chase dreams and dads who chase tail, dads who are just plain sons of bitches, dads who are dead. Even "Hungry Eyes" is at least as much about the father who works so diligently to satisfy the mother's hunger, and fails, as it is about "Mama."

It's the father in "The Roots of My Raising" who keeps pulling me back. Or rather the father I imagine Merle is imagining, a father who died young and whom he barely knew but who here is alive and enjoying peaceful golden years. "The roots of my raisin' run deep," he sings, and on that word *deep*, Merle flies up to what may just be the highest falsetto of his career. "I've come back for the strength that I need / And hope comes no matter how far down I sink / The roots of my raisin' run deep."

The redundant phrasing of that title is probably just a reflection of Tommy Collins's own melodic demands and southwestern vernacular. Still, the distance that wording creates resonates. The song title promises that Haggard will find sustenance and inspiration not in his roots, and not in his raising, both of which are California stories, but in something more at arm's-length: the roots *of* his raising. Those roots run deep indeed, all the way back to the Oklahoma of family legend. Haggard found in that imagined state—in the tales he inherited from the real people who loved it and left it—a kind of prehistory for himself that, going forward, he could reshape as reality and myth.

CHAPTER 3

"MAMA TRIED," 1968

Among the songs most closely associated with Haggard today, "Mama Tried" is hands down his most purely autobiographical. Even the song's one well-known fiction—Merle wasn't doing "life without parole"—is every bit as much a concession to artistic demands as an embrace of artistic license. "Instead of life in prison I was doing one-to-fifteen years," he once told Wayne Bledsoe of the *Knoxville News-Sentinel*. "I just couldn't get that to rhyme."

"Mama Tried" certainly has that It-Happened-Just-This-Way feel. The romantic triumvirate of rhymes that launches the song ("First thing I remember knowin'…lonesome whistle blowin'…a young'un's dream of growin'"); the in memoriam of its second verse ("dear old Daddy, rest his soul"); the shout-out to a woman who struggled to be both mom and dad to the boy, who saw to it he went to church, who tried to raise him right; even the bit about a twenty-first birthday behind bars—it's all Merle, all true, right up to and including his owning up to being such a headstrong fool that no one, not even his mother, could tell him a damn thing.

Ironic, then, that Merle penned this musical memoir on commission for *Killers Three*, the B-movie in which Merle made his acting debut in 1968. "Just some PUNKS from the PECKERWOODS out for a picnic," read advertisements in some southern newspapers. "Before it was over, 37 men were dead." Adding to the irony, and then multiplying it by a factor of about a thousand, real-life ex-con Merle Haggard switches sides in the film and portrays a Smokey the Bear–hat-wearing North Carolina state trooper. This might have gone down as the greatest case of miscasting in Hollywood history if only *Killers Three* didn't also star Dick Clark, America's Oldest Teenager and the movie's producer, as a pyromaniac who may or may not be gay and who (spoiler alert!) shoots officer Haggard dead in a country diner. An instrumental version of "Mama Tried," billed as "The Ballad of Killers Three," plays over the opening credits while another song Merle wrote, "Killers Three Theme," is dropped between scenes a verse or two at a time to provide exposition or narrate the on-screen action: "He dreamed of California and the new life there would be," or "Johnny drove hard and fast to make his getaway," like that.

Back in the real world, or at least back in a Los Angeles recording studio, Merle gave "Mama Tried" lyrics that are a far cry from its reputation as an ideal Mother's Day radio request. "Mama Tried" isn't the simple and touching apology, however hard-won, of an older-but-wiser son paying rueful tribute to the ever-loving, long-suffering mama who knew best all along. "Mama Tried" doesn't sound rueful at all, not with James Burton kicking off the record with a Dobro lick that skips in breathless anticipation toward whatever adventure the open road holds in store, not with Roy Nichols squeezing off electrical sparks that sound like Merle's once more chasing down a freight train and shouting, "Wait for me."

Turns out, "Mama Tried" is less an acknowledgment of all the pain and trouble Merle put Flossie through and more a celebration of his own willfulness, his refusal to be broken. "Mama tried. Mama Tried!! MAMA TRIED!!!" After all these years, those indelible ascending shouts—they may speak of regret, but they *sing* like victory—strike me less like pangs of a guilty conscience and more and more like a boast. Everyone tried to change his mind, to set him straight, but no one could. *Not even his mother.* "She tried to raise me right but I refused," he sings. He appreciates what his mama tried to do, of course. Really, he does. But not one note here says he wouldn't refuse her again.

CHAPTER 4

TOWARD THE BAD HE KEPT ON TURNIN'

Merle was nine when his father died. He ran away for the first time when he was ten. Merle and a buddy hopped "a freight train leaving town" after school one day, not knowing where they'd end up. But the trains must have been calling out to Haggard for a while before he found the guts to make his break. The Santa Fe reefer that Jim and Flossie had repurposed into a house sat just yards off the Oildale tracks: the last of the steam locomotives, and the newfangled diesel and electric engines that were rapidly replacing them, clanged by daily, like a siren's call. He clambered aboard.

Lots of kids run away if only in hopes they'll be better appreciated upon return, and as a fair number of Merle Haggard songs remind, it's not just young people who feel the urge to roam. Grown-ups, too, harbor dreams of taking off someday for somewhere, anywhere, as long as it's not here. Indeed, what one 1977 Haggard hit diagnosed as "Ramblin' Fever" is something of an American affliction. We aren't supposed to know our place in this country; we're supposed to seek it out, find or invent it. Instructed from the cradle that we needn't, maybe even that we shouldn't, be content with our lot, Americans like to sing and dream along with that most quintessential of American songs, "Over the Rainbow." Not that we entirely believe it. Eventually, whether our dreams take wing or remain mere flights of fancy, the moral we're expected to take from our wish for escape is that there's no place like home. Sure, the 1939 film version of *The Wizard of Oz* begins with Dorothy Gale dreaming of getting up and out, over the rainbow to some Big Rock Candy Mountain "where troubles melt like lemon drops," but it ends with Dorothy back where she started, where she was born and, we're to understand, where she belongs. "If I ever go looking for my heart's desire again, I won't look any further than my own backyard," Dorothy attests, "because if it isn't there, I never really lost it to begin with." We might fairly object to this line of reasoning (Lost? Who said anything about *lost?*), but the contradiction's revealing. Dorothy's hard-traveling trip over the rainbow and back enacts an endlessly repeated version of the American Dream: in this country, you can be anything you want to be, but isn't what you already are plenty good enough? When Merle's backing band the Strangers cut an instrumental-only "Somewhere over the Rainbow" in 1973, they made it sound, at first, like someone crying over abandoned hopes and then like someone snickering at the foolishness of tears.

All of Merle Haggard's music, I think, springs from this same American Dream and ends bound by the same American dilemma. For when Merle went poking around in search of his heart's desire, what he found, and right in his own backyard, was a freight train leaving town.

Merle Haggard was a noted train buff as well as a collector of toy trains and other railroad memorabilia. I count sixteen train-alluding tracks in his catalogue even before he devoted an album to the theme, *My Love Affair with Trains*, in 1976. This number includes his own Hag-defining "Workin' Man Blues" and "Mama Tried," but the bulk of the tally is composed of Jimmie Rodgers train songs, with the remainder coming from songwriting masters Curly Putman, Roger Miller, and Dallas Frazier.

My Love Affair with Trains is typical in this regard. Of the album's ten tracks, Merle wrote only one: the autobiographical-as-all-get-out "No More Trains to Ride" waves to the boxcar of his youth and to the dad who worked the rails. The rest of the album only sounds autobiographical, the title track most of all. "Ev'rytime I hear the sound of a train a-comin' down that railroad track, I get that faraway look in my eye," Haggard sings, pining to escape his wage slavery. "I'd like to throw my hammer down and take off to some distant town." That's pure Merle, but the words and music are courtesy of Dolly Parton.

The single from Haggard's *My Love Affair with Trains*, "Here Comes the Freedom Train," was written by one Stephen Lemberg. A top-ten country hit, "Here Comes the Freedom Train" was every bit as provincial and optimistic as you'd expect a song with that title to be during the bicentennial summer, scooting along a boom-chuck rhythm track through "200 years of glory, never to turn back," on its way to a conclusion that, like any good American, is more than happy to conflate national pride with national superiority and historical inheritance with personal achievement: "We stand tall, Americans all," Merle talk-sings. "No honor can be higher!"

Train songs like these, and the prison songs that are their emotional opposite, are in country music's DNA. The recordings now recognized as the genre's first nationwide successes are "The Prisoner's Song" and "The Wreck of the Old '97," a two-sided hit for Vernon Dalhart, the light-opera-warbling Texan turned ur-countrypolitan crooner, in 1925. The Old '97 was a real train, and, in 1903, it really crashed. Other country trains, though, were made-up metaphors of national locomotion. "The Wabash Cannonball," for instance, hightails it so rapidly through Roy Acuff's 1947 classic that it can get from the Atlantic to the Pacific in scarcely two and a half minutes. (A 1968 version by Merle's longtime backing singer and second wife Bonnie Owens travels faster still!) The Orange Blossom Special was an actual train, running along the Eastern Seaboard from New York to Miami, but in the oft-performed song that real train inspired, specific destinations aren't the point. "Talk about travelin'," countless country vocalists have bragged in "The Orange Blossom Special," "it's the fastest train on the line." Insert impossibly speedy fiddle solo here.

Movement *is* the point. Trains in country music tend to be valued simply for carrying riders rapidly down the track, for getting them gone. Sick of obligations and people telling you what to do? Start fresh a little farther down the line. If a lover's left you flat, hit the road after her, and if you're tired of her mess, hit the road again. If you're burnt or baked out in Oklahoma, maybe California's the place you ought to be. If you don't love it, leave it. "The train is called America," Merle explains helpfully in "Here Comes the Freedom Train." By this way of thinking, movement, and the unencumbered individualism it implies, *is* freedom.

Country music freedom has its allure, but it can be a profoundly circumscribed condition as well, and deeply lonely. In Black culture, freedom is typically presented as a destination, a goal, a human condition to be achieved, and trains (the Underground Railroad, the Gospel Train) are the means by which we might arrive there together, free at last. Sometimes that freedom is to be found in heaven one day, but other times it can be achieved right here on earth, and sooner rather than later. Often, as in the Impressions' "People Get Ready," it seems headed to both destinations at once. The impulse of African American train songs is overwhelmingly collective, aspirational, and leaning toward the utopian. The struggle is to climb aboard. Freedom, as James Baldwin wrote of the country itself, is something we must achieve.

The southern white working class's most prominent traditions are closer to what Tex Sample calls "populist anarchism"—always on the side of the little guy but understanding that little guy as properly being all on his own. The country audience most often rides the rails not as a beloved community but as individuals who don't need to travel somewhere else to become free. If you're on board, it means you're American, born with a ticket in your pocket and free already. Or at least as free as you've got any right to expect.

That first time he hopped a freight, Merle made it all the way to Fresno before a "yard bull" caught him and notified his terrified mother her son was safe. "Why in the world would you run away?" is what Flossie wanted to know, particularly since, as a child of a deceased railroad employee, Merle had a pass to ride free until he turned twenty-one. But to Merle her question made no sense. He couldn't make Flossie see that he hadn't run away but was only looking for the adventure he'd find, or that might find him, somewhere down the track.

Whatever he called it, running away quickly became a way of life for Merle. Grown-ups rise each morning and go to work; Merle got up each day and ran. He ran from teachers and homework and the truant officer, and he ran from the rules and expectations of his mother and older siblings. He ran from anyone and everyone, it appears, who demanded he stand still long enough to be told what to do. A teacher complained on one of his report cards that he was forever staring out the window, he told *Look* in 1971. "But I was writing songs."

Or plotting his next escape. During his freshman year at Bakersfield High, Merle showed up a grand total of ten days. Confounded by his chronic truancy, the principal suggested that perhaps a weekend in juvenile hall would scare the boy straight. Merle's family agreed, but the plan backfired badly. Merle knew he'd done nothing to warrant what felt to him like a jail sentence—like Flannery O'Connor's Misfit, the young Merle couldn't make "what all I done wrong fit what all I gone through in punishment"—and from then on, when Merle was sent to juvenile hall for skipping school, he tried to escape from there as well, usually successfully. There was no sophomore year.

Why was Merle running? He was running, the Haggard family determined, from the thunder-strike pain of losing his dad, but by their own account it took them far too many years to see it. They knew Jim Haggard's death hit his youngest child hard, of course, but because Merle was a boy who kept things to himself, who chewed frantically on the past like a starving dog gnaws on a bone and all without ever breaking silence on his fears and regrets, it hit him much harder even than the family realized at the time. As Merle spiraled out of their control, the Haggards became increasingly protective, overprotective in Merle's view, and he resented it. He resented most any authority figure who wasn't his father. Since teenage boys who run wild, get drunk, "borrow" cars, and hop freights are pretty much guaranteed to run up against authority figures at every turn, this would prove an ongoing problem—one compounded by his being from the wrong side of the Bakersfield tracks. "I probably wouldn't have done any time at all if I'd been a rich boy," he concludes, not unreasonably, in *Sing Me Back Home*. "But I was just a poor kid."

"Freedom is not free," he observed in the 2010 documentary *Learning to Live with Myself*. "And, you know, if you want to take advantage of the law, you got to have a lawyer to help you. Poor people don't get justice in America, and I was one of those poor people."

There's a crumply black-and-white arrest photo of Merle from around this time: a little punk wearing a leather jacket and a sneer, and with an oily curl hanging down his forehead. The teenage Hag looks a lot like actor Robert Blake as he appeared when portraying murderer Perry Smith in 1967's *In Cold Blood*, or, closer yet, like Charlie Starkweather, who had modeled his look after James Dean's and who in early 1958 rampaged murderously across the upper Midwest. You can imagine Flossie, middle-class-aspiring and sternly religious, looking at that image of the boy she'd hoped might become a minister and seeing something along the lines of her worst nightmare.

Flossie's dreams were of the solidly bourgeois variety. Back in Oklahoma, a sixteen-year-old Flossie Harp had been a state penmanship champ. The prize was a college scholarship, but her father refused to let her accept it. A year later, in 1919, she married James Haggard, a "footloose person," she told Dale Vinicur, who "didn't worry about tomorrow at all" and whom she'd first met while he was fiddling at a party. For her part, Flossie was about as footloose as a man in leg irons, worried about almost everything, and could come off as emotionally cold: in 1973, a thirty-something Merle told journalist Donn Pearce that he could not remember his mother having ever kissed him. Comfort and safety could only come, she thought, "when a person settles down in one place, at one job, and makes somethin' of themselves." So while Flossie was a music lover herself—she chorded along on the organ at the Church of Christ—she insisted her musician husband lay the fiddle down more or less for good. When Jim died, Flossie found work keeping the books for the Quality Meat Company in Bakersfield, but she was not one for getting above her raising. "I told her I wanted to buy her a Lincoln with my first royalty payment [for "Mama Tried"]," Merle recalled long afterward to journalist Paul Zollo. "She said, 'The ladies in church will make fun of me if you get me a Lincoln. I want a Dodge Dart.'"

With his father gone, siblings grown, and mom at work, Merle became what we'd today call a latchkey kid, which made skipping school a breeze. To keep him out of trouble, the family nurtured his interest in music. Flossie got him violin lessons for a time, but Merle only wanted to play hillbilly tunings, fought with his teacher, and gave it up. When Merle was twelve, his brother gave him his first guitar, a Sears Roebuck job called a "Bronson" that some down-on-his-luck fellow had left for payment at the gas station where Lowell worked. But while music was a fun diversion, it wasn't work. "People like us," Merle said his family told him more than once, would never find success—they meant security, some material comfort, acceptance, pride—in the music business. Work and the future it purchased were to be found only in the fields or an office, on a factory floor or in a store, and by doing well in school. Typical of many Okie families, the Haggards valued education as the clearest path their children had to make something of themselves, so the more Merle Ronald wanted to play and sing, the more his mother and siblings insisted he march his butt back to school. But school felt like a trap to Merle. The older he got, the more he began to think that middle-class stability felt like a kind of trap, too. He kept running.

In 1951 fourteen-year-old Merle and another boy, nineteen-year-old Bob

Teague, hitched all the way from Oildale to Texas. The plan was to visit mutual hero Lefty Frizzell, but either because they had the town wrong or because their idol had moved, the boys settled for visiting Teague's grandfather instead. He sent them on their way with a sawbuck and "a half a stick of bologna." It was a coming-of-age adventure Haggard never forgot, a picaresque he featured in both of his autobiographies: on the way out, he had sex for the first time (at a brothel in Amarillo); on the way back, he and Teague were arrested around Los Angeles for armed robbery. They were released a week later when the actual criminals were found, and from there, Merle thumbed a ride back to Bakersfield. "I loved the freedom of the road" is how Haggard summarized the experience in *Sing Me Back Home*. "No family telling me to do this or that. No teachers trying to tell me to learn something I didn't want to know. No truant officers grabbing me by the elbow. No authority figures trying to size me up. There are many definitions of the word 'freedom' but at that particular time, I thought this was it."

There were fights and court appearances and more trips to juvenile hall. He was such a regular there, he had his own stash of 78s in the rec room. At fifteen he escaped from juvie, stole a car, and drove it to Arizona, making his way back home by hopping freights and hobnobbing with hoboes. Another time, after another escape, he stole a car and went to Las Vegas. After he was caught that time, he was sent to the Fred C. Nellis School for Boys in Whittier, part of the California Youth Authority, but it couldn't hold him either. After four escape attempts, he was declared "incorrigible" and sent to the Preston School of Industry, a notorious reform school where Haggard acquired a tattoo he wore on his hand to the day he died: "P.S.I."

The stories Merle Haggard told about his misspent youth, complete with car chases and close shaves and cases of mistaken identity, sound like scripts for a Burt Reynolds or Steve McQueen movie and are cast with sadistic guards and heartless wardens straight out of *Cool Hand Luke*. (After one escape and capture, he was forced by a guard to jog for hours while being beaten with a leaf rake: "So you boys like to run, do you?") He told his stories in 1981's *Sing Me Back Home* and told them all again in 1999's *My House of Memories*, but he'd been telling the best of them in interviews for decades—since at least 1971, when "We Don't Smoke Marijuana in Muskogee. We Steal." appeared in *Rolling Stone*. Some of the tales are broadly comic (like the time he tried to steal a car that, unbeknownst to him, was chained to a tree); some are poignant (in 1951 fourteen-year-old Merle celebrated Christmas in juvie); and others are terrifying (after one Nellis escape, he cowered under a shed while just feet away a local posse searched for another man who had raped a young girl). But setting and plot remain the same. Merle Haggard is in a cage: He's out of work or hates his work; he's in juvie or in a relationship; all he wants to do is to go home. Somehow, he slips his bonds and makes a break for it only to discover upon arrival that home, too, feels like a cage.

He was perpetually feeling in these years "a clear and simple pull back to Bakersfield," he wrote. "Usually followed by a burning need to leave Bakersfield."

The story of how Merle Haggard finally got sent up the river, as he told it in *Sing Me Back Home*, is like an episode of *America's Dumbest Criminals*. It's Christmastime 1957, and Merle is at the kitchen table killing a bottle or three of cheap wine with an old acquaintance he'd run into earlier in the day and invited up to the house, and with Leona Haggard (née Hobbs), Merle's wife of just over a year and the mother of his eight-month-old daughter, Dana. Merle had been in the Ventura County Jail, doing nine months for grand theft auto, when Dana was born, and he'd just finished a three-month stint on a road gang after trying to seed his own scrap metal business by helping himself to someone else's scrap.

Now, Merle and his buddy are bitching about how America's going all to hell—no money in their pockets and no jobs that pay decent, "the school mess down in Little Rock," *Sputnik* and Khrushchev and the Soviets. "A workin' man just can't make it no more and that's the God's truth," Merle's friend declares, good and drunk and then some. Every drop as drunk himself, Merle announces he's had it with just sitting around and griping about the way things ought to be. He has a plan, and while it won't fix America it'll goddamn fill their empty wallets.

The three of them stagger out to the car and head down old Highway 99 to Fred & Gene's Café. Merle knows the place well—it's run by a cousin of a buddy—and all they have to do is crowbar open the back door, clean out the register, and hightail it home. Easy as 1, 2, 3. Step one is well underway when, to their three-sheets surprise, the diner's back door bursts open. It's then Merle realizes that, in their inebriation, they'd made one small miscalculation. While they had it in their heads that it's two or three in the morning, it is in fact still only ten or eleven, Fred & Gene's is open, full of customers, and here stands the owner in front of them. The guy recognizes Merle right off but isn't sure what he and his pal are up to: "Why don't you boys come around to the front door like everybody else?"

At this point, if Merle had been sober enough to retain possession of a few of his wits, the thing to do would have been to quick crack a joke: "Hey, what's a fellow got to do to get a sandwich around this dump anyway?" Merle wasn't sober, though, so instead of talking his way out of trouble, he proceeded to do what he'd been doing pretty much all his life. He ran.

And was quickly apprehended. Exacerbating his case, police found in Haggard's car a stolen check protector machine, hidden not very well under a blanket in the backseat. The same blanket, according to the Bakersfield *Californian*, that covered "the Haggards' 8-month-old daughter, with her parents at the time of the arrest." That was the week before Christmas. On the eve of Christmas Eve, Merle made one last break for it. Again, from the *Californian*: Haggard "apparently joined a detail of prisoners on their way to court at 10 A.M. Monday, replacing a man who was being interviewed by a parole officer. [He] joined the group as it was leaving the jail to enter the prison transportation van, and officers said Haggard apparently made his escape at that time." He spent the night at a motel with his wife, Leona. Thirty hours later, he was back in custody.

If this had been his first encounter with law enforcement, and if his family had had connections, or at least money for a lawyer, Haggard might have served only a short sentence. But because his rap sheet was already so long, he got a maximum of fifteen years, and because of his well-documented habit of escape, he was assigned to serve his time at San Quentin State Prison. Merle Haggard entered there in March 1958, prisoner #A-45200.

Stories from Merle's time in San Quentin are well known among fans. He saw Johnny Cash perform an inspiring New Year's Day show there in 1959, as most sources have it, or possibly in 1960, according to Cash biographer Robert Hilburn, and maybe even another time, too: in his autobiography Cash remembers Merle telling him he "had been in the front row for three of those concerts." In the versions of the story Merle shared again and again with profile writers through the decades, Cash's prison show bill included the rockabilly Collins Kids for an opening act, plus a couple of strippers.

During his first year Merle seriously contemplated escaping but was advised against it by fellow inmate Jimmy "Rabbit" Hendricks: "You can sing and write songs and play the guitar real good. You can be somebody someday." Hendricks saw no such future for himself: he escaped, shot a cop while on the lam, and was eventually executed in the San Quentin gas chamber.

For a time, Haggard didn't see a future either. Back in Bakersfield Leona had given birth to their second child, Marty (named after singer Marty Robbins), but had stopped visiting or writing, and now he learned she was pregnant again—with another man's baby. He became involved with a gambling ring in the prison, working the beer concession. When he was discovered blotto on his own homebrew, he was punished with seven days' isolation, housed in a concrete block of a room with nothing but a blanket, pajama bottoms, and a Bible. "You know you're in jail," he told journalist Christopher Wren in 1971.

It was a turning point in his life. As San Quentin's isolation cells abutted Death Row on what was known as the Shelf, Haggard could hear the talk of the doomed men. One of these was Caryl Chessman, the accused Red Light Bandit, who in 1948 had been convicted of robbery and rape and sentenced to die. He never ceased claiming his innocence, however, and became something of a culture hero to critics of the death penalty and, after several last-minute stays of execution, to the prisoners in San Quentin. Haggard spoke to Chessman while in isolation, identified with him (they'd both spent time at PSI), and began to fear his life was headed in the same direction. "My death flashed before me" is how he puts it in *Sing Me Back Home*.

When the week ended, Merle vowed to change the direction of his life. He volunteered to work in the prison's textile mill and auditioned successfully for the official prison band. After two years and pushing nine months, he was released early, for good behavior, on November 3, 1960.

Merle Haggard and prison go together, in the popular imagination, like Robert Johnson and a certain crossroads in the Mississippi delta. Even casual admirers, who may know next to nothing about the details of the man's life, can readily affirm that he's an ex-con. The Hag's backstory grants him instant artistic credibility and is inseparable from his appeal: he doesn't just play an outlaw; he's authentic. Never mind that, in Merle's opinion, his prison record reads as his life's most humiliating chapter.

Shame may help explain why Haggard, personal history and public reputation aside, recorded so few prison songs in his career, certainly no more than many other country artists of his generation, and why he wrote even fewer. I count only a baker's dozen among the three hundred or so sides he cut during his tenure at Capitol Records, a rate that slowed even further in the decades afterward. The exceptions to this rule, of course, are exemplars of his legend. "Sing Me Back Home" is a prison song of the first order and represents Haggard at his definitive best. So does "Mama Tried," though save for its famous half-truth, it's not properly a prison song so much as a blueprint for how to wind up in one. From the other direction, the same goes for "Branded Man," about the disgrace that hounds an ex-con who, presumably, has already paid his debt.

The first explicit prison song Merle released, in 1967, was one he wrote. About an imprisoned individual who'd rather swing than live, "Life in Prison" is a harrowing number, but no more harrowing, and no less generic, really, than "Life to Go," a song written by Merle's eventual pal George Jones that was a big country hit for Stonewall Jackson just as Merle entered San Quentin. Prison life, in particular the details of Merle's life in prison— what it felt like for him to be trapped there, week after month after year—is a songwriting subject he mostly avoided. No doubt he revived memories when he sang a prison song, whether it was his own or by Dallas Frazier ("Will You Visit Me on Sundays?"), Curly Putman ("Green, Green Grass of Home"), Whitey Shafer ("I'll Break Out Tonight"), or Mel Tillis ("I Could Have Gone Right"). Yet when it comes to setting down the words and melodies of his own songs, the concrete details of Merle's trip up the river are stories he mostly kept to himself.

Merle did cut a number called "I Made the Prison Band" in 1967: "I been planning a break since Christmas . . . but now I know that I ain't gonna go!" That lines up perfectly with Merle's real life, but in a twist we've seen before, it was actually written by Tommy Collins, who clearly recognized a good song idea when he heard one.

Haggard sang and wrote relatively few literal prison songs. But as a state of mind, Prison competed with Freedom as his paramount artistic focus. Feeling cornered, followed by a burning desire to escape, was what Merle was normally going on about in the many train songs he recorded, but those represent merely a subset within the great overarching theme of his career. Merle Haggard was "The Running Kind." "Within me there's a prison, surrounding me alone," he shudders in that hit 1978 single. "As real as any walls of stone."

In American popular music, living out on the road, running and rambling 'round, is almost always presented as just an easy, peaceful blast. In such songs—I have in mind Haggard-relevant numbers like the Allman Brothers' "Ramblin' Man," Waylon Jennings's "I'm a Ramblin' Man," Lynyrd Skynyrd's "Free Bird," and Glen Campbell's "Gentle on My Mind," but there are hundreds to choose from—in such songs, to be a man of constant movement, to have nothing and no one to tie you down and no need for anyone's help, least of all a woman's, is a self-evident good. Anyone who misunderstands is just one more trap to avoid, one more good reason to hit the road.

Merle sang similar blues, over and over. In "Ramblin' Fever" and "White Line Fever," in Dallas Frazier's "Too Many Bridges to Cross Over," in "I Can't Get Away" and "The Running Kind," and two or three dozen more, Merle is fed up with where he is or who he's with, and, to prove he was free all along, he lights out. But his music's rule-of-thumb definition of freedom—not "Do your own thing" so much as "Every man for himself"; not individuality but individualism—can feel like no freedom at all. The next town down the line, with its same demands for survival and its new versions of the same demanding people, inevitably begins to feel as cramped and suffocating as the last. So the Hag takes off again, hops a freight or thumbs a ride, until running itself becomes a cage he can't escape, until running becomes its own prison and the only way out is to run. Repeat as necessary.

And it is always necessary. Merle tells us over and over again that running is in his DNA the way train and prison songs are in country music's. Freedom, in the commonsense sense of freedom of choice, of free will and subjective agency, and in the not-so-common-as-it-should-be sense of the development of one's human distinctiveness and the achievement of one's potential, is perpetually insisted on in Merle's recordings even as its possibility is denied. In Merle's music, freedom is movement, the freedom to leave a situation if you don't like it and to be left alone to do it. But, at least as he presents the case in his music, Merle couldn't stay put if he wanted to. The Hag has no choice in the matter. What the Hag does have is "Ramblin' *Fever*," "White Line *Fever*." "Jammin' gears has got to be a fever," he says in one of his several contributions to country music's trucking industry, "Movin' On." There's no cure for this disease; it's just the way he came. "I know running's not the answer," he sings in "The Running Kind," his bravado slipping for just a moment, "but running's been my nature and the part of me that keeps me moving on."

There is an honesty in those lines, and a real misery in the way he delivers them, that doesn't romanticize the running at all. He is at once freedom defending and freedom denying; his slavery remains the essence of his freedom. Merle Haggard's music is so powerful, in part, because he never resolves the contradiction. To his credit, and unlike any artist I know, Haggard lays it out there *as* a contradiction. "Every front door found me hopin' that I'd find the back door open," Merle croons, with great weariness, in "The Running Kind," his gift for escape extolled with a swagger indistinguishable from regret. "There just had to be an exit for the running kind," he concludes, which is not to say he ever really found one.

Never forget. In Merle Haggard's vision, as laid out in "Mama Tried" and reaffirmed for nearly half a century afterward, it was "a lonesome whistle blowin' and a young'un's dream of growin' up to ride" that led him directly, inevitably, to San Quentin, the way a train can keep on a-movin', but only along its tracks. All those train songs, all that running.... Merle never ends up anywhere any better. But he does get gone.

CHAPTER 5

HE LOVES THEM SO

A PLAYLIST OF EARLY INFLUENCES

In 2002 Merle was doing press interviews in promotion of the just-released *Roots, Volume 1*, an album honoring the C&W records he fell in love with as a working-class California kid halfway through the previous century. "I'm looking back on my life," he told me then, "and the music I used before I had music of my own." What music was that, exactly? *Roots* offered some answers, but Merle had been scattering clues all along. Like many country artists, Haggard went out of his way to present himself as a link in a chain of tradition. That traditionalist posture was sometimes established by the sincerest form of flattery and sometimes through the recording of tribute songs and albums, but always through continued recourse to a shared repertoire.

Let's play some records.

1. "Mom and Dad's Waltz," Lefty Frizzell (Columbia, 1951)
2. "Mom and Dad's Waltz," Merle Haggard (from *Sing Me Back Home*, Capitol, 1968)
3. "Always Late (with Your Kisses)," Lefty Frizzell (Columbia, 1951)
4. "Always Late (with Your Kisses)," Merle Haggard (from *Roots, Volume 1*, Anti-, 2001)

The first time he saw Lefty Frizzell, Merle Haggard was just fourteen. On a summer night in 1951, he squirmed his way near the front of Bakersfield's Rainbow Gardens, but the club was so packed, and the cramped stage set so low, that he was only able to see Lefty after someone handed up a chair for the star to perch on. Included in Frizzell's set was a pair of soon-to-be country standards: "Always Late (with Your Kisses)" and "Mom and Dad's Waltz," a for-the-ages two-sided single that debuted on the national country charts that August. Years later, in his first autobiography, Merle wrote that he gazed upon Frizzell that night "in absolute wonder" and that "when he told us that was the first time he'd ever done those songs in public, I felt like I was being included in country music history in some way. It was a feeling I've never forgotten."

"He was dressed in white," Merle enthused. "Heroes usually are."

"His songs hit me right in the heart," Haggard explained to me in 2002. "And his voice…It was strange. It was like listening to my own voice. I had some soul connection with Lefty. It was like somebody had turned on the light. It was like somebody reached around and turned on a switch on my back."

As we've seen, his Be-a-Good-Boy-Now-and-Go-to-School switch was already off by this time. That's how a year or so after seeing Frizzell, Merle Haggard found himself just outside Modesto, California, on a break from bringing in the hay, at a cinder-block dive bar with the trying-too-hard name The Fun Center. When the bartender asked if that guitar slung on his back was just for show or if he could actually play the thing, the fifteen-year-old chose to prove it was the latter by strumming and singing his way through "Always Late (with Your Kisses)." The guy must've liked what he heard well enough, because he offered Merle five bucks to keep going—Merle Haggard's professional debut. A half century later, when Merle released *Roots, Volume 1*, that album devoted to honoring music "I used before I had music of my own," he made "Always Late" the lead track.

He cut the other song he'd heard Frizzell test drive at the Rainbow Gardens, "Mom and Dad's Waltz," much sooner. Haggard would eventually record Frizzell songs nearly twenty times, not to mention a half dozen or so of his own songs that name-drop ol' Lefty. But in 1968, when he'd only just established himself as a consistent hit maker and country star, it was "Mom and Dad's Waltz" he chose to be the first.

Merle covered the signature songs of this or that musical hero at every stage of his career, and in most cases, he made certain to turn the old music he loved into new music. He transformed classic music into Haggard music. But there's one glaring exception to the rule: when Merle sang a Lefty song, he was likely as not to say to hell with interpretation and to straight-up copy it.

Even though he recorded them more than forty years apart, Merle's versions of "Mom and Dad's Waltz" and "Always Late" are both covers in the old-fashioned sense: they try to sound as close to the original singles as possible. Merle made certain his 2001 version of "Always Late (with Your Kisses)" begins with the same gravity-defying, Looney Tunes steel lick that boomeranged Lefty's record to life a half century before. The abridged, small-combo edition of the Strangers that backs him here forgoes the improvisational soloing typical of his late-period recordings for low-key, almost lazy restatements of the melody—first by twin guitars, then by the piano, then fiddle. These restatements are note-for-note copies of the trio of aching solos—guitars to piano to fiddle—that laze about the middle of Frizzell's hit.

Merle also tended to *sing* Lefty songs the way many of us sing along with our favorite records—by impersonating the singer. On that twenty-first-century "Always Late," Merle's sixty-something voice cracks unpredictably, but he's still doing Lefty as close to note-for-note as he's able. On "Mom and Dad's Waltz," cut at that late-sixties moment when he was approaching his prime, a youthful-sounding Merle has his Lefty impersonation down cold. He doesn't merely reveal himself to be influenced by Frizzell's hushed and conversational, almost fragile, croon; he is deliberately, lovingly bent upon sounding *exactly like Lefty*, like their voices are the same voice. Replicating most of his hero's curlicued vocal lines, Haggard hugs the song's key words and phrases as if reluctant to set them free. The a cappella "I love them so" that ends the record is stretched and squeezed ever so gently until, just as on Lefty's 1951 original, it seems determined to encapsulate a lifetime of gratitude and devotion: Lefty turns and twists the final two syllables into half a dozen, a melismatic mark of which Merle lands just shy. Merle cherishes the melody, the notes themselves, sounding convinced that if he releases these words too soon, he'll risk losing forever the feelings they convey. And the people who inspired them, by whom I mean Mom and Dad Haggard, of course, but also Lefty Frizzell.

When Merle first began to sing, he sounded just like Lefty. Everybody said so. Once, a friend of his mother's heard him singing in the car to Lefty's first hit, "I Love You a Thousand Ways," and told him he "sounded just like that guy on the radio." Many years later, after Merle and his idol became friends, Frizzell's own mother confessed to Merle that "when I heard you sing [on the radio], I said why that's Sonny. And they said to me, no Mom, that's not Sonny, that's Merle Haggard."

A kid looking to emulate a hero, Merle consciously nurtured the resemblance. Naturally so, since Frizzell was the greatest, coolest singer he'd ever heard—but there was also a part of him that just naturally couldn't help it. Merle's voice seemed to fall into Lefty's without his trying. The teenage Haggard would "borrow" a car for a joyride with a buddy, or head out to Oildale's Beer Can Hill to drink till sunup with pals, but wherever he went he was always singing, always working out an ever-more-precise impersonation of Lefty Frizzell.

What we approvingly call "influence" often starts with what we unfavorably term "imitation." The youthful impersonation of a hero is such a common backstory for aspiring country singers that it nearly counts as a rite of passage. The countrypolitan crooner née honky-tonk shuffler Ray Price sang on his earliest recordings in a voice that was at times all but indistinguishable from that of Hank Williams. George Jones idolized Williams and Frizzell both, and sounded like it: "Can you sing," his producer asked at the start of his career, "like George Jones?" Merle had to overcome the same obstacle. Or, to phrase it closer to the way Merle experienced it, he benefited from similar inspiration. When Merle started recording, his manager and first producer, Fuzzy Owen, would stop him midtake to warn him, again, that he was maybe sounding a bit too much like ol' Lefty.

5. "Cotton Picker" (from *Totally Instrumental with One Exception*, Capitol, 1973)
6. "White Man Singin' the Blues" (from *Merle Haggard Presents His 30th Album*, Capitol, 1974)
7. "White Man Singin' the Blues" (from *Chicago Wind*, Capitol, 2005)

This is one way country music understood itself when Haggard was coming up: the path to a distinctive voice, your voice, was inseparable from a knowledge of just where that voice came from. Merle's voice came from Lefty.

Where did Lefty's voice come from? The short answer is from Jimmie

Rodgers. Frizzell grew up spinning and respinning the Rodgers 78s in his father's record collection. Rodgers's trademark was his "blue yodel," which he tagged to the end of lines or choruses as a wordless but endlessly evocative hook. As Frizzell biographer Daniel Cooper describes it, Lefty's key innovation was to modernize Rodgers's yodel, not by yodeling himself but "by internalizing the sound within his own ballad—not blues—lyric…a deceptively simple maneuver, yet revolutionary in country music." Heard this way, Frizzell's distinctive multisyllabic runs are like little blue yodels sprinkled throughout his phrasing.

This makes a great deal of sense—and is delightful to boot. But it overlooks an additional, even obvious, building block of the Frizzell singing style. Frizzell's melismatic phrasing is typically characterized as "unprecedented," "unique," something that "no one had ever heard." Yet countless Black singers—jazz vocalists, bluesmen and blueswomen, gospel singers most often of all—had bent their notes for years before Frizzell appears to have adopted the technique.

This is *not* one of the ways country music tended to understand itself when Merle was coming up and, mostly, it still isn't. There is a short list today of Black men who are at least acknowledged as essential to the creation of country music as we know it: Lesley Riddle helped shape the guitar stylings and songbook of the Carter Family; Arnold Schultz mentored and performed with Bill Monroe; Rufus Payne tutored Hank Williams. Belated acknowledgment, of course, beats no acknowledgment. But actual careers for Black performers in country music, not to mention a level of fame or fortune commensurate to their contributions, has been nearly nonexistent. The country genre has most often told a story about its tradition that commits repeatedly a sin of omission, and even of erasure.

While white country acts are routinely indebted to Black musicians, the names of the specific men and women who did the mentoring, tutoring, collaborating, and inspiring have mostly remained a mystery. Jimmie Rodgers, for example, heard the music of Black musicians in the medicine shows and carnivals that passed through his hometown of Meridian, Mississippi, and as a water boy and brakeman, he absorbed the talk and the blues he heard among African American laborers. But what songs or styles he learned precisely from those men are nearly as impossible to know as the identities of the men he learned them from. Similarly, we're told, a twelve-year-old Lefty liked to sneak off come Sunday to visit a "Black tenant farmer." Cooper reports that the man taught the boy his first chords and even supplied him with his first guitar, after Frizzell's uncle offered to buy it from the man.

We can hear Haggard acting out just this sort of cultural appropriation on "Cotton Picker," from a 1973 album by his backing band the Strangers. Picking dreamy, absent-minded blues and swapping jokes about old times with guitarist Roy Nichols, Merle speaks a story about "an old black man, used to pick the same field every year, along with my bunch." As he worked the California cotton fields, Merle says, the man would "get to hummin' the blues" and "the faster he'd hum, the faster he'd pick." Then: "Sounds something like this right here." As the Strangers join in—their accompaniment is both thrilling and completely familiar, those good ol' "Generic Acoustic Blues"—Merle hums and moans a melody, a wordless expression of emotions, everything from joy to sorrow and back, that's as old as work songs and field hollers. "Lord, Lord," he interjects. Merle is impersonating that "old black man," but, tellingly, he also sounds a lot like Merle Haggard. And as it's Haggard who's doing this imitation of African American style, it sounds just a little like ol' Lefty, too. And like Jimmie Rodgers.

Beyond encounters with named or unnamed Black musicians, white country acts have most often been influenced by Black music simply by hearing it on radio, on records, and by existing in a world where everyone else is knowingly lifting or, if it's popular and widespread enough, consciously or unconsciously absorbing the often cutting-edge styles and sounds of African Americans. Lefty was no exception. After Frizzell's first recording session in 1950, which resulted in big but notably melisma-free country hits like "I Love You a Thousand Ways" and "If You've Got the Money (I've Got the Time)," Lefty passed the time till his next session managing a small club in Dallas, Texas. The club—Cooper locates it "in one of the Hispanic sections of town"—came with "a working jukebox stocked with race records....He spent months with his life and career on hold...spinning the likes of Ivory Joe Hunter's 'I Almost Lost My Mind.'"

That cool-and-blue smash by Hunter aside, we've no way to know what specific platters were in that stocked machine. What we do know is that it was at just this midcentury moment when the note-bending curlicues of Black gospel—not just the splitting of notes in half but the twisting of single syllables to three, four, even more—were finding their way like never before onto the secular recordings crowding R&B jukeboxes. Listen closely to Sonny Till on the Orioles' "It's Too Soon to Know" or to Percy Mayfield's

"Please Send Me Someone to Love." Check Ruth Brown's "So Long" and Dinah Washington's "Baby Get Lost" and Sister Rosetta Tharpe's gospel crossover "Up above My Head." All of these R&B hits from 1948, '49, and '50, and many more besides, include notes that are bent and stretched, warped and slurred into polysyllables. Not on every line or word the way contemporary singers often do, but, like Lefty would, in a selected spot or two for emotional emphasis and rhythmic fun. Even smooth-singing Ivory Joe springs up and down and up the melody of his "I Almost Lost My Mind." Each iteration by Hunter of his title line sounds something like a little slow-motion blue yodel.

We know something else, too: when Frizzell finished binging those "race records" and returned to the studio for sessions in 1951, his previously melismaless singing style now included the taffy-twisting of key words that became his vocal signature—on the sides "Always Late (with Your Kisses)" and "Mom and Dad's Waltz," specifically. Noting this detracts not a whit from the power of Frizzell's singular style or legacy: he's the most influential vocalist in country history. But it does remind us how multidetermined musical influence tends to be and how difficult it can be to identify. And it is revealing, too, of how the country tradition has maintained its seeming whiteness. Some links in the chain of tradition are named and treasured, worried over and polished, while some links remain uninitialed and left to rust.

Though Black influence is a constant of the country story, country singers have rarely written or sung of that experience. Merle was an exception. His "White Man Singin' the Blues," from 1974, sings out loud what normally goes unmentioned. Almost as rare, the song's lyric posits the possibility of interracial class and cultural solidarity. Merle is telling us the story, invented or recalled it's hard to say, of a time when he met an "old black man" and the pair bonded over music ("The Blues was one thing we both understood"), as well as over the knowledge that they've both "been down and out," "both done a heap-a-hard livin'."

Not that Merle's song is as honest about these matters as it might be. Its opening, "The old man paid no mind to color," feels like Merle could well be reading his desired point of view into the man's head. Perhaps when "old Joe" calls Merle "a soul brother," the man is merely rehearsing what his own hard living has taught him this random white person likely wants to hear. And is "old Joe," as the song refers to the man once, really the man's name or just another white man's age-old default for "old black man," as the song identifies him twice? The song bridges all manner of important distinctions by eliding them. "From the same side of the railroad tracks where people have nothing to lose," Merle sings in a spirit of working-class unity. But even on the poor side of town, the poor white folks and poor Black folks tend to live in different neighborhoods.

Still, the song's title alone, "White Man Singin' the Blues," summarizes succinctly something true about Merle Haggard and about country singers generally. The song mattered enough to Merle that thirty-one years later he cut it again. The 1974 version of the song was acoustic country soul, loose and playful and complete under two minutes, though not without an undertow of gravitas. Nearly twice that length, the 2005 version was electric with booming drums, and, instead of playful, it was earnest. Reggie Young, the Memphis-to-Nashville studio legend, sears his way through two roadhouse blues solos, the second resurrecting the recording after a dramatic false ending. In both versions of the song, Merle moans, "Together we hummed out an old-timey blues." Then he hums and moans his way right through the spot where Lefty would have turned and twisted a note into notes and where Jimmie Rodgers would've yodeled.

8. "My Rough and Rowdy Ways," Jimmie Rodgers (Victor, 1929)
9. "My Rough and Rowdy Ways," Lefty Frizzell (Columbia, 1950)
10. "My Rough and Rowdy Ways," Merle Haggard (from *I'm a Lonesome Fugitive*, Capitol, 1967)

Individual style discovered via a period of imitation is a key to tracking country music. Witness, for example, the genre's collective homage to Jimmie Rodgers, the man regarded today as the Father of Country Music. The distinctive vocal styles of country's most recognized genres are each exemplified by men who began their singing careers as undisguised Rodgers mimics: Ernest Tubb, whose quavering twang became the very model for how a Texas honky-tonker should sound; Tommy Duncan, whose easy-does-it croon helped define western swing; Gene Autry, whose dusty alto became the model for singing cowboys; and Hank Snow, who synthesized all these styles into the broad mainstream category marketed, for a time, as Country & Western.

One more son of the music's father, Lefty Frizzell was never an out-and-out Rodgers impersonator, at least not on record, but he was profoundly influenced by the Rodgers style. It was Lefty's infatuation with Jimmie's singing and songs that moved him to record the album that led directly to Merle's own Jimmie infatuation. *Songs of Jimmie Rodgers, Sung by Lefty Frizzell* (1951) was one of country music's earliest LPs and its first tribute album. Haggard told author Barry Mazor that the first time he heard Frizzell's tribute was also the first time he'd ever heard of Jimmie Rodgers:

> One day my mother and I were standing around in the kitchen and on the radio [Rodgers] came, singing "Blue Yodel No. 6." I said, "That's Lefty with a new record; Mom—*Lefty's got a new song.*" And she had a funny look on her face and said, "That's Jimmie Rodgers' song." She had some sort of indifferent posture about it, so I said, "I don't understand. Who's Jimmie Rodgers?" And she said, "Why he's—*the best!*"

This was probably in the fall or winter of 1951. "Blue Yodel No. 6" was the B-side to Frizzell's version of "Travelin' Blues," one of the single releases from sessions that led to the *Songs of Jimmie* album and a top-ten country hit late that year.

Prodded by Lefty's endorsement, the young Merle set to learning as many Rodgers songs as he could, though of course he sang them, as he sang everything then, by borrowing Lefty's voice. Later, Haggard famously recorded his own Rodgers tribute, *Same Train, a Different Time*, in a voice unmistakably his own. Back in '51, he'd yet to discover a distinctive style, but he was beginning to intuit that Frizzell's sound and Rodgers's songs might serve like signs pointing the way. "My Rough and Rowdy Ways" especially provided a clue to solving himself.

"The second time I went to see [Lefty] in Bakersfield I was sixteen years old, and he got me up to sing," Haggard told me in 2002, still sounding more than a little amazed five decades later. With the help of a buddy, Merle finagled his way backstage to meet the star of the show. Then, after his pal bragged to the singer that Merle did a pretty swell Lefty impersonation, the kid was kindly asked to prove it. Lefty must have been impressed, or maybe he just spotted a way to have another couple of drinks before he had to take the stage. In any event, the star decided he wanted the kid to sing a number on stage before the start of the next set.

"The owner looked at Lefty like he was crazy," Haggard explained to *Penthouse* in 1976. "He told him, 'Hey, that crowd didn't pay to hear their own local yokel sing. They came to hear Frizzell.' " That's when the headliner pulled rank, replying with some version or other of "Either the kid sings or I don't." The next thing Merle knew, he was doing his Lefty imitation for Lefty's audience. "I got to use his guitar and have his band play behind me. It was quite a thrill. I did two or three songs, and they were well accepted." They were more than just well accepted, apparently, and beyond being a thrill, the experience was self-affirming. As he told Dale Vinicur: "I went out on this show and they ripped the seats out—they loved it. And I was a nobody. I went right out in front of Lefty when they were wanting Lefty. Everything was against me and everything went for me. I seen that and I knew that's probably what I was going to do."

"Other than Frizzell's songs, I only knew songs by Jimmie Rodgers," is how he told it to Mazor. "And I remember singing one of 'em, called 'My Rough and Rowdy Ways.' " He'd learned it off the 78 Flossie had given him that year for Christmas.

Listen to Rodgers singing "My Rough and Rowdy Ways" in 1929. Compare it to Frizzell singing the same song at the century's midpoint. Then play Haggard's version cut in 1966. Right there, in just three records and not even nine minutes, you have a pretty nifty capsule history of a genre: its prime movers moving west—Mississippi to Texas to California; its technology improving—brittle to cool to warm; and the style of its Black influences evolving—from vaudeville and blues to hot pickin' to a pulsing and electric country-soul thump.

My favorite part of Rodgers's song is its clever second verse: "Sometimes I meet a bounder who knew me when I was a rounder / He grabs my hand and says 'Boy, have a drink.' …The daylight comes before I've had a wink." Lefty's "Rough and Rowdy" ditches that economical sketch of how temptation can overwhelm good intentions, just as it passes on attempting Rodgers's signature yodel. A smarter edit is the way Lefty switches out Jimmie's clunky "I may be tough and counted vile" for the smoother "I may be rough but that's just my style." Still, amidst the alterations is "My Rough and Rowdy Ways" itself. Jimmie and Lefty recorded the song approximately two decades apart, but the song remains the same because human beings still wrestle with the same tensions. Jimmie and Lefty both wish to quit their carousing and settle down with their girl in the old hometown. Then they turn right around and no less tenderly sing of their good old ramblin' days and ways.

Two decades down the road, Merle sings Lefty's version. He wants to straighten up and fly right, he really does. But right beside Merle's "I thought I would settle down" sits his "Somehow I can't give up," each iteration of which inches Merle closer to leaving his gal behind—to tossing his bills and catching a train for another town, as he'd later phrase it in "Workin' Man Blues." By the last chorus, you can almost hear the door hitting his butt as he hightails it to freedom. This doesn't mean Merle won't be back as soon as his rough and rowdy ways start to feel a bit too rough, too rowdy, when he hears again the calming call of Home Sweet Home. It does mean that, for as long as he can get away with it, he's damn well going to have it both ways. Because both ways is how he feels.

The old Jimmie Rodgers songs that the teenage Haggard learned from Lefty and the new songs that Lefty wrote in conversation with Rodgers—these songs spoke to young Merle Haggard. They spoke to him plainly of fear and betrayal, of miscommunications and missed opportunities, of promises made and broken, of loss and sweat and sickness and death—of all the limits built into the world. But the old songs hinted at possibilities, too, and provided the tools to realize them. The world would demand a great deal, those songs said, but in Lefty's voice, Merle found a hint he needn't settle merely for what the world demanded. If Lefty could feel and contain within him both contentment and dissatisfaction, both "I thought I would settle down" and "I can't give up my good old ramblin' ways," then couldn't he feel and contain, and perhaps even resolve, those tensions as well? If he could sing just like Lefty, then why couldn't he sing like whomever he chose? Even like himself.

"More and more," Merle writes in Sing Me Back Home, "I found myself trying to sound like him, sometimes without even realizing it. Lefty gave me the courage to dream."

11. "My Mary," Stuart Hamblen (RCA Victor, 1931)
12. "My Mary," Merle Haggard (from Pancho & Lefty, Epic, 1982)

Haggard lore has it that the family's youngest child seemed drawn to music from very nearly his first breaths. Early on, they noticed that the new baby kicked his legs happily along with whatever music might be on the radio; they found it especially amusing that they could start and stop his little legs by switching on and off the radio.

When Merle was just learning to talk, the story goes, he came to his mom demanding "stewed ham." Flossie was surprised by the request, but assumed Merle was just trying to say he was hungry. "Stewed Ham, Stewed Ham," he repeated, now pointing at the radio. Flossie got the message: it was time for Stuart Hamblen's daily radio show.

Hailing from East Texas, Hamblen was at first another singer deeply in thrall to Jimmie Rodgers, and like so many others, he soon built on that imitative foundation a persona of his own, Cowboy Joe, one of the early singing cowboys. When Hamblen arrived in California in 1930, he was exactly the sort of singer who'd soon take country music nationwide throughout the 1930s and '40s, joining a steady stream of Hollywood movies and Gene Autry platters. He was quickly enlisted as one of the Beverly Hill Billies, California's original country music stars. The schtick was that they were primitives discovered way back in the hills of Beverly. Hamblen played "Dave Donner," the lone survivor of the cannibalized Donner Party.

In 1934, feeling homesick, he wrote "Texas Plains," then cut it during the debut country music session for Decca Records. For the next two decades, Hamblen was a major presence in the Southern and Central California country scene, and his songwriting credits eventually boasted a trio of standards: "This Ole House," the oft-covered hymn "It Is No Secret (What God Can Do)," and "(Remember Me) I'm the One Who Loves You," a #2 country hit that lingered on the national charts for half of 1950.

Hamblen's first songwriting success, though, came much earlier. Hamblen cut "My Mary," his wistful reminiscence of a girlfriend back east, in 1930, at his first California session and performed it regularly on his radio programs over the years. "My Mary" has a lullaby melody, dreamy and hummable, of the sort that reminds just how closely intertwined commercial country music has always been with the songs of minstrelsy, vaudeville, and Tin Pan Alley. It's a sentimental song, and Hamblen sings it sentimentally, strolling down a twinkling memory lane and imagining his darling is again awaiting his return at the garden gate. You picture Hamblen sitting alone, probably in a darkened room, his eyes closed, wearing a dazed and goofy grin, and pretending. Especially so midway through, when Hamblen delivers a recitation that moves the song beyond mere nostalgia to fantasies of time travel: "Oh gee! Wouldn't it be great to open the door to the past? And live again? In yesterday?" He pronounces this wish in full-on Ted "Is-Everybody-Happy" Lewis mode, a stylized approach that in the day signified reverie and revelry but that to contemporary ears leaves Hamblen sounding about half nuts. But then he starts to sing again, his sanity restored, though perhaps a little tipsy, too. Blearily, beautifully, dreamily tipsy, and crooning his heart out.

Merle heard "My Mary" countless times as a boy, and on *Pancho & Lefty*, a 1982 project with Willie Nelson, he sings it solo. (Willie provides harmony, but from somewhere so far away he barely registers.) Merle passes on Hamblen's recitation and lets his musicians toss back and forth the phrases of the melody instead. During the verses he pulls even further back from Hamblen's fantasy ("living those days again") in favor of simple remembrance ("dreaming those dreams"). Those are telling edits: Haggard likes to look back at least as much as the next guy, and often a good deal more, but his brand of nostalgia is rarely escapist.

Merle's baritone retained in the early 1980s its youthful suppleness, but it was deeper too and comfortably scuffed a bit by age. "My Mary" is Merle at the peak of his vocal powers. On Hamblen's song, Merle's voice is oh-so-tender as he recalls what he loves but can't regain. Yet each word also resounds with strength and a kind of wisdom. He conveys an appreciation for the fact, a respect for it even, that while loss lingers and stings, it will ever be the necessary price for memories so sweet.

13. "San Antonio Rose," Bob Wills and His Texas Playboys (Vocallion, 1939)
14. "New San Antonio Rose," Bob Wills and His Texas Playboys (Okeh, 1940)
15. "New San Antonio Rose," Bing Crosby (Decca, 1941)
16. "San Antonio Rose," Merle Haggard (from *The Best Damn Fiddle Player in the World*, Capitol, 1970)

Merle cut "My Mary" near the beginning of his 1980s tenure with Epic Records, but his vocal style, generally speaking, is the same at any career point you choose: relaxed, warm, and rugged; intensely felt, unmistakably masculine, and unabashedly Okie-accented; but smooth, too, for all that, and tending toward what we might fairly term pretty. Haggard's a crooner.

This may seem counterintuitive. The expectation is that classic country singers are nasal and exaggeratedly melismatic: hillbilly soul singers, in effect, like George Jones and his not-so-many-as-you'd-think honky-tonk descendants. Either that or they're nasal and exaggeratedly declamatory: like

Hank Williams singing "Hey, Good Lookin'," they're basically down-home, white equivalents to big-city blues shouters. And whether considered nasal note-benders or nasal shouters, country singers have been widely perceived as either cartoonishly overwrought or cartoonishly taciturn, lacking entirely in affect, energy, or corresponding intelligence.

These categories of country vocalizing do exist, broadly speaking, sort of, and thank goodness. But they wind up revealing a lot less about country music than they do about common attitudes toward it, those held by listeners outside country's core fan base in particular. For starters, the line that separates one listener's too-wrought from another's wrought-just-right is often indistinguishable, aesthetically speaking, from genre boundaries themselves. Note, too, how often and perfectly such caricatures of the music and its musicians—dumb as a rock, lazy as sin, and laughably stoic but prone to swinging on a dime to childishly sentimental or rootin'-tootin' violent—rehearse prejudices against Okies and poor folk generally, white and Black and brown alike: *Another class of people put us somewhere just below.*

The condescension here becomes more blatant when we notice that country singers have been, in the main, neither melismatic nor declamatory but have valued instead the not-quite quiet, the straight and smooth, with intermittent note-twisting embellishments—"relaxed American," as Barry Mazor calls it. It's not nearly so true these days as it once was, but for the bulk of its history, country music has favored a never-let-them-see-you-sweat vocal aesthetic. Its singers worked hard to make the work of singing appear like no work at all. An easy front-porch croon is the genre's default vocal mode, a norm as true for honky-tonkers, outlaws, and a fair number of bluegrassers as it is for singing cowboys and tuxedoed country-clubbers. Even ol' Lefty, a master of the twang-heavy vocal filigree, is at base a crooner who picks his spots for the fancy stuff and delivers his lines relaxed and smooth even then.

Another way of arriving at the same point: no singer had more direct influence on the development of country vocalizing than Bing Crosby. Crosby's impact is unavoidable across American popular music, of course, but his croon, comfortable and approachable and middle-class-defining, found an early home in country, and in the homes of many middle-class-aspiring country fans, the Haggards included. Asked once what records his parents had when he was young, Merle recalled that "the first thing that was a hit must have been a Crosby record." He "had as much influence on me as anybody did," Merle told country music journalist Bob Allen in 1984.

Like Jimmie Rodgers, Bing Crosby was also profoundly influenced by Black singers and musicians, particularly by the one-time Rodgers collaborator Louis Armstrong. Biographer Gary Giddins positions superstar Crosby as a prime example of "an axiom that defined—and continues to define—American music" ever since minstrelsy became the soundtrack of the nineteenth century: "African-American innovations metamorphose into American popular culture when white performers learn to mimic black ones."

Bing Crosby was especially important to the western swingers and singing cowboys, those most pop-minded of country crooners who in the 1930s and '40s trailed their southwestern audiences to Hollywood and the Pacific Coast. All parties concerned sang "relaxed American," in part because they understood that, together, "relaxed" and "American" telegraphed "middle-class." In return, Crosby found many of his biggest records in the country repertoire, including "New San Antonio Rose" in 1941.

"San Antonio Rose" was initially a breakout hit for Bob Wills in a fiddle-fueled, small-group instrumental version in 1939, a rearrangement of one of his first recordings, "Spanish Two-Step." Wills wrote that earlier "mariachi-flavored fiddle instrumental," country critic John Morthland informs, after noticing "local Chicanos weren't dancing to his more traditional fiddle breakdowns because the beat was wrong." A fan both of blues queen Bessie Smith and minstrelsy remnant Emmett Miller, Wills joined string-band music and cowboy melodies to the driving swing of territory bands and other big-band jazz outfits—creating a country subgenre eventually dubbed western swing. He became a star in Texas and Oklahoma, but after World War II he followed the Okies to California where he and his band regularly appeared at Bakersfield's Beardsley Ballroom. "I used to catch their 7 P.M. *Bob Wills Show* with my dad, and then listen to *The Lone Ranger*," Haggard told journalist Gary Eskow in 2009. "Bob is still the best performer I ever saw."

Wills's "San Antonio Rose" became a hit again (peaking in 1941) when singer Tommy Duncan and other members of Wills's Texas Playboys fitted words to their boss's tune, replaced the formerly dominant fiddle with sax, clarinet, and Tex-Mex trumpets, and chugged the rhythm hard like a fast-moving train: "*New* San Antonio Rose." Crosby covered the song by year's end, with orchestral backing from his brother Bob, who softened the beat considerably but heightened the dreamy swoon of the melody, underscoring the dreamy croon of the singer.

Haggard was a Crosby fan as a boy, but Bob Wills was a hero. "Bob Wills was all over the radio, all day," Haggard explained to one interviewer. "There was a…station that broadcast from Rosarita Beach in Baja, Mexico, just across the border from where my family lived in southern California." Much later, after "Okie from Muskogee" made him into a country music superstar, Haggard chose to spend some of his new artistic capital on *The Best Damn Fiddle Player in the World*, an album tribute to Wills and his music. It was no coincidence that Haggard's band began to be described as a swing band almost instantly. It's worth noting, however, that prior to the Wills project, western swing had barely registered as part of the Strangers' live sound or studio repertoire. The singing of Tommy Duncan, on the other hand, left its mark on Haggard much sooner. In 1955, in fact, Haggard played guitar in a pickup band behind Duncan for a sparsely attended Bakersfield solo gig.

A shorthand description of Duncan's vocal approach would say it was a cross between Jimmie Rodgers and Bing Crosby—American, extra relaxed—and like both of those singers, he sang, as has been said, thought by thought rather than word by word, not only emphasizing the emotions of a lyric but adding emotions the words never addressed. When Crosby sings "New San Antonio Rose," he at first takes the lyric sheet literally—it's "a broken song of love" for the Rose he's had to leave at the Alamo. But he doubles down on the loss—he elongates words with a sustained note here, a quivering mordant note there—and before long the song ceases to be about words at all. "Deep within my heart lies a melody," the song begins, and Bing sings it so the melody, and the aching beauty of Crosby's voice, is the point.

Duncan's version, by contrast, is plainspoken, unadorned, and not especially pained at all. The Playboys' rhythm bounces the singer through his lines rapidly, egged on by Wills's smiling falsetto "ah-ha's," and when Duncan comes to the bridge, wishing the moon would once more shine upon his lover, he's smiling big himself. Duncan's version is all about the melody, too, but as a tool for dancing on your troubles, rather than feeling them more intensely.

On 1970's *The Best Damn Fiddle Player in the World*, Merle chooses to move the crowd with the Playboys' train-track rhythms, but after the opening, he drops the big-band charts for guitar and fiddle solos nearer to the song's instrumental origins, and while his phrasing and timbre are all Duncan's, his feeling is all Crosby. "Call back my Rose, Rose of San Antone," he cries—he sounds as if he might be *about* to cry—but as the song puts it, those are "empty words." It's the melody that matters. And the held-in anguish of Merle's voice, fighting back tears and trying hard to sound relaxed.

17. "Sally Let Your Bangs Hang Down," The Maddox Brothers & Rose (Four Star, 1949)
18. "Sally Let Your Bangs Hang Down," Merle Haggard and Leona Williams (from *Heart to Heart*, Mercury, 1983)

Country music wasn't all smooth and easy. It could get gone, too, when it had a mind, and no act better stands for the rough-and-raucous streak in California country than the Maddox Brothers & Rose. They were known as "America's Most Colorful Hillbilly Band," a slogan that you'd figure had to be hyperbole—until you saw and heard them. Merle heard them on the radio all the time as a kid and loved them so much he begged his brother, Lowell, to take him to one of their appearances when he was twelve. This was Merle's first show, an electrified riot of volume, dim lights (and bright ones, too, blazing off the group's rhinestone-studded suits), thick smoke, and loud music presented at breakneck speed and with lascivious commentary pinballing between Maddoxes. All of this was punctuated with maniacal laughter.

The Maddoxes came to California from Alabama early in the Depression, in the vanguard of Okie migration. They were so far ahead of the deluge that when they hit Oakland in 1933, their plight was considered newsworthy ("Family Roams U.S. for Work"), and they got their picture in the paper. Desperately poor, the family was forced to give daughter Rose to the local postmaster for a time. As she explained it to author Nicholas Dawidoff, "They couldn't afford to feed me."

The Maddox Brothers & Rose—brothers Fred, Cliff, Don, Cal (who died in 1949), and Henry ("Friendly Henry," Cal's replacement, "The Working Girl's Friend!"), plus little sister Rose ("The Sweetheart of Hillbilly Swing")—were tailor-made for the San Joaquin Valley's newcomers. Their broad stage accents and unabashed hillbilly identity, their family lineup and penchant for oldish songs (covers of Bob Wills's "Cherokee Maiden" and Jimmie Rodgers's "Mule Skinner Blues"), helped transplants keep in emotional touch with home. At the same time, the Maddoxes' fancy duds and knowing humor, their clamorous locomotive rhythms and hopped-up covers of brand-new hits, evangelized for a new home. The Maddoxes' hillbilly boogie—prototype for rockabilly and the Bakersfield Sound both—offered up hot, delirious, grab-it-while-you-can fun. And it was loud. "Nobody else turned it up as loud as they did, and [mandolin man] Henry would *really* crank it up," Roy Nichols told Maddox biographer Jonny Whiteside. Nichols knew this firsthand. Long before joining Merle Haggard's Strangers, he played lead guitar for the Maddoxes, on record and on stage, in 1949, when he was still a teen.

The Maddoxes made a lasting impression on Merle. Nineteen seventy-one's chart-topping "Daddy Frank" was inspired, in part, by stories he had heard of the family's journeys, and his 1974 "Old Man from the Mountain," also a #1, with its hot rhythm and "Don't want no Friendly Henrys warmin' up my bed," paid tribute to their sound and randy attitude. But what really impressed Merle when he saw the band was Roy Nichols, a kid barely older than himself, on electric lead guitar.

Haggard fell into singing because he was a gifted mimic, but also, he would say with frustration, because he wasn't all that great a guitarist. As Merle grew up, the West Coast country scene was just taking shape, distinguishing itself by electric guitar licks and runs, usually played on Fender Telecasters (made just down the road in Fullerton, California), and by a who's who of hot country pickers: Kentucky transplant Merle Travis, Joe Maphis, Speedy West, and Larry Collins (of the Collins Kids); Buck Owens, Buckaroo Don Rich, Roy Clark, and future Haggard sidemen James Burton and Glen Campbell; and, later on, country rockers Roy Buchanan, Clarence White, and Roger McGuinn, among many others. In this hotbed of six-string mastery, an aspiring picker like Merle was as likely to wind up second-rate as he was to dream of guitar stardom in the first place.

Roy Nichols was as good as any of them. Born in Arizona but raised in Fresno, California, Nichols cited gypsy-jazzer Django Reinhardt as a key influence, but it was Lester "Junior" Barnard, Bob Wills's lead guitarist during the Playboys' years on the West Coast, who became his model closest to home. Nichols worked with the Maddox Brothers & Rose for only a year but parlayed the experience into session work and eventually into a gig with Lefty Frizzell, both in the studio (including "California Blues" on Lefty's Rodgers tribute) and on the road as one of his Tune Toppers. In fact, Nichols was in the band in 1953 when Merle regaled the Rainbow Gardens with his Lefty routine. What was it like working for Lefty, the sixteen-year-old Merle asked the eighteen-year-old Roy. "Not worth a shit," Nichols told him. The young Nichols's playing won Merle's respect, but cocky and jaded, too? Now *that* was the kind of musician Merle wanted to be.

You can hear a fine early example of Nichols's work on the Maddox Brothers & Rose's 1949 "Sally Let Your Bangs Hang Down," a single with a reputation at the time as something of a "dirty record." That was because of bawdy lyrics—"I saw Sally change her clothes / She was in a perfect pose"— and also because Sally was so game: "She loves 'em and she leaves 'em," the song says, in language anticipating a famous Haggard line to come. But if "dirty" is what you're after, check out Nichols's break at the end of the first verse. The whole record seems to slow down as the sixteen-year-old makes his guitar pant and thrust and wiggle. "Swing 'em low," yells brother Cal, and sister Rose fans herself: "Wooooo!"

Thirty years on, when Merle covered "Sally" with his then-wife Leona Williams, he dropped the Maddoxes' fiddle intro and added solos on piano and pedal steel, even penny-whistle, but kept the randy, growling intensity of the Maddox version he'd loved as a boy. Halfway through he introduces a by-then fifty-year-old Roy Nichols, and his old friend proves he's still got the moves while Haggard cackles his approval.

19. "Devil Woman," Marty Robbins (Columbia, 1962)
20. "I'm Moving On," Hank Snow and His Rainbow Ranch Boys (RCA Victor, 1950)
21. "Folsom Prison Blues," "Jackson," and "Orange Blossom Special," Johnny Cash (from *At Folsom Prison*, Columbia, 1968)
22. "Love's Gonna Live Here," Buck Owens (Capitol, 1963)
23. "Medley," Merle Haggard with Bonnie Owens and the Strangers (from *The Fightin' Side of Me*, Capitol, 1970)

Haggard's career argues that musical indebtedness felt personally should be proclaimed publicly. Eliminate all his albums and songs intended to express gratitude and admiration for other artists, particularly artists he loved as a teenager, and you'd very nearly halve his catalogue. And even after landing a recording contract and scoring his first national hits, he was still borrowing voices and sounds, still tinkering with Haggard. We can hear some of that, and what feels like a letting go of it, on 1970's live *The Fightin' Side of Me*. He tells the crowd:

> We haven't been doing them on our show, but we promised we'd do them the next time we were here in Philadelphia. Would you all like to see some impersonations for a second or two?

The imitation of country stars by country hopefuls, as in Merle mimicking Lefty, is one thing. The impersonation of big stars by other big stars with already well-defined styles of their own is something else. There was a time when this was fairly common in country circles, an adjunct of country comedy generally. But unlike the way an impersonator such as Rich Little might tweak, say, Richard Nixon on *The Tonight Show*, country singers favored verisimilitude over laughs. Their takeoffs weren't so much funny as amusing and affirming, an opportunity for artist and audience to honor shared heroes. The ensuing smiles and chuckles are tingles of recognition: "Sounds just like that, don't he?" Or: "Ah hell, we got *that* record at the house!"

"This is one of my very favorite singers," Merle avows at that 1970 Philadelphia concert. "If I don't sound like him, I'm going to be mad at me, I guarantee you." This very favorite singer turns out to be Marty Robbins, and he wasn't kidding about the singer being a favorite: Merle's second child, about to turn twelve at the time of the concert, was named after the singer. Here Merle doesn't merely try to sound like Marty, he sets out to re-create Robbins's 1962 record, "Devil Woman": "If I wanted my freedom, I could be free ever more," his Mary tells him. "But I don't want to be." With the Strangers' help, it's a passable job, but his next impersonation is uncanny, Merle's voice all but indistinguishable from the clipped, speedy croon of Hank Snow singing the 1950 freedom-seeking train hit "I'm Moving On." Next, Merle does the Man in Black, and the bit is greeted by stomps and roars of approval—not because of the fidelity of Merle's imitation, which is sketchy at best, but because it's so game, so fond, and so identifiable as aping specifically the versions of "Folsom Prison Blues," "Jackson" (with Bonnie Owens playing June Carter), and "Orange Blossom Special" ("I don't care if I do-die-do-die-do-die-do-die-do") heard on Cash's own wildly successful live album, *At Folsom Prison,* from a couple of years earlier. The segment ends with Merle and the Strangers catching a lift on the freight-train sound of one of the records that first brought the Bakersfield Sound to national attention, a spot-on re-creation of Buck Owens & the Buckaroos' 1963 "Love's Gonna Live Here."

Impersonations like these were already quaint when Merle had performed them on a 1969 episode of *The Glen Campbell Goodtime Hour* (with Buck Owens and Johnny Cash on hand to feign annoyance). He was well aware of this ("We haven't been doing them on our show"), so Merle rushed ahead to breaking news: the Nashville Songwriters' Association had just named him Songwriter of the Year. "I'm very proud of it," he told the crowd. "And this is one of the songs that I think maybe took a little notice or something." He crooned "Today I Started Loving You Again" then, a ballad that had been recorded by some two dozen acts in just the last year and a half. It was a sign that from now on, the country singer people would be covering, and even copying, was Merle Haggard.

CHAPTER 6

"LEONARD," 1981

Many artists provided Merle Haggard with aesthetic and emotional options in the years before he'd developed those qualities in himself. Later, after he emerged as a star in his own right, a tiny group of other acts influenced him further. "Leonard," a top-ten country hit at the dawn of the Reagan era, was Merle's musical raising of the glass to someone who belongs in both camps, a man who'd been inspiring him damn near his whole life—first as a local hero, then as a professional role model, and finally as a colleague and friend.

Leonard Sipes was born in Oklahoma in 1930. He followed the hordes to California in 1952, riding out with his girlfriend at the time, the future rock-and-roll and country star Wanda Jackson, and her family. Sipes arrived just in time to witness the Bakersfield scene's national coming-out party. That was the woebegone Korean War–era hit "A Dear John Letter," which not only topped the country survey in 1953 but went top-five on the pop charts as well. Sung with matter-of-fact cruelty by Jean Shepard and recited with it-just-figures pathos by Ferlin Husky, "Dear John" was additionally the creation of some of the very men who figured later among Merle's closest musical confidantes, several of whom were also his business partners: Ken Nelson produced it for Capitol Records, and Fuzzy Owen and Lewis

Talley (who'd earlier cut the song with young "girl singer" Bonnie Owens) split the writer's credit. Fuzzy and Lewis played on the record as well, on steel and acoustic guitar, as did two more guitarists, Buck Owens and... Leonard Sipes, though by then he was going by an intoxicating stage name Husky had suggested: Tommy Collins.

The early Bakersfield scene was small and more or less self-contained, but that doesn't mean it wouldn't help to have a scorecard. Bonnie Owens (with an "s," maiden name Campbell) had once been married to Buck Owens (also with an "s," real name Alvis), but wasn't married anymore when she moved to California and began to date Fuzzy Owen (no "s," real name Charles). Per Bear Family, "A Dear John Letter" was first recorded in 1953 for the Mar-Vel label and credited to "Fuzzy and Bonnie Owens" (with an "s" for both; it was just easier). Writer Gerald Haslam reports that "Dear John" was actually written by Bakersfield's Johnny Grimes (stage name Hillbilly Barton). However, before the song became a hit for Jean Shepard (real name Ollie) and Ferlin Husky (his real name, believe it or not, though he'd briefly used the stage name Terry Preston and would one day record comedy sides as Simon Crum), Grimes traded the song to the apparently nickname-deprived Lewis Talley in exchange for either a scooter or, depending on who's telling the tale, a "Kaiser automobile." Talley, in turn, sold half the copyright to Fuzzy Owen for 150 bucks. Fuzzy played steel guitar in the Orange Blossom Playboys, the Blackboard house band run by Bill Woods, aka "The Father of the Bakersfield Sound," who at various points had also employed Buck Owens, Merle Haggard, and Red Simpson (real name Joe), aka Suitcase Simpson because of the satchel of songs for sale he always carried. (In 1972 Merle recorded a Simpson-penned tribute number called "Bill Woods from Bakersfield.") The studio lineup for Shepard and Husky's "Dear John" session was rounded out by bassist Herman Snyder (stage name Herman the Hermit), whose son Clifford Snyder (stage name Cliffie Stone) was the longtime host of *Hometown Jamboree,* a Los Angeles–based TV show that regularly featured Leonard Sipes, aka Tommy Collins, and was a regular as well on another seminal television show, Bakersfield's own *Cousin Herb Henson's Trading Post.* Wikipedia claims that host Cousin Herb (real name Herbert Henson) was the first cousin once removed of alt.country band Wilco's frontperson, Jeff Tweedy (real name Jeff Tweedy).

*   *   *

Collins joined the hit parade himself soon after "Dear John," landing a #2 hit with his own "You Better Not Do That" and succeeding it with the like-minded #4 hit "Whatcha Gonna Do Now," both in 1954. In other words, the very year in which Merle's impromptu opening gig for Lefty Frizzell had him deciding he wanted to play music for a living was also the year that jukebox-crowding Tommy Collins offered hometown proof it could be done. For a time Collins continued to pen hits for himself and others: "Untied" and "It Tickles," which like "Whatcha Gonna Do Now" feature hot hillbilly licks by Buck Owens, went top-ten for Collins in 1955. That same year his "If You Ain't Lovin' (You Ain't Livin')" was a big record for Capitol label mate Faron Young.

But Collins had a religious conversion the following year. By decade's end, he'd attended a seminary, pastored several congregations, and, finally, set aside professional music altogether. By the time Merle was out of prison, though, Collins was trying to get back in the game, and after catching Merle's "Sing a Sad Song" on the radio, he tracked down the young singer. "I had never heard a voice that good and I just had to meet the man who owned that voice," he told Dale Vinicur.

This had to be a big deal for Merle—at that very moment the nation's best-selling country album was the debt-repaying *Buck Owens Sings Tommy Collins*. Soon Haggard and Collins were taking regular fishing trips along the Kern, the older man helping out the ambitious young ex-con with his songwriting and musicianship and just being generally supportive in ways Merle needed. As Merle put it in "Leonard," a tribute song to his friend, Tommy Collins "even brought around a bag of groceries (Hey!) / Back before Muskogee came along."

At first glance the two seem a poor match. Haggard, even early on, was a notably smooth crooner, down-to-earth but with a soaring and wide vocal range, whereas Collins sang with a self-consciously rural accent, high and pinched thin. What's more, while Haggard's best known today for material that marks him as about as earnest a singer-songwriter as you'll find, Collins leaned wacky. His specialty was the G-rated wink at R-rated activity, for which "You Better Not Do That" was the model: there, Collins tells his pawing and petting girlfriend that she'd better stop her pawing and petting, PDQ, the never-stated but always obvious reason being that if she doesn't, he is, at the very least, going to be sporting a big ol' boner—and then what'll they do? The subsequent "Whatcha Gonna Do Now" ("Then I saw a gleam that I never saw before!") and "It Tickles" ("That's what she said") were variations on the theme. So was "Sam Hill," in which the title character heads up the mountain to see his sweetheart for years on end, returning home each evening with a smile on his face: the townsfolk wonder "what the Sam Hill's goin' on," but we know. In 1964 that Collins novelty would provide Merle with a minor follow-up hit to his career-launching "Sing a Sad Song."

But Merle and Tommy were an odd couple only at first glance. Behind the grin, Collins was an adept interpreter of wickedly mournful balladry. Country just doesn't come much more completely licked by circumstance than his "I Wish I Had Died in My Cradle," or more betrayed and self-righteously pissed than his "High on a Hilltop." These titles are much nearer in style and sentiment to the more than a dozen Collins numbers Haggard would later record—the cynical and game-playing "Carolyn," for instance, or "Wine Take Me Away," which they wrote together. Including that cowrite (and one more, "My Hands Are Tied," which the pair wrote with fellow Capitol artist Kay "Little Pink Mac" Adams), Merle cut eighteen Collins songs in his career. When asked by *Rolling Stone* in 2011 to list ten songs he wished he'd written, Merle chose a series of classics by the likes of Jimmie Rodgers and Lefty Frizzell, Tom T. Hall, Kris Kristofferson, Hank Williams, and others, but he saved the #10 spot for Collins's "When No Flowers Grow." It's "about a woman who accidentally kills her child by backing over him. She goes crazy, picking flowers in the snow, when no flowers grow," Haggard explains, noting, "It's an expert piece of work."

Returning the autobiographical assist Collins had earlier given Haggard in songs like "The Roots of My Raising" and "I Made the Prison Band," "Leonard," a top-ten hit in 1981, allowed Merle to sing Collins's story with reverence, good humor, and a keen sense of how hard a world it is: Sipes nearly became a star ("Hey, once he even followed Elvis Presley!"); he gave it all up to preach the gospel before figuring out that wasn't his calling after all ("How in the hell was Leonard supposed to know?"); he lost his wife and kids to addiction and the road ("I saw what pills and booze can really do"); and then he got himself back on track after all ("I'd forgot about a Friend that Leonard knew")—all of this, and more, in a mere three dozen lines. It's an expert piece of work.

CHAPTER 7

THE BAKERSFIELD SOUND AND FURY

Merle Haggard walked out of San Quentin on November 3, 1960, and caught a bus back home to Bakersfield. He was twenty-three. Leona hadn't met him at the prison gates as planned, but the couple had already decided to give their marriage another try. With a growing family to feed, Merle had no time to ease into his liberty. He signed on at the electrical contracting business belonging to his brother, Lowell, digging ditches and doing other odd jobs for a solid eighty a week.

Bakersfield in 1960 was a very different place from the one Merle's folks emigrated to in 1935 and where he'd been born in '37. Haggard noted some more recent changes on 1972's *Let Me Tell You about a Song* during a spoken introduction to "They're Tearing the Labor Camps Down." "The freeways were wider and the old steam engines were gone forever," he observed. Women wore their dresses shorter, too, he smiled, though perhaps it just seemed that way to a man who'd been in stir for three years.

"One thing I noticed most of all down through the San Joaquin Valley," he continued, "was the disappearance of so many labor camps where once I'd lived from time to time myself." It set Merle to worrying about the migrant workers, the men "with the big family who can't afford the old high standard of living," who still followed the harvest and needed places to live. An ongoing problem, as it's turned out, though one increasingly less pressing for Okies than for Black and Hispanic laborers.

That was because of another development. The coming of the Okies created much nativist hostility through the Great Depression and World War II, but it also put the little oil town on the map. Thirty years down the road, the Okies were more and more identified (by their former tormentors and by themselves) as assimilated middle-class-aspiring Californians—like immigrants before them, they had "become white"—and many of them had the mortgages and lawn mowers to prove it. A related development: many Okies defended their rising standards of living and tenuous new status by putting a boot on the throats of those who'd never shared even their limited privileges to begin with. In 1964, only months after President Lyndon B. Johnson signed the Civil Rights Act and just months before riots in the Watts section of Los Angeles, Californians voted two-to-one in favor of Proposition 14, which repealed the state's open housing law and made it legal for property owners to reject prospective renters or home buyers on the basis of race. Two years later, as gubernatorial candidate Ronald Reagan campaigned against open housing, two thousand Black Bakersfieldians protested the city's failure to distribute federal poverty funds by setting fire to a school bus. Local whites reacted first with a Molotov cocktail assault on Black neighborhoods, and second by passing an initiative to refuse any future federal poverty assistance. One way Okies signaled to themselves and the world they'd arrived, relatively speaking, was to purchase tract homes in Southern California's "crabgrass frontier" and to fill them with shiny new appliances. A way for Okies to defend their toehold in that world was to inflict class- and race-based wounds that were like evil twins to the ones they still nursed themselves.

It's been said that California's conservative turn in the 1960s, soon taken nationwide by Richard Nixon and Ronald Reagan, should be blamed on the arrival of the Okies and their conservative worldviews, a new political reality—the southernization of America, Golden State division—exploited by Republican southern strategies ever since. Historian Peter La Chapelle shows that the catalyst for the shift was at least as much the other way around: "the southern California-ization of…transplanted southerners" working overtime to achieve the American Dream and the respectability that proved it had come true. With good prospects and a little luck, they could maybe even contemplate a level of success that would let them become Republicans, of all things, albeit ones likely lacking country club memberships. By 1969 music journalist John Grissim was able to report, in his *Country Music: White Man's Blues*, on preparations for the official declaration of Bakersfield as the Country Music Capital of the West, with organizers eager to mark their new status by inviting Governor Reagan and Vice President Spiro Agnew to the celebration.

These new attitudes and ambitions, reinforced by new subdivisions and strip malls, new financial security and political clout, were forward-looking but tentatively so and tetchy. Any optimism was mitigated by its opposite being only a few missed paychecks away. The mood was bright-eyed but vigilant and with a giant chip on its shoulder. "I'm proud to be an Okie," Merle would sing in 1969, only months after recalling in "Hungry Eyes" how "another class of people put us somewhere just below." All through the golden age of the Bakersfield Sound is a pride in collective roots that's inseparable, indistinguishable really, from an anxiety that the Okies could still be sent, if only metaphorically, back where they came from.

These were the decades when the trade category "Hillbilly" was replaced by Country & Western in evocation of the tonier Town & Country, and it's when Okie references in band names and song titles all but disappeared from the rollicking Bakersfield scene. Those rhinestone-bejeweled Western suits—designed by Los Angeles–based tailor Nudie Cohn and so closely identified with Buck Owens, Porter Wagoner, and other 1960s country acts—are a neon-bright symbol of economic apprehension. A Nudie suit is both a salt-of-the-earth signifier of hillbilly style and a flashy advertisement for upward mobility.

Merle had dabbled at becoming a professional musician before he went to prison—a poor boy's dream fueled by a handful of high-profile homegrown hits. The scene's coming-out party was "A Dear John Letter," a duet for Okie-to-Cali migrant Jean Shepard and Bakersfield's own Ferlin Husky in 1953. Ferlin plays a poor G.I. stuck in Korea who gets a letter from his girl back home, informing him that she's dumping him for his brother. Ferlin gets most of the record, spilling his heartache via recitation, but Jean stars because she gets to sing the hook: "Dear John, Oh how I hate to write." In signs of both aspirational Bakersfield ambition and country crossover potential, "Dear John" topped the national country charts and climbed all the way to #4 on the pop side. A string of country hits by Tommy Collins over the next few years solidified the Capitol Records–Bakersfield connection.

A teenage Merle played some around town through these years and appeared, once, on TV's *The Billy Mize Show*, singing Lefty's "King without a Queen." (Small world: Mize had been the leader of the house band that night years earlier when Lefty Frizzell insisted that Merle sing to his audience.) In 1956 an eighteen-year-old Haggard relocated to Springfield, Missouri, with the intention of auditioning for the *Ozark Jubilee*, the nationally televised program hosted there by that great country Crosby, Red Foley. "I got a Greyhound bus ticket," he told journalist and filmmaker Dave Hoekstra, "but it never happened." That was because local personality Jack Tyree hired him first for his *The Smilin' Jack Tyree Radio Show*. The new gig ended almost as soon as it had begun, though, and that, Merle said, was because Tyree claimed he couldn't afford to pay him what he'd promised. In a tale he delighted in telling and retelling through the decades, Merle said he yanked up Tyree's pants leg, grabbed the wad of bills he kept in his sock, peeled off what he was owed, and tossed the rest back on his now former boss's desk. The entire heartland adventure lasted less than a month.

In 1957 Merle even cut a demo with the hopes of landing a record deal with some small Bakersfield label. But, as Fuzzy Owen recalls in his own autobiography, he and his cousin Lewis Talley thought long and hard about signing the young singer but turned him down. To their ears, the young Haggard sounded too much like Buck Owens. It was just a few months later that his ill-fated burglary attempt sent Merle up the river.

Now a free man again, inspired by Cash's San Quentin appearance and newly confident in his abilities, Merle set to scrounging for pickup gigs in earnest. His first break came a few months after his release when a visitor showed up at Merle's house needing a singer for his band and wanting to hear if Haggard was as good as recommended. Merle had just recorded himself singing Jimmie Rodgers's "Nobody Knows but Me" on a borrowed Webcore reel-to-reel and offered to play it for the fellow. After some initial disbelief ("That's not you," the guy replies in *House of Memories*, "that's Lefty Frizzell."), Merle was tapped to sing lead and play rhythm guitar four nights a week at a club called the High Pockets. Things moved quickly from there. He entered a talent contest at the Rainbow Gardens, singing "Smoking Cigarettes and Drinkin' Coffee Blues," a Marty Robbins–penned Lefty Frizzell hit from the year before. He came in second, but the exposure helped win him a job spelling singer Johnny Barnett nights at the Lucky Spot. Before he knew it, Merle was working six or seven nights a week, and, as he wrote in *Sing Me Back Home*, "I quit my som'bitchin' ditch-diggin' job real quick." All of this was in 1961.

Sometime in '62 Haggard recorded his first single—with the same man who'd rejected his demo half a decade earlier. An Arkie transplant, Fuzzy Owen was now the steel guitarist at the Lucky Spot, a regular on Cousin Herb Henson's television program, and a fixture of the Bakersfield club scene. He had ambitions beyond making it as a working musician, too. He headed a local record label and had even found significant success as a songwriter: his "The Same Old Me" had been a country chart-topper for Ray Price while Merle was in prison, and Jan Howard had landed a sizable national hit with Fuzzy's "The One You Slip Around With," cowritten with another local boy about to make good, Jan's husband at the time, Harlan Howard.

Fuzzy didn't think Merle sounded like Buck Owens now. The more he heard Merle sing at the Lucky Spot, the more excited he became. The two struck up a friendship and soon decided to cut some sides for release on Tally Records, the label Owen had cofounded with, and recently bought outright from, his cousin Lewis Talley. For the A-side they picked one of Merle's songs, "Skid Row," and the B was Owen's "Singin' My Heart Out." The latter is like a thousand other records of the moment that echoed the Nashville Sound—tinkling slip-note piano, female chorus, smooth Marty Robbins–style vocal. But "Skid Row" is another matter. It's kicked off by electric guitar that's thick and twisty like taffy, like the lick from George Jones's "Tall, Tall Trees" played in quicksand. At the same time, it has a by-then-mainstream rock-and-roll energy and feel, with backing singers doing their best to suggest Nashville's the Jordanaires and with a lyric that swipes an image from Memphis's Carl Perkins: Merle admits he's "got a great big hole in my blue-suede shoes." "Skid Row" is about a guy who's fallen on harder-than-hard times, a common enough theme for country music. What makes it a standout, and what holds it back from being fairly termed a novelty, even with all its jokes and good humor, is Merle's tart, pointed vocal and its unexpectedly mature lyric. His girl tells Merle she's leaving because he's "got *no class*," and in a song he sometimes said he wrote when he was just fourteen, maybe fifteen (other times he dated it to his prison years), Merle's voice lets us know he agrees with her. Merle's so rock-bottom that when people pass on the street, "they stop and stare." Then he cops to a humiliation many Okies would recall all too well: "They giggle and snicker at the clothes I wear."

Haggard now had earned enough of a reputation that Buck Owens hired him to play bass. Haggard only lasted a few months with Owens on the road—in Milwaukee he got a standing "O" singing George Jones's new hit, "She Thinks I Still Care"—but stuck around long enough to dub Buck's band the Buckaroos. (The Buckaroos repaid this debt with the release in 1971 of an instrumental album entitled *The Songs of Merle Haggard*.)

Buck Owens's emergence as country music's brightest young star was the most consequential change to the Bakersfield scene of all. Buck had been a familiar face in area clubs well before Merle jimmied Fred & Gene's back door, and Capitol Records producer Ken Nelson had A-listed Owens for studio work as well: Buck played hot-dog guitar on rockabilly-influenced sessions for Gene Vincent, Wanda Jackson, and Tommy Collins. But Owens didn't hit with a cut of his own until spring 1959, about a year into Merle's sentence, when "Second Fiddle" registered briefly on the charts. He solidified that minor success with a trio of major ones—"Under Your Spell Again," "Above and Beyond," and "Excuse Me (I Think I've Got a Heartache)"—before Merle was released the following year. Owens was on his way to becoming a hometown star so big that locals began referring to "Buckersfield."

An eight-year-old Owens and his parents had headed to California from Texas in 1937, the year Haggard was born, but their car lasted only to Arizona, adding a decade-and-a-half layover to Buck's itinerary. The Owenses spent years in desperate poverty in Arizona, working when they could get work in fruit and vegetable fields they didn't own. Buck played music for fun and extra cash and eventually married the girl singer in one of his first bands, a swingy little string band known by the self-consciously rural moniker the Skillet Lickers. Buck and Bonnie Owens had two children in Arizona, but they were on the outs when Bonnie took the kids to Bakersfield early in 1951, and they were legally separated by the time Buck moved there in May.

It's fun to imagine Buck and Merle passing one another out there on the road somewhere that spring—Buck twenty-one and Bakersfield-bound, Merle barely a teenager and road-tripping to Texas. In many ways the two men most identified with the Bakersfield Sound were always moving in different directions. Buck Owens was a savvy music entrepreneur who would eventually make millions in publishing and radio, in artist promotion, and as cohost of the TV series *Hee Haw*. Merle was indifferent to money matters and ended up declaring bankruptcy in the 1990s. The men were musically very different, too. Merle was born with a technically great voice, offering broad range and arresting texture, and he sang with deep nuance, variety, and emotional presence. Buck was a highly effective singer, as well, but more limited. He had two speeds, so to speak. One was effervescent and bubbly, which was good because Buck liked effervescent, bubbly songs: "My Heart Skips a Beat," "Love's Gonna Live Here," "We're Gonna Let the Good Times Roll," and so on.

Buck's other speed was a plaintive solemnity he adopted for ballads. Typically, Owens sang "Together Again" in 1964 pretty much the same way he sang "Crying Time" the year after, even though the former ballad is presumably happy and the latter very unhappy indeed. He sings both songs pleasantly, agreeably, his aim to entertain, not to challenge. Always, Owens sings with a palpable sense of wanting to be liked.

That was another difference between Buck and Merle, who himself wanted to be liked as much as anyone, but who went about it by stressing how much he didn't give a damn what you think. In 1969, in "Workin' Man Blues," for instance, a prickly Merle took a stand and bragged he'd never been on welfare. But when Buck acknowledged the same issue in "Waitin' in Your Welfare Line," a chart-topper in the months prior to passage of Bakersfield's antiwelfare initiative, he made it a sweetly shuffling joke. Haggard, who as a boy experienced similar if not nearly so desperate deprivation as Owens had in Arizona, grew up to write introspective, angry songs about what it's like to be poor. Owens was about getting up and out. "Act Naturally," "Johnny B. Goode," "Above and Beyond," "Big in Vegas"—the songs Buck Owens wrote and sang—are about class, too, but from the perspective of a poor man who wants desperately to be rich. These differences between Haggard and Owens mirror the conflicted emotions of white working-class communities generally. Merle Haggard wore his carefully guarded outsider status like a scab. Buck Owens wanted to belong.

Haggard's first single for Tally sold out, but since Fuzzy Owen had printed only two hundred copies and sold those mostly off the stage and out of his trunk, that wasn't saying much. Merle wanted to record again, but Owen kept putting him off, saying the songs Merle was writing were fine but not hits. Bring me a song that we can make some money on, Fuzzy kept saying. Merle kept writing and kept looking.

Merle visited Las Vegas around then, stopping in at the Nashville Nevada Club, home base for another important Bakersfield figure, Wynn Stewart. Stewart came to California from Missouri in the late 1940s, and by the time Merle visited Vegas, he'd had one honest-to-goodness hit, a haunting, fiddle-driven shuffle called "Wishful Thinking" in 1959, and a string of middling ones just as strong, including most recently two inestimable boot scooters: "Big, Big Love" and "Another Day, Another Dollar" paired Wynn's pinched tenor with searing electric licks from pedal steel pioneer Ralph Mooney and Merle's childhood guitar hero, Roy Nichols.

Merle says Nichols spotted him right off that night, enlisting him to play guitar for a few numbers so Roy could hit the bathroom. "Can you sing?" Mooney wanted to know, and when Merle said sure, they ran through a series of Marty Robbins hits, ending with "Devil Woman," a song that, as Merle explained to Colin Escott, "you won't hear too many guys singing because it's got a high note in there that will embarrass you if you don't hit it." As the song ended, Merle noticed Stewart was listening from in front of the bandstand, impressed.

Stewart's West Coast Playboys were one of the best country bands on the planet. Mooney (cowriter of Ray Price's "Crazy Arms" and later the main man in Waylon Jennings's the Waylors) and Nichols were two of the finest soloists in the business; Bobby Austin, who'd just informed Stewart he was planning to leave, played bass; and Helen "Peaches" Price was the "lady drummer"—a lineup that foretold Merle's fortune twice over: first, because Stewart hired Merle on the spot as Austin's replacement and second, because within the year this lineup became the core of his own studio band.

Merle moved his family (now including daughter Kelli, his and Leona's third child) to Vegas, but though his Lefty and Marty impersonations were well received, he stayed there only about six months. One reason for calling short his Vegas stay was that the $250 a week Stewart paid him ("More money than I'd ever earned," he writes in *My House of Memories*, "or even imagined I'd earn") was promptly being lost in the casinos. His main prompt for returning to Bakersfield, though, was "Sing a Sad Song," a swooning, heartbroken ballad his boss finished at the bar one night between sets and introduced to the band just as they went back on. Merle sensed right away that the song Stewart had in mind for a next single was the song he and Fuzzy were searching for. It took him a few days to gin up his courage, but Merle finally approached Stewart (only "about halfway jokin'," he later told music journalist Alanna Nash) with what he had in mind. "Wynn," he asked, "if it was in your power to make me a star, would you do it?" Of course he would, Stewart said. "It *is* within your power," Merle replied. "Give me that song you wrote. Let me record it." Stewart agreed, and Merle walked straight to a pay phone, called Fuzzy, and told him to schedule a session. "We got the song."

In 1996, at a concert in Bakersfield, Merle and Buck Owens performed on stage together for the first time in thirty years. Buck and Merle, along with acolyte Dwight Yoakam (who'd teamed with Buck in 1988 for the hit "Streets of Bakersfield"), were all in town to help Merle make a video for one of his recent recordings, "Beer Can Hill," the Hag's proud party song about growing up rough and rowdy in the Okie stronghold. During an interview about the event for the Nashville Network, television reporter Stormy Warren asked the pair a good question: "What *is* the Bakersfield Sound?"

"It's what Merle and I do," Buck said. "Good answer," Merle replied.

That *is* a good answer. Still, there's more to say that might prove helpful. And one familiar way to do that is to juxtapose the Bakersfield Sound with what, we're told, it is not.

For nearly as long as there has been something called the "Bakersfield Sound," it's been contrasted with what people have in mind when they refer to the "Nashville Sound." The former is described with words like "raw" and "real," "traditional" and "twangy," while the latter's deemed "over-produced" and "fake," "poppy" (a bad thing, in this context) and "twang-less," or twang's presumed opposite, "smooth." In sociologist Richard Peterson's spot-on categorizing, it's "hard core" versus "soft shell."

Now, in the 1950s and '60s, Bakersfield did possess a much rowdier music culture, typified by what Tommy Collins once described to country journalist Tom Roland as the "redneck, scared-to-death, honky-tonk, skull orchard, barely-making-a-living places of Okie entertainment." Bakersfield prized the big beats of western swing and boogie-woogie, and it embraced the loud guitars and even louder rhythms of rockabilly, too, and of rock and roll generally. Just like Joe Maphis's hit says, it was "Dim Lights, Thick Smoke and Loud, Loud Music." Bakersfield was Get Up and Dance whereas Nashville, at least when limited to the Grand Ole Opry, leaned toward Sit and Clap. Buck Owens, who favored a big beat and "Freight Train" rhythms, and who set loose Buckaroo Don Rich's fiddle on classic Harlan Howard shuffles but traded it in for Rich's Telecaster when covering Chuck Berry, is the exemplary figure.

All true, but all exaggerated. Company town Music City and upstart Bakersfield were never as far apart sonically as either's patrons have been willing to allow. It's not that Nashville was less receptive to rock and roll than Bakersfield, but that it was receptive to different types of rock and roll. Per Charlie Gillett's "Five Styles of Rock 'n' Roll," Bakersfield favored "the Chicago rhythm & blues style of Chuck Berry" and "the Northern band rock 'n' roll" of western-swing fiend Billy Haley & His Comets, while Nashville was into "the New Orleans dance blues style," particularly the rock and *roll* of Fats Domino (and the bluesy croon of Ivory Joe Hunter across the Gulf), and the ballad-loving "vocal group style" most of all. The two camps will just have to agree to share the Memphis-centered rockabilly that Gillett called "country rock."

What's more, as Bakersfield came into its own in the early to mid-1960s (it should be noted that Bakersfield had the clubs and much of the talent but that the hit-making happened almost exclusively in Los Angeles, or, as locals cheekily called it, "a town south of Bakersfield"), fans of sharp electric leads and hotshot picking would've found more twang-centric hits coming out of Nashville than what was sometimes dubbed Nashville West. Buck Owens had his first two national #1's, "Act Naturally" and "Love's Gonna Live Here," in 1963. But look what Nashville put out that same year and the year before: Porter Wagoner's "Misery Loves Company," George Jones's "She Thinks I Still Care," Carl Butler & Pearl's "Don't Let Me Cross Over," Marty Robbins's "Ruby Ann," Johnny Cash's "Ring of Fire"—and those are just the #1's, each of which swings or rocks as hard as, is as twangy or traditional or raw (and in some cases a good deal more so) as Buck's hits. Not to deny that Nashville was just then making a lot more of the country-pop stuff, too. Nashville made a lot more of everything.

Bakersfield was more diverse than its reputation, as well. Take Billy Mize. He migrated west to Bakersfield from Kansas during the Depression and, in the 1950s and '60s, became one of Southern California's most beloved country figures. This was due chiefly to his nearly daily appearances as a host on various country television series through the years, where he eschewed the Nudie suits, cowboy hats, and neckerchiefs most associated with the hard-core Bakersfield scene in favor of a look that was sport-coat sharp and solidly middle class. And his singing style, a warm and smooth croon indebted to his hero Tommy Duncan, fit his look. No ultra-twangy hillbilly reacting to country-pop Nashville, Mize sounded just like country-pop Nashville—like Marty Robbins, say, or Don Gibson—and he favored similarly buttery ballads. In 1965, when he cut a version of Merle's "You Don't Have Very Far to Go," it sounded like the finest Eddy Arnold record that Eddy Arnold never made.

Better yet, take Merle Haggard. "Sing a Sad Song," a small national hit in 1964, Merle's first, stands as Exhibit A to illustrate the ways the Bakersfield Sound engaged with, rather than rejected, the Nashville Sound. Merle, Fuzzy, and Stewart's Playboys met in Hollywood for the session, and the result was a Nashville Sound–ing masterpiece. Appropriately so, as Stewart's lyric alludes to "The End of the World," Skeeter Davis's lush-and-then-some Nashville pop smash from the year before. "Pretend it's the end of the world," Merle pleads, alone in some bar, playing the jukebox and trying to forget the woman who's told him off. "She's unhappy with me," he confesses. Then, with sheepish understatement: "She told me so." The song's heavy acoustic strum and Price's relentlessly simple beat weigh on Merle—you imagine his head bobbing as he fights the whiskey for consciousness—and then with great force of will his voice skies, riding the melody to a self-involved falsetto. Strings drip off the track like grease down the walls of an old diner, and when Ralph Mooney plays the melody on pedal steel, the strings play along until it sounds like Mooney is playing a thousand steel guitars, like the orchestra's been electrified, and like the world as Merle's known it really is coming to an end.

In September 1963, when "Sing a Sad Song" was earning local airplay but had yet to crack the national charts, Cousin Herb Henson celebrated the tenth anniversary of his *Trading Post* program with a concert recording for Capitol Records. *Country Music Hootenanny* is like a time capsule of the new Bakersfield. Buck Owens and the Buckaroos race through their soon-to-be chart-topper "Act Naturally." Tommy Collins hams it up through appropriate-to-the-occasion novelty "I Got Mine," and the evening also includes performances by Bakersfield stalwarts Jean Shepard and Buddy Cagle, among others, plus a very young and very pop Glen Campbell. Roy Nichols is there, too, fronting the *Trading Post* band. His furious rock-and-roll guitar on Rose Maddox's "Down to the River" (a Buck Owens song) is a model of controlled, real-real-gone aggression.

Maddox and her brother Cal, "the laughing cowboy," who joined her in the performance, were still-thriving remnants of the audience's Okie past at its over-the-top hillbilly-est. When Cousin Herb presented the colorful pair, though, he made a point of guaranteeing they would "be big city all the way!" That tension between newfound community self-esteem and small-town inferiority was present all night. "Welcome to the beautiful new civic auditorium in Bakersfield, California," Henson gushed, "one hundred miles north of Los Angeles. *We have our own airport, thank you very much.*"

Merle was on the bill that night, as well, performing "Sing Me Back Home." He didn't make the album, though, for the simple reason that he wasn't a Capitol Records artist. When Ken Nelson, up from Hollywood to record the show, spotted the singer, he buttonholed Haggard, telling him what a fine record "Sing a Sad Song" was and counseling him to leave Tally for Capitol, where he'd get the promotion he needed. Perhaps, to put a point on that argument, he let slip plans to record the song with Capitol artist Buddy Cagle. Merle thought about it, then told Nelson thanks but no thank you. Fuzzy had done right by him and was a friend to boot. He was going to try both to make it and to stay put.

CHAPTER 8

SOMEONE TOLD HIS STORY IN A SONG

"Sing a Sad Song" hinted at possible big things to come for Haggard, just barely, charting a measly three weeks and reaching only #19. Perhaps it would've managed a bit better if it hadn't competed for airplay against that Buddy Cagle single. But even with a distributional and promotional disadvantage of David-versus-Goliath proportions, Merle's "Sing a Sad Song" bested Cagle's Capitol version, which didn't crack the top 25. Still, competition from major labels was always going to be an existential problem for tiny, cash-poor labels like Tally.

If Owen and Haggard hadn't known that going in, they learned it for sure in the early summer of 1964. Merle's "Sam Hill," the silly Tommy Collins number that was the follow-up to "Sing a Sad Song," couldn't breach the country top 40 even as a version from Columbia artist Claude King peaked at #11. Then again, King's Nashville version was more driving and electric, more hard-core and Bakersfieldy, and at the same time more understated, than Merle's more broadly comic, novelty-*sounding*, soft-shell rendition. "Sam Hill" did well enough, though, that Merle quit Stewart and returned to Bakersfield. For the next year, many of his show posters and newspaper ads heralded appearances by "Merle Haggard and the Sam Hill Boys." "I'm glad 'Sam Hill' wasn't a big hit," Merle writes in *My House of Memories*.

"I didn't much like the song and had it been a giant hit I would've hated to have sung it for the next fifty years."

Merle brought his own new songs to Fuzzy all the time in these early years, and Fuzzy, now his manager, steadily turned them down. The two, often joined by Bonnie Owens, the ex–Mrs. Buck Owens and Fuzzy's longtime girlfriend, spent a lot of time talking about songwriting. Fuzzy liked to comb the pages of *Billboard* or *Cashbox*, pointing out trends and explaining to his pupils why hits were hits and why Merle's songs weren't. Haggard would listen closely and try again. Is *this* song any good? Merle asked, and Fuzzy would allow that, yeah, it's a pretty good song. When Merle pushed, though, wondering if the song was good enough to be a *hit*, Fuzzy delivered the same deflating reply: "Naaaaw." Merle kept writing and kept looking.

Liz Anderson was living in North Dakota when she and husband Casey and four-year-old daughter (and future country-pop star) Lynn moved to California in 1951, settling around Sacramento. That's where she started writing country songs, because, as she told historians Mary Bufwack and Robert Oermann, there weren't any country radio stations around, and she missed the music. "I just started writing," she explained, "so I'd have some to sing to myself." By the early 1960s she was getting some of those songs recorded. Del Reeves took her "Be Quiet Mind," one of those hard country records Nashville wasn't supposed to make, top ten in 1961, and the not-hard-at-all Roy Drusky scored a hit in '64 with Anderson's "Pick of the Week."

Haggard and Anderson were introduced to one another at a gig outside Sacramento by Bonnie Owens, who'd recently cut Anderson's "Lie a Little" for Tally. Merle "kind of turned his back on the audience," Anderson recalled when I spoke to her in 2011. "He was a little mad no one was there. But when he sang, we flipped out!" Casey Anderson invited Bonnie and Merle back to the house after the show, offering to cook breakfast if they'd check out some of his wife's songs. "I was set to be bored to death," Merle writes in *Sing Me Back Home*, "especially when she went over to an old pump organ." To his amazement, though, Anderson proceeded to play, by his estimation, "one hit after another." Merle and Bonnie would eventually record as duets several songs Anderson shared that night, most notably "Just between the Two of Us." But it was a song called "(My Friends Are

Gonna Be) Strangers" that grabbed Merle by the collar. "He had it learned on the guitar before he left the house," Anderson said.

Today, "(My Friends Are Gonna Be) Strangers" sounds like a Merle Haggard record to a degree his earlier singles don't. Merle seems relaxed, sings in a slightly lower register, and sounds earthier, too. His voice sounds haggard like it hadn't before, but not so much that it rejects polish, embellishment, or other nice things like the ooh-ing female chorus seconding his emotions. This rough beauty is shared by the music. Roy Nichols's fancy-free acoustic guitar lines keep snagging on his barbed-wire chords, and his fellow West Coast Playboys play gritty and pretty by turns.

His woman has left him, Merle sings, after promising she'd stay with him forever. Hardly a new story, but Liz Anderson's lyric conveys those age-old feelings of betrayal and loss with special bitterness. "It sure turned out to be a short forever," Merle deadpans on the way to making a promise of his own. From here on out, he's never going to trust anyone, ever: "All my friends are gonna be strangers." He means it. At the same time Merle makes plain that he doesn't mean it, his confident tone covering unmistakably for intense self-loathing borne of who knows how many other humiliations. What had he been thinking? He knew she was bad news, should have seen her treachery coming, and should now be relieved she's gone. But, oh, what he wouldn't be willing to do if she would only come back…

"Strangers" came out on Tally late in 1964, and it was immediately clear that the new record wouldn't merely hint at something big, as "Sing a Sad Song" had done. "Strangers" *was* big, a top-ten hit for Merle in the first part of '65. Even so, the old problem of the big label stealing the little label's thunder remained. In a detail mostly forgotten today, the artist who had the really big record that year with "Strangers" was Roy Drusky, the deep-voiced Mercury Records crooner who had a concurrent #6 hit with the song. Ken Nelson saw his chance and approached Merle and Fuzzy again about signing to Capitol: "I started to notice this Tally Records on the Billboard charts," Nelson told author Michael Jarrett. "I said, 'This is ridiculous.' I called Fuzzy, 'Hey, get down here. You're blowing your stack. You don't have the distribution or the ability to promote these records. Get down here and let's talk.'" This time Haggard saw his own chance and agreed, though not before ensuring Fuzzy Owen would continue to produce his records in cooperation with Nelson.

SOMEONE TOLD HIS STORY IN A SONG **85**

The switch to Capitol is a big reason why it's Haggard's version of Anderson's song we know so well today, not Drusky's. Moving to Capitol allowed Haggard to release more and better-sounding records, to reach a wider audience, and to have a career that would eventually include not only one hit after another but theme albums and double albums and tributes—and, taking the long view, catalogue reissues and best-of collections, quite a few of them including "(My Friends Are Gonna Be) Strangers." Then again, there's the little matter of Haggard's version of "Strangers" simply being more arresting than Drusky's. When Drusky tells us he "should be taken out and tarred and feathered" for his foolishness, we take him as self-effacing. When Haggard sings the line, it's as if he's identifying exactly the punishment he deserves.

Strangers, Haggard's album debut, arrived late in 1965. It joined his early singles—including the follow-up to "Strangers," the joyously embittered but commercially unsuccessful Merle original "I'm Gonna Break Every Heart I Can"—with a few new Capitol recordings and a couple of Tally leftovers. It was a remarkable debut in many ways, in the consistently high emotional intelligence of Haggard's vocals most of all. *Strangers* is also very much of a piece with most country music in the middle sixties.

For starters, and in contrast to his and his scene's hard-core mythology, *Strangers* is more than anything else a pretty swell Nashville Sound album. Five of the album's dozen tracks are sweetened by strings (bitter-sweetened, actually); supper-club piano is prominent throughout; and Roy Nichols's acoustic picking cops regularly from Music City sides by Hank Snow and Marty Robbins. Merle borrows a good deal himself: he's doing Robbins on a cover of the early 1950s Eddy Arnold hit "I'd Trade All of My Tomorrows," doing him again on the chorus to Liz Anderson's "The Worst Is Yet to Come," and yet again throughout one of his own songs, the peevish and accusing "You Don't Even Try." On his less peevish but more accusing "If I'd Left It Up to You," he channels Wynn Stewart.

Like almost any country album of the period, *Strangers* is topped off with covers—Merle's go at Ernest Tubb's "Walking the Floor over You" paces about its room with considerable agitation. But at this point in his career, even Merle's originals draw heavily on other styles and songs. His "Hey Mr. D.J.," for example, follows in the path of recent disc-jockey-themed hits like Stonewall Jackson's "B.J. the D.J." and Jimmy C. Newman's "D.J. for a

Day"—proof, perhaps, that Merle had been taking notes when Fuzzy was picking winners in *Billboard*. It's a clever touch when Merle slips a request for his own first hit into each chorus of "Hey Mr. D.J.": "Play me that *song of sadness*, and I'll be grateful to you, sir!"

Haggard comes off as an intermittently distinctive artist on *Strangers*, but his derivativeness was of a high and promising quality. It was his own songs that showed greatest promise of all. "I'm Gonna Break Every Heart I Can," for instance. Merle dedicates his life to hurting women before they have a chance to hurt him, but does it in such broad strokes—he predicts his dick moves will even make the news or "my name ain't Merle"—you can't help but laugh with and at him both. Another Merle original, "You Don't Have Very Far to Go," would turn out to be recorded by others a dozen or more times through the years, plus twice more by Merle himself. Cowritten with Bakersfield's Red Simpson, it's the earliest Haggard composition to have legs. The song also provides an early glimpse of Merle working a theme he'd return to for life, worrying his most-prized possession: "You always find a way to hurt my *pride*."

Merle kept working on his writing throughout 1965, and Fuzzy kept repeating the songs were good, just not good enough. But late in the year Merle sang his friend a new song that made Fuzzy gush, at last: "I believe it might be a number one song." As it turned out, "Swinging Doors" peaked that summer only at #5, but close enough. Its follow-up single, "The Bottle Let Me Down," went to #3 in the fall, and Merle's second solo album, *Swinging Doors and the Bottle Let Me Down*, credited for the first time to "Merle Haggard and the Strangers," reached #1 on the country album chart in December.

These early artistic and commercial breakthroughs aside, *Swinging Doors/The Bottle* is no less derivative than *Strangers* had been, and, if anything, it is less memorable. Excepting, of course, the pair of drinking songs that provide the album with its title: by 1966 those consecutive top-five singles had elevated Merle's profile from Rising Star to Consistent Hit Maker. They were first-rate Haggard originals, to boot, with melodies and sentiments that even now prove timeless.

"Swinging Doors" is a very Bakersfield sounding number—critic Dave Marsh crowned it "probably the best Buck Owens record anybody but Buck ever recorded"—but the Strangers sound heavier here than the Buckaroos, more on edge and on guard. It was also right in line with several recent making-the-most-of-nothing tavern hits from Porter Wagoner ("Misery Loves Company," "Sorrow on the Rocks," "I'll Go Down Swinging"): the honky-tonk "Swinging Doors" finds Merle planted at the bar, crowing the virtues of his limits. "I got swinging doors, a jukebox and a bar stool," he shouts as Ralph Mooney's pedal steel flashes bright, then dark, like the neon out front. What more could a loser ask for? At least until they kick him out at closing time?

That's where "The Bottle Let Me Down" picks up the story. "Each night I leave the barroom when it's over," Merle moans like he's just pulled another drunken double shift. Mooney kicks it off, out of his head, and studio ace James Burton, making his debut on a Haggard session, slaps the singer to his senses with lacerating Telecaster. Then Merle tells us that all those bottles have betrayed his faith and let him remember the woman who busted his heart. The bottle, his "one true friend," has turned out to be as untrustworthy as any other random stranger. These numbers stare as deeply into their respective shot glasses as almost any drinking songs out there. And two more songs from the album—"I Can't Stand Me," where Burton's revved-up guitar chases after a self-hating Merle ("I gotta get away from myself!"), and Merle's haunting rendition of Tommy Collins's imperious "High on a Hilltop"—are nearly as powerful. But the rest of the album is rote. The songs, all but two by Merle, are solid and competent, and so are the arrangements and performances, but at this remove, if they didn't happen to be by Merle Haggard, no one would care. On "I'll Look Over You" Merle is Marty once again, while "This Town's Not Big Enough" isn't up to Liz Anderson's songwriting best.

The joke songs don't work, either—as a comedian Merle makes a great straight man. Still, a randy novelty called "Shade Tree Fix-It Man" scoots along nicely, making up in the momentum of its groove for what it lacks in laughs. With Merle pulling over for both quick repairs on his "hooptie" and a quick tumble with his girl, it's an Okie's country-song answer to all those fun cars-and-girls songs put out at around the same time by the Beach Boys, Merle's fellow Southern Californians and Capitol Records label mates. "The Girl Turned Ripe [when the pickers came today]," though, is just creepy and misogynist, a low point in his catalogue.

Liz Anderson's greatest song, and certainly her greatest contribution to the Merle Haggard story, was a song she wrote with her husband, Casey—and its genesis lay in that staple of sixties American culture, prime-time television. One of the most popular shows in the nation in the winter of 1965–1966 was *The Fugitive*, starring David Jansen as Richard Kimble, on the run and trying to prove he hadn't murdered his wife. Casey kept suggesting to Liz that she should write a song about it, but she couldn't think of an idea she liked. During a car trip from Nashville back home to Sacramento, though, the Andersons read a Montana historical marker describing an Indian tribe whose chief crop had been children. Or so it seemed to the area's white settlers, who prayed, the sign explained, that "their crops would fail." Liz had a brainstorm then—the song's centerpiece line, "I raised a lot of Cain back in my younger days while Mama used to pray my crops would fail." By the time the Andersons stopped in Nevada for breakfast, they'd written "The Fugitive."

Liz Anderson would cut a version of the song herself in 1967, including it on an album of her own songs entitled *Cookin' Up the Hits*. What was the recipe for "The Fugitive"? Start with the television show, then add that roadside inspiration. Emphasize the show's episodic weekly structure ("Down every road there's always one more city") and mix in some imagined empathy born of the Andersons' wearying cross-country drive. Toss in a line recalled from Rudyard Kipling ("He who travels fastest goes [*sic*] alone") and pour in a touch of the zeitgeist too: clichés about moss-gathering aside, is "a fugitive must be a rolling stone" alluding to the Dylan hit from the summer before or to the British rock band first topping the charts at the same time?

When they presented the song to Merle, the Andersons had no idea he'd ever been in prison or spent his teenage years fleeing law enforcement. But Merle felt a connection to the song immediately, and it set him to thinking how he might harvest life experience for songs of his own. He took his first stab at "The Fugitive" in the studio that March, recording a clip-clopping, 'round-the-campfire take that's pretty and delicate and has lots of harmonica and backing singers. Merle, Ken Nelson, and Fuzzy Owen decided to come back to it later. When Merle next visited Capitol in June, he brought along a new song he'd written, "Someone Told My Story in a Song," that sounds inspired by that night Liz Anderson had killed him softly with her songs, "Fugitive" especially. "I scarcely could believe the song I heard," Merle gasps, replying in the world of the song to some new record just played on the jukebox. "It was almost like I'd written every word." He cleverly namechecks "Swinging Doors," a song to which he did write every word, as well as "I Almost Lost My Mind," the Ivory Joe Hunter R&B hit that a young Lefty Frizzell had studied so closely in 1950 and that, in the decade and a half since, had been widely adopted as a country standard.

A couple of months later Merle and company took another crack at "The Fugitive," now identified as "I'm a Lonesome Fugitive," and they got the hounded take we know today. The drums feel insistent but stationary, locked in, as Glen Campbell's acoustic guitar tumbles aimlessly on. Merle sounds world-weary and increasingly out of breath—"I'm a hunted fugitive with just two ways: outrun the law or spend my life in jail"—and James Burton offers a short, sharp Telecaster run that screams like a siren. In the spring "I'm a Lonesome Fugitive" became Haggard's first #1 single.

With "Strangers" and "Fugitive," Liz Anderson had helped teach Haggard how to cook up hits. Now he set to teaching himself how to fashion an image. The day after cutting "Fugitive," Merle recorded two songs that made use of his outlaw past like never before. The first of these, "Life in Prison," he'd attempted back on his second Tally session in 1963, but with "Fugitive" fresh on his mind, he gave it another try. In a writing choice that would soon emerge as a pattern, "Life in Prison" exaggerated the specifics of Merle's actual sentence and invented a crime from whole cloth, too: "Insane with rage I took my darlin's life." The song also articulates a hard way of feeling the world that Merle would succumb to often, though only intermittently, for the rest of his days: "My life will be a burden every day / If I could die my pain might go away."

Haggard turned next to "House of Memories," his first use of penal imagery to convey not a building but a mindset: "My house is a prison"—the guards apparently reside in his head—and "there's no place to hide where your memory can't find me." Down every road there's always one more misery, the song says. Like Richard Kimble, he's always on the run, and without even having to leave the house.

After *Strangers* went top ten, Ken Nelson suggested to Haggard that he might next do an album of truck-driving numbers of the sort being popularized by Dave Dudley, Del Reeves, and, soon enough, Bakersfield's own Kay Adams. Hag didn't think so, and Nelson gave the assignment to sometime Haggard collaborator Red Simpson, who rode the idea to success aboard the Tommy Collins–penned "Roll Truck, Roll."

There would be plenty of themed Haggard long-players to come, of course, and in hindsight, 1967's *I'm a Lonesome Fugitive* looks a little like a first try. In addition to the on-the-run title track, Haggard's third solo album includes "Life in Prison" and "House of Memories," and nearly every other track finds Merle caught in some sort of trap: even coming upon that secret-revealing song in "Someone Told My Story" freezes him in his tracks. He's on the run or looking to go throughout, an inmate or a fugitive. His "All of Me Belongs to You" alludes to the old Tin Pan Alley jazz standard, except that Merle's iteration of the image is nightmarish ("Fingers claw the darkness in my dreams") rather than fanciful, agitated rather than slyly seductive. And even though it's about being caged in a body controlled by another, it still somehow outswings Frank Sinatra.

Two songs Merle wrote when he was a teen manage to out rock anything he'd yet recorded. With James Burton on electric guitar, a new version of "Skid Row" makes those "giggles and snickers" sting like needles and underscores that when snobs say you've "got no class," what they mean is you do too have a class—*beneath them*. In "If You Want to Be My Woman," Merle complains to a girl that she needs to give him "something equal in return" to all the money he's been spending on her. "Don't look at me like maybe you don't understand," he snaps when she plays confused. Burton and pianist Glen D. Hardin, laying down whirlwind parts that suggest a Smash-era Charlie Rich side, have his back. His would-be woman may have other ideas.

The whole album's like that, hurtling and out of control even when standing still. Merle can do nothing but sit and wait for phone calls that never come, or he answers the call of a railroad train he couldn't resist if he wanted to—and, if only on "My Rough and Rowdy Ways" (his first release of a Jimmie Rodgers song), he swears to God he wants to. On "Drink Up and Be Somebody," he determines to pretend a woman hasn't wounded his self-esteem again (first line: "Well, I gotta keep my reputation, gotta keep my *pride*"), but allows he's going to need another drink or three to do it.

Even the record's loving testimonials come with warnings in the fine print. "I once lived a life without meaning," Merle admits in "Mary's Mine," a song by Jerry Ward. Now that Mary's his, he's been "given reason for living." But if Mary being "mine" is the only motivation he can find to keep breathing—Merle's hesitant delivery and brooding arrangement all but demand we consider the possibility—then what happens when, someday, Mary isn't?

It's a fantastic album, start to end, but it was the title track that made Merle a star. More to the point, it was Liz and Casey Anderson's song that suggested to Haggard an artistic persona his third album made good on. In a shot that could be a screen grab from David Jansen's TV show, *I'm a Lonesome Fugitive*'s album cover stars Merle Haggard, as the Running Kind, hanging off the side of a boxcar and peering warily down the tracks.

CHAPTER 9

"I STARTED LOVING YOU AGAIN," 1968

F alling back into love. What could be better, right? People sometimes sing "I Started Loving You Again," or, as it is commonly
called, "*Today* I Started Loving You Again," just that way—all happily,
gratefully in love. Upbeat readings are only half the story, though. Listen
to a cross-section of the versions of this standard cut over four decades,
and you can find almost any emotional take you're looking for. Between
1968, when "Today" was the B-side to Merle's "The Legend of Bonnie and
Clyde" single, and 1975, when it belatedly made the country top ten in a
not-happy-in-the-least rendition by Sammi Smith, at least sixty recordings
of the song were released. There have been hundreds in the decades since,
and that's without counting the times it's been performed on television
through the years, or during megastar arena shows and don't-forget-to-
tip-your-waitress bar sets, or the just-for-fun semipro and amateur versions
YouTube lists into the thousands. "Today I Started Loving You Again" is,
hands down, the most performed song in Haggard's catalogue.

Considered from one angle, that makes "Today" Merle Haggard's most
valuable copyright. Less crassly, it's one of his contributions to the Great
American Songbook, a song that's proven irresistible to a wide variety
of singers, in all sorts of settings and interpretations, from old-school
Italian American crooner Al Martino, who scored a minor crossover hit

with the song in 1968, to trippy Canadian folk-poppers the Poppy Family a few years later, to Belizean brukdown legend Wilfred Peters in 1997, to latter-day jazz songbird Diane Schuur, scatting Merle's melody up to high Cs, in 2011.

In 1975 Bobby "Blue" Bland rasped his way through the song, trying at first to ignore the brassy and bass-heavy R&B house party throwing down around him, then seemingly deciding "If you can't beat 'em" and volunteering to make a liquor run. All the way back in 1968, Jerry Lee Lewis used the song to help him transition from rock and roller to country star—and to make plain that by loving his woman again he was doing her a favor. In 1973, on the album *Obie from Senatobie*, O. B. McClinton borrowed the song to frame a rambling tale that ends "in a lonely room watching a faded photograph of your wedding...Oh sugar! I'm right back where I've really always been." In 2004 an African American gospel singer named Patrick Reid rewrote about half the words and set his Casio to "reggae." Merle's song was born again as a backslider's rededication to Christ: "Lord, I'm back where I always should've been."

The song's indestructible. On the *Louisiana Hayride* once in the late 1960s, Ferlin Husky told the live audience that he had time for one more number, "my favorite song," before the news at the top of the hour. He started to sing "Today I Started...," but interrupted himself after the opening chorus to introduce an impersonation of the song as it might be performed by Fats Domino. Then he sang the final verse as Walter Brennan. The audience never stopped singing along.

On her syndicated 1976 television variety series, Dolly Parton performed "Today" with musical guest the Hues Corporation—a good choice for her and the trio, she explained, because it was a "soulful country song" and because "you've got the soul and I've got the country." "And I got the hair to match," she added, patting the giant blonde Afro wig that she "wore... just for you. I thought it'd be appropriate." Toss in jokes about the guests' "California tan" and Dolly advising the group that *they* "need to get the soul in it" because *she's* "the wrong color," and it's all a queasy postcard from Old Seventies America. Yet when Dolly sings a verse, and is backed by the Hues harmonies, all that vanishes. It's just "What a fooool I was."

There's Billie Jo Spears in 1968, moving about the song in slow motion, padded by echo and sounding stoned out of her mind; and John Fogerty, rock and roll's great fatalist, sounding more resigned in 1973 than anyone's ever been; and Tom Jones, also in '73, sounding resigned himself before overpowering resignation with a gale-force voice that introduces Elvis to Otis; and Clive Gregson and Christine Collister in 1990, both of them back in love, one with the other, and both of them miserable; and Artie "Blues Boy" White, in 1990, turning a confession of weakness into one hell of a seductive pickup line; and in 1989 the groan-inducing-named Beasts of Bourbon, an Aussie punk outfit, doing the song all sloppy and slurry, like a drunk spoiling for a bar fight, talking far louder than necessary and hoping like hell somebody will make something of it. In 2012 I heard Bryan and the Haggards, a hard-bop and acid jazz group that does nothing but Merle songs, squawk and squeal their way through the song in a tiny bar in the Red Hook section of Brooklyn. All my favorite versions travel the same melody but map new worlds.

A state-of-the-art pop-country ballad in its day, "Today I Started Loving You Again" has been naturalized into the repertoires of a variety of twang- and melody-appreciating subgenres. Most versions live in one or another style or era of straight-up country, but it's made major inroads into all sorts of related roots genres, from swamp pop (Johnnie Allan, Joe Barry) and bluegrass (the Osborne Brothers) to country soul (Bettye Swann, Percy Sledge) and especially the contemporary grown-ass blues (Lavelle White, Rufus Thomas, Junior Wells, Magic Slim). The song's now a shared language for a variety of communities, connecting then to now, them to us, me to you—and most of all highlighting our individuality. This is what all standards can do. Lining up to be the umpteenth singer to do "At Last," say, or "White Christmas," is the vocal equivalent to dancing down the Soul Train Line. Everyone doing the same thing shines a white-hot spot on the varied ways that everyone does their own thing.

"Today I Started Loving You Again" has especially allowed country singers to stand out by joining in. The song's brief, conversational phrases allow singers to emphasize subtle and not so subtle differences in texture and phrasing. Indeed, when its melody is unspooled, as it usually is, at a barely midtempo stroll, the song encourages such treatment, cultivates and rewards distinctiveness. This is true whether we're listening to country singers with sky-high ranges (Marty Robbins, Jack Greene, Gene Watson, Martina McBride) or more earthbound instruments (Ernest Tubb, Jean Shepard, Buck Owens), or iconoclastic styles (Willie, Waylon, Emmylou, Wanda, Loretta, Buck, Jerry Lee). "Great song," each interpreter agrees. "But have you heard *me* do it?"

Listen to Merle do it. You'll wonder how anyone ever had the guts to sing it again. As Bonnie and Merle tell the story, he wrote the song as the newlyweds were just pulling out of a rough patch in their relationship. See? Happy! But that's not the song Merle wrote, or the record he chose to make. The Strangers begin the original 1968 recording slowly, playing steadily at a singing-cowboy trot but herky-jerky too. Guitars weave unsteadily, and when Merle begins, he likewise lists side to side. If you just read his title on the page, it would seem to signal straightforwardly what's ahead—a moment of joyful clarity following some bout of temporary insanity. But listen to Merle crawl across that opening line—"Today I...started loving you...again..."—and you understand that here love isn't the solution to his problem. It *is* the problem, a shrinking of life's possibilities to only one: love unrequited.

Soon enough Merle says all this straight out. He was a fool to think his broken heart would ever mend. He knew better than to think "these few million tears I'd cried" would be payment anywhere near enough to get him out from under the pain. He "should have known the worst was yet to come." He even reveals his song to be a prequel to Buck Owens's 1965 hit "Crying Time." "I should have known," he tells us, "that crying time for me had just begun." But by then he's just fleshing out what his shaky, halting voice revealed from the start.

He loves her. Again. She doesn't love him. Still. What could be worse?

CHAPTER 10

THE LEGEND OF BONNIE AND HIM

In the Merle Haggard story, Bonnie Owens is a key supporting character, the lead's longtime harmony singer and onetime wife. But it's worth remembering that when they recorded Liz Anderson's "Just between the Two of Us" together in 1964, it was actually Bonnie who was the better-known performer—a fixture of the Bakersfield club scene, a decade-long semipro recording artist, and a regular cast member on *Cousin Herb Henson's Trading Post* television show. Her boyfriend, Fuzzy Owen, was a member of the house band, too, and they were known around town the way Henson introduced them on the show: "Our sweethearts." She recorded for Fuzzy's Tally label, as well, and helped with day-to-day operations. When she sent copies of her latest singles to DJs, she liked to slip one of Haggard's into the envelope too. The kid had real talent, she thought, and she was happy to do him the favor.

Owens was born Bonnie Campbell in Oklahoma City in 1929, but she grew up in a series of small Oklahoma towns and came of age in Arizona, where her family migrated during the war. Her dad cropped shares, labored for the WPA, and wound up doing a bit of everything through the years: he had a big job just getting by, with eight kids and a wife. They were a musical bunch—Mr. Campbell sang, for fun, and could play about anything that made sound—but Bonnie was the one who as a little girl talked about growing up to sing for a living. In her early teens she won a state yodeling competition, and you can hear how good she was on the rollicking version of the Patsy Montana classic "I Want to Be a Cowboy's Sweetheart" that concludes her 1965 album *Don't Take Advantage of Me*.

Montana was a hero of Bonnie's, as was all but inevitable for young women who wanted to sing country music in those days. Any moderately successful male country act included a "girl singer" in his program, but when it came to female stars, Patsy Montana was about it. When Bonnie and new husband Buck Owens went to see the Maddox Brothers & Rose in Mesa one night in the late forties, it was a revelation. "I never took my eyes off Rose Maddox," she told Deke Dickerson. "And Buck never took his eyes off Roy Nichols."

Buck and Bonnie had been musical partners for a while by that point, working together in a string band sponsored by a local service station. Bonnie married Buck in 1948, gave birth to a boy, Buddy, soon after, and the couple had a second son, Michael, two years after that. They divorced in 1953. It was just like Bonnie, though, that she stayed friendly with her ex. On Capitol Records' *Buck Owens Sings Tommy Collins*, the former spouses duet charmingly on "It Tickles."

That 1963 cameo was Bonnie's major label debut, but she'd been recording off and on for years. She first gained local attention as the "singing waitress" at Bakersfield's Clover Club, and throughout the fifties she released a handful of singles on a series of tinier-than-tiny local labels, including "X," Del-Fi, and Mar-Vel, where she and Fuzzy cut the original "Dear John Letter" in 1953. In 1956 her keening, reverent duet on "Father" with JoAnn Miller ("the Kern County Sweethearts") was the debut release from Lewis Talley's Tally records, and several years later, when Fuzzy purchased the dormant label, one of its first releases was another Bonnie single, a Kitty Wells–styled, tear-jerking cowrite from Fuzzy and Dallas Frazier called "Why Don't Daddy Live Here Anymore." The brutal answer—"Because Daddy loves another woman now and he left us to be with her"—was delivered via recitation and became a top-30 country hit for Bonnie in 1963. The following year her twice-shy "Don't Take Advantage of Me" did the same, as did her and Merle's "Just between the Two of Us," one of the numbers Liz Anderson auditioned for them in Sacramento. That single had Bonnie and Merle warning listeners not to judge a book by its cover: everyone thinks they're the perfect couple, yet they get along so well only because they really don't care about each other anymore. When their voices come together at the chorus, though—Merle's youthful, reedy, high tenor, Bonnie's brassy alto—they harmonize their indifference with obvious affection.

Nineteen sixty-five was the turning point in Owens's career, for better and for worse. "Just between the Two of Us" had been a big deal for Tally: it hadn't climbed as high as Merle's "Sing a Sad Song" but had stuck around the charts for half a year. When Ken Nelson put out Merle's *Strangers* in the fall of '65, he simultaneously released Bonnie's first full-length record, *Don't Take Advantage of Me*. Like Merle's debut, Bonnie's was composed of old Tally recordings and new Capitol ones—though unlike Merle's, Bonnie's was a top-five entry on the country album chart. Before the year was out, she won the new Academy of Country Music's first-ever award for female vocalist (Buck was the male winner), and as 1965 ended she seemed poised for greater successes.

It didn't happen for several reasons. The most immediate was that in the middle of it all, she up and moved to Alaska. Bonnie was torn. She says she knew more success in the music business would mean more time both with Fuzzy—whom she cared for very much but who she suspected was seeing another woman and who she wasn't sure she wanted to be with anyway—and with Merle, who she sensed had feelings for her she didn't think she felt in return. (Merle writes in *My House of Memories*: "She thought that I had the hots for her, and she thought Fuzzy was cheating on her.") Plus, Merle and Fuzzy were such good friends—the whole situation could get ugly in a hurry. Bonnie decided maybe the best course was to leave the situation altogether, so she booked herself a long engagement at a club in Alaska. Merle followed after a month or so, telephoning from Seattle that he was coming to see her. She said don't. He said I'm on my way. They married in June.

The new couple's first weeks were a preview of the on-the-road-again decades to come. They played a few dates together while still up north (a March 27, 1965, ad in the *Fairbanks Daily News Miner*: "This Weekend— Last Chance to See Bonnie Owens...with [in smaller type] Merle Haggard at [in large type again] the Silver Dollar Bar"). They were married on a rush trip to Mexico, then spent their honeymoon touring together on the East Coast, driving from gig to gig in the Chrysler station wagon Fuzzy loaned them.

Merle's career took off at this point, but Bonnie's didn't have a chance. The following spring their duet album came out. In addition to its indelible title hit, it featured a light-as-air take on Chester Smith's "Wait a Little Longer, Please Jesus" and a knockout version of Hank Williams's "A House without Love Is Not a Home." But though the golden age of male-female duets was just ahead—teams like Porter Wagoner and Dolly Parton, Conway Twitty and Loretta Lynn, and George Jones and Tammy Wynette dominated country radio in the early 1970s—there was no follow-up Merle and Bonnie album, or even a follow-up single. As Merle's career strengthened, Bonnie's faded. Increasingly, she didn't get dedicated recording dates, instead cutting a side or two with any leftover time on Merle's sessions. Capitol continued to release singles on her: "Number One Heel" and "Consider the Children" (a Merle composition) charted in '65 and '66, and "Lead Me On" got some spins in '69. And she kept putting out albums, the most commercially successful being two that featured Haggard-written title tracks, 1967's *All of Me Belongs to You* and 1968's *Somewhere Between.* But her releases sold less and less—the albums above charted only in the mid-30s and the singles fared worse—victims at first of scant promotion and then no promotion at all. Bonnie's image probably didn't help either; she was demure and dressed in crinoline when that version of the girl singer was becoming an antique. Now, her records were slipped into Merle's mailings.

On record and on the road, though, Bonnie's harmonies became a defining and beloved part of Haggard's sound, a contribution as important in its way as the playing of Hamlet and Nichols. The contrast between Merle's tempered-steel voice and her rusty one was bracing, and the two worked out a distinctive way of falling in and out of harmony together. Bonnie would join Merle to sing, say, "Tonight, the bottle…" but then fall silent for the conclusion of the line, making Merle's "…let me down" hit like a crash landing. "Sing me back home…," they harmonize, sounding universal and bigger than life, "…with a song I used to hear," Merle finishes, sounding very small and alone.

Owens seemed content to play second fiddle after she and Merle married. She liked to sing, she liked to tour, she thought her husband was a rare talent, and she didn't desire the spotlight. For his part, Merle, eight years her junior, liked to have the reliable, motherly Bonnie around, keeping track of his lyrics and ideas and just generally counteracting the rough masculinity of the road family. In a 1973 *Penthouse* profile of Haggard, journalist Donn Pearce summarized her role this way:

> And Bonnie. Poor Bonnie. The mother of them all. She always knew who was hungry, who was tired, who had troubles. She doled out Merle's vitamin pills. She handed out advances. She paid for rooms and ordered meals. Merle called her a "gosh darn dad burn good mama."

For her part, Bonnie seems to have well understood who she married. She knew Merle slept with other women, regularly, and only requested that he not rub it in her face or humiliate her. "We had a little deal, Bonnie and me," is how Merle describes the marriage in *Sing Me Back Home*. "To be frank, I had what some of my friends called a perfect situation."

The situation was less perfect for Bonnie. That *Penthouse* feature spent much of its word count on Merle's attempts to hook up with "two wild sisters" in their Peoria hotel without Bonnie knowing. It's hard to read, particularly as its writer presents himself as an accomplice to Merle's plotting. But not nearly so hard as it must have been for Bonnie to have experienced in real time on a more or less regular basis. Music journalist Dave Samuelson writes that the final straw for Bonnie was Dolly Parton, who went on the road in support of Merle and the Strangers after she ended her association with Porter Wagoner in 1974: "Haggard's relentless (and ultimately futile) pursuit of his nubile opening act was more than Bonnie could handle. She left the road troupe that year and filed for a legal separation the following summer."

"When I decided to quit the road in '74," Bonnie writes in one of her contributions to her former husband's first autobiography, "it was as much for Merle as it was for me....I felt like Merle had outgrown me. I did feel the kids [Merle's children, her stepchildren] needed me at home and I needed them....I didn't know what was happening out there on the road and I didn't try to find out."

Bonnie Owens released six solo albums on Capitol between 1965 and '70. They're not as consistently strong as they might be—cramming at the end of Merle's sessions, the Strangers didn't have time to work out the inventive arrangements they were capable of, and their rhythm beds for Bonnie typically have a lot less spring—but each album comes with marvelous moments. She had a lot going for her, what with her pick of Merle Haggard songs and her own voice's unmistakable brassy twang. (Merle once described it as so unique that if you heard it just once, you'd instantly recognize it three hundred years later, and in the dark.) Bonnie's vocal on "Somewhere Between," for example, will stop you in your tracks, just an achingly beautiful performance that should have gone down as a career record.

I think my favorite of her solo albums was her last, *Mother's Favorite Hymns*. That 1971 gospel collection includes backing vocals by southern gospel group the Victors and by a female chorus composed of Gloria "Tainted Love" Jones, onetime Ikette Venetta Fields, and the great Merry Clayton, just months removed from outsinging Mick Jagger on "Gimme Shelter." The picking throughout the album is hot and acoustic, the rhythms jump with the spirit-girding energy of a Wednesday-night church service, and the songs ("I Saw the Light," "Farther Along," "I'll Fly Away") are as sturdy, as welcoming and forgiving and reliable, as the one-of-a-kind voice of Miss Bonnie Owens.

CHAPTER 11

"SING ME BACK HOME," 1967

"**S**ing Me Back Home" cracked the *Billboard* Hot Country
Singles chart the week before Thanksgiving 1967, topped
the chart before 1968 was three weeks old, and over the next year or so
would be recorded by such country heavyweights as Conway Twitty, Ernest
Tubb, Buck Owens, and Porter Wagoner. "Okie" and, perhaps, "Mama
Tried" excepted, it's the song most closely identified with Merle Haggard.

In the first verse, a Death Row prisoner asks a warden, "Can my
guitar-playin' friend do my request?" In the second, the prisoner asks a
visiting choir if they will sing him "a song my mama sang." The chorus is
as fine, economical, and mournful as any Merle Haggard ever wrote, as
any written:

> *Sing me back home with a song I used to hear*
> *Make my old memories come alive.*
> *Take me away and turn back the years*
> *Sing me back home before I die.*

Throughout, Stranger Eddie Burris's kick drum pounds, throbs, like the
doomed man's heart.

In the documentary *Learning to Live with Myself*, Merle tells director

Gandulf Hennig that "Sing Me Back Home" was "written years after I was out of the joint...from a conglomeration of information that I'd gathered while I was there."

Merle identified a bit of that conglomeration in a 1977 *Billboard* interview with Bob Eubanks. Remembering his friend "Rabbit" Hendricks—the San Quentin inmate who escaped and killed a police officer before he was recaptured and sentenced to die in the gas chamber—Merle told Eubanks:

> Even though the crime was brutal and the guy was an incorrigible criminal, it's a feeling you never forget when you see someone you know make that last walk. They bring him through the yard, and there's a guard in front and a guard behind—that's how you know a death prisoner. They brought Rabbit out...taking him to see the Father,...prior to his execution. That was a strong picture that was left in my mind.

"Sing Me Back Home" is a eulogy, then, for "Rabbit" Hendricks, and for Caryl Chessman, and for all of the condemned men up on the Shelf. Merle is sharing with us what he saw when he was there with them—or something akin to what he saw that later inspired a song with images of its own. Yet the song feels so much bigger than that. There is something within Merle's song, and within the grooves of the record he cut, that can't be caged.

In the 1936 film *Pennies from Heaven*, Haggard favorite Bing Crosby plays a con who can't stand to be tied down: "You see, with me, when I leave a place, I get myself a feather," Crosby's character tells us. "I toss it up and whichever way the wind blows, that's where I go." It's a role Haggard himself could have played. We might say it's a role he did play for half a century. *Down every road there's always one more city.* And it's revealing that while Merle only infrequently recorded selections from the Great American Songbook—Tin Pan Hollywood edition, that is—he twice cut "Pennies from Heaven," the Arthur Johnston and Johnny Burke pop standard Crosby sings in the film.

Pennies from Heaven, the movie, begins like this. There's a shot of a menacing-looking prison on a dark and stormy night, then of a newspaper headline: "Hart Dies Tonight—Goes to Chair at State Prison." Cut to inside the prison where, as "Sing Me Back Home" would one day phrase it, we see "the warden [lead] a prisoner down the hallway to his doom."

"Where does that fellow with the guitar hang out?" the prisoner asks, and the warden and the prison chaplain escort him to Crosby's cell. "Many's a time I heard you out there in the yard," the prisoner tells him. "It kind of took my mind off of things." Now he hopes Crosby will do him one more favor and deliver a letter of apology to the family of the man he murdered.

"Why me?" Crosby wants to know.

"Because you're the only guy around here I can trust," the prisoner answers. "Anybody who can sing sappy, sentimental songs in a prison wouldn't double-cross a guy taking his Last Walk!"

And then he takes the walk. *Down the hallway to his doom.*

"Sing Me Back Home" finds Merle detailing an archetypal narrative— inspired by real life, sure, but long familiar from a thousand novels, movies, comic books, and television shows. It's the earnest, hymn-like melody of its chorus...the way the arrangement advances the lyric at a cadence conveying great respect and great sorrow, at once solemn and on edge, like a funeral procession...and the song's repeated appeals to memory as anodyne: "Take me away and turn back the years...before I die." These carry Merle's song beyond cliché and free the record from any one era or situation. "Sing Me Back Home" unfolds like a dream you somehow understand everyone else is having, too, like a folk song that seems always to have been there. No one teaches you the words. You fall in and sing along.

Prison songs were a country music staple long before Merle Haggard made them a personal specialty—at least since Vernon Dalhart's "The Prisoner's Song" ("Now if I had wings like an angel over these prison walls I would fly") in 1925, and straight along to Johnny Cash moaning "Folsom Prison Blues" at Sun Records in 1956 and then singing it three years later to a San Quentin audience that included Merle Haggard. It's an especially poetic coincidence that one week after Cash cut his famed live album, *At Folsom Prison*, in January 1968, Merle's "Sing Me Back Home" became the #1 country song in the nation.

"Sing Me Back Home" feels timeless but is a song very much of its genre and moment. The record's insistent kick drum, for example, booms out of the mix like Robert Blake's heart as he swung from the end of a rope in *In Cold Blood*, the film version of Truman Capote's "nonfiction novel" that was released at the very moment "Sing Me Back Home" was debuting on the charts.

In the year and a half leading up to the release of "Sing Me Back Home," the prison number that left the most indelible impression was the Curly Putman–penned "Green, Green Grass of Home." A major country hit for Porter Wagoner in the summer of 1965, and then a pop hit for the Welsh rock-and-soul belter Tom Jones in 1967, Putman's song was soon covered by virtually every country act going, and by a host of pop, rock, and soul singers, too. "Green, Green Grass of Home" was from the start a favorite of troops fighting the escalating war in Vietnam, and it almost instantly earned a spot in the Great American Songbook, Nashville edition.

It's also a song with a great deal in common with Haggard's "Sing Me Back Home." Merle included "Green, Green Grass" (and "Folsom Prison") on his successor to the *Sing Me Back Home* album, 1968's *Mama Tried*. In both Haggard's and Putman's songs, men dream of going home. Literally dream, in the case of Putman's convict: in the final verse, he awakes from sweet dreams of the old hometown only to discover he's still on Death Row. Merle's prisoner longs for home, too, is seeking desperately for a song that will let him imagine his way there. But both men know the only way they'll really ever make it home is in a box.

I've often wondered what song, exactly, the prisoner in "Sing Me Back Home" asks his "guitar-playing friend" to play? And what song did his mama like that he requests the street choir to sing in the song's second verse? Haggard doesn't say, letting that omitted detail stand as one more piece of the song's mystery and power—all the better for us to hear our own requests echoing off cold stone walls. I can think of songs that might do the imaginative work necessary to lead the prisoner home. "Precious Memories," for instance, might make "the sacred past unfold." It would need to be a gospel song, in any case, for the practical reason that the "choir from off the street" would have to know it, but also because this Dead Man Walking is surely pondering more than one kind of home, more than one kind of freedom. "I'll Fly Away," by the great gospel songwriter Albert Brumley, would fit the bill. "I'll fly away like a bird from prison bars has flown" to a new "home on God's celestial shore."

The particular title doesn't matter, of course. What matters is that this man's life, however spent, deserves a song—and that the taking of his life will spur others to sing in mourning. It is loss, sharp and inevitable, that overwhelms any plea for memory whenever I listen to "Sing Me Back Home." On record, every word passes from Merle as if it hurts him deeply, but he holds in his tears, out of respect. For just under three minutes, the whole world feels like a prison; each note a separate trial, a new sentence. "Sing me back home," Merle has the prisoner plead. Glen Campbell's acoustic guitar attempts an encouraging smile, settles for grim tenderness. Norman Hamlet's pedal steel cries a pure, high note. Eddie Burris's kick drum beats one final time, and another man is gone, out of this hard world and headed home.

So maybe it was another Albert Brumley song that Mama used to sing, one Merle would himself record in 2003, a gospel standard typically sung not funereally but at a pace spirit-lifting and impatient—"This World Is Not My Home":

> *This world is not my home, I'm just passing through ...*
> *Angels beckon me from Heaven's open door*
> *And I can't feel at home in this world anymore.*

CHAPTER 12

THEY WON'T LET HIS SECRET GO UNTOLD

One way to get at the importance of Merle Haggard in the last years of the 1960s is to marvel at his indelible hit singles, which, after "Fugitive" topped the country charts in early 1967, came in a rush. For the next three years, between the Summer of Love and the release of "The Fightin' Side of Me" in the spring of 1970, Haggard had a new #1 single every four months: "Branded Man," "Sing Me Back Home," "The Legend of Bonnie and Clyde," "Mama Tried," "Hungry Eyes," "Workin' Man Blues," and "Okie from Muskogee." These records have defined Haggard—and, to a large degree, country music—ever since. Or we could look at his albums, which in these years were as strong as his radio hits and accumulated as rapidly. The immediate successors to *I'm a Lonesome Fugitive*—*Branded Man* in 1967 and, in '68, *Sing Me Back Home* and *The Legend of Bonnie and Clyde*—were among the very finest country albums of their respective years. The albums that followed—1968's *Mama Tried*, then *Pride in What I Am*, the Jimmie Rodgers tribute *Same Train, a Different Time*, and *A Portrait of Merle Haggard*—should all be chiseled in stone as masterpieces.

This isn't how conventional narratives of the era are told. The pop music of the late sixties is known today as overflowing with classic albums. Yet when those albums get listed and ranked, pop music critics and historians typically whiff on country altogether. Country albums, especially ones released before the rise of Outlaw Country in the midseventies, tend to get dismissed as "hits plus filler," a single or two padded out by an LP's worth of decades-old country standards, plus maybe a couple of versions of someone else's recent hits. This was true of some country albums, but hardly all of them. More to the point, such dismissals are deaf to all the times and ways an old song, delivered by a new singer in a new arrangement for a new moment, can allow listeners to hear that old song as if for the first time—or to discover new meanings altogether.

In any event, Merle's albums don't fit the clichés. His albums became increasingly top-heavy with originals. And when he did cut the well-known songs of others—*Mama Tried*, for example, is one-third covers, and of course his Rodgers tribute is covers all the way down—Merle's versions are distinctive and modern. What's more, as the sixties progressed to the seventies, Haggard's writing was now as smart in its way as Dylan's or Lennon and McCartney's, his singing was as powerful as Aretha Franklin's or Van Morrison's, his attitude as sharp and dissolute as the Stones', his soundscapes and emotional intensity as arresting as those of Jimi Hendrix or the Family Stone or the Band—or even of James Brown, Haggard's only peer at the time in terms of producing such a high quantity of quality work.

In 1967 Merle followed the persona-creating success of Liz Anderson's "I'm a Lonesome Fugitive" with a pair of singles he'd written himself: "I Threw Away the Rose" and "Branded Man" each consolidated recent themes and successes. In '66 "Swinging Doors" and "The Bottle Let Me Down" had tracked a drunk's descent. Now, in "I Threw Away the Rose," Merle shows that same sot hitting bottom. "Once I lived a life of wine and roses," Merle begins, alluding to both the 1962 film starring Jack Lemon and its title song by Henry Mancini and Johnny Mercer. But Merle isn't recommending a movie; he's deep in his cups, in danger of drowning. Though bleary-eyed, he recognizes that all his fine former pals now put him somewhere just below: "Now all my social friends look down their noses." Merle sings the lines of the song with uncharacteristic formality, attempting to play sober in compensation for his shame. But his stately enunciation can't hide the shakes. Ralph Mooney, meanwhile, commiserates with Merle's humiliation, barring his pedal steel on tiptoe, careful not to crash.

"Rose" climbed to #3 on the charts and was followed by "Branded Man," the second #1 of Merle's career and a record reminiscent in many ways of his first. "Branded Man" shares with "I'm a Lonesome Fugitive" a relentless, loping rhythm and a liberty-seeking narrative. The cuts are so alike that Liz Anderson liked to joke "Branded Man" was just the basic track for "Fugitive," with her words switched out for Merle's. "Branded Man" even seems to allude to a contemporary TV show—*Branded*, starring Chuck Connors—the way Anderson's song had. And "Branded Man" is reminiscent of another song Merle likely knew, "Branded Wherever I Go"—an old Roy Acuff number that producer Ken Nelson had cut in 1962 with Charlie and Ira Louvin but that was only just then preparing for fall release.

In Merle's song, instead of being pursued by police as he had been in "The Fugitive," he has paid his debt and been set free only to find himself hounded still—by the stigma of having done time. "I'd like to hold my head up and be *proud* of who I am," but wherever he goes, no matter what he does, people treat him like a marked man: "If I live to be a hundred, I guess I'll never clear my name."

The desire to feel proud, but beaten back by the reality-based fear of people treating you like you're no-account, was on Haggard's mind during this period more than usual. As "Branded Man" further personalized the "Fugitive" theme, Merle was nervous about releasing it. It might give away his past and ruin his career. That fear of being found out, of being forever unable to outrun your past, was exactly what "Branded Man" was about: "They won't let my secret go untold." Haggard's anxieties only intensified when, in 1967, he spent most of a week in a Sacramento jail for driving without a license. The press didn't get wind of the story, but those five days he spent back behind bars, Merle told writer Chris Heath some four decades after the fact, felt "like five years."

Still, word about his prison record did begin to emerge as Merle confided in friends, band members, and others he trusted. When he first met Johnny Cash—the two were on the same Chicago bill in the midsixties—Merle gushed that he would tell Cash, someday, about the first time he'd seen him. "Hell, I know where it was," Cash replied, according to Dale Vinicur. "It was San Quentin." When Merle's face flushed instantly red, Cash realized that what he'd intended as a joke was no joke at all. "Hell, I'd never said it if I thought it was really true." As the two men got to know each other,

Cash advised the younger singer to come clean about his prison record before any controversy could arise.

It's unclear how Merle's story finally did come out. Within the year following "Branded Man," though, Haggard was being described in press accounts as an ex-con, as if Merle's prison past was already familiar to readers rather than breaking news. Peter La Chapelle points to two Haggard pieces in *Music City News*, one from May 1967 and the other in July 1968: "The first article does not mention his prison record, while the second talks of it as though it were common knowledge." One thing we do know is that between those publications, Merle wasn't trying all that hard to keep his secret: according to journalist Donn Pearce, Merle gave a dancing-with-the-one-that-brung-you concert for the San Quentin inmates on New Year's Day, 1968. He gave a concert at the Correctional Training Facility at Soledad, California, later that year. "Bonnie and some of the boys are scared to death playing for you here in prison," Merle told the inmates, as reported by Tom Grein for *Country Song Roundup*. But: "Myself, I feel right at home."

What a relief it was, not having to hide his record any longer. And what a boon. What Merle hadn't anticipated was that his outlaw past didn't seem to matter much to the country audience. It may have helped. As he summarized it years later, "I found out that my past was one of the most interesting things about me."

When the *Branded Man* album charted just after Labor Day 1967, it included the two recent singles, "I Threw Away the Rose" and the title track, along with a few more prison songs, most notably a pair of Tommy Collins numbers: "Don't Get Married," where Merle steals a jewelry store engagement ring but is sent up before he can propose, and the be-proud-of-what-you-got closing track, "I Made the Prison Band," a kind of country "Jailhouse Rock" that costars cellmates "Bashful Bill on the doghouse bass" and "Two-Time Tom, our rimshot tempo man." But the album had a bit of everything, as if Merle, having figured out who he was in the previous two years, was now trying to figure who he could be. "Loneliness Is Eating Me Alive" is a Hank Cochran song that features the bluesy piano of Glen Hardin and a vocal that shows Hag could glide through a melody like Frank Sinatra or Dean Martin if he wanted. The oft-recorded "Long Black Limousine," covered memorably a year and a half later by Elvis, was a class-based morality tale that in Merle's version reminds that we can all run but we can't hide. A recut version of his "You Don't Have Very Far to Go" (first line: "You always find a way to hurt my *pride*") begins with a heavy minor-key acoustic strum and shimmers with pop potential. "Somewhere Between," a deep country-soul ballad that has Merle and Bonnie trying to scale "a wall so high, it reaches the sky" with harmonies that soar almost but not quite high enough, deserves a spot alongside "Today I Started Loving You Again" and "Silver Wings" as the most deserving Hag hits that never were.

Two weeks before *Branded Man* charted, Haggard was already in the studio recording most of the tracks for what would become his next album. Out in January 1968, *Sing Me Back Home* was solid enough but also felt, for the most part, like Merle was stuck in a bit of a holding pattern. It includes numbers from some familiar sources: "Mom and Dad's Waltz," for instance, and "Son of Hickory Holler's Tramp," a Dallas Frazier song from the point of view of a boy who loves his working-girl mom ("When [she] sacrificed her *pride* the neighbors started talkin'") every bit as much as Lefty loves his. Most everything else was by Merle, either a sturdy cowrite with an old friend—"My Past Is Present" with Wynn Stewart, "Wine Take Me Away" with Tommy Collins—or some only so-so Hag originals. "Home Is Where a Kid Grows Up," for example, has nothing to tell us that isn't in the title; "I'll Leave the Bottle on the Bar" sounds like someone trying to write another "The Bottle Let Me Down" and failing. With the album's title track as a notable exception, only Merle's "Good Times," a slinky, shushed blues about for once not feeling blue at all, is up to Merle's own high standards.

That title track, though, didn't just match Merle's standards. It set new ones. "Sing Me Back Home" was a defining work for Haggard, both commercially (it topped the country charts a couple of weeks into the new year) and artistically, but that can't really convey how amazing it must have been to hear it on the radio as 1967 gave way to '68. Few country records of its time sound even remotely like it. For example, while "Sing Me Back Home" stands today as an exemplar of the Bakersfield Sound, it doesn't sound like any Bakersfield records to that point. It doesn't *feel* like any either. "Sing Me Back Home" has hooks and emotional heft; it combines gravitas with fun, delicacy with doom: on the top 40 station of my dreams, it would segue best with weighty 1968 hits such as the Beatles' "Hey Jude" or the Temptations' "I Wish It Would Rain," Glen Campbell's "Wichita Lineman," Aretha Franklin's "I Say a Little Prayer," or, most of all, Otis Redding's "(Sittin' on)

The Dock of the Bay." Redding's record and Haggard's possess a similarly earnest accessibility. Redding's hard-travelin' tale, with its determination that nothing is going to change, its singer least of all, and with its passing ships perhaps calling to mind Merle's many metaphorical trains, is, in a word, Haggardesque. "Sing Me Back Home" and "Dock of the Bay" pose kindred existential questions, as well: Where *is* home, exactly? How will I get there? Who am I if I never make it back there again? You could say the same for Otis's spirit-buoying whistle and the woebegone, soul-lifting pedal steel guitar on "Sing Me Back Home," performed here for the first time on a Haggard session by Norman Hamlet, a perfect Stranger from here on out.

Where did Haggard's sound come from? Producer Ken Nelson is one part of the answer. Nelson wasn't much of a musician himself, though he did sometimes strum jazz banjo at parties thrown by "Voice of the Southland" Gene Austin, world-famous for "My Blue Heaven." He wasn't a knob-twirling auteur, either. Merle recalled, in a 1986 conversation with journalist Alanna Nash, that Nelson once told him, "I don't sign people who I have to produce, I sign people who are capable of producin' themselves." His standard operating procedure was to set the tape rolling, doodle on scrap paper during the performance, then either suggest another take or declare it "a master and a joy to behold. Come in and be proud."

His artists quickly learned to trust such estimations. Nelson had an ear for talent and material and for sounds that would do well on the radio, not just right now but *soon*. He brought Jean Shepard and Ferlin Husky together at Capitol Recording Studio in Hollywood to record that all's-fair-in-love-and-war melodrama "A Dear John Letter," launching the Bakersfield scene. In 1956, as head of Capitol's country division but often recording in Nashville, he signed rockabilly Gene Vincent and released "Be-Bop-a-Lula" in the wake of Elvis's initial breakthrough; the following year he produced "Gone," the swelling Ferlin Husky dreamscape that would prove a key template for the Nashville Sound. A couple of years later, working in Los Angeles almost exclusively, he was the producer behind more or less every significant Bakersfield Sound hit for most of a decade. (According to Fuzzy Owen, Nelson was even the man who gave the subgenre its name.) These were all wildly different country records, but Nelson's job wasn't to enforce a house style. He was an old-school A&R man, artist and repertoire, and he had the role's key skill: he could hear *pop*.

So could Haggard's longtime session leader, studio guitar ace James Burton. A member of the *Louisiana Hayride*'s backing band when he was fifteen and the lead guitarist on Dale Hawkins's germinal "Susie Q" a couple of years later, Burton had spent his career blurring the blurry-to-begin-with lines between blues, rock and roll, and country, then refocusing the lines into hits. By the time he was eighteen, he was a Californian and playing Fender Telecaster on many of Ricky Nelson's defining records. That's Burton's economical solo on "Travelin' Man," for example, a major radio presence in the months after Merle's release from San Quentin that expounded on a theme Merle knew a thing or two about. Soon Burton had joined the house band on the L.A.-based musical series *Shindig!* while logging countless sessions with everyone from Martin and Sinatra to Buffalo Springfield, the Monkees, Johnny Rivers, and the Everly Brothers: Burton picked out the lead to the Everlys' version of "Mama Tried" six months after playing on Merle's. An impressive résumé, each bullet point anticipating Burton's work with Elvis Presley in the '70s.

His work with Haggard might be his greatest of all. Ken Nelson had used Burton on sessions for a while, including some with Buck Owens, and recommended him as someone with a knack for coming up with memorable, radio-ruling guitar licks. Merle didn't need persuading. Deke Dickerson notes that Merle was already nuts about Burton's playing, especially his work on one of Rick Nelson's first stabs at country, 1966's "You Just Can't Quit." Burton's searing sound on that record predicts dozens of Haggard sides to come. As Merle explained to *Downbeat* in 1980, James "was doing a thing called chicken-pickin'. But he wasn't really bending strings. Roy [Nichols], on the other hand, was doing the string bending but wasn't doing the chicken-pickin'.... Our guitar style came out of a marriage between the styles." Though Nichols played lead on stage, he typically sat out or played a supporting role when James Burton was on the session—and most of the time, from '66 to '70, when he left to head Presley's band, Burton was on the session: he played most of the Haggard licks we recognize today. The doom-saying acoustic figure that sends "Sing Me Back Home" to its date with the gallows; the weaving lines of "The Bottle Let Me Down" or the weeping ones of "Hungry Eyes"; the belligerence that begins "The Fightin' Side of Me"—in the last half of the sixties, it was almost always James Burton announcing Haggard records *as* Haggard records. And, typically from note one, as hits.

*   *   *

Haggard followed "Sing Me Back Home" with "The Legend of Bonnie and Clyde," another country #1 in April 1968 and the rare hit to emerge in these years from a Burton-less recording session: the reckless acoustic guitar that springs the single is by Merle's old Bakersfield pal Billy Mize, and Glen Campbell gives the record its hurtling, wind-in-your-hair feel on banjo. Campbell was poised to become a star himself—his "By the Time I Get to Phoenix" was on the charts with "Sing Me Back" and "Legend" both—and Merle helped all he could, including his fellow Capitol artist's record in his DJ mailings. But while "By the Time I Get to Phoenix" cracked the pop top 40, none of Merle's records did. Perhaps a gorgeous Al De Lory string arrangement of the sort gracing Campbell's hit would've helped Merle's similarly moody and melodic "Today I Started Loving You Again" get wider airplay. Maybe it was the banjo that killed any of the pop potential in "The Legend of Bonnie and Clyde," although it hadn't stopped Flatt & Scruggs's "Foggy Mountain Breakdown (Theme from *Bonnie & Clyde*)" from becoming a minor sensation around the same time. Fuzzy Owen recalled Merle insisting his record needed a banjo *because* the instrument was so prominent a part of the film and its popular soundtrack album.

In 1968 this must have seemed like the way of the world. The fetishization of small differences *is* pop culture at any given moment, though those differences can sometimes be tough to pin down only a short time later. That was especially true for "Sing Me Back Home," a one-of-a-kind record but one that features an acoustic-plus-electric blend, leaning heavily to the former, and laid over thumping bass and drum that made it of a sonic piece, generally speaking, with contemporaneous country records that did go pop: "Harper Valley PTA," for instance, or Capitol releases like "Ode to Billie Joe" and "Gentle on My Mind." Nothing on Haggard's *Sing Me Back Home* and its successor, *The Legend of Bonnie and Clyde*, had similar successes, but the two albums did similarly survey pop-relevant subjects with similar folky, pop-minded arrangements.

The same was true of Haggard's next album, *Mama Tried*, in 1968. The title track became Merle's fifth career #1 single that summer, and has it all: Mama, a misspent youth, trains, prison, a musical arrangement that seamlessly combines the plugged and unplugged and that identifies itself from its first notes. James Burton's heart-racing Dobro calls out like the open road, then Roy Nichols's Fender doubles you over like a sucker punch to the gut. The album cover—Merle posed in a jail cell, clad in prison garb and strumming a guitar—would have been recognized by country fans as in conversation to a similar shot on the cover of *Soul of a Convict and Other Great Prison Songs*, by Porter Wagoner, released just the year before.

But "Mama Tried" had potential to reach beyond the country audience that went unrealized, at least in Merle's version, though it's assembled from clearly pop elements. "I was trying to land somewhere in between Peter, Paul & Mary and Johnny Cash," Merle told Paul Zollo. James Burton's launching lick is jangly, supercharged folk rock. The two quick notes that Norman Hamlet hits to snap the intro closed, then repeats to end the record—the only pedal steel notes on the entire single—were known in the band as the "Batman lick" because they mimicked the urgent hook of the TV show's theme song: "Bat! Man!"

Mama Tried betrays pop ambitions all through. It's worth noting that its hit title track is followed by covers of two songs that had been pop hits the previous year—"Green, Green Grass of Home" (by Tom Jones) and "Little Ole Wine Drinker Me" (for Dean Martin)—and the album's side one ends with Merle's version of "Folsom Prison Blues," which Johnny Cash had returned to the top 40, this time via a live recording, only months before. The trapped soul Haggard portrays in "Folsom Prison" is haunted by the lonesome whistle of the train he hears rolling by each day, year after year after year. Its riders are bound for San Antonio, says Cash's lyric, but the hell of it for the Hag is that folks are free to move about the country at all. "Those people keep a-*movin'*," Merle groans through gritted teeth, "and *that's* what tortures me."

On *Mama Tried* Merle feels tortured in so many ways. "Run 'Em Off," an Onie Wheeler and Tony Lee song that had been a top-ten hit for Lefty Frizzell in 1954, presents a husband scared to death his wife is cheating on him—with the iceman, the milkman, and basically every other "two-footed wolf" who knocks at the door. Frizzell's version is a charming, catchy shuffle and is played for laughs: this hubby's misgivings seem exaggerated and ridiculous, his pleas ineffectual. Merle's version, a rare instance of him singing a Lefty number in his own voice, simmers with anxiety and anger and, paranoid or not, feels like a real threat to his wife. The cut's mocking electric guitar lines are nagging suspicions, needling him relentlessly. Then, on his own "I'll Always Know," Merle comes off again as suspicious as all hell, paranoid to the point of being out of his mind. "Someday soon I know you plan to hurt me," he declares, presumably because hurting him is just what people do. "But I'll always know when you've been cheatin'," he threatens. His and Bonnie's harmonies are terrifying.

Only two tracks earlier he'd sounded considered and wise, too—on "In the Good Old Days (When Times Were Bad)," the first of several Dolly Parton songs he'd record over the years. Parton's song articulates a way of using, and feeling, a hard-scrabble history that is every bit as nuanced as his own: "No amount of money could buy from me the memories that I have of then, no amount of money could pay me to go back and live through it again." Like Dolly, Merle found strength in his past, not because poverty or prison was any place he wished to return to, but because he knew those things made him, for worse and for better, who he was.

Who he was, was the running kind, as free and unfree as a bird on the wing. On the album's closing track, another Dallas Frazier song called "Too Many Bridges to Cross Over," Haggard advises the woman he's with not to grow accustomed to having him around. "Like an eagle," he warns her, "I'm a prisoner of the wind." You could listen to Merle sing that line for the rest of your days—he's bragging and complaining both—and never get to the bottom of all it suggests regarding the hot-wired relationship between human freedom and the limits, man-made or built-in, that go with simply being alive.

CHAPTER 13

HE'S LIVING IN THE GOOD OLD DAYS

COUNTRYPOLITAN, COUNTRY SOUL, COUNTRY ROCK

I n July 1968 Merle Haggard marked a career milestone when Ken Nelson and Capitol released *The Best of Merle Haggard*. Merle's first greatest-hits album gathered eleven commercial and artistic high points from his brief half-decade as a recording act: three country chart-toppers, four additional top tens, plus "House of Memories," "Shade Tree Fix-It Man," "High on a Hilltop," and "Sam Hill." In its moment, this early retrospective underlined what today may be only faintly grasped: Merle Haggard was a major figure in country music even before he released "Mama Tried," "Hungry Eyes," "Workin' Man Blues," "Okie from Muskogee," and all that followed. In 1969, in liner notes for Haggard's Jimmie Rodgers tribute *Same Train, a Different Time*, disc jockey Hugh Cherry compares Merle's standing enthusiastically, though not inaccurately, to the "Father of Country Music" himself: "Today, Merle Haggard enjoys a position of eminence in his chosen art, equal to the Rodgers of forty years ago." Country radio listeners and record buyers didn't need this explained to them. Only albums from the red-hot Johnny Cash and Glen Campbell stopped *The Best of Merle Haggard* from topping *Billboard*'s Hot Country LP's chart—in 1972 the album became his first to be certified gold. Merle's colleagues recognized his "position of eminence," too, and codified it. Mainstream country artists recorded Haggard songs at least fifty times in 1968 alone.

*   *   *

Haggard flirted with mainstream pop success throughout his Muskogee Moment. In September 1968, he became one of the few country acts to appear on *American Bandstand,* performing "The Legend of Bonnie and Clyde" and "The Fugitive." He did not perform "Mama Tried," even though it was the nation's #1 country hit at the time. The omission, host Dick Clark explained, was to avoid any "conflict of interest": the song, the title of which he couldn't name, had been written by Merle for a movie, which he also couldn't name, that he had produced and that they had both starred in. "You'll come back and do it another day when the heat's off," Dick promised. Merle thought that was pretty funny: "When the *heat's* off?"

After working with Haggard on *Killers Three,* Clark had insisted he could transform the country star into a pop star, if Merle was willing. That was a more realistic possibility than might be remembered today. In 1968 country and country-adjacent stars Tammy Wynette, Jeannie C. Riley, Bobbie Gentry, Johnny Cash, Henson Cargill, Bobby Goldsboro, and Glen Campbell all placed big records in both the pop and country top 40s. Then, through 1974, Charlie Rich, Anne Murray, Sammi Smith, Ray Price, Olivia Newton-John, John Denver, Kris Kristofferson, Donna Fargo, Conway Twitty, Freddie Hart, Jerry Reed, Tom T. Hall, Lynn Anderson, and Elvis Presley, among several others, did the same. The line between the country and pop formats in those years was quite permeable, musically speaking, even as the line between audiences became more politically rigid.

This fluidity between genre and format was because country had entered what became known as its crossover-minded "countrypolitan" phase, when the music achieved more success on pop radio than at any time before or since. In part, countrypolitan could more easily negotiate format barriers in this era because of its frequent string arrangements rather than twin fiddles, and because of its big vocal choruses and other pop accessories. As a result, the style was understood, sometimes dismissively, as only the latest itera-tion of soft-shell country. That characterization wasn't wrong. What such characterizations overlooked was that countrypolitan embraced hard-core country elements at least as often as softer ones. Countrypolitan recordings reinserted pedal steel and resonator guitars and other hyper-twangy color instruments that the earlier Nashville Sound eschewed. Countrypolitan also favored vocalists, placed way out front in the mix, with far twangier singing voices than those of, say, Patsy Cline, Eddy Arnold, or Jim Reeves.

Exemplary recordings of the countrypolitan style include Sammi Smith's "Help Me Make It through the Night," its humid cellos and doomed pulse either easing or exacerbating an existentialist crisis; Ray Price's "For the Good Times," where a clip-clopping, steady-as-she-goes beat drives an easy-listening orchestral arrangement to suggest that the middle of the road, presumably safe to a fault, is precisely where many relationships become roadkill; and Johnny Cash's "Sunday Morning Coming Down," a hangover-induced accounting, cut live on TV with a brass band and a fleet of violins. These records are uniformly lush but sonically quite varied. The songs, all written by Nashville newcomer Kris Kristofferson, a hippie-lookalike Rhodes Scholar and former army officer, take up themes and points of view that are strikingly mature—even within a genre long known as "grown-up music."

The same is true for a trio of star-making hits by Merle's old Capitol Records studio pal Glen Campbell: "By the Time I Get to Phoenix," "Wichita Lineman," and "Galveston," each written by Jimmy Webb. But perhaps it is "Rose Garden," a #1 country hit in 1970 (#3 on the pop charts), written by Joe South and performed by Liz and Casey Anderson's daughter, Lynn, that is countrypolitan's beau ideal: sunny vocals, hurtling pedal steel, harrying strings. Like so many countrypolitan hits, "Rose Garden" provides a soundtrack either for suburban dreams or for diminished expectations, as needed.

Because Merle's reputation is fixed so tightly to the rough-and-tumble Bakersfield scene, his music has almost never been considered countrypolitan. But, sometimes, the term captures precisely what Merle's and Ken Nelson's records are up to. Take, for example, "Hungry Eyes," which knocked Campbell's "Galveston" from atop the country chart in May 1969, and "Silver Wings": each string bejeweled, each with twangy guitar and voice, each invigorated by the contrast.

What was happening on radio was both cause and result of what was happening on television: country singers were frequent guests on, and even hosted their own, national TV shows during the Muskogee Moment. Haggard benefited as much as anyone from country's newfound cachet. After "Okie" and through the summer of 1971, Haggard released seven consecutive singles that at least "Bubbled Under" on *Billboard*'s Hot 100. In the same stretch, Haggard appeared on ABC's *Music Scene*, Campbell's

Goodtime Hour, and the syndicated *The Porter Wagoner Show*. He appeared, seven times, on *Hee Haw*, CBS's cross between *Rowan & Martin's Laugh-In* and an old-time medicine show. And he showed up three times on *The Johnny Cash Show* as well, and once, singing "Workin' Man Blues," on *Jimmy Durante Presents the Lennon Sisters*. Hag was on the big screen, too. In the 1970 John Wayne vehicle *Chisum*, Haggard's voice can be heard singing "Turn Around," a string-swollen ballad à la Glen Campbell's title song from Wayne's previous film, *True Grit*.

Country acts were also being covered by big-city newspapers and general-interest magazines as never before. Merle saw *Sing Me Back Home* reviewed in that bastion of middle-class, middle-American, "middlebrow" middle-ness, *Life*, and in '71 he was featured in one of the final issues of *Life*'s poor cousin, *Look*. In the same period Haggard was reviewed and profiled several times in *Rolling Stone*, at this point still growing its hair long and shaggy out in San Francisco, and in Atlanta's underground weekly, *The Great Speckled Bird*. The Hag played well on both the hip and square sides of the street.

He had the looks to be a star: publicity photos from this period have him looking like a blue-collar James Dean; one writer described him as "a cross between Audie Murphy and Warren Beatty." He had the songs, too. "Swinging Doors," "The Bottle Let Me Down," and "Hungry Eyes," among others, were cut often by Nashville types, and "Sing Me Back Home" and "Mama Tried" were endlessly covered by rock and country acts alike. Corny, old-school pop crooners cut his tunes: Dean Martin's "I Take a Lot of Pride in What I Am" beat "Okie" to the pop charts by a couple of months, and a couple of months later, Al Martino crept onto the charts with one of the first noncountry covers of "Today I Started Loving You Again." In fact, Haggard had so many good songs that other country singers had taken to cherry-picking the best of his leftovers for hits of their own. In 1967 Maine-based country singer Dick Curless landed a #28 country hit with Merle's "All of Me Belongs to You," then followed it with "House of Memories." Ernest Tubb made "One Sweet Hello" the title track of an album in 1971, and in '73, Charley Pride topped the country countdown with "Shoulder to Cry On." "I'd Rather Be Gone" went top-five for Hank Williams Jr. in 1970, and Conway Twitty did the same a year later with "I Wonder What She'll Think about Me Leaving." Most of these songs wouldn't make it onto Hag's own albums for years.

More important than the songs, as far as pop success was concerned, not to mention the larger cultural conversation such success allowed, was that Haggard had the *records*. The 1968 *Sing Me Back Home* review that ran in *Life* said its title track "could be a Top 40 hit tomorrow if the big-city stations would play it." The same was true for the following year's "Hungry Eyes" and for "Workin' Man Blues," with its rocking Elvis-in-Vegas rhythm, and for its B-side, "Silver Wings," as pure pop a record as Haggard ever made. "Don't leave me, I cried, don't take that airplane ride," Merle sings, his baritone borne aloft by strings that roar and shimmer. A brooding piano lick keeps circling back around, though, and the record ends with Merle wingless and earthbound and watching the sky.

For Merle, it was the sky that seemed the limit.

Haggard's next two albums were released only three months apart in the first half of 1969. *Pride in What I Am* came first. A single, "I Take a Lot of Pride in What I Am," climbed only to #3, Merle's lowest entry in three years, and the album itself went only to #11. Then, *Same Train, a Different Time*, Merle's annotated salute to "Father of Country Music" Jimmie Rodgers, topped the country album chart. In terms of both longevity and peak position, only *Swinging Doors/The Bottle Let Me Down*, back in 1966, had to date fared as well on the country album chart as *Same Train*. The album even climbed to #67 on *Billboard*'s Top LP's chart, the first time a Merle Haggard album had climbed any higher there than #165, *I'm a Lonesome Fugitive*'s showing in 1967.

This success was all unexpected, to put it mildly. A tribute to a forty-years-dead yodeler, sprinkled with narrated, momentum-killing history lessons, in a double-album format that priced it a couple bucks more than a regular LP and released without so much as a supporting single? *Same Train* should have been a bad bet. The album had been encouraged anyway by producer Ken Nelson, himself a longtime Rodgers fan. Nelson and Capitol's willingness to indulge their star was proof of Merle's increased professional clout, and the album's success only furthered his pull.

The tribute was proof, too, of Haggard's growing ambitions. As Merle achieved the freedom to do what he wished as an artist, one thing he wished to do was to evangelize for an idol. "I guess I was being sort of a professor in some ways," Merle told Barry Mazor. "There were a lot of people who didn't know about Jimmie Rodgers who ought to. It didn't satisfy me—and it doesn't satisfy me yet."

Merle had been inching toward the Rodgers album for a while. He'd included the Blue Yodeler's "Rough and Rowdy Ways" on *Fugitive* in 1967, and *Pride in What I Am* included the same version of "California Blues" that opened *Same Train*. We've seen how Rodgers's music, learned from the Lefty Frizzell 78s his mother bought him, was a formative influence on young Haggard, so let's note here that on *Same Train, a Different Time*, Merle doesn't try to re-create those Lefty performances, and mostly only waves in the direction of Rodgers's originals. The album's narrations do allow Merle to model for contemporary listeners a way into hearing that hoariest feature of the Rodgers style, the blue yodel: "Jimmie made the yodel *work* for him. His yodel could display pain, loneliness or even a happy frame of mind."

The Strangers' modern arrangements demonstrated how Jimmie's songs might still be made to work for us. On "California Blues" and "Waiting for a Train," on "Train Whistle Blues" and "Frankie and Johnny" and the rest, the album is built on contemporary rhythms that swing and thump—hard, thanks to Eddie Burris's kick drum and brush work and to Jerry Ward's electric bass. The album also showcases more than ever James Burton's very full and electric-*sounding* Dobro and, a few times, gives it up for Roy Nichols on electric. Along with Merle's knowing, state-of-the-art country croon, augmented here and there by Roy's harmonica, these elements had been identifying features of the Strangers' studio sound for a couple of years already. The Rodgers project was traditional rather than retro, in other words, connected to the past but planted in the present. Merle was riding the *Same Train*, but his emphasis was on *a Different Time*. Now.

Occasional electric guitar aside, the primary way Merle and the Strangers announced that their Rodgers take was a modern one can be summed up in a word no one has ever used to praise the Singing Brakeman's own records: groove. And the Strangers achieved that different-time effect on *Same Train*, as they did on most of Haggard's Muskogee Moment music, with their version of another dominant sound of the time: country soul.

Emerging from Muscle Shoals, Alabama, and Memphis, Tennessee, in the early 1960s, country soul was first heard on R&B hits such as Arthur Alexander's "You Better Move On," Jimmy Hughes's "Steal Away," and William Bell's "You Don't Miss Your Water." These and scores more country-soul recordings are marked by their straightforward melodies and by twangy guitar and piano licks that plainly evoke country music, but they are sung in the melismatic style of the Black church and set atop rhythms—played just on the backside of the beat instead of square on—that plainly evoke soul music. This fusion of white and Black styles was an easy, inviting fit, musically and thematically. But country soul resonated socially and politically, as well, because it wasn't supposed to fit at all: country music in the sixties was associated with the states of the former Confederacy and with segregation during the last days of Jim Crow; soul music stood with civil rights and integration and Black power.

Country soul's power as a symbol—Black and white Americans making beautiful music together—was further enhanced in recording sessions that often employed white musicians in support of Black stars. Yet as historian Charles Hughes has shown, the reality was far uglier than the metaphor. In the "Country Soul Triangle," Hughes's term for the relevant recording centers in Muscle Shoals, Memphis, and, a bit later, Nashville, the racism and power imbalances of American society were replicated in the recording studio. In late 1964, when the session musicians of the Original Muscle Shoals Rhythm Section transplanted to Nashville, they became part of country music's rhythmic avant-garde. At the same time, the appropriation of country soul by country musicians wasn't new in the least. Country had long helped itself to Black rhythms and styles—swing, boogie, rock and roll, plus generation after generation of variations on the blues—to freshen its sound and broaden its reach. Now country soul was tapped to update the modified rock-and-roll beats that both the Bakersfield and Nashville Sounds had embraced, albeit dissimilarly, a decade prior.

As the sixties moved into the seventies, country soul was just how a lot of country records sounded, from Tammy Wynette's "Stand by Your Man" in 1968 to Conway Twitty's answer record, "How Much More Can She Stand," in 1971. A country-soul rhythm section formed the pop-minded foundation for so many countrypolitan hits that way: Smith's "Help Me Make It through the Night," Dolly Parton's "Jolene," Charlie Rich's "Behind Closed Doors," Elvis Presley's "There Goes My Everything." And Merle Haggard's "Hungry Eyes," a country-soul track dusted with countrypolitan strings. Merle and the studio Strangers cut it while on a break from the *Same Train* sessions, so it hardly seems coincidental that the song works with Depression-era subject matter Rodgers would surely have appreciated.

Country-soulish arrangements didn't just become a norm in the country, pop, and soul fields. Switch out that Dobro on the Rodgers tribute for a slide guitar, or strip the strings from "Hungry Eyes," and you've got the basic template for a bulk of the tracks on the Rolling Stones' *Beggars Banquet*. That rock album was released only a few months prior to *Same Train*, itself released the same month "Hungry Eyes" sat atop the country singles chart. The biggest sonic differences between these projects come down to the Stones' simpler lines and louder drums and their self-consciously rougher and rowdier textures—a British art student's notion, per "Street Fighting Man," of what a poor boy could do. Merle and the Strangers' recordings were every bit as fussed-over but with more clean-and-polished tones and fancier picking. Haggard's ideal of what a poor boy could do, once he'd made it, was to have some nice things and show them off.

Pride in What I Am was released in February 1969, three months before *Same Train, a Different Time*, and worked similar grooves. "Country music is white folk's soul!" shouted newspaper advertisements for the album, alongside art that made it look as if Merle had a tree growing out the top of his skull. "And Merle Haggard is the soul of the country!" The ads pointed to Merle and the album's country-soul sound, to country and soul as related American forms, and at least hinted at country's longstanding appropriations of Black style. All selling points, in the view of Capitol's marketing department.

Pride stands among Haggard's very best. Its not-quite-title track was contemporary country at its most cutting-edge, simultaneously embracing a country-soul pulse and pretty folk pop—the single's sprightly, rolling guitar figure is reminiscent of Glen Campbell's "Gentle on My Mind"—and rebellious rock subject matter: "Things I learned in a hobo jungle are things they never taught me in a classroom." As usual, Merle fudges some of the details, autobiographically speaking: "I don't remember ever havin' any folks around" and "I've never been nobody's idol" do not speak of Merle's actual life, not by a long shot, but they do help draw a character who *feels* alone and insecure and who does not feel falsely. "I Take a Lot of Pride in What I Am" finds Merle uncharacteristically humble, peaceful, satisfied, sleeping on benches and happy to be "living off the fat of our great land." Unlike the business- and plowmen in Bob Dylan's and Jimi Hendrix's versions of

"All Along the Watchtower" from the year before, Merle knows the land's worth, knows his own worth, too, and is proud of both.

"The Day the Rains Came," meanwhile, is wondrous, weird, and lovely. Merle and a lover take refuge in a cave during a storm, amidst idyllic folk guitar and otherworldly backing vocals that haunt until they soothe. If he can only hold on in memory to what he found with her in that cave, Merle sings, then he'd be happy forever. If he can remember that, and if the world should give him nothing more, then the world has given him enough. At the end of the album, on "I Think We're Living in the Good Old Days," Merle even suggests that we should "cheer up and be glad" and seize the day. In 1969, mind you, amidst an increasingly unpopular war and growing social unrest. Nine consecutive top-five country singles made it easier, perhaps, to feel such good vibrations.

But contentment is a state of mind that came and went for Merle. On a brutal cover of the 1960 Charlie Walker hit "Who Will Buy the Wine?," written by Bakersfield friend Billy Mize, Merle sounds bitter as poison. On another cover of an old Lefty song, "It Meant Goodbye to Me When You Said Hello to Him," he's bed-sick pale. Boasting red-hot picking and an everybody-now chorus, "I'm Free" keeps declaring what the song fails to illustrate: Merle insists he's happy with no expectations and no social ties, with no one telling him what to do and no obligations, but this just sounds like a kid's idea of freedom—no real agency but (yay!) a lack of supervision. In "I'm Bringing Home Good News," Merle's "sittin' downtown in a tav-run" when it comes to him that he's going to leave his girl for good, and he races home to pack. On Jimmie Rodgers's "California Blues," he's gone.

"I'm going off of the deep end....I disagree with the way that I'm living," he half laughs, half chokes on a dissolute country blues called "I Can't Hold Myself in Line." Just the same, he intends to "head full speed ahead down the wrong road of life." His weakness is stronger than he is, he allows. Then he chuckles again, just a little, though not because he thinks it's all that funny.

By the end of the sixties, much of Haggard's music could fairly be termed "country rock." That doesn't just mean rock and roll with some country thrown in. Country music had been present at rock and roll's national coming-out party, what with Chuck Berry copping "Ida Red" for

"Maybelline" and Elvis Presley's first single featuring countrified blues on its A-side and bluesy country on the flip. Rock and rollers have been mixing the forms quite explicitly ever since. Again, James Burton with Ricky Nelson stands out, but so does the instrumental electric guitar work of Duane Eddy, Dick Dale, any number of rockin' little surfer bands, and especially of the Seattle-based instrumental group the Ventures, who learned their first hit, 1960's "Walk, Don't Run," off a Chet Atkins LP and who two years later cut an album of country songs, including Cash's "I Walk the Line" and Bob Wills's "San Antonio Rose." The group's principal guitarist, Nokie Edwards, was a transplanted Oklahoman who'd played with Buck Owens.

For country music, all those electric guitars, Fender Telecasters as often as not, quickly became just another tool for producing the genre's defining aesthetic effect: twang. This was particularly true in the Okie-dominated San Joaquin. Bakersfield bar bands mixed plenty of rock and roll into their country sets because audiences enjoyed dancing to both and because, increasingly, it was hard to tell the difference. Long before Buck Owens was charged with hypocrisy for swearing allegiance to country music in advance of an album that included a Chuck Berry song, he'd already covered the Coasters and the Drifters. Before stardom, Buck sang and played guitar for years in what was perhaps Bakersfield's definitive local band, Bill Woods and the Orange Blossom Playboys, and, after Buck moved on to front his own group, Merle too served a brief stint as a Playboy. "Though we were a Country-Western band," Woods clarified to journalist John Grissim in 1970, "we always played about 75 percent rock in clubs. Still do." Or, as Owens himself calculated it for journalist Liane Hansen, the Buckaroos' driving, big-beat sound was "a mix of Bob Wills and the Texas Playboys and Little Richard." Coming from the rock-and-roll side of this synthesis, Owens and Haggard's Capitol label mates, the Beatles, covered Buck's "Act Naturally" and went all Bakersfield Sounding on one of their own songs, "Run for Your Life," in 1965.

The Beatles, along with Bob Dylan, are key here, since country rock requires, technically speaking, something called *rock*, as distinguished from *rock and roll*, for existence in the first place. Perhaps Haggard seems an odd fit in this context? We have a strong sense today that Haggard was about as country as they come. And, thanks to hippie-jabbing hits ahead, about as antithetical to rock music, too, what with the style's necessarily Dylan-inspired songwriting; its indulgence of guitar distortion, louder volumes, and longer jams; and its identification with the drug culture, the sexual revolution, the political left, and other phenomena, primarily youth-oriented and middle-class-associated, we today term the sixties. The differences were real.

But that didn't mean distinctions were always easily made in real time. Just before "Okie from Muskogee" hit in the fall of 1969, and to an only slightly diminished degree afterward, Haggard was a greatly admired songwriter among those rock musicians experimenting with returns to rock and roll's rootsy origins, country roots included, and away from highfalutin works like *Sgt. Pepper's Lonely Hearts' Club Band* and *Days of Future Passed*. Some counterculture kids had been turned on to country when Dylan began cutting albums with session cats in Nashville. Rock bands like Creedence Clearwater Revival (they gave a shout-out to Buck on 1970's "Lookin' Out My Back Door") and the Rolling Stones were scoring hits with unabashedly twangy LPs like *Bayou Country* and *Green River*, *Beggars Banquet* and *Let It Bleed*, respectively. The Band, who had covered both Dylan songs and Lefty Frizzell's ghost-story hit "Long Black Veil" on their debut, *Music from Big Pink*, even made the cover of *Time* in January 1970: "Canada's Contribution to Country Rock."

Merle was a cult hero to these acts—a proletarian poet, a rebel—an assessment that carried over to later-arriving country rockers like the Gram Parsons–led Flying Burrito Brothers, Buffalo Springfield (and two of its progeny, Poco and Neil Young), as well as Linda Ronstadt and the Eagles. Like Merle, all of these acts were California-based rather than southern, and often at odds with the Nashville establishment. But this didn't mean they felt or used the music in the same ways. Merle's pride in "livin' off the fat of our great land," for example, might be heard by some as promoting individualism and self-sufficiency, and even perhaps turning a blind eye to living outside the law: think of the similarly themed "King of the Road," for instance, where Roger Miller brags that "I know every lock that ain't locked when no one's around." Others might catch in Merle's lyric an echo of Woody Guthrie's "This Land Is Your Land," while still others might decide that, for them, it was proof that Merle shared their conviction that America should get back to the garden. As Geoffrey Stokes would summarize it much later, country rockers adopted a stance toward country material that was sincere, even envious of its presumed simpler world, but held at arm's length. They performed their brands of country music, as critic Ellen

Willis observed in real time, with "ironic affection." Either way, as the 1960s ended, Merle had the ear of a lot of the same people his "Okie" and "Fightin' Side" would openly disdain.

The Byrds, for example, had turned from Dylan-inflected folk rock to Haggard-loving country rock with the help of Parsons, who'd done Merle's "I Must Be Somebody Else You've Known" while leading the International Submarine Band in 1966. The Byrds were scheduled to perform Merle's "Sing Me Back Home" at the Grand Ole Opry in March 1968—with Merle's record still lingering on the charts—but didn't because Gram Parsons, shocking his bandmates and host Tompall Glaser, stepped to the mic and announced they'd instead be playing one of his songs, "Hickory Wind." When the group's *Sweetheart of the Rodeo* was released in August, it included Haggard's "Life in Prison."

Most remarkably, the Grateful Dead included "Mama Tried" in their storm-shortened set at that crowning glory of the rock era, Woodstock: "Three Days of Peace and Music" and, for a couple of minutes there, Merle Haggard. The Dead put an unaccountably funky "Mama Tried" on a self-titled 1971 album. For decades afterward the song stayed nearly as predictable a part of the Grateful Dead concert experience as the fragrance of weed on the wind. And a year after Merle had "Workin' Man Blues," these quintessential long-and-shaggy-haired San Fran hippies had *Workingman's Dead*.

Haggard was thirty-two in 1969, but had connections, briefly, with the never-trust-anyone-over-thirty youth culture, nonetheless. *Killers Three*, the movie for which "Mama Tried" was written, played a role in boosting Merle's Love Generation credibility, for instance, or at least that was part of the idea. A movie where the youthful outlaw protagonists are troubled and violent but basically good kids, *Killers Three* was Dick Clark's attempt to ride the coattails of *Bonnie and Clyde*. That 1967 Arthur Penn film was, in some ways, deeply nostalgic, but, typical of the way nostalgia works in American culture, its backward glance wasn't about the Past so much as it was an attempt to process the Now. Nearly everyone who saw *Bonnie and Clyde* understood it was commenting on the era's increasingly violent Generation Gap and, what's more, was actively rooting for the kids. Merle was obsessed with the film. Drawn to its Depression-era setting (much of it in Oklahoma) and its doomed young outlaws (fugitives!), he saw it six times—he was especially enamored of Faye Dunaway's Bonnie—and determined to translate it into song.

"The Legend of Bonnie and Clyde" was cut early in 1968. By April it was another country #1, Merle's third in a row, and he and Ken Nelson made it the title track to his next album. Merle plays dress-up in gangster pinstripes on the cover, wielding a tommy gun and posing with a Dunaway look-alike. The following spring Merle performed the song before a national audience on *The Glen Campbell Goodtime Hour*. Campbell replicated the single's running-for-their-lives acoustic guitar lick, while on banjo, to Merle's left, sat freak-flag-flying folkie and *Goodtime Hour* regular John Hartford.

Merle's reading of the Bonnie and Clyde legend omits key details from the film: the impotence of Warren Beatty's Clyde, most obviously, and for that matter any sex at all. Merle draws markedly different conclusions from the tale, too. The film has us siding with the kids, hoping they escape with their lives and without punishment, but Merle intones a moral he presents as unavoidable: "For robbin' and killin', they both had to pay." Still, in the wake of *Bonnie and Clyde*, any mention of the outlaw duo came with sympathetic connections to youthful rebellion. For country rock's early adopters, and for anyone else paying attention, "The Legend of Bonnie and Clyde" was one more bit of evidence that Merle Haggard, just maybe, was on the kids' side, too.

But those differences persisted and could be tough to negotiate. Gram Parsons was a trust-fund Florida kid and Harvard dropout who became a devoted Haggard fan. While playing with the Flying Burrito Brothers, he'd cut "Sing Me Back Home" like everyone else and had spent several months introducing the Stones' Keith Richards to his hero's music. Parsons was such a Haggard man that while preparing to record his 1971 solo debut, he sought out Merle to produce. The two even met to discuss the project but decided against it. In some versions of the story, that was because Merle was too busy to fit Parsons in. Though he was actively looking to try his hand at producing other acts at the time, that was actually a likely story: Merle was booked on the road almost constantly while also finishing up several albums of his own. Plus, Gram the rocker was thinking along the lines of weeks to make his record, whereas Merle the country singer was much more of a three-tracks-in-a-four-hour-session cultural worker. Complicating matters further, according to Parsons's biographer Ben Fong-Torres, when time came to begin the project, Merle and Bonnie were on the outs, and, upset that his wife had walked out on him, he refused to leave the hotel and head to the studio. In another version of the story, Parsons's Byrds and

Burrito Brothers partner Chris Hillman told Peter Doggett what finally sank
the collaboration: "Gram was drunk. So Merle quit." That could be, too.
Haggard liked to drink himself, among other diversions, but he believed
in getting up and going to work, doing the job the best you could—and
figured you'd need to be something like sober to do it.

The patron saint of country rock didn't get Haggard to produce, but
he did get the next best thing: Merle's longtime Capitol engineer, Hugh
Davies. He also landed James Burton and Glen Hardin, who'd played on
nearly all the Hag's signature records, and drummer Ronnie Tutt, who'd
been on "Okie from Muskogee," all three on a break from backing Elvis
on the road. Nineteen seventy-three's *GP* is a gem of a record, laconic and
anguished, tight as a drum but pleasantly rag-ass when it needs to be, and
what it lacks in fullness of tragicomic vision, it embraces entirely by being
very, very serious. Still, I do sometimes wish it swung, grooved, or rocked
as hard as one of Merle's records.

Merle's final LP of the decade made the country album chart in October
1969, just one week before "Okie from Muskogee" cracked the singles
countdown and changed his life. Though the hit studio version of that song
wouldn't be collected on an LP for many years, *A Portrait of Merle Haggard*
did collect his other most recent #1's: the for-the-ages, one-two punch of
"Hungry Eyes" and "Workin' Man Blues," plus its beautiful B-side, "Silver
Wings," along with several of the strong stray tracks he had lying around
in seemingly unlimited supply. Some, like a Nashville Sound-ing version of
the George Jones hit "She Thinks I Still Care," were more than a year old,
while others, like the dreamy, countrypolitan "Every Fool Has a Rainbow,"
were brand-new.

The melody for "Every Fool" seems to present the song as Merle's contribution to that now-quaint record-store category, Inspirational. "Every
Fool Has a Rainbow" is his "You'll Never Walk Alone" or "I Believe," or
his go at something like "If I Can Dream" from Elvis's comeback Christmas
special back in December. Except Merle's lyric mitigates such dreams with
warnings of folly and the all-too-human. People go chasing rainbows all
the time, he warns, losing their good things along the way. "And the rule
applies to me," Merle confesses of his own over-the-rainbow dreams. He
doesn't know whether to laugh or cry. A string section that elsewhere might

lift the spirit here sounds an elegy. Merle's croon, meanwhile, resists the cautions of his own lyric and casts his lot with the fools.

Side one of Merle's *Portrait* recounts a drama of domestic devotion and loss. Merle plays a poor sap who busts his tail for wife and kids ("Workin' Man Blues"), even preferring to stay in evenings with his wife instead of making the bars ("What's Wrong with Stayin' Home?"). Merle's wife flies on him anyway ("Silver Wings"). The story's unhappy ending leaves Merle alone and miserable, casting about for fleeting affection (Glenn Martin and Willie Nelson's "Who Do I Know in Dallas"), and not a little pathetic, too, reduced to stalking his ex or maybe drunk-dialing her ("She Thinks I Still Care")—all accidently on purpose, of course. It's a hoary old tale, parts of which you've perhaps even told yourself.

There are no happy endings on *Portrait*. Side two begins with "Hungry Eyes," American dreams forever deferred, and ends with "Montego Bay," a Hank Cochran and Glenn Martin number about an exotic locale stealing a poor boy's girl away from him. "I even thought of stealing," Merle confesses, "so I could show her more." Trumpets sway, Jamaica lures, but he's stuck alone in Tennessee. In between are a trio of the slinking, country-soul-type ballads that Haggard took to after the success of "Today I Started Loving You Again" the year before. "Every Fool Has a Rainbow" was Merle's; "I Die Ten Thousand Times a Day" was written by "Lost Highway" songwriter Leon Payne; and "I Came So Close to Failure" was by Jimmie "You Are My Sunshine" Davis. They feature skittering acoustic guitar lines and weeping pedal steel, and their unhurried, even crawling paces and spare settings accentuate Merle's emotional presence on key lines. Scared to death on "Without soul a life comes to its end," bemused and bittersweet at "He'll give up a bed of roses for a hammock filled with thorns," wailing and hoarse on "When I think of what I've done a chill runs through me." These ballads were, to date, among the most aching, most beautiful vocal performances of his career. Though not well known today, they have remained so.

By the fall of 1969 Merle was setting the pace in country music. He was a master of the rough croon, he was acknowledged as one of country's finest-ever songwriters, and he was a country traditionalist of the first rank. Tethering to the past while playing the present, he embraced countrypolitan, as needed, when he felt it benefited his songs and his records. He'd adopted a distinctive version of the new country soul. And he'd helped seed the new country rock. What next?

"My father came from the [Muskogee] area, worked hard on his farm, was proud of it, and got called white trash once he took to the road as an Okie," Haggard recalled to Nat Hentoff when his Muskogee Moment was ten years in the rearview. "And there were a lot of other Okies from around there, proud people whose farms and homes were foreclosed by eastern bankers. And then got treated like dirt.

"Listen to that line: 'I'm proud to be an Okie from Muskogee.'

"Nobody had ever *said* that before in a song."

CHAPTER 14

"WORKIN' MAN BLUES," 1969

Haggard wrote "Workin' Man Blues" because, after Johnny Cash charted anew with "Folsom Prison Blues," he'd begun to dream of an identity-solidifying, common-man anthem of his own. "I needed my own 'Folsom Prison Blues,' " he told Deke Dickerson. "I needed a song that would express my way of life."

That Johnny Cash connection explains why studio Stranger James Burton kicks off "Workin' Man" with a lick in the same, extra fat, echoey tone he'd used a year before to launch Merle's own version of "Folsom Prison," a production choice that was itself a louder, more muscular version of Luther Perkins's echoing opening lick to Cash's 1956 original. But it isn't Burton's "Workin' Man" heralding lick, as insistently melodic as it is, that matters as much as the rhythm part that drives the record to its conclusion.

There are antecedents for what Haggard and Burton do here, starting with old rock and roll generally. "Chuck Berry and Carl Perkins were the kings of the kind of rock and roll I liked," Merle once explained to Peter Cooper. "Songs that I later wrote, like 'Workin' Man Blues,' were patterned after listening to 'Blue Suede Shoes.' " More specifically, think of the skittering, indomitable rhythm guitar that Scotty Moore used to power Elvis's Sun Records–era sides like "Mystery Train" and "Milk Cow Blues" and think, especially, of Ricky Nelson's own "Milk Cow Blues," with guitar provided by James Burton. On "Workin' Man Blues," Burton solders these ideas to his own lacerating lines, and, together with session bassist Chuck Berghofer, he propels the Hag headlong to his future. Burton and the Strangers had ridden a kindred rocking guitar groove on 1968's "I'm Bringing Home Good News," but "Workin' Man" sets the standard.

And not just for Merle. For all practical purposes, Burton loaded up the sound he helped create for "Workin' Man Blues" and drove it straight over to Elvis Presley. "Workin' Man Blues" was cut at Capitol on May 19, 1969. At Merle's next trip to the studio, on July 16 and 17, Burton played sessions for "Okie from Muskogee," along with pianist Glen D. Hardin and, on the second day, drummer Ronnie Tutt. Then, on July 18, Burton, Hardin, and Tutt began rehearsals for Elvis's return to the stage, across town at RCA's Hollywood Boulevard studio. Soon enough, the rhythm that propelled Merle's "Workin' Man Blues" would be recognized the world over as Elvis Presley's fanfare.

At the end of each verse, Haggard stops singing for a moment. The band pauses, too, as if they've all stepped outside for a smoke break, but Burton keeps playing, insisting everyone get back to work. "Here comes that working man," Merle says to introduce a solo, probably from Roy Nichols, that's heedless yet somehow controlled—a Fender Telecaster screaming the blues, then shaking them off to dance instead.

We hear a hammer dinging repetitively against an anvil throughout, homage to Wynn Stewart's "Another Day, Another Dollar." Merle hears a train, and it has him longing to take off. Is it the Mystery Train? Is it the train that mocks Cash's Folsom Prison con? Doesn't matter. Merle's got work to do, nine kids and a wife to feed and clothe, and rainbow dreams notwithstanding, he isn't going anywhere. On Friday, he'll cash his check, drink a few beers with buddies before heading home, and come Monday, he'll be at work.

That's where you'll be too, if you're lucky. "Workin' Man Blues" admits a cruel capitalist truth: you have to sell your labor to live. Not to thrive or to chase your dreams, not because of "freedom," but simply in order to exist. In America wage slavery is an individual mandate. It's why the song is called "Workin' Man *Blues*."

"I ain't never been on welfare," he infamously boasts in the final verse.

"And that's one place I won't be." Then he explains why: "I'll be workin'."
His voice flattens at the thought, his spirit crushed by the necessity of it.
He sounds shaky and old. "I'll be workin' as long as my two hands are fit
to use." He sips his beer, accepts the years of work ahead, and prays his
hands stay fit as long as he's going to need them.

CHAPTER 15

HE LIKES LIVING RIGHT AND BEING FREE

In the fall of 1969, as "Okie from Muskogee" rocketed up the country charts on its way to becoming a minor crossover hit, and as the song he envisioned as his common-man signature, "Workin' Man Blues," fell from the charts entirely, Merle Haggard appeared on the short-lived ABC series *Music Scene*. Hosted by a cast of presumably counterculture-cool comedians (including David Steinberg and Lily Tomlin) and focused around performances of each week's higher-charting records on *Billboard*'s various singles charts, *Music Scene* survives on DVD as a snapshot of American pop culture at that moment when the sixties gave way to the seventies. The show's comedy intros—Nixon jabs, "bad needle" jokes—have dated badly, but the music remains amazing.

Music Scene's October 20, 1969, episode kicks off with musical guest Sly & the Family Stone, who tear through a take-no-prisoners live performance that skips the group's smash of the moment, "Hot Fun in the Summertime," in favor of a pair of hits from the year before. Sly himself is a sight to behold, resplendent in a puffy-sleeved goldenrod blouse kind of thing that cinches in front, exposing his stomach. The Family Stone race through an abbreviated "Everyday People," their Love Crowd embrace of we're-all-in-this-togetherness: "Different strokes for different folks... We got to live together!" The group then veers quickly into "Dance to the Music," an even more irresistible call, though one that builds to a less inviting exhortation from trumpeter Cynthia Robinson: "All the squares go home!" As Sly keyboards the song to a close, the dancing-to-the-music studio audience nearly crowds the band off the stage. No squares here.

Music Scene's guest host that week was Tom Smothers, one half of the folk-revival comedy duo the Smothers Brothers. The Smothers' establishment-tweaking series, *The Smothers Brothers Comedy Hour*, had been canceled only that April: for tardy script submission, CBS said; for pissing on the president, and middle-American values generally, everyone understood. Adding insult to injury, the *Comedy Hour* was replaced by that antithesis of counterculture cool, *Hee Haw*, a frozen-in-amber bit of C&W vaudeville that was almost instantly more popular than the Smothers' show had been. Now, on *Music Scene*, Tom Smothers has to introduce Merle Haggard, *Hee Haw*'s second-episode guest star back in June and a performer on the show three more times by Labor Day. Normally Tom played a naïve dummy to the comic exasperation of his brother, Dick, but not tonight. Tonight Tom's playing himself, a persona oozing bitterness. Understandably so, given recent developments, but harder to cotton is Smothers's condescension, a sneer he aims not only at the man he's introducing but at any of the everyday people viewing at home who might be inclined to endorse, or just enjoy, what's to follow.

"Throughout the time the show's been on the air, it has had some really groovy aware guests on the show," Smothers begins. He's sitting on the studio floor, surrounded by an integrated group of with-it-looking youth. No beads or Roman sandals can be seen, but there are smock-tops and long hair. "You know, the Beatles and John Lennon singing 'Give Peace a Chance,'" Smothers continues. "And very hip people…

"Uh, now, under the Equal Time Provision set up by the, uh, Bureaucratic, uh, Establishment"—Smothers is mumbling—"uh, Orientation of America, we've got to make adjustments and give equal time to the other side. So, here's Merle Haggard with a song that jumped from #30 to #7 on the Hot Country, uh, Singles Chart of *Billboard*." Smothers feigns a cough and, after covering his mouth in mock politeness, mimes taking a hit off a joint. Finally, still holding make-believe smoke in his lungs, Smothers chokes, "Ladies and Gentlemen. Merle Haggard. 'Okie from Muskogee.'" Smothers fake releases fake smoke and grins.

I expected the camera to pan right or left now, revealing Merle Haggard and the Strangers set up to play live in the studio just as Sly and the Family Stone had a moment before. The screen instead goes black, save a circle of spotlight that bounces in and out of center as the camera begins a slow zoom. Probably a pre- or post-taped segment, I realize. Which means, too, that Haggard likely wasn't there to hear Smothers introduce him as the government-mandated "other side." He doesn't know, as viewers at home do, that his performance has been presented as a joke and that he's the punch line.

The camera moves closer. Following Sly Stone would be a nearly impossible task under the best circumstances, but Merle has been triply handicapped in the attempt, sitting down (on a white-railed porch), without his Strangers, and with a bloodhound sitting inexplicably at his side. Merle croons gently, almost sweetly, and he punctuates his song's details—"We don't smoke marijuana...We still wave Old Glory...holdin' hands and pitchin' woo"—with frequent bemused grins, as if to say, "I know, I know. Hard to believe, huh? But we really are this square." The song, this night, feels like an embracing of, accompanied by a chuckle at, the out-of-fashion ways of small-town America. When Merle declares in the title line how proud he is of all this, he mugs broadly, even rolls his eyes just a bit, like he knows all of it—the pride, the song, the Hag—must be just about the corniest thing you ever heard. Old Glory? White lightnin'? *Woo?* After Sly's miniriot, Merle Haggard comes off less like a representative of another side and more like an ambassador from another planet. The name of this alien world is "Muskogee, Oklahoma, U.S.A."

"A place where *even squares* can have a ball."

Then, lights come up, and what's revealed isn't alien at all, but distressingly familiar. Merle's white-railed porch is surrounded by American flags—as the camera retreats, there are more and more of them until it's as if Merle has been singing from the middle of a military cemetery. And just like that, a song in part protesting antiwar protesters has been commandeered by the show's set designer *into* an antiwar protest.

In 2008's *Nixonland*, historian Rick Perlstein identifies the immediate origins of America's past half century of polarized politics in Richard Nixon's rise to the White House and particularly in his Republican Party's enlisting of the so-called Silent Majority in a to-the-death culture war. "What one side" in this fight "saw as liberation, the other saw as apocalypse. And what the other saw as apocalypse, the first saw as liberation." "Nixonland" is Perlstein's term for "what happens when these two groups try to occupy a country together." Here's another way to think of it: as the sixties gave way to the seventies, Nixonland was where Merle Haggard singing "Okie from Muskogee" was either heavenly music to your ears or your idea of hell.

Of course, it was far more complicated than that. There were a hundred, a thousand, different sides, so many sides it was never easy to predict where real people would align themselves from one situation to the next. There were those who supported the Vietnam War and those who didn't. Increasingly, there were mainstream Americans who hated the war but were repulsed by the war-protesting counterculture. It was hard hats versus hippies, *The Smothers Brothers Comedy Hour* versus *Hee Haw*, rednecks and blue-collar ethnics enraged by Panthers, Black and white. It was Black versus white. Teenage peaceniks faced off against teenage National Guardsmen. Archie Bunker argued with Meathead. Law-and-order types despised draft dodgers. *Ms.* challenged *Ladies Home Journal*. Liberal Democrats were challenged by the New Left while moderate Republicans fought conservative Republicans—and they all fought George Wallace, except when they didn't. It was straights and suits versus longhairs and druggies, Frazier versus Ali, and it was Getting Involved and Getting Ahead versus Dropping Out and Dropping Acid. The Way We've Always Done It was pitted against It's Time We Do It Better, and both of those positions squared off against Burn the Whole Thing Down, starting with the flags. It was "all the squares go home" versus "a place where even squares can have a ball." And so on versus so on. As much as anything, it was a fight between wildly differing conceptions of what it meant, as Haggard put it, to live right and be free.

"Okie from Muskogee" mentions little of this directly but suggests it all. It became an instant rallying cry *and* instant bête noire. It also turned "Merle Haggard" into a household name, though in some homes *it wasn't all that friendly when they said it*.

The "Okie from Muskogee" origin story changes slightly from telling to telling, but it always begins in spring 1969, with Merle and the Strangers driving through eastern Oklahoma on their tour bus. Or maybe they were still on the Arkansas side of the state line headed west, but in any event one of the Strangers spots a road sign that informs them Muskogee, thataway, thirty miles (or maybe it was a hundred), and then somebody, maybe it was drummer Roy "Eddie" Burris but it might've been somebody else, maybe even Merle, makes a joke: "I bet they don't smoke marijuana in Muskogee."

Everyone aboard agrees that's pretty damn funny. Funny, presumably, because at that very moment a joint was being passed among them, but perhaps it was just that a busload of California musicians, blue-collar and small-town bred but now worldly and big-time, could laugh with relief at how far they'd come and in sympathy with where they'd come from: as in, "There but for the grace of God…" Everyone starts brainstorming what else they probably don't do in Muskogee—drop acid, throw orgies, grow long hair, protest. In some versions Merle writes the song right then, doesn't take him but about twenty minutes. At one point (this according to Deke Dickerson's Bear Family liner notes), Merle can't remember what it is you call those dang fool things hippies wear on their feet, and when Burris chimes in with "Roman sandals," Merle thanks his drummer by awarding him 25 percent of the publishing.

Other versions of the "Okie" story don't have Merle finishing the song until later. In 1970 he told Michael Ochs that he heard Garner Ted Armstrong, the evangelical host of radio's *The World Tomorrow*, claim that small-town southern colleges hadn't experienced unrest like the Berkeleys and Madisons of the world. That's when Merle added the bits about football being "the roughest thing on campus" (as opposed, say, to blowing up the science building) and kids still respecting the college dean (as opposed to occupying his offices). When he played the finished product for Fuzzy Owen and asked what he thought, the manager said, "I *think* it needs to be *out*."

Sometime early that summer, the stories go, Merle, Bonnie, and the boys are playing an NCO club at Fort Bragg, North Carolina, but nothing's connecting. The officers just sit there, staring and applauding politely, so Haggard figures, what the hell, let's try that new one. And then…"The whole place went berserk"; the officers are on their feet, cheering and whooping, like to tear the place down. The NCOs storm the stage to shake Merle's hand, slap him on the back, hug his neck. Play it again, they tell him. You just got to play that song again; we're not going to let you leave if you don't. Haggard and the band have never in their lives experienced anything like this. They play "Okie" again, perhaps four times, the military men repeating favorite lines and shouting with the chorus. Afterward, on the bus to the next gig, a time when people are normally wiped and just want to get some shut-eye ahead of tomorrow's show, no one sleeps, everyone's laughing and talking at once: What the hell just *happened*?

"The next night at a regular stage show, we got the same reaction," Merle told Ochs. "'Okie' certainly started something for me, and it hasn't seemed to quit yet."

The Haggard camp knew they were on to something. Everywhere they went, every show, "Okie" did more than prompt enthusiastic applause. There was an unanticipated adulation racing through the crowds now, standing ovations that went on and on and sometimes left audience and band members alike teary-eyed. Merle had somehow stumbled on a song that expressed previously inchoate fears, spoke out loud gripes and anxieties otherwise only whispered, and now people were using his song, they were using *him*, to connect themselves to these larger concerns and to one another. It was absolutely thrilling, the kind of validation he'd craved all along. But it was scary, too.

They recorded the song at Capitol, mid-July. Merle took the recording to Nashville the next month for mastering, though not before overdubbing a nylon-string guitar track there that he dictated to Jerry Reed: "Listen real close, to the studio version," Merle noted to Deke Dickerson, "and it doesn't have much gusto...as much gusto as [it would've had with] Roy Nichols or James Burton." Then "Okie from Muskogee" was released as a single on August 15. Merle and Fuzzy were so sure it was going to be a monster that they actually arranged to record what became the *Okie from Muskogee* concert album, the one where Muskogee's mayor declares Merle an official Okie, on October 10, one day *before* the single even made the national country charts. A month later the studio version of "Okie" was #1. A month passed, and it was still #1.

Later, a far more aggressive, even hostile, version of "Okie," cut live and cocksure, with a key change for extra oomph and the audience clapping time and rebel-yelling its approval, got a fair amount of airplay. On that one, cut at a concert in Philadelphia for 1970's live *Fightin' Side of Me*, Merle punctuated the next-to-final "We still wave Old Glory down at the courthouse" with an angry "*By Golly!*"

The studio version that became the hit, though, is an altogether different affair, quiet and acoustic and with a harmony group ooh-ooh-ing us through chord changes. James Burton tickles the single to life on acoustic, Ronnie Tutt brushes time and provides nary a fill. It does lack a bit of gusto. *Billboard*'s tin-eared description aside—a "bouncy rhythm item"—nobody was going to be cutting a rug to this "Okie." For his part, Merle sings quietly, prettily really, while Roy Nichols and pianist Glen Hardin pick and plunk their way through an arrangement that calls to mind summer breezes and trickling brooks. The arrangement hints at the song's implicit antagonism between big city and small town, but only subtly. If anything, the "Okie from Muskogee" single sounds like a folk-revival leftover. Heard today, it's hard to believe such a gentle, delicate record could've pissed off anybody, but it did. No way does it sound like it could empower anyone. But it did.

Haggard claimed then, as later, that "Okie" was a joke, or that it began as one anyway. His lyrical choices back him up. The song's first line—"We don't smoke marijuana in Muskogee"—doesn't reflect Merle's personal taste in intoxicants; he told one reporter in the early seventies that Muskogee was about the *only* place he didn't smoke pot. More to the point, the antiquated "pitching woo" is cornball, even for country music; the decidedly un-Haggard-ish phrase "manly footwear" just has to be deliberately farcical; and since when did Merle, a longtime disdainer of bourgeois authority figures, give a shit about college deans or courthouses?

All of this, combined with Merle's pretty but uncharacteristically flat reading of the lyric—not a whiff of anger—suggests that he was joking, at least to some degree, when he wrote the song. It's worth noting, though, that if "Okie" is a Generation Gap–inspired novelty, it's one that pokes fun not at the longhairs but at the fuddy-duddy citizens of Muskogee. "We like living right and being free," after all, is a parody of patriotic provincialism and starchy middle-class values if ever there was one. In small towns like Muskogee, the song tells us, *being free* is equated with a version of conformity called *living right*. Anyone who disobeys the rules of right-living, or who dares challenge the authority of those who declare and enforce the rules, is not exercising "freedom" but threatening it. Haggard, who spent so much of his life fleeing and defying just such "civilizing" attitudes, would've appreciated the irony, could've conceived the line as a joke: if you're coerced to live by your neighbor's definition of "free," then "free" is the one thing you ain't. What the hippies do in the song, meanwhile, is just what hippies do. Hippie behavior is so obviously *wrong*, so plainly *not* living right by Muskogee's standards, that jokes at its expense are neither needed in the song nor attempted.

Which is why Merle's audience didn't take "Okie" as a joke, let alone a joke on themselves. Haggard released the song into an America that seemed, depending upon one's point of view, on the verge of a new age or about to explode. On October 10 and 11, the very moment "Okie from Musk-ogee" was debuting on the country charts and the same weekend *Live in Muskogee* was recorded, the Weathermen waged Days of Rage in Chicago. The following week saw the Moratorium to End the War in Vietnam, two million mostly young Americans holding protests around the nation to stop the fighting. The week after that found Merle presenting the Other Side on *Music Scene*. "Okie" crossed over pop the same week to #91 on the Hot 100, only a few spots behind "Tonight I'll Be Staying Here with You" and just ahead of "Ballad of Easy Rider," from Haggard fans Bob Dylan and the Byrds, respectively. (Creedence Clearwater Revival's not unrelated "Fortunate Son" debuted at #58 the same week.)

It was unlikely many of Merle's rock fans were fans of *this* single, though, and Merle knew it. In May 1970, in possibly his first nationally published interview in the wake of "Okie from Muskogee," *Rolling Stone*'s John Grissim asked Merle if he had given any consideration to how the song might impact his image. Merle replied that, yes, he'd given it quite a bit of thought. "I'm thinking possibly there'll be a bad taste left with a certain class of people," he explained. "I'm thinking possibly here of hippies—not hip type people—but these barefooted bums walking around. That's my definition in the song."

That alone would have left an unpleasant taste in the mouths of many *Rolling Stone* readers, but Merle couldn't leave it alone. "I didn't put out the record to reprimand or anything," he said, then went on to do just that:

> What I don't understand is where did they all come from? We didn't have 'em ten years ago. I don't know what they done back then....I don't like their views on life, their filth, their visible self-disrespect, y'know. They don't give a shit what they look like or what they smell like....What do they have to offer humanity?

Of course, what Merle had been doing ten years ago was time.

Merle warmed to the topic again the following month, for trade publication *Coast FM & Fine Arts*:

> Some of the hippies have good minds, but I don't believe in filth and some of the other things they seem to represent sometimes. I'm not against long hair; I might decide to wear my hair long next week. I have nothing against long hair as long as there's nothing growing in it.

And this from a 1973 profile in *Penthouse*:

> It's like the words of the song. We don't let our hair grow long and shaggy. *Shaggy.* That's the thing. Shaggy means dirty. Right? Ain't that whut it means?

None of which sounds very jokey.

This isn't to suggest the song didn't begin as a joke, or that Haggard didn't intend it seriously, or that the truth is one or the other. What *did* "Okie" mean? People used it all sorts of ways; as Merle observed a few years later, "There are about 18 different meanings in that song." So was "Okie from Muskogee" a joke, as he explained from the beginning? Or was it, as he also claimed, an endorsement of small-town values in response to countercultural threats? If it was a joke, was it mocking the freaks or tweaking the yokels? Was that damn song meant to be sung with your tongue in your cheek or with your hand over your heart?

Yes.

Not all of the conflicts of the Muskogee Moment were as trivial as hippie hygiene or as seemingly quaint as the Generation Gap. Indeed, as the sixties slouched toward its denouement in the first half of the seventies, and with the civil rights movement having long since split into integrationist and Black-nationalist camps, middle- and upper-class America was discovering class, specifically its *white* working class. This was a rediscovery, of a sort, a late twentieth-century reminder that the common folk depicted in the works of John Steinbeck, Woody Guthrie, and Dorothea Lange were still with us, still struggling.

But what a difference thirty years made. *All in the Family* made its television debut in January 1971, offering up Archie Bunker as a kinder, goofier version of the working-class slob presented in the homicidal *Joe*, a film out the previous summer. John Updike's *Rabbit Redux*—about a printing plant employee who doesn't understand the crazy world he's living in and who echoes the guy in Merle's "Fightin' Side of Me" when he avows, "I love my country and can't stand to have it knocked"—was a 1972 finalist for the National Book Award. A rash of news stories began to appear, as well, fretting over the Troubled Americans (a *Newsweek* "Special Report on the White Majority"), over the Middle Americans (*Time*'s "Man and Woman of the Year" for 1969) and the Forgotten Americans (per *Harper's*)—or, putting a not-fine-in-the-least point on it, over "these forgotten whites" (as Nixon advisor and Republican strategist Kevin Phillips wrote in the *Washington Post*). That is, fretting over ethnic or rural white, blue-collar workers as alienated as ever but pissed off like never before. In April, Peter Hamill published "The Revolt of the White Lower Middle Class," a prescient and widely discussed *New York* magazine piece that warned something must be done about "the growing alienation and paranoia of these people." If not, "the next round of race riots might not be between people and property, but between people and people."

A representative sample:

> "I'm going out of my mind," an ironworker friend…told me. "I work my ass off. But I can't make it. I come home at the end of the week, I start paying bills, I give my wife some money for food. And there's nothin' left. They take $65 a week out of my pay. I have to come up with $90 a month rent. But every time I turn around, one of the kids needs shoes or a dress or something for school. And then I pick up the paper and read about a million people on welfare in New York or some spades rioting in some college or some fat welfare bitch demanding—you know, not askin', *demanding*—a credit card at Korvette's [department store]….I *work* for a livin' and *I* can't get a credit card at Korvette's….You see that and you want to go out and strangle someone."

Ladies and Gentlemen…The Other Side.

That same month, Merle's latest single seemed to diagnose Hamill's ironworker as suffering from what it called "Workin' Man Blues." Richard Nixon called it a political opportunity. When he read "The Revolt of the White Lower Middle Class," the president saw his chance to win over those members of the white working class who *liked living right and being free*, but who were seeing their wages stagnate or decline; who were sick to death of Moratoriums and Days of Rage, disgusted by hippies, and fed up with sneering high-class liberal elites (*Another class of people put us somewhere just below*); and who harbored racial resentments that the decade's civil rights advances had only inflamed. That those resentments now had to be expressed in code like *I ain't never been on welfare* was both a sign of progress and a mile-marker for how far there was to go.

As Perlstein notes, a study Nixon ordered in the new year, "The Problem of the Blue Collar Worker," confirmed that the white working stiffs Nixon particularly wanted to woo felt taken advantage of, abused, neglected. Blacks had civil rights, the hippies had their marches, but who spoke for *them*? Who even remembered them? Nixon determined that he would. Or, closer to true, he would make sure they *felt* remembered.

On November 3, two days after "Okie" cracked the pop Hot 100, Nixon delivered his famous Pat Buchanan–penned "Silent Majority" speech: "So, tonight, to you, the great silent majority of my fellow Americans, I ask for your support," he read, effectively stoking grievances already smoldering within so many current Merle Haggard fans and within countless new ones the singer was, if only temporarily, about to acquire.

"*They* were loud. *You* were quiet" is Perlstein's translation of the emotional hook to Nixon's Silent Majority pitch:

> *They* proclaimed their virtue. *You*, simply, lived virtuously. Thus Nixon made political capital of a certain experience of humiliation; the humiliation of having to defend values that seemed to you self-evident, then finding you had no words to defend them, precisely because they seemed so self-evident. Nixon gave you the words.

Now, thanks to "Okie from Muskogee," so had Merle Haggard, whether he'd meant to or not.

The song had been inspired by a joke, but Merle adapted quickly when he saw how earnestly the presumed butts of that joke received it. Through the years he would intermittently talk about "Okie" both ways—it's actually kind of a humorous song, he'd explain; hell, it's an anthem of pride is what it is—because both ways, deep down, was how he felt about it. He described himself, repeatedly through the decades, as some version or other of "dumb as a rock" back when he wrote it. In 2001 he told journalist Keith Phipps, "Oh, I must have been an idiot. It's documentation of the uneducated that lived in the America at the time, and I mirror that. I always have."

Sometimes he would even admit to wishing he hadn't written it at all. But, as he told Brock Ruggles:

> Willie Nelson said, "Hey, if you don't want the son of a bitch, I'll trade you 'Crazy' for it!" If I was to do it over again, it would take a lot more thought. I thought it was funny. The song was humorous. It was like the epitome of ignorance on certain subjects. But I'll be damned if people like Wallace and Nixon didn't take it for the truth.

That interview was in 2002. Yet the very next year, speaking to the Country Music Television documentary series *Controversy*, he did not sound at all like a songwriter discussing a lyric he'd thought was humorous:

> To have the audacity to go downtown and fix yourself up different just to protest a war that you probably don't know anything about! And I felt like I knew more about being away from freedom than they did. I'd been in jail. And it really irritated me to see these spoiled brats, you know, rich kids, down there doing everything they could to irritate their parents and irritate society.

He alternately embraced the song and shoved it away like that for the rest of his life. "Sometimes, out of a little bit of rebellious meanness, you know, I say I'm not going to do it," he told Bryan DiSalvatore in 1990, describing the tension. "But very seldom. Your own songs become like living creatures. They are like children. They are individuals. You forgive them. God dang, you fall back in love with 'em, you know?"

For its part, Capitol Records always leaned hard into the more earnest side of that equation. In liner notes to *Okie from Muskogee: Recorded Live in Muskogee, Oklahoma*, released during the last week of 1969, writer K. Vincent took no truck with irony and assumed Haggard's fans didn't either:

> It took Merle about half a man's lifetime to get around to Muskogee and discover his father's people...the people who are proud to be pinned with the name "Okies." Those people came in great crowds to see Merle.

Many had to stand for the entire time. They came because they knew he had written a song about their town and about how they lived. They came to hear about themselves from a man who had come from themselves.

Billboard predicted the new album would have an appeal far beyond Okies, self-proclaimed or otherwise: "Package should garner big sales not only in country, but also in the pop field."

CHAPTER 16

"IRMA JACKSON," 1969

Merle headed into Capitol Studios in early November to record a follow-up single as "Okie from Muskogee" was still a week away from topping *Billboard*'s Country Singles chart. This was "Irma Jackson." "Of all the songs I've written, this may be my favorite," Merle would say a few years later, "because it tells it like it is." Quite a statement, considering the competition, but listen to "Irma Jackson" and you understand the appeal. The song has a universal theme—individual freedom, sought and crushed, represented by our nation's great manifestation of that theme, white supremacy and the legacy of Jim Crow—all in a compact narrative that speaks to its moment. Only two years after the Supreme Court had declared laws prohibiting interracial marriage to be unconstitutional, "Irma Jackson" shows us something all but unheard of in country music, and rare even in pop: a Black woman and a white man in love.

Merle got the idea for the song after seeing an in-flight presentation of *Guess Who's Coming to Dinner*, though it's telling that the love story Merle invents lacks the happy ending of Stanley Kramer's 1967 movie. "Irma Jackson," he told Michael Ochs in 1970, was about "a plantation-owner's son falling for one of the colored help":

They played together, went to school together, nobody paid any attention to it until they became somewhat of age. They actually fell into a true, deep love....They were intelligent people and realized that their families were different, and...they decided to sever, more out of respect for their families than society....I thought it was a beautiful story.

This may be the backstory Merle imagined, but "Irma Jackson" makes no mention of a "plantation" or "colored help" or disapproving parents. And he thought the story was beautiful, I take it, not because it's inspirational or romantic, but because, as he explained later, its tragic scenario tells it like it is. "If my loving Irma Jackson is a sin," Merle nearly wails on the record, "then I don't understand this crazy world we're living in." Faced with "this crazy world we're living in"—Merle tries to spit the line from his mouth, fails, swallows the "in"—his narrator can only conclude that "there's a mighty wall between us standing high," a wall that cannot be scaled, just as the world, crazy or not, can't be defeated or even engaged in battle. "I'd love to shout my feelings from a mountain high, and tell her that I love her and will until I die," Merle sings. He breathes that "her" like a gentle kiss, that "die" like a longer one, so you believe that he has love to shout about. But he croons quietly nonetheless, certain as he is of the world's reply and resigned to it. "A mighty wall between us, standing high," he repeats, dipping from his well of the-world-is-a-prison imagery. "And that's why Irma Jackson can't be mine."

It's also why "Irma Jackson" isn't quite the liberal counterweight to "Okie" and other conservative Haggard songs it's regularly made out to be. The song does depict an interracial couple in love, no small thing, even today, and even suggests that white Americans, too, are imprisoned by racism—their own. Racism thwarts white desire, too, and breaks white hearts. In the song, Merle wants to be set free, and if the world says it's a sin for a white man to love a Black woman, Merle's song replies, all right then, he'll go to hell.

But the song also strongly implies that such relationships are bound to fail, their lovers born to lose. So when Irma decides to go away, Merle vows he'll love her forever but lets her go. "I guess it's right that she alone should have the final say," he concludes, granting her agency in the situation but also not putting up much of a fight. Perhaps Ms. Jackson has determined to leave because, love aside, she understands the world better than Merle does, knows this white man better than he thinks he knows himself. Push has come to shove, and Merle hasn't even asked Irma if he could go with her.

Merle wanted "Irma" to be his next single, but it didn't happen. The reason repeated through the years is that Capitol wouldn't put it out, but that's never struck me as entirely plausible.

Merle had already proven he had the power to make the music he wanted in the style he wanted. Earlier that year Capitol had released *Same Train, a Different Time*, the double tribute album to a forty-years-dead singer most people had barely heard of and that had Merle delivering little lectures between the tracks. After "Okie" Merle wielded even greater creative control—and used it. Witness 1971's *Land of Many Churches*, surely one of the least commercial projects ever realized by a mainstream country act: another double album of what amounts to glorified field recordings cut in four different churches and including minister introductions and sermons. And don't forget that between *Same Train* and *Many Churches* came Merle's Bob Wills album, another tribute to an out-of-favor artist and style that didn't exactly drip with commercial potential. And yet Capitol refused its number one cash-cow country star...a seven-inch single?

What seems likely isn't that Merle was denied but that he was persuaded by Nelson and Capitol that "Irma" was a bad idea. Merle, understandably anxious about the song's subject matter and just then learning of the press's tendency to demand further comment on politically minded radio hits, probably didn't need his arm twisted. As Earl C. Gottschalk wrote at the time in the *Wall Street Journal*:

> Mr. Haggard wanted to release the song, but Capitol marketing executives held a long, agonizing meeting and decided it would be dangerous to the Haggard image to do so. "People are narrow-minded," says the singer, who went along with the decision. "Down South, they might have called me a n[*****] lover."

Indeed, they might have, and not only down South. The backlash among some portion of Merle's audience would likely have been brutal. All the more reason, one might imagine, for this instinctively contrarian artist to dig in his heels and reaffirm his commitment to Ms. Jackson. Instead: *They might have called me a...* This explanation, notice, finds Haggard, who could well be rehearsing arguments he'd heard from Ken Nelson and others, neither endorsing the racism behind that slur nor condemning it. It does show him attempting to distance himself from such a charge, though, while also accepting it as a fact of life he could do nothing about. That, it seems, is why "Irma Jackson" couldn't be his next single. It was a real-life outcome that mirrored the doomed relationship in the song itself.

What if Merle *had* followed "Okie from Muskogee" with "Irma Jackson"?

According to music journalist Daniel Cooper, Merle called Johnny Cash and played the song for his friend over the phone. "It's a smash!" Cash told him. I suspect Johnny was right. Haggard surely would have lost some fans, at least for the moment, but he would have gained many more. "Irma" would've been a hit, a big one, if it had been released right then: the TV appearances; the covers of his songs by a wide variety of acts; the news coverage; the movie tie-ins; and all of it compounded by the crossover controversy surrounding "Okie from Muskogee." At the dawn of the seventies, Merle Haggard was poised to become a major star of the pop-but-still-country sort Cash himself was then perfecting.

"Irma" would have sounded great on top 40 radio, too. Its pulsing rhythm and swollen-hearted electric-meets-acoustic arrangement, its high-and-haunting female harmony shouting "Amen!" to Merle's confusion and punctuating one of the more infectious melodies this melody-master ever wrote—"Irma" would've fit comfortably between early 1970 singles like CCR's "Who'll Stop the Rain," say, and Brook Benton's "Rainy Night in Georgia." And "Irma" wasn't just topical. Like "Okie," it was ambiguous enough to allow listeners to hear what they wanted: *See, prejudice is terrible*, or *See, I knew those relationships couldn't work*. In Cash's words, "Irma" could've been a smash.

"Ken Nelson never interfered with my music," Merle told me when I asked him about "Irma Jackson" in 2001. "But this *one time* he came out and said, 'Merle...I don't believe the world is ready for this yet.'...And he may have been right. I might've canceled out where I was headed in my career." I suspect this is right, too, though maybe not the way Merle meant it. In 1970 it would have taken a song declaring his love for Jane Fonda to have significantly diminished Haggard's country appeal. Country stardom was where he already was. Where Merle was headed in his career was *pop* stardom.

The single that replaced "Irma" put an end to that.

CHAPTER 17

HIS FIGHTIN' SIDE

"The Fightin' Side of Me," the last-minute replacement for "Irma Jackson," let Merle once again woo a white, square, blue-collar, and small-town-identifying demographic. It was cut a couple of days before Christmas 1969, with a lineup of mostly L.A. session pros serving as studio Strangers, and was released at the beginning of February as "Muskogee" slipped from the charts. By the middle of March it had hit #1, just like Merle's three previous singles—"Hungry Eyes," "Workin' Man Blues," and "Okie from Muskogee"—and eight of his last ten, all in just three years.

"Okie from Muskogee" and "The Fightin' Side of Me" have rightly been lumped together ever since. If "Okie" had been chased by "Irma Jackson" instead, as Haggard had planned, attitudes toward the former would have grown instantly more tolerant; its satire, however halfhearted, would have been more easily discerned. "I always thought everybody got 'Okie from Muskogee' wrong," Bob Dylan told Jason Fine in 2009. "If Randy Newman would have written and sung it, nobody would have thought twice." After "Fightin' Side" was substituted for "Irma," though, it became harder to hear "Okie" with any generosity at all. "Okie" and "Fightin' Side" together became anti-counterculture teammates.

The overwhelming success of the former, after all, and not only at the cash register, made some sort of sequel more or less inevitable. Merle admitted as much that Valentine's Day 1970 during a concert at Philadelphia's Civic Center, a performance that became Haggard's next album, *The Fightin' Side of Me*, itself an attempt to capitalize on the previous year's live, and platinum-selling, *Okie from Muskogee*. In Philly that evening, as applause for "Okie" died away, Merle introduced "a brand-new record" (it had charted only the week before) "that's, uh, much on the same thought. We hope that you like it as much as you did 'Muskogee.'"

"The Fightin' Side of Me" was along the same lines. But it was also a different sort of song—and a damn near unprecedented one, at least as far as country music went. The most obvious difference was in tone. Where "Okie" had condescended to any and all listeners, and had done so with enough aw-shucks humor and good old-fashioned irony to leave it at least slightly open to question just who was being condescended to, "The Fightin' Side of Me" addressed one audience by unambiguously laying into another. "Okie" had been playful and at least partially in jest, where "Fightin' Side" sounded mad as hell. The difference was between "I'm proud" and "Let this song be a warning."

"Fightin' Side" took the grievances "Okie" had revealed and doubled down on them. We'd say today that it throws red meat to the base; it's an attack ad with melody. There are real Americans who love this land just the way it is, Merle's song insists. And then there are those side-switching, blame-America-first types:

> People talkin' bad about the way we have to live here in this country,
> Harpin' on the wars we fight, gripin' 'bout the way things oughta be.

The way we *have* to live. Yet the hippies "preach about some other way of living."

"When you're runnin' down my country, hoss," Merle growled, "you're walkin' on the fightin' side of me."

This was less than two months after the infamous Altamont Free Concert and only three months before Kent State. It was a year after some redneck shotgunned that hippie Captain America at the end of *Easy Rider* and a year before San Francisco's *Dirty Harry* snarled, "Do [you] feel lucky? Well, do ya, punk?" at a Black bank robber. "I read about some squirrelly guy who claims that he just don't believe in fightin'," Merle sneers, disbelieving.

That "claim" is priceless, as subtly sharp in its way as, barely half a year after the Stonewall riots, that "squirrelly guy" is dickish and homophobic.

The end of the sixties and the start of the backlash seventies are now half a century in the rearview, but like any number of Muskogee Moment artifacts, "The Fightin' Side of Me" emotes as familiarly today as if it had been released last month, or tomorrow. If you catch Merle's drift, if you place yourself to one side of the line he draws, you can feel attacked, all these years later, as if Merle's just poked you hard in the chest and dared you to do something about it. On the other hand, if you place yourself on the Other Side, if you feel like you belong on the side of the song, you may hear Merle's carping and suddenly stand up a little straighter, feel a charge that someone's finally saying it like you're feeling it. You might feel like it's *you* poking someone in the chest.

"Fightin' Side" can still stop you in your tracks, in part, because it's so sonically gripping. It's a great record, far more rocking and pop-inclined than "Okie," and nearly as catchy. James Burton launches the studio version with a clarion Fender lick that would sound right at home on a Creedence Clearwater track. Bassist Chuck Berghofer enters next, playing a burbling, counting-to-three Fender bass lick that's reminiscent of the indelible double bass part he'd played a few years earlier on Nancy Sinatra's "These Boots Are Made for Walking." Drummer Sam Goldstein (the year before he'd backed the Flying Burrito Brothers on "Wheels") keeps impatient time. "The Fightin' Side of Me," like "Workin' Man Blues" before it, is dance music for a bar fight in some suburban tavern where the Wurlitzer is as crowded with rock-and-soul records as C&W discs. Its rocking rhythms incite Merle onward and second his threats, while Burton's Fender keeps showily flexing its muscles, but saving its strength, too, should the song's title need making good on after all.

The Philadelphia version's even more charged. Its accelerated pace and the call-and-response electricity of its boisterous arena crowd leave that concluding key change sounding like liftoff. Roy Nichols swaggers the lick on this version, and Dennis Hromek's jeering bass—flipping off the hippies, flicking them in their foreheads, laughing—sounds full-on Dixie fried. *All the squares go home?* Like hell.

Even while still on the charts, "Fightin' Side" left Merle worried it was a mistake and that people misunderstood it. He attempted to clarify things in an interview with Michael Ochs in spring 1970. "I don't believe in communism, and I'm fighting *it*, not the hippies," he stressed, though many of his fans would no doubt have been perplexed by the distinction. What's the difference? "And if any of the protestors ever come up with a solution," Merle continued, "then I might be able to listen to them, but all they do is gripe about the way things are." This may have been more confusing to readers than clarifying. For starters, what did Merle mean by "communism"? Ho Chi Minh? "From each according to their ability, to each according to their needs"? And exactly who on Merle's fighting side was arguing *for* communism anyway? Angela Davis? In a town just south of Bakersfield, only days before "Okie" was released, the young professor had been fired from UCLA, with Gov. Ronald Reagan's encouragement, for being a communist—but "Fightin' Side" mentions neither Davis nor communism. For that matter, Merle's "Hungry Eyes" had itself griped about the way things ought to be without offering any solutions, either. So had "Workin' Man Blues" and "Irma Jackson." *All of them had only wanted things they really needed.* In Ochs's view, with "Okie" Merle "could have become another Dylan, but his follow-up…was far too fascist even for the 'majority.'" Then as now, "Fightin' Side" is reactionary in any number of ugly ways.

It was part of something new, as well, and something that's been commonplace ever since. Not the borrowing from rock and roll. Country music had been doing that for as long as there had been a rock and roll to cop, but Haggard took that appropriation several steps further. "The Fightin' Side of Me" deploys *rock-and-roll* sounds to assert, with great defiance and without contradiction, that it is by-golly *country* to the core. Haggard was onto something else, too. Country musicians had long proclaimed collective identities—southern, rural, down-home and down-and-out, patriotic—but these claims to distinction were hardly threatening and determinedly apolitical. "Okie" and, especially, "Fightin' Side" were another matter. For the first time these Haggard hits presented the country audience to itself as an explicitly political grouping. In "Okie" and "Fightin' Side," and in countless country radio hits since, the country audience is conceived not only as distinct from other groups but as standing in contemptuous opposition to them. Its members are not merely patriotic—they are true Americans, defending their values from derision and assault. This new sense of class consciousness was extremely limited, not to mention limiting, but it was empowering for all that. Haggard expressed it best simply by shouting to the world that such a demographic existed at all and by giving the shout a name.

Pride.

"Fightin' Side" had the music to be an even bigger hit than "Okie" had been, but its words squandered one of the best rhythm tracks of Merle's life. This isn't to say his lyrics were deaf to pop potential. He was articulating grievances well known today, but he was speaking in the commercial language of his day. Since the early 1960s, for instance, Americans had seen a print and television ad campaign for Tareyton cigarettes: a man or woman sporting a shiner and smoking a Tareyton, with the catchphrase "Us Tareyton smokers would rather fight than switch." The slogan became so well known it was recycled by everyone from the Goldwater Girls on the right to, most famously, Thomas "TNT" Todd on the left. (The civil rights activist's fierce interpolation of the cigarette slogan was sampled much later by Public Enemy to introduce their even fiercer "Fight the Power" in 1989: "Yet our best-trained, best-educated, best-equipped, best-prepared troops refuse to fight. Matter of fact, it's safe to say that they would rather switccccccch...than fight!") Merle was playing with the Tareyton slogan when he magnanimously allowed, or at least agreed to tolerate, that the protesters had freedom of thought and expression just as he did: "I don't mind 'em switching sides and standin' up for things that they believe in." But if that free speech was critical of the United States, he cautioned, then they could invariably expect to feel the wrath of his "fightin' side." Either that or they could just shut the hell up. Or move.

In 2003 the harpin'-on-the-wars-we-fight Dixie Chicks would be infamously advised to "shut up and sing"—and Merle came to their defense! But in 1970 Merle offered Vietnam protesters what amounted to the same advice: "If you don't love it, leave it." The precise origins of that expression are unclear, though it was certainly in circulation (Walter Winchell had speed-read something similar during World War II) well before Merle Haggard set it to music. After "Fightin' Side," it entered the zeitgeist.

On May 4, with "Fightin' Side" still a week from sliding off the national country charts, National Guardsmen shot and killed four young people and wounded nine others following a campus protest at Kent State University against the invasion of Cambodia. Responses to the tragedy ran overwhelmingly in favor of the Guard. On May 8 New York City mayor John

Lindsay ordered all city flags lowered to half-mast in memory of the Kent State victims, while downtown that morning maybe a thousand college kids sat applauding speeches calling for peace. Just before noon, according to the *New York Times*, "a large group of construction workers, most of them wearing…orange and yellow hard hats, descended on Wall Street from four directions…marching behind a cluster of American flags." The Hard Hats, as they became known almost on the spot, pulled hammers, pliers, and other tools of their trades from the fronts of their overalls and began to beat, kick, and punch the protesters. As many as eighty were injured, while the Hard Hats, many from the nearly finished World Trade Center nearby, chanted, "All the way, USA" and "Love it or leave it." The following week two thousand Hard Hats stomped angrily about the financial district, shouting slanders and carrying signs, mostly saying a very specific version of hurray for our side: "America: Love It or Leave It."

The Hard Hats' public language lacked logic—"Love it or leave it" is a textbook example of a false dilemma—but it conveyed absolute emotional clarity. Most working stiffs who sat down, after another day, another dollar, to watch developments on the evening news would've never joined even a peaceful protest—who could afford the time off? ("The people who work don't have time to protest," Haggard told Christopher Wren. "Too busy working.") But the Hard Hats stood out because they shoved back: against women yapping on about equal rights; against Blacks and other minorities who wouldn't shut up, either (and after all they'd been given!); against homosexuals who all of a sudden thought they had rights too; against kids who'd been handed everything on a silver platter and couldn't stop complaining about it; against anyone and everyone who wanted something they didn't have coming, who wanted that something for nothing, and who now seemed prepared to get it by helping themselves to what normal people had already earned for themselves fair and square. This was freedom as a zero-sum game.

Nixon, eager to shore up support for his reelection among the white working-class voters who'd voted solidly Democratic for decades, spotted a chance. Before the month was out, representatives of the AFL-CIO and the International Longshoremen's Association had awarded him with an honorary hard hat, "a symbol, along with our great flag, for freedom and patriotism to our beloved country." To help win away similar voters from George Wallace down south and out west, the president also proclaimed

October 1970 "Country Music Month," then did it again the next two Octobers.

In 1972 the Country Music Association returned the favor, officially signing on to the reelection cause and presenting Nixon with a personalized album. *Thank You, Mr. President* was narrated by Haggard's fellow Capitol recording artist Tex Ritter ("Country music, which in reality is the voice of your Silent Majority"), and the set also included Johnny Horton's 1959 all-charts smash "The Battle of New Orleans," Bill Anderson's 1961 hit "Po' Folks" (a paean to the character-building importance of growing up poor, not to be confused with *being* poor, *now*, and maybe being on welfare as a result), and a rousing, slyly funky singalong version of "Okie from Muskogee" pulled from *The Fightin' Side of Me*.

"We still wave Old Glory down at the courthouse. *By golly!*"

During the Muskogee Moment, rock became associated with protest in the popular imagination, a perception that remains entrenched. But it's also true that, save for Country Joe McDonald's "Fixin' to Die Rag," or hits like CCR's "Fortunate Son" or Crosby, Stills, Nash & Young's "Ohio," the rock scene proper produced surprisingly few explicitly political protest songs. Country radio, by contrast, sounded for a while there like a musical version of a Hard Hats rally, grudgingly behind the war but wholeheartedly against the protesters.

Country music has always had something of a sentimental side when it comes to war. In the decades before Haggard showed up, this was almost entirely of the flag-saluting and morale-inspiring type, as in the World War II–era hits "There's a Star-Spangled Banner Waving Somewhere" by Elton Britt and "Stars and Stripes on Iwo Jima" by Bob Wills, with Tommy Duncan singing lead. These were hand-over-heart patriotic. They took consensus for granted but mostly weren't hawkish or belligerent.

More common in country music were songs that confronted war not so much patriotically as personally. Southerners, both pre- and postdiaspora, have long served disproportionately in the military. It makes sense that the people doing so much of the fighting and dying would crave songs reflecting that experience, so a number of now-classic country records—Gene Autry's "At Mail Call Today," for instance, or Floyd Tillman's "Each Night at Nine" or Bakersfield's own "Dear John"—have expressed the homesickness of soldiers overseas. Far and away, though, country music's soundtrack to war has offered condolences to those mourning their dead. The Father of Country Music's very first recording was just such a record, "The Soldier's Sweetheart"; and from Ernest Tubb's World War II–era "The Soldier's Last Letter" to the Dixie Chicks' Iraq War hit "Travelin' Soldier," country music has cried over war's fatal consequences in almost exclusively individual terms. None of the country songs above could be fairly characterized as against their respective wars, but each of them is indisputably against dead American soldiers.

Country music's apolitical posture toward war began to erode in the middle 1960s, as the United States, via troop escalations and the implementation of the bombing campaigns called Operation Rolling Thunder, initiated the so-called Americanization of the Vietnam conflict. Johnny Wright led the way in late 1965 with "Hello Vietnam," a country #1 written by Tom T. Hall that defended the war in language that could have been quoting President Lyndon B. Johnson: "We must stop communism in that land or freedom will start slipping through our hands." The following year songs about the personal costs of war still resonated. In "Dear Uncle Sam," Loretta Lynn pleaded that she needed her man much more than the Pentagon did. But 1966 also saw a new brand of country song on the charts, one that stepped beyond expressing loss or patriotism in favor of unequivocally supporting the war in Vietnam, or at least—it amounts to the same thing—the absolute necessity of supporting the troops. Sgt. Barry Sadler's "The Ballad of the Green Berets," a major country radio hit, framed Vietnam fatalities as almost purely national rather than individual losses. Dave Dudley, a macho baritone who with "Six Days on the Road" and "Truck Drivin' Son-of-a-Gun" had found great success in Nashville with a modified version of the Bakersfield Sound, was a key figure in this transition. His "What We're Fighting For," another Tom T. song and a top-five single, shook its head and fist at simpleminded demonstrators. Dudley's follow-up single, the Kris Kristofferson–penned "Vietnam Blues," did the same, but it was angry and bitter where the former was wearily resigned. As on Stonewall Jackson's "The Minute Men (Are Turning in Their Graves)," these 1966 hits struck an apocalyptic tone. Nothing less than American freedom was at stake in Southeast Asia: dissenters were at best naïve and quite possibly traitorous.

All of this was in the air as Merle Haggard rose to country stardom, and it's this context that helps explain why his "Okie from Muskogee" and "The Fightin' Side of Me" were successful in the country market. But these hits did more than extend preexisting conditions. First of all, Haggard's music had the undeniable hooks, indelible imagery, and country-rock sound to take those concerns nationwide in a way the music of old squares like Dave Dudley and Johnny Wright most definitely didn't. What's more, his songs escalated hostilities over the war to full-scale Culture War. "Okie" and "Fightin' Side" weren't only about Vietnam, not then and certainly not in the years since. They were about hair and fashion, authority and hierarchy and tradition, about warring conceptions of freedom. And they expressed an anti-elitist class loyalty bordering on the clannish.

More immediately, "Muskogee" and its infamous follow-up were catalysts for several dozen like-minded country records, starting most obviously with the couple of dozen big-time country stars who raced to lay down their own versions of "Workin' Man Blues" (Jerry Lee Lewis, Charlie Louvin, etc.), "Okie" (Conway Twitty, Jeannie C. Riley), "Fightin' Side" (George Jones, Jeannie Seely), or, in the case of Johnny Cash's little brother, Tommy, all three. Haggard's language inspired records like Rusty Adams's "Hippie from Mississippi," whose folks are so ashamed of their longhaired boy they've changed their name, and Ernest Tubb's "It's America (Love It or Leave It)." Merle's themes and tone inspired many more hits, including a pair of top-ten recitations from 1970: the earnest "Where Have All Our Heroes Gone," in which Bill Anderson gets sick to his stomach about the radicals admired by the "Now Generation," and the wacky "Welfare Cadillac," in which Guy Drake plays a hillbilly freeloader who has a falling-down shack but still manages to drive a new car.

Haggard's "Okie from Muskogee" also inspired a number of answer songs from a counterculture perspective: Big Brother and the Holding Company recorded "I'll Change Your Flat Tire, Merle" in 1970, and Pure Prairie League covered it in '75. Hippies all—but still more than happy to help out "the greatest country singer alive." The Youngbloods took "Hippie from Olema" to #5 in 1971: they claimed they didn't "watch commercials…or buy the plastic crap they sell," and they wanted squares and straights everywhere to know that "we bathe often, therefore we don't smell." David Peel & the Lower East Side cut the inevitable "The Hippie from New York City" in 1972 ("We don't like your country-western hits!"), and Chinga Chavin declared himself an "Asshole from El Paso" in 1976. In 1971 the Beach Boys had "Disney Girls (1957)," which critic Tom Smucker calls a "perfectly executed wish list for escaping the '60s," a West Coast "bourgeois companion" to Merle's heartland but already pretty bourgeois "Okie."

Plenty of artists figured their best answer was just to sing the song. The Grateful Dead and the Beach Boys played it live together on stage, and Mike Love led the Beach Boys through it alone, too, though as Merle well knew when people sang "Okie" you sometimes had to listen closely to discern if it was meant as a counter-counterculture protest or as a slightly ironic counterculture party starter. Phil Ochs sang it at Carnegie Hall; Arlo Guthrie, Woody's boy, sang it at the Hollywood Bowl; Okie born-and-bred Leon Russell sang it in Anaheim, California, on tour with Joe Cocker; and Kris Kristofferson rewrote the song for a performance at Philharmonic Hall in New York City. "We always have to do that one with apologies to our good friend Merle Haggard, who is neither a redneck nor a racist," Kristofferson clarified to the crowd. "He just happens to be known for probably the only bad song he ever wrote. He's written many great ones. Very soulful dude."

Kristofferson eventually revised his estimation of the song. "I was wrong," he told Jason Fine in 2009. "That song is saying 'I'm proud to be an Okie from Muskogee.' Coming from [Haggard's] background in California, that's like saying I'm Black and I'm proud." Eventually Merle revised how he performed the song, too. In the last years of his life—singing it with Marty Stuart and Willie Nelson in 2014, with Willie again on the *An Intimate Evening with Willie and Merle* television special, and, just weeks before he died, with Toby Keith—Merle proudly sang his song as if Kristofferson's verse had been there all along: "We don't shoot that deadly marijuana / We get drunk like God wants us to do."

But even during the Muskogee Moment, country music was less monolithic toward the war and other cultural conflicts than is usually remembered. Merle session-hand Glen Campbell had "Galveston," a countrypolitan smash that instead of taking a stand on the war pictured a kid soldier "so afraid of dying." Johnny Cash had something for everyone, supporting the troops in "Singing in Vietnam Talking Blues," while allowing in "What Is Truth?" that maybe the younger generation had a point. He introduced the song on *The Johnny Cash Show* during the same 1970 episode where guest star Merle Haggard sang "Okie" and "Fightin' Side" both, the two country stars in respectful conversation with one another. Cash's marvelously self-mythologizing "The Man in Black," meanwhile, worked both sides of the street at once, protesting the war in one line, protesting the protesters in the next, but dressed for mourning either way: "Each week we lose a hundred fine young men!"

Ambivalence and confusion were as prominent as certainty among country emotions during the Muskogee Moment. People often hold tightly to a position because it makes them feel less helpless than it would to embrace conflicted emotions wholeheartedly—and then feel doubly at sea as a result. "Okie from Muskogee" had toed a line in the dirt and cultivated home soil. "The Fightin' Side of Me" had cast stones across the divide. But Haggard began to bridle under his new persona. He hated the way left-leaning rock fans figured he was a warmonger and bigot, a real-life Lonesome Rhodes: one editorial writer called him "the Spiro Agnew of music," a designation bound to give any artist second thoughts, and peace protesters were picketing some of his shows.

He disliked the assumptions many country fans made about his politics, too. According to the 2003 documentary *Controversy*, the Nixon administration made "numerous requests" in the winter of 1971–1972 for Haggard to officially join the president's reelection campaign, but Merle declined each time. In 1970 Georgia governor George Wallace, the segregationist whose success as a third-party presidential candidate had helped Nixon conceive his Southern Strategy, had approached Merle to join his own reelection campaign. Merle passed. "Any time I represent George Wallace, man, I'm liable to lose a lot of my fans," he told Christopher Wren for *Look* in 1971. "Wallace is unrefined and uncontemporary. He's strictly against the black man." Merle's thinking here was evolving. Only months before he'd accepted advice not to release "Irma Jackson" for fear the song's sympathetic portrayal of an interracial romance, and its implicit rejection of segregation, would harm his career. Now, Merle determined that actually it was an association with a notorious supporter of segregation, not with hippies or Black folks, that would wind up costing him fans. This was the proletarian poet as a work in progress—and with work still to do. Wallace "wants to keep 'em n[******]," Merle added in that *Look* piece, coming off terribly "unrefined and uncontemporary" himself. "He don't want 'em to be colored people."

Merle began working on a song with room to move. He cut it in August, then toyed with the lyrics and tried again a year later, punching up the chorus with harmonies from Bonnie Owens. But "Somewhere in Between" (similar name, different song from 1967's "Somewhere Between") was a dud. It was didactic and vague where "Okie" was farcical and specific, and it was measured and abstract where "Fightin' Side" was animated and ready to rumble. Strike three was that it wasn't even very catchy. Merle moved on.

"I haven't heard an answer that'll change things overnight," Haggard sings in the unreleased recordings. "That's one thing I know for sure is right," he continues, an admission sure to please no one.

> *I stand somewhere between divided wings*
> *The liberal left, the narrow right, and the young of 17*
> *And I'm not too old to understand the young who disagree*
> *It leaves me standing somewhere in between*

And there he was, cornered again.

CHAPTER 18

HE'D RATHER BE GONE

Conventional wisdom has it that Haggard reacted to controversy by fleeing his fightin' side almost as quickly as he'd stepped in it and running as fast as he could into new apolitical work. After a pair of live albums that had become flashpoints in the cultural present, Haggard's next album was going to be all about the music—and music from the past to boot, specifically the swinging sounds of Merle's boyhood hero, Bob Wills.

This bit of Haggard lore isn't quite right for a couple of reasons, the most obvious being that the time line doesn't work. The new tribute project, inspired partly by Wills's 1968 induction into the Country Music Hall of Fame, was conceived before "Okie" was recorded, was well into the planning stages before "Fightin' Side" made the charts, and was already in the can for four months by the time the live *Fightin' Side* album was released. When Merle and the Strangers played that concert on Valentine's Day 1970, they included Wills favorite "Corrine, Corrina" in anticipation of sessions already scheduled for April. Merle made sure to feature his guest fiddler, the legendary Chubby Wise, and to introduce Roy Nichols and Norman Hamlet for solos, just as bandleader Wills liked to do.

As to being about the music of the past, *A Tribute to the Best Damn Fiddle Player in the World (Or My Salute to Bob Wills)* can only plead guilty as charged. Like its tribute-paying predecessor, *Same Train, a Different*

Time, the Wills set was part love letter, part history lesson. Merle's narrated preface on the album links the projects explicitly: "About the time the late and great Jimmie Rodgers's career came to an end, another young fellow by the name of Bob Wills was making preparations unknowingly to become a legend in his own time." Unlike the earlier record, which fuses Rodgers's old songs to the Strangers' modern country-rock-and-soul sound, *Best Damn Fiddle Player* isn't interested in updating its material. It's more like *Same Train, Same Sound.*

To get the old sound right, Haggard enlisted several former Playboys, fiddler Johnny Gimble and electric mandolin man Tiny Moore among them. Wills was in the hospital at the time, but Merle made up for his absence by visiting him for advice and by teaching himself to play the fiddle—in just a few months, too, an achievement only slightly mitigated by the head start he'd been given by childhood violin lessons. As Merle explained at its start, the album was an attempt "to turn back the pages of time and recapture some of the great sounds of the legendary Bob Wills and the Texas Playboys."

Wills and the Playboys were stars up and down the San Joaquin Valley when Merle was a boy. Haggard's overly enthusiastic mouthful of an album title aside, Wills usually wasn't even the best fiddler in his own band, let alone the world, but he was a pretty damn good one. He was a first-rate songwriter, too, with an ear for melodies that stick in your head and stay stuck. Wills had a fine voice, strong and bluesy, and was not averse to showmanship (his idols were Queen of the Blues Bessie Smith and minstrel Emmett Miller), and he was an accomplished bandleader—an expert self-promoter, a savvy entrepreneur, and a keen talent scout. The self-evident boss even when he wasn't the center of attention, Wills was a charismatic front man, chomping his cigar, twirling his bow like a baton, tossing off jive interjections, and calling out his musicians for solos. His constant stream of chatter (and in particular his frequent "Ah-haaaaaa's") still sets detractors' teeth on edge, but for his Okie fan base, it was all key to what made Bob so attractive. Wills was one of them, a hell of a regular guy, feeling his pain, but ironic and on top of it—a man's man. The Playboys moved the crowd, but Bob Wills was the show, and with sense enough to stay out of singer Tommy Duncan's way on the slow ones.

Judged by its stated standards—the album's a "salute to Bob Wills" and means to "recapture" his sound—*The Best Damn Fiddle Player* is a success. As a Merle Haggard album, it's a disappointment. The album's most charming quality, its attention to authentic period detail, is a built-in limitation it never entirely transcends. Merle doesn't merely throw in intros and asides à la Wills; he quotes Bob's patter straight off the old 78s, even mimics his voice. "I'm gonna try to do Tommy Duncan's part," Merle says to introduce "Misery," by which he means Duncan's part exactly. He's doing impersonations again, in other words, except what was in concert a diverting interlude is here the whole gig. Several times the album replicates original Playboys arrangements so precisely that Wills's sides and Haggard's remakes are exactly the same length or off by only a second or two.

My favorite moment comes in "Stay a Little Longer." Merle and his Playboy-augmented Strangers are again expertly playing the record, but then Roy Nichols, who'd been busy doubling Tiny Moore's mandolin on his electric guitar just as it had been doubled on disc a quarter century before, suddenly falls into playing that state-of-the-art, Elvisy rhythm lick from "Workin' Man Blues." Instantly, the history lesson jolts into breaking news, a hint of what might have been if Merle had chosen to honor Wills in the modernizing way he had the Singing Brakeman. *The Best Damn Fiddle Player* is retro bordering on vintage, but when Nichols quotes Haggard's own catalogue, retro becomes traditional, connects new to old, values both. This only lasts a split second, though, a good musical joke, but that's all. "Heeey," Merle mock-warns, sending Nichols back to school.

Still, in that brief moment is a glimpse of where Haggard would take his music. After the Wills tribute, Merle began to highlight his Strangers more than ever, pointing them out by name on record and encouraging them to stretch out and improvise on the road, like the country-jazz-loving Texas Playboys would have done it but in the Strangers' own style. He soon began experimenting with horns, too, and enlisted some old Playboys—Gimble and Moore, especially—as official Strangers for a time on tour and in the studio. The album mostly makes you eager to revisit the originals, but it let Merle imagine options for himself.

Of course, getting folks to check out Bob Wills was another of the album's intentions—and another success. *The Best Damn Fiddle Player* prompted a western swing revival, sending younger musicians—many of them of the noticeably long-haired type, like members of Asleep at the Wheel and Commander Cody and His Lost Planet Airmen—back to modernize the old sounds of Wills, Milton Brown, Spade Cooley, and other legends of

what otherwise might have been a dead genre. Merle contributed further
to the Wills legacy when he helped organize, and then participated on, the
sessions for what would be Wills's final album, 1974's *For the Last Time*.
Western swing has played a role in most every country development since,
from the rise of the Outlaws onward, and has helped keep dance music
alive in the genre, as well. Ironic that the most backward-looking Haggard
album would turn out to be among his most prescient. Or rather it would
be ironic if Haggard hadn't been self-consciously employing the past to
invent the future all along.

There were no singles from the Wills project. Merle's radio follow-up to
"Fightin' Side of Me" was "Street Singer," a hot acoustic blues pulled from
the Strangers' second instrumental album, *Introducing My Friends the
Strangers*, on which Merle says nothing more polemical than "Hey, hey," and
"Blow my mind one more time!" But in April 1971 Merle's next proper solo
album, called *Hag*, marked a return to the state-of-the-art country-rockin'
country he'd been developing since "Sing Me Back Home"—and to politics.
Hag is the most sustained and closest-to-coherent political statement of his
career. Showcasing some of his finest songs, split about evenly between his
tender and fightin' sides, and some of his most evocative singing, it's also
among the half-dozen best of his career.

The world Hag portrays on *Hag* is one teetering on the brink. From
atop some middle-American watchtower, Merle delivers a nearly despairing
state of the union. "The mighty roar of gunfire is now a local sound, and
our city streets are filled with angry men," he observes wearily on "Jesus,
Take a Hold," as Roy Nichols sounds the alarm on harmonica and guitar.
"Destruction seems to be the current trend. This world has never been in
the awful shape it's in!" Merle's characters here have it at least as bad as
their nation, nursing insults, mourning losses, bracing for failure and pain
to come. On the desolate "Shelly's Winter Love," the title character comes
and goes like the seasons, leaving Merle cold and depressed all year 'round:
"She'll leave when love has thawed the winter ground," he predicts as pianist Glen Hardin plays an icy drip, drip, drip. On Dave Kirby's "Sidewalks
of Chicago," Merle is homeless, dissolute, distilled. "If I buy the bread, I
can't afford the wine," he sings, and the way he gives that last word the
shakes, we know the wine is nonnegotiable. On "If You've Got Time," Merle
leans hard into his chorus's internal rhymes—"Let me brace my heart, so I

can face the part, that I've been dreading"—while riding twin fiddles that feel like a melancholy chamber group. Halfway through the album, an unaccountably buoyant Merle ("Don't worry 'bout my *pride*") declares, "I'm a Good Loser." We understand instantly that's not out of sportsmanship; it's just that lately he's had so much practice.

Each of these individual hurts spirals outward on *Hag*, binding personal trouble to public issue. In "I've Done It All," Merle recalls that, in addition to picking his share of cotton and "driving one railroad spike," he's "been to Frisco wearin' regular clothes [and] felt them modern hippie folks starin' down their nose." "I can *proudly* say I answered my patriotic call," he adds with a sneer.

On the clarion "I Can't Be Myself," Haggard boasts again of his rough and rowdy ways: "It's a way of mine to say just what I'm thinkin' and to do the things I really want to do." His woman wants to change him, though—to change the very parts of him of which he's most proud, in fact—and he can't allow that. "I can't be myself and be what pleases you," he claims, almost breaking into a beautiful blue yodel. The song's a testament to Merle's rugged individualism, but he makes it sound like Sartre: hell is other people wanting you to change.

Hag begins with "Soldier's Last Letter." Originally a World War II–era hit for Ernest Tubb, Merle transforms it into a Vietnam hit simply by singing it in 1970. In the song, a mother excitedly reads a letter from a son stationed overseas, then realizes, rather implausibly, that he's died in action because the letter is unfinished. "Dear God," she prays, falling to her knees, "keep America free." Patriotic hokum, that, but it's also a kind of psychological realism: people understandably invest a great deal in the conviction that loved ones have sacrificed for a good cause, that they are heroic rather than merely dead. And it's toward that mother's fall to her knees, her tears and trembling hands, where Merle directs our focus. Merle's "Soldier's Last Letter" is musical testimony that, as Barbara Kingsolver has written, "every war is both won and lost and that loss is a pure, high note of anguish like a mother singing to an empty bed."

Near *Hag*'s end is "The Farmer's Daughter," in which reverent and ragged acoustic guitar picking and Johnny Gimble's bittersweet fiddle evoke the setting: a ramshackle but candlelit country church that's about to host a wedding. A widowed farmer is hesitant to give away his daughter, his "one possession," to "that city boy from town." "His hair's a little longer than we're used to," Merle complains, and you figure you know where Merle's train of thought must be heading. But then something remarkable happens. As he'd attempted earlier, Merle positions himself somewhere between: his tribalism eases a bit, his tolerance blooms, and instead of feeling cornered, his world seems to expand. Gimble's fiddle leaps and swells, and Merle, knowing how dearly he loves and trusts his daughter, allows himself to be changed. This young man, Merle sings at the end, his heart breaking and mending all at once, "says he really loves the farmer's daughter."

More to the point: "I *know* the farmer's daughter loves the man."

Hag was a #1 country album and boasted four hit singles, more than any album of his career to that point: "Soldier's Last Letter," "Jesus, Take a Hold," and "I Can't Be Myself" were #3 hits across the board, and the latter's flip, "Sidewalks of Chicago," received a lot of play too. These days, though, if people remember *Hag* at all it's as one more example of what used to be called Nixon music, an opprobrium taking in everything from the cultishly clean-cut mass choir Up with People singing "Freedom Isn't Free" at the 1968 Republican convention ("You got to pay the price, you got to sacrifice, for your liberty") to Johnny Cash being asked to perform "Welfare Cadillac" and "Okie from Muskogee" at a White House performance in July 1972 (he declined) to Merle himself performing for Nixon the following spring.

"An Evening with Merle Haggard" was held at the White House on the occasion of First Lady Patricia Nixon's birthday. Opening act the Osborne Brothers was received politely but not at all enthusiastically, and when Merle and the Strangers took their turn, the audience of DC officials and dignitaries appeared "like a bunch of department store mannequins." "I felt like I was coming out for hand-to-hand combat with the enemy," Merle remembered in *Sing Me Back Home*. "I searched the faces in the crowd, hoping to find at least one that was interested in what I was doing," he wrote. "No luck." And: "There *he* sat, the president of the United States, the most powerful man in the world. His face was a mask I couldn't read. It was blank." But that was only what Merle was thinking. In public, the Haggard visit to the White House was covered widely, his association with Nixon's Silent Majority further entrenched.

Those connections are all fair enough, but when I listen to *Hag* these days what leaps out at me is how it seems to be in deliberate conversation with *What's Going On*, Marvin Gaye's album from the same year. It wasn't deliberate—again, the time line's wrong; Haggard's album came out the month before Gaye's—but the themes the albums address seem like family to one another, at times almost eerily. *Hag* begins with a mother weeping for a dead son in Vietnam, Gaye's album with "Mother, mother, there's too many of you cryin'." Merle sings, "His hair's a little longer than we're used to," and Gaye snaps back, "Who are *they* to judge us simply 'cause our hair is long?" Both albums, too, are to some degree frightened to the point of fatalism about where America stands in 1971. Marvin inquires despairingly, "Who is willing to try to save a world that's destined to die?" Merle warns that "like the mighty Roman Empire, this world is doomed to fall." Both recommend Jesus is our best bet.

"Father, father, we don't need to escalate," Gaye pleads, and Merle's future father-in-law says amen: "I know the farmer's daughter loves the man."

In the fall of 1971, as the sixties transformed themselves irretrievably into the seventies, as his Muskogee Moment dribbled to an end, Merle followed *Hag* with one more masterpiece. *Someday We'll Look Back* is the album I'd nominate as Merle's greatest ever and (no disrespect to *There's a Riot Goin' On* or *Every Picture Tells a Story* or to *Blue, Tapestry*, or *Tupelo Honey*) the finest of that year. Its title track, a #2 hit, sees Merle promising better days to a lover or a wife...someday. A couple getting by in the meantime on "love and pennies" is a durable country subject, and Merle's sweet-tempered reading of his melody joins Norman Hamlet's soothing pedal steel in a model of patience and optimism even while settling in for the hard, long haul and no promises. "If we both pull together...," Haggard sings, pausing before adding, "tomorrow will surely come." Hamlet fills the pause with a wink so that we won't miss that Haggard's making a joke about the limits of human plans and agency, and a particularly grim joke at that: tomorrow tends to come whether we pull together or not. "When our dream world finds us, and these hard times are gone," Merle predicts, we'll look back at our fraught shared histories and tell ourselves a story about how these were the good old days. As people will. "Someday We'll Look Back" is a nostalgic song that makes gentle fun of nostalgia.

The whole album is dark and bright like that, doomed and hopeful at once, all down the line. A quartet of songs—"Train of Life," by Roger Miller; "One Row at a Time," by Red Lane; "California Cottonfields," by

Dallas Frazier; and the brooding, alternately childish and bullying "Caro-lyn," a #1 single from the Tommy Collins songbook—underscores Merle's gift at identifying songs by other people that sound like they just have to be ones he wrote himself. "Carolyn, let me tell you what I heard about a man today," Collins has a husband sing to his wife. This man, Merle explains, "didn't come home from work and he went away" to cheat on his spouse. That, the song's game-playing narrator warns, is just what men will do sometimes when their wives are mean to them. The power of the song comes from the way its countrypolitan violins and cellos shrink Merle's menace to pomposity, making him come off like the ridiculous villain in a melodrama. The poignancy of the record lies in the chasm between this baby-man's not-so-veiled threat and our imagining of his wife's mocking laughter.

The songs Merle did write are remarkable. Each Haggard tune here is an imperative to sing along, each lyric a reason to keep silence and reflect. His "One Sweet Hello" couples with "one sad goodbye" to elevate a cliché into a worldview, and his "I'd Rather Be Gone" (as opposed to "in your way") is an elegant statement of that old escape route, it's-not-you-it's-me. "Tulare Dust" stands shoulder-to-Okie-shoulder with "Hungry Eyes" as the greatest contribution to his Kern County Suite. "Huntsville," cut at the same 1969 session that produced "Irma Jackson" and featuring James Burton's coiled-to-strike Telecaster, is deep-down-in-the-dirt country funk. And definitively Merle. He's playing an outlaw being escorted to prison in leg irons—"I guess they got a good excuse"—and he's waiting patiently for his chance to break: "They're gonna lose old Hag." He swears he doesn't care if he gets killed in the attempt, and he makes even that suicide mission sound like freedom instead of just an end to hurt.

The album's centerpiece is "Big Time Annie's Square," a generous Musk-ogee Moment fantasy in which small-town Merle visits a former girlfriend who's now living with a bunch of LSD-tripping hippies in "San Somethin' Somethin', close to east L.A." In Merle's dream these previously warring camps all get along just swell—and without anyone having to change their minds or ways of living right to do it. Well, that's not quite true. Because if an "old Checotah boy" can imagine himself singing live-and-let-live instead of love-it-or-leave-it, and can even imagine himself enjoying it, then Merle Haggard had changed, just a little, and so had America.

CHAPTER 19

"IT'S NOT LOVE (BUT IT'S NOT BAD)," 1972

The least romantic, most cynical love song ever to top the country chart isn't a love song at all so much as a song about settling. Nashville Cat Hargus "Pig" Robbins announces the record with a classic gospel piano run, lifting Merle's spirits with a sprightly right-hand flourish before tumbling into depressed bass notes with his left. Merle repeats the cycle: his first line begins steadfast and grateful ("She was always there each time..."), then pulls the rug out from under itself ("...I needed *you*"). The record keeps lowering our expectations and shifting our attention downward. You can't always get what you want, this Hank Cochran and Glenn Martin–penned song argues, but sometimes, if you try, you can get...some.

"I don't have to wonder who she's had," Merle declares about the woman he's been seeing in lieu of the woman he wants. Not because he believes she's any more faithful than the one who's broken his heart, but because he doesn't really care what she does. In the chorus, each time he sings, "I don't have to wonder," Merle's voice free-falls out of itself again and back into Lefty's. For just that instant, he sounds free from want, free from fear, even free from having to be Merle Haggard.

CHAPTER 20

HE WISHES HE WAS SANTA CLAUS

"If We Make It through December," a #28 pop hit in 1973, was the biggest crossover hit of Haggard's career, even bigger than "Okie from Muskogee." It might also be the quintessential presentation of his hard-nosed Poet of the Common Man concerns. It's a Christmas song, but it feels almost like an anti-Christmas song. The character he plays isn't just feeling blue this holiday season like we've seen in hundreds of other Christmas numbers. He *hates* Christmas, hates the whole idea of it, at least this year. "Got laid off down at the factory," he growls with a sigh. Now, he can't buy his wife and kids any presents—hell, he doesn't know how they'll make it to the new year, even without gifts—and it's bringing him down like the plummeting temperature. Roy Nichols's acoustic guitar sounds pretty as falling flakes, but pings and stings like an ice storm. "If we make it through Decem-brrrr," Merle keeps repeating, trying to convince himself. *Then*, we'll pack up and move on to someplace warm, maybe even to California.

After the recording of "If We Make It through December" turned out so well—it became Merle's sixteenth country #1 that holiday season, then did double duty as the title track to an LP released the following spring—Ken Nelson suggested an entire Christmas album. Merle embraced the project wholeheartedly. On the front of 1973's *Merle Haggard's Christmas Present (Something Old, Something New)*, he's posed in front of a roaring fire, Bonnie and kids at his side, and sporting a cardigan straight out of a Bing Crosby special. On the back cover is a note from Santa, in which St. Nick explains that whether you asked for it or not, he's giving "you Merle Haggard's *first* Christmas album." The "first" is italicized like that, too, as if recording a second in 1982, *Goin' Home for Christmas*, and a third in 2004, *I Wish I Was Santa Claus*, was on Merle's wish list all along.

Merle's commitment to Christmas music seems a little out of character, doesn't it? The emotions associated with holiday music have a kind of split personality to them: earnest competes with zany, only one of which we think of as being especially Haggardian.

On the one hand, the Christmas aesthetic favors the sorts of grown-up Christmas wishes that emerged on the radio during World War II, when Merle was a little boy and his father was still alive. Merle's big Christmas hit springs from common ground: "*If we make it through December* [we've] got plans to be in a warmer town" finds an antecedent in the contingent cheer of "I'll be home for Christmas, *if only in my dreams*" and "Someday soon we all will be together, *if the fates allow*." Christmas songs like these are arm's-length utopian. They yearn for peace, for families safely reunited amidst pretty Currier & Ives backdrops, but their key lines almost always begin with *if* or strongly imply one. Bing is "*dreaming* of a white Christmas," as is Merle on his three versions of the standard—his dreamiest being the one from a 1986 various-artist anthology called *Nashville's Greatest Christmas Hits* that decorates Merle's croon with nothing but Clint Strong's Django Reinhardt–styled guitar.

At the same time, the Christmas aesthetic spikes its sobriety with healthy pours of full-on goofy wonder. The childlike ditties that dominated the pop charts just before the tweenage Merle began elbowing his way to adulthood—"Here Comes Santa Claus," "Rudolph, the Red-Nosed Reindeer," and "Frosty the Snowman," all from Okie-turned-Cali-cowboy Gene Autry in 1948, '49, and '50, respectively—each evoke those week-of-the-twenty-fifth moments when, as writer Mike Warren phrases it, "that one kid spazzing out of control...hears some sleigh bells...and freezes." That doesn't sound very Haggard.

Then again, doing the Christmas thing has long been a good way for Great American Artists to throw down on their American Greatness in the first place. Think Bing, Elvis, and James Brown. Think Bob Dylan, whose

2009 *Christmas in the Heart* prompted many to wonder, "What in the world is he thinking?" when a better question might have been "What took him so long?" The greatest artists all tend to get around to childlike wonder, playful silliness, rainbow dreams of the peace-on-earth variety at some point if for no other reason than that those qualities are all part of what it means to be human. The return engagements of Christmas music in the Haggard catalogue are enriching and functional in just that way. "As dancing," per Andre Dubus, "allows the tongue-tied man a ceremony of love," Christmas music allows Haggard to express emotions tamped down or absent in the rest of his work. His Christmas aesthetic allows the normally pessimistic Hag access to a variety of utopianism that's collective by definition, and it also gives the self-serious Haggard a chance to cut up and use silly voices and embrace his inner kid. It lets him have fun.

The Haggard Christmas catalogue includes ten tracks each from *Christmas Present* and *Goin' Home*, twelve more from *I Wish I Was Santa Claus*, plus a "Blue Christmas" from his 1977 Elvis tribute and that 1986 "White Christmas." That comes to thirty-four tracks, but, thanks to multiple versions, just eighteen distinct songs. Not unexpectedly, each Haggard Christmas album includes a fresh take on "If We Make It through December," and it's hardly surprising that this Crosby nut would tackle "White Christmas" three times. He turned to "Blue Christmas" three times, as well, a natural choice for a big fan of Elvis Presley, who first released his version of the song in 1957, that same holiday season Merle was arrested for trying to rob Fred & Gene's Café. And a big fan of Ernest Tubb, too. The Texas Troubadour had the original hit with the song in 1949, then saw it return to the country top ten in December 1950 and '51—all as Merle was transitioning from hooky-playing tween to larcenous teen.

Most of the holiday duplication, though, comes down to rerecording his own songs. *Merle Haggard's Christmas Present* includes a quintet of Haggard originals: "If We Make It," plus "Santa Claus and Popcorn," "Bobby Wants a Puppy Dog for Christmas," "Daddy Won't Be Home Again for Christmas" (he's on the road, but at least remembered to send a check), and "Grandma's Christmas Card" comprise the set's "Something New" first side. The "Something Old" side two is devoted to holiday standards done up in glittery, festive string arrangements courtesy of Billy Walker and His Orchestra. Merle reprised them all not quite a decade later on *Goin'*

Home for Christmas—not as strong as its predecessor, but it gets points for unabashed Christmas spirit: shimmering strings and glockenspiel, the Carpenters-sounding backing singers throughout, the dog arf-arf-arfing at the end of "Bobby Wants a Puppy," and most of all the wonderfully dorky toothless grampa voice Merle adopts for the title track.

You could look at all this, I suppose, and see nothing more than a time-tested seasonal marketing strategy, but I think that misses a big part of the point of Christmas albums generally and of Merle's holiday releases in particular. In all of pop music, commercial motivations are rarely mutually exclusive of emotional and aesthetic ones. Blatant seasonal marketing items may not be *only* blatant seasonal marketing items—indeed, they are successful at parting people from their money each holiday season precisely because audiences find them useful, even enriching.

In the same commercial vein, recording and rerecording his own songs lets Merle work his publishing, but there's something perfectly Christmassy in the repetition, too. Christmas is a holiday that people celebrate traditionally, rehearsing the rituals that keep families connected to themselves and their own histories in a fatally dynamic world. "Grandma's Christmas Card" is about exactly this experience. With "O Little Town of Bethlehem" caroling in the background—the melody picked out simply by Roy Nichols on *Christmas Present*, performed lushly by Walker and company on *Goin' Home*—Merle recites in homage to a departed matriarch, ensuring hers is "the only card we keep from year to year."

Time changes everything: new ornaments replace damaged old ones; a real tree gives way to an artificial one; this year there's an empty chair at the table where Grandma always sat, but, just think, next December there'll be a newborn. Singing along to the same records, viewing the same animated TV specials, insisting on the same sugar cookie recipe—celebrating the *same*—honors forefathers and -mothers, eases transitions, connects each year's isolated chapter to an ongoing narrative bigger than oneself.

The all-American Christmas is a gesture, reminding us that even though the world is a cold place, we have each other to keep us warm. Though our lives are far too often determined by material conditions beyond our control—the first line of Merle's Xmas hit is, after all, "Got laid off down at the factory"—we have each other. Merle's Christmas music is a gesture, too, insisting that while life is fragile, fleeting, tragic, it sure is fun to have fun. And I'd add that, at least in Merle's case, it's a gesture that's overwhelmingly secular and Santa-centric. Of Merle's thirty-four Christmas tracks, only two are of the purely Baby Jesus sort—a 2004 go at Willie Nelson's "El Niño" that feels more menacing than grateful, and an almost more sprightly than somber "Silent Night" that has all of its sacred power undercut by the "Jingle Bells" that's *Christmas Present*'s final word. Much more typical is the title track to *I Wish I Was Santa Claus*: Merle figures Santa's got the game beat because he only has to work one day a year.

"Santa Claus and Popcorn," the Haggard original that appears on all three holiday sets, glorifies the newborn king but juxtaposes the nativity every step of the way with temporal cheer. "Carolers singing 'Silent Night' " and "Jesus loves me, this I know" butt up against "Crosby dreams of Christmas white" and "Christmas trees and mistletoe." The song begins on its knees, slow and humble, like it's going to be a hymn. "We celebrate because a king was born," Merle croons, reverently, then floors it to sleigh-ride speed, explaining giddily that, sure, Christ is the reason for the season, but..."Snowballs! Crosby! Sleigh bells and reindeer horns!"

And maybe next year in California, if that job comes through, some presents under the tree.

CHAPTER 21

MERLE LOVES DOLLY

On the choruses to "Always Wanting You"—next line: "But never having you"—Merle drops his tenor to a quavering baritone, creeping cautiously across notes, straight-up worrying each of them from a specific word into a long, painful moan, each "you" most painful of all. "Always loving you," he wails exquisitely. Next line: "But never touching you."

His voice speeds in the verses, his phrases become short and clipped, his voice high and thin, breathy: "Better off"…"if I"…"turned away"…"never looked"…"at you." The record features a Spanish guitar intro and fiddles that play like they're violins; Louise Mandrell's lone harmony somehow sounds like a choir singing along miles away. The music feels like a soap opera, either in solemn sympathy with Merle's distress or in subtle melodramatic mockery of his misery. He's trying very hard to maintain some dignity, to not appear hysterical or pathetic.

One of Haggard's saddest ballads, a descendant of "Today I Started Loving You Again" and "Everybody's Had the Blues," "Always Wanting You" throbs with unmistakable loss but keeps its songwriting inspiration a secret: in the midseventies Merle Haggard spent a couple of years attempting to woo Dolly Parton, advances she consistently rebuffed. No one in the audience could have known about Merle's crush at the time.

(Bonnie Owens, of course, who first left Merle's road show and then filed for divorce in precisely this period, surely knew about it all too well.) But when it came to appreciating Dolly Parton, the artist, Merle was an early adopter, first seeing her perform when he played a show in her Tennessee mountain hometown in the midsixties: "She was a cute little thing with a little girl voice," he recalls in *Sing Me Back Home*. "I thought she was best when she worked on stage alone, just her and her guitar." It was at the same 1968 session where he cut his nostalgic anti-nostalgia song "Mama Tried" that Merle also recorded Parton's nostalgic anti-nostalgia song "In the Good Old Days (When Times Were Bad)." That was a few months before she'd even recorded it herself and more than two years before she had any significant solo hits of her own.

Parton and Wagoner recorded Haggard's "Somewhere Between" that same year, and in 1970 they presented him with the album of the year prize, for *Okie from Muskogee*, during the televised Country Music Association awards. It wasn't until 1974 and '75 that modern country music's two greatest artists really began to get to know each other. Merle and Dolly were booked together regularly in the time immediately following her break from the television and road shows of her longtime boss and duet partner, Porter Wagoner. By then she had plenty of hits to her credit, including such jewels of her catalogue as the autobiographical story-song "Coat of Many Colors," the imagination-inspired tale of "Jolene," and the autobiographically inspired feelings of "I Will Always Love You." Country fans didn't know the impetus behind Parton's song when it topped the charts in 1974 any more than they would know what inspired Merle's "Always Wanting You" a year later. But "I Will Always Love You" was a breakthrough for Parton. First, because it served as a tender tendering of written notice to her mentor. But also because the song was an expression of Parton's feelings rather than a step-by-step recounting of a narrative, like the stories in many of her early singles ("Coat" and "Jolene," of course, but also "My Blue Ridge Mountain Boy," "Daddy, Come and Get Me," "Jeannie's Afraid of the Dark") or some of her finest early album tracks (all hail "Down from Dover"). In this way Haggard's and Parton's songwriting developed along similar lines. They both began their careers scoring a lot of stories, either remembered or imagined but often about being working-class and poor. They both developed into writers who more often wrote about their emotions or states of mind—and mostly kept their stories to themselves.

On the road, Merle writes in *Sing Me Back Home,* the two artists spent hours together on one or the other's tour bus, with Merle fondly recalling that Parton "would sit herself down on the floor of my bus aisle, lay her head on my knee, and talk on and on about her dreams and that plan of hers to be a STAR." As we'll see, Merle was, at that very moment, entertaining the possibility that what he wanted to do with stardom was to flee it, as quickly as possible. But Merle was gaga for her anyway. Unsurprisingly, he can't resist panting in his memoir over Parton's physical appearance, "all that bunch of fluffy hair, fluttery eyelashes and super boobs," but he then spends the next four-and-a-half pages going on about her songs, her drive, her charisma—and his infatuation: "I would have carved 'Merle loves Dolly' on every damn tree in the country if she'd asked me to." He was especially struck by Parton's confidence that nothing and nobody would stand in her way when it came to her career plans, "both a statement and a kind of warning," as he took it. Besides, as she kept reminding him, she was married and loved her husband. He was married, too, but wouldn't let it drop. He shares an embarrassing story on himself about phoning her at home, at three in the morning, to confess his feelings yet again and how he refused to hang up until she agreed to listen to him sing the new song he'd written because of her. "Always Wanting You" didn't change Parton's mind, but the song did top the country charts for a couple of weeks in April 1975.

For a time the two formed something of an on-record mutual admiration society. Dolly's recording of Merle's "You'll Always Be Special to Me" (as in, "To you I may never be more than a friend, but…") beat his own version to market by a couple of months. Merle's single just prior to his Parton-pining "Always Wanting You" was the Parton-penned "Kentucky Gambler," and in 1976 he concluded his *It's All in the Movies* with Dolly's "The Seeker." That same year he made another of her songs the title track to his *My Love Affair with Trains* while she recorded Merle's "Life's Like Poetry."

Today the origin stories behind "I Will Always Love You" and "Always Wanting You"—even the echoing titles hint Merle had eyes for Dolly's songwriting—are well known even by casual fans. But while *Behind the Music* trivia is interesting, and can be revelatory about how art is created, it also has the potential to shrink a work's power. Back before we knew what we know about Dolly's farewell-to-Porter song and Merle's in-love-with-Dolly song, the meanings those songs expressed were limited only by the life experiences of people singing along. The stories were ours to tell.

CHAPTER 22

SONGS HE'LL ALWAYS SING

Between June and October, 1972, an hour-long syndicated Merle Haggard documentary found its way to most US television markets. Produced "in association with Merle Haggard Inc." and "brought to you by the small car and truck experts" at Datsun, *Let Me Tell You about a Song* offered a portrait of the artist as a thirty-five-year-old man—and of how he was choosing, in that moment, to present himself to a national audience. Much of the program is devoted to an arena concert at Kiel Auditorium in St. Louis, Missouri. Merle takes the stage wearing a black jean jacket, sporting a moustache and a spit curl, and the set begins with a groovy "Workin' Man Blues" that's right in line with Merle's Elvisy muttonchops. The evening concludes, inevitably, with "Okie from Muskogee" and is just as inevitably punctuated by a standing "O."

It's the behind-the-scenes footage and voice-over commentary that's most revealing. Narrator Jefferson Kaye, later of NFL Films fame, informs us that Merle is a road warrior: "His days are six hundred miles apart." He's also a composing and singing country superstar, and he's an ex-convict: "Merle Haggard's Mama *did* try. And *failed*." And he sings for "the people: truck drivers, farmers, hard hats, factory workers."

"I want to be on the level of the working man," Merle tells us in one voice-over. "That's the people I'm singing to. It's like saying, 'Hello working people, glad to have you.' A person can only talk about what he knows about. The only type of life that I am *sure* of is the working class 'cause I've been there. I don't know any other way to sing. Or anything else to sing about."

"The *music* is Merle Haggard," Kaye intones. "Merle Haggard *is* his music."

We get glimpses of Merle at his new mansion outside Bakersfield (it cost $700,000, *Time* reported) and tinkering with his model train set (worth fifty grand). We see him fishing along the Kern River, sawing a bit of "Today I Started Loving You Again" on the fiddle at the request of Fuzzy Owen, and writing (or more likely just reenacting the writing of) his by then year-old hit "Someday We'll Look Back." We visit Merle in the studio, too, cutting "I Forget You Every Day" (Bear Family's discographers mark the session "lost"), and we see him performing before a shoulder-to-shoulder dance floor at J.D.'s, a small "country & western night club...on the edge of the Mojave Desert." As he croons a rousing version of the old western-swing number "What's the Matter at the Mill," Merle beams with undisguised joy. It's a stark contrast to the self-serious persona he adopts on stage in St. Louis. The scenes at J.D.'s are the only time Merle really smiles in the entire documentary.

The television special shares a title with a record released earlier that year. *Let Me Tell You about a Song*, the album, is the one that includes spoken introductions to songs like "Irma Jackson" and "They're Tearing the Labor Camps Down" and that would be named album of the year that fall by the Country Music Association. The documentary does not show Merle singing the multiracial "Irma" for his monoracial audiences, but he does perform "They're Tearing the Labor Camps Down." "It's kind of like we don't need the man with the two hands anymore," Merle explains in another voice-over. "It's another insinuation of the machine replacing the man, you know. But we've still got that man. He's still here."

This is Merle going all-in on a way of reading his art that, by this point in his career, was well established: Poet of the Common Man. Right on cue, he recorded "If We Make It through December" just a few months later, in January 1973. But very quickly even that subject matter began to feel like a bit of a trap. As the seventies progressed, Haggard wrote less and less often about explicitly working-class themes and recorded fewer obviously working-class songs. "I didn't want to be Nixon's poet laureate," he recalled in 1980 to journalist Jim Auchmutey.

How the world perceived him and his music wouldn't change at all, though. The white working class was Merle Haggard. Merle Haggard *was* the white working class—no matter what he was singing about or how he sounded doing it.

Once James Burton left his studio lineup and signed on with Elvis, Haggard never had another crossover hit—with one enormous exception. "If We Make It through December" became the biggest crossover hit of his career in the winter of 1973 and has proved perennially popular ever since. Like "Okie," it has a sharp political edge, but instead of seeming to align itself with the college-and-courthouse values of the petite bourgeoisie, "December" voices the struggles of American proles to provide the things their families really need. "If We Make It through December," critic Dave Marsh later wrote,

> was the first record—perhaps the first meaningful piece of pop culture— to come to grips with the fears, frustrations, and hopes-against-hope of the workers thrown into disarray by the initial round of deprivation as the world economy cooled after three decades of post–World War II expansion. In other words, this is Bruce Springsteen country, but Haggard is speaking ten years sooner, and in the voice of someone for whom rebellion isn't an idea, let alone an option.

In the real world, of course, the real Merle did rebel against poverty and unemployment, albeit meagerly and counterproductively. Haggard's reputation as an autobiographical songwriter, particularly in the years that first earned him that reputation, is almost always overstated. That's another way "If We Make It through December" stands out. The song's specific scenario—a blue-collar worker, unemployed during the holiday season and with a family to consider, including a young daughter—is precisely the autobiographical predicament that prompted Merle's attempted robbery of Fred & Gene's Café in 1957: "My little girl don't understand why Daddy can't afford no Christmas cheer."

The same year that Merle repurposed his outlaw past into a universal Christmas song about hard times also witnessed the emergence of a very different sort of outlaw. By then some radio stations were already programming acts they identified as "progressive country." These were appreciators of twang, especially if it swung a little, who came off more self-consciously literate than typical mainstream country stars and who were presumably smarter, hipper, and hippie-embracing, too—remnants of a counterculture audience largely drawn to country by Haggard in the first place. One of those artists, Austin singer-songwriter Michael Martin Murphy, aspired to be what he dubbed a "Cosmic Cowboy." Up in Nashville, Charlie Daniels threw some good-ol'-boy southern rock into the mix and declared himself a "Long Haired Country Boy." But when Nashville publicist Hazel Smith was asked by a journalist about such performers, she recalled a Waylon Jennings album, *Ladies Love Outlaws*, from the year before. The members of this new breed were called "Outlaws," Smith told the reporter, and that was the brand people remembered.

"Well, 'outlaw' has a dual meaning with me because of the fact that I had some real run-ins with the law earlier in my life," Haggard once reminded Alanna Nash. "Every time they say 'outlaw,' I have to stop and think what they're talkin' about." The artists identified as Outlaws—stars Waylon Jennings and Willie Nelson were who they were talking about most—were not criminals the way Haggard had been, though a few of them had been busted for possession. They weren't out of work, either, or trapped by a shitty labor market in jobs they loathed, the way the narrators in Merle's songs often were. One Outlaw-adjacent singer-songwriter, James Talley, did memorably connect both Haggardian impulses, the criminal and the impoverished, in the same song. "Are They Gonna Make Us Outlaws Again," a negligible country hit in 1976, references breadlines and the blues, boxcars and gas prices and hunger. It seems designed to answer the musical question, "What if Merle and the Strangers collaborated with Woody Guthrie?"

Far more routinely, the Outlaws avoided politics in favor of good-old-boy basics, like carousing 'round with their running buddies and bedding all the ladies drawn to their "Lonesome, On'ry and Mean" charms, as a song by Outlaw Steve Young has it. It wasn't just, or even mostly, the sound of the new music that prompted Hazel Smith to flash back on *Ladies Love Outlaws*. The salient association was to Waylon's subject matter and point of view. "If you don't love me, woman, just say so—that's all," Jennings snarled a couple of years later, singing Jimmie Rodgers's "T for Texas" on one of the new country subgenre's finest albums, *Waylon Live*. As Rodgers critic Barry Mazor summarizes it, Jennings's attitude there was "no problem, no fuss" because "he could get more women than a passenger train can haul."

Jessi Colter's notable inclusion on the breakthrough *Wanted: The Outlaws* compilation (1976) notwithstanding, the Outlaw movement was even more heavy on testosterone than mainstream country had normally been.

Haggard had romanticized a cantankerous sort of romantic individualism, too, of course, in the songs he sang as in his life, and he was one contemporary inspiration for the Outlaws. The same Steve Young album that introduced "Lonesome, On'ry and Mean" included a cover of "I Can't Be Myself," a Merle song that, joined with his "I Can't Hold Myself in Line," seems almost to have invented Outlaw singer-songwriter Billy Joe Shaver. Like Haggard and the Outlaws' mutual hero, Jimmie Rodgers, but notably unlike most Outlaws, Haggard was characteristically conflicted with that stance, belaboring its contradictions rather than eliding them:

> *I thought I would settle down.... But, somehow, I can't give up my good old ramblin' ways.*

*   *   *

> *There was a clear and simple pull back to Bakersfield—usually followed by a burning need to leave Bakersfield.*

*   *   *

> *I'd like to settle down but they won't let me.*

*   *   *

> *Like an eagle, I'm a prisoner of the wind.*

The Outlaws didn't really do conflicted. Their recalcitrant individualism was in support of their macho liberty on record and, behind the scenes, in support of their artistic freedom—like that recently won, for instance, by Marvin Gaye and Stevie Wonder at Motown. For an example closer to hand, they wanted to choose their style, session personnel, and repertoire the way Merle Haggard had been doing it for almost a decade already at Capitol. Now and then the freedoms won by Waylon, Willie, and the boys translated into different sonics, though as a rule of thumb only connoisseurs would hear a big difference on that front. The real victory won by the Outlaws was greater control over the length of their hair and the conditions of their labor.

"Are they talkin' about 'outlaw' outlaw," Merle asked Nash in 1986 when she told him some folks figured he was the "last authentic outlaw." "Or are they talkin' about a guy that don't do it the same way everybody else does it? I think they mean the latter one." Definitely the latter: the Hag was the Fugitive, the Branded Man, the Running Kind. His catalogue is full of live sets and longform tributes and concept albums. The Hag was the boss of his own sessions and the author of songs both classic and idiosyncratic, a lover of western swing and country blues, of Rodgers and Presley, and a primary source for country rock, too. If Outlaw Country hadn't stuck, "Haggard Country" might've been just as good.

As the Outlaws began their rise, Merle's Muskogee Moment was mostly over. He was just a country star again, though of a rare sort: to many, Merle Haggard now stood for country music, a function he served for people who never listened to the genre if they could help it and for those who listened to nothing else. When *Time*, late to the party, did a 1974 story called "Country Music: Songs of Love, Loyalty & Doubt," it was thirty-seven-year-old Merle Haggard who was on the cover. When *Reader's Digest* republished the article, it was titled "The King of Country Music."

Merle had become shorthand for country music and what it stood for. On the 1974 country hit "(We're Not) The Jet Set," George Jones and Tammy Wynette jokingly proclaimed their downhome authenticity with "Our Bach and Tchaikovsky are Haggard and Husky." Tex Ritter, not joking in the least, cut a talking blues that "Amen-ed" Merle and his working-man laments: "After a week down at the Ford plant, I'm a little Haggard, too." Cledus Maggard, meanwhile, listed a few of his favorite things in a chart-topping 1976 hickface novelty called "The White Knight": "Now, ahead uh yer chil'ren and ahead uh yer wife, on the list of the Ten Best Things in Life, yer CB's gotta rate right around number fo'. 'Course beavers, hot biscuits and Merle Haggard come one, two, three, y'know."

Haggard enjoyed a burst of high-profile television appearances through the middle of the decade, as well. In 1974 he starred on one of the first episodes of a new syndicated country music program, *Pop! Goes the Country*, and the next year he was on *The Midnight Special*, duetting with host Helen Reddy on "Today I Started Loving You Again." In January 1976 he mouthed along to his recording of "If We Make It through December" while sporting a chunky, shawl-collared and sash-belted cardigan on *The*

Donny and Marie Show. Then he joined the sibling duo ("Hey! You like trains!") for an inexplicably disco rendering of "I've Been Working on the Railroad." Back in November 1970, after nearly a week of rehearsals, Merle had walked away from a special episode of *The Ed Sullivan Show*, a tribute to Richard Rodgers at the Hollywood Bowl, because he was uncomfortable performing the required *Oklahoma!* dance routines. Now, though, he gamely put on a big Instamatic grin for the Osmonds, bobbing and jerking along in a manner suggestive of dance.

Later in '76 he played a Depression-era country singer, "the incomparable Red Turner," on an episode of *The Waltons*. Portraying a father who has given up music in grief over his son's death, Merle is coaxed out of retirement and sings a grateful, perfect verse and chorus of Jimmie Davis's "Nobody's Darling but Mine" in his comeback performance at the Dew Drop Inn. It was probably the best acting performance of Merle's career, allowing him to play a guarded, hurting character and to pick and sing—all right in his wheelhouse. His role the year before in a made-for-television *Huckleberry Finn*, starring Ron Howard as Huck and Antonio Fargas as Jim, was considered less successful. "Merle Haggard, the country singer, playing the Duke," John O'Connor wrote in the *New York Times*, "merely looks inconsolable without his guitar."

For Haggard, the hits in the seventies didn't just keep coming, as the saying goes; they came relentlessly. Between the time "Carolyn" topped the country charts in 1972 and the release of his final Capitol singles, "A Working Man Can't Get Nowhere Today," "The Running Kind," and "The Way It Was in '51," in 1977 and '78, Haggard racked up a baker's dozen more #1's to go with the ten he already had, and there were other fantastic if less successful singles along the way. Some of these we've already noted: "It's Not Love (But It's Not Bad)," "The Roots of His Raising," "Everybody's Had the Blues," "Cherokee Maiden," "Always Wanting You."

There were so many. "It's All in the Movies" topped the country charts late in 1975, just as Outlaw Country was enjoying its breakout moment. Waylon's Outlaw manifesto, "Are You Sure Hank Done It This Way," had been #1 a couple weeks earlier. His and Willie's "Good Hearted Woman" did the same a few weeks later. Anticipating the sexy hum of Merle's Quiet Storm–impacted records to come, "Movies" floats by on lazy congas and loungy saxophone, rather than thumping along, and its gently swooning melody hints at fifties R&B balladry but in the contemporary vein of, say, Neil Sedaka. Or perhaps like a duo Merle told journalist Susan Scott he'd been enjoying lately, Loggins and Messina. "Disco-era easy listening," Deke Dickerson calls it, and with its lyrical promise of romantic constancy, "It's All in the Movies" could not have been less Outlaw. With its rejection of current Outlaw musical trends, it could not have been more Outlaw.

In 1972 Haggard had a #1 with "Grandma Harp," a short-and-very-sweet ode to his mama's mama. The next year he had "I Wonder If They Ever Think of Me," a prison ballad that, in a topical twist sprung on listeners in the bridge, was actually about a "rotten prison camp in Vietnam." The line where the prisoner imagines his folks wondering if he's "still proud to be a part of Uncle Sam," as if that would be what kept his parents awake nights, is patriotic pandering at its dumbest. But the line where the POW worries his parents might not even know he's alive will punch you in the gut. That #1 was followed by "The Emptiest Arms in the World," a honky-tonk throwback to his Bakersfield breakthroughs that climbed only to #3. Across half a decade, from 1971 to '76, Haggard charted fifteen singles, and "Emptiest Arms" was the only one that failed to top *Billboard*'s Hot Country Singles chart.

Haggard kept releasing good-to-great to not-so-great albums through the remainder of his Capitol tenure. Some of these, such as the reverent gospel set *Land of Many Churches*, remain gems of the country canon. The double album was cut live across half a year, during services at four different houses of worship: Big Creek Baptist Church in Millington, Tennessee, outside Memphis; the Garden Chapel, located within Merle's old digs at San Quentin prison; the Union Rescue Mission in Nashville; and the Assembly of God Tabernacle in Keyes, California. Merle is backed across the board, one album side per church, by stripped-down Strangers lineups and joined on a couple of sides by Mother Maybelle Carter and her daughters Anita and Helen—the Carter Family. On side one he makes a point of characterizing the project not as another Merle Haggard concert album but as his third tribute project. "In the past, I've done a couple of tribute albums," he tells the Big Creek attendants. "And this is sort of a tribute to an old friend of mine who is truly number one. Of course, I'm speaking of our Lord, Jesus Christ." That's as close as Merle comes to evangelizing; he shares no personal testimony. But he does keep coming back to one big reason why these hymns and other gospel numbers matter to him. "My mother has told me many times with tears in her eyes that this was my daddy's favorite song," he says before crooning Albert E. Brumley's "If We Never Meet Again." Later, Merle tells those gathered at the Nashville Union Rescue Mission that DJ Ralph Emery refers to him as a "no-stall-o-gist." Merle figures that's about right, adding that one of his most precious memories was his dad singing "On the Jericho Road."

The other standout album in the post-Muskogee years was *Merle Haggard Presents His 30th Album*, from 1974. The album finds Merle doing nearly all his Merle things with the strongest batch of originals since *Someday We'll Look Back*, just three years but seven albums earlier. In "Holding Things Together," the heart-wrenching lament of a struggling single father, Merle signs a birthday gift to his daughter "Love from Mama" so she won't know her mom's forgotten her again. In "Honky Tonk Night Time Man" he updates his Jimmie Rodgers mode for the kick-drum thumping Outlaw era, while on "The Old Man from the Mountain," Merle similarly tweaks his Maddoxes mode, too. He plays an "all uptight and tense" sawmill-working cuss who calls his wife to warn he's headed home, and she'd better get any and all "Joe the Grinders" and "Friendly Henrys" out of his bed and off the premises. Piano-and-fiddle ballad "Things Aren't Funny Anymore" is another suffering country-soul descendant of "Today I Started Loving You Again." There's a Bob Wills cover, "A King without a Queen," too, and a rare Haggard gospel original called "Don't Give Up on Me." There also are takes on two songs he'd make a point to come back to: "White Man Singin' the Blues" and "Seashores of Old Mexico." ("Seashores" was also recorded in 1974, along with "The Running Kind" and the title track "Love and Honor," by Kenny Seratt, on an album Merle produced.)

Merle Haggard Presents His 30th Album is one of the Haggard catalogue's most underrated albums, but its title, inflected with exhaustion, predicted the future. As a rule of thumb, Merle's albums were consistently less focused and strong during these years, the very models of "hits plus filler," the tired Nashville assembly-line approach his earlier albums had begun to avoid. *Keep Movin' On*, for instance, produced a trio of impressive chart-toppers in 1975: his love letter to Dolly, "Always Loving You"; the Parton-penned "Kentucky Gambler" (its narrator wants rid of his blue-collar life but winds up losing his shirt); and the theme song for the Claude Akins–starring television series *Movin' On*, about two small business owner-operators. Merle wrote that one on commission, assigned to spell out the show's eighteen-wheeling premise: "The white line is the lifeline to a nation. And men like Will and Sonny make it move!" But it was songs of love and commitment, such as the lovely "Life's Like Poetry," that he was writing most often in these years, sometimes in unexpected ways. On the steadfast rock and roll of "A Man's Got to Give Up a Lot," Merle complains, again, about the liberty he has to sacrifice in order to preserve domestic tranquility. But stepping out of character, he then advises men to make the sacrifice, to see things through a woman's eyes and "go ahead and give up some ground." That makes for five unforgettable Haggard tracks on *Keep Movin' On*. But the rest of the album has a half-dozen more dreary cuts still to go and barely registers.

More and more, his albums were like that, fewer highs and more lows. You want the hits on *Let Me Tell You about a Song, It's Not Love (But It's Not Bad), If We Make It through December, Keep Movin' On, It's All in the Movies, The Roots of My Raising, A Working Man Can't Get Nowhere Today*, and *The Way It Was in '51*, and you probably want another track or two from each of those titles as well. Then again, on *My Love Affair with Trains*, with the low-grade *Schoolhouse Rock* flag-waver "Here Comes the Freedom Train," you may not even want the hit.

Still, the next keeper album track was never far away. Merle was at his cynical best on "Love and Honor" (he's betting it never crossed her mind), from *If We Make It through December*. Haggard's take on Hank Williams's "Moanin' the Blues," on *A Working Man Can't Get Nowhere Today*, professes misery while enacting freedom's headlong rush like nothing he'd ever recorded: it swings *hard*. "Turning Off a Memory," from *Let Me Tell You about a Song*, was a memorable late-Capitol drinker. It was covered three years later by British folk-rock duo Richard and Linda Thompson, and the rock and country covers of Haggard tunes kept on like that as well. Earl Scruggs and friend Linda Ronstadt used "Silver Wings" to travel from Laurel Canyon to the Blue Ridge Mountains and back in '72, and Elvin Bishop ambled through a rickety "I Can't Hold Myself in Line" in '74. Emmylou Harris chose "The Bottle Let Me Down" for her first album; Lynyrd Skynyrd roared through "Honky Tonk Night Time Man" on their last ("Ever been to Bakersfield?" Ronnie Van Zandt asks at the kickoff); and Merle's own "Life's Like Poetry" became Lefty Frizzell's next-to-last charting single in 1975.

Frizzell died only a few months later. Merle's in memoriam, the lovely "Goodbye Lefty," is one of those old-school tribute songs composed more or less entirely of the honoree's most famous song titles: "I'd love to hear a jukebox play…," Merle begins with head bowed. Then he counts off Lefty's greatest hits, all while recycling and recombining Lefty's melodies, licks, and phrasing, love-struck still.

Merle left Capitol, after twelve years with the label, in 1976, and signed with MCA (née Decca) Records. A prime motivation for the switch was that Ken Nelson, who'd nearly always given him his head in the studio, was nearing retirement. According to Haggard chronicler Dave Samuelson, Merle feared a new Capitol-appointed producer would translate to less artistic freedom. Ironic, then, or maybe just all too apt, that Merle's final new recording for the label wound up being "Here Comes the Freedom Train," cut April Fool's Day 1976. An insipid "political" novelty, "Freedom Train," even with its bicentennial bump, couldn't manage any better on the country charts than #10. That made it Merle's weakest performing chart single since his first for the label, "I'm Gonna Break Every Heart I Can," all the way back in 1965.

In the two years following his departure, Capitol released two more "new" Haggard albums, with the singer's input. *A Working Man Can't Get Nowhere Today,* released in '77, comprises previously unreleased material cut as far back as 1972, including "The Running Kind" and "I'm a White Boy." *The Way It Was in '51,* released the next year, is a half Hank Williams, half Lefty Frizzell tribute collection; it includes Merle's recently cut title track (at midcentury "Hank 'n' Lefty crowded every jukebox") but is otherwise filled with previously released sides, including a version of Hank's "I Saw the Light" from *Land of Many Churches* and his career-first Lefty cover, "Mom and Dad's Waltz," cut in 1967. Standouts "Moanin' the Blues" and "Goodbye Lefty" appear on both albums.

In 1977 Merle and his former label also put together the double album *Songs I'll Always Sing,* a summary of his Capitol years. It was meant to be more than another greatest-hits package, though. Like *Decade,* the Neil Young set it beat to stores by a few months, and like *Chronicle,* the Creedence Clearwater Revival collection from a year earlier, *Songs* distills an aesthetic while demonstrating its expansiveness. The Merle Haggard of *Songs I'll Always Sing* isn't merely a country hitmaker: nonsingle album tracks, such as "Love and Honor" and "Honky Tonk Night Time Man," take up a fourth of the available slots. Its version of Merle can't be reduced to labels like Poet of the Common Man, either. Seven of the album's twenty tracks are brokenhearted ballads, poetic for sure but "common" only because of who is singing them. The "conservative" "Okie from Muskogee" makes the cut, of course, but so does the "liberal" "Uncle Lem." The nationalist "Fightin' Side of Me" is instantly complicated by the humanist "Sing Me Back Home" and the betrayed "Branded Man."

Despite its necessarily missing most of his finest work, *Songs I'll Always Sing* gained an almost immediate reputation for representing, as Fred Schruers advises in the 1979 *Rolling Stone Record Guide*, "the pick of Haggard's formidable output." "God damn it—," Robert Christgau writes in his "Consumer Guide" column, "I could put together *four* discs that would never go below A-." If anything, that understates the case: Capitol could easily have released a double-album sequel, *More Songs I'll Always Sing*, say, and even a *Songs I'll Always Sing, Volume 3*. Such theoretical collections would certainly have been less iconic, what with "Workin' Man Blues," "Okie," and "Mama Tried" already accounted for, but there wouldn't have been an appreciable drop in quality. Haggard had put together a Hall of Fame–worthy career even *without* the songs included on *Songs I'll Always Sing*.

As it turned out, the album title's pledge wasn't even true. At least half of the album's great songs would soon drop from Haggard's set lists, more or less permanently.

"If you were to want just one Haggard album, this would be the one," John Morthland wrote a few years later in his inestimable genre guide *The Best of Country Music*. "But you'd still be missing too much."

And there was still so much to come.

CHAPTER 23

HE TAKES A LOT OF PRIDE IN WHAT HE IS (HINT: HE'S A WHITE BOY)

In August 1971 Merle appeared on an episode of *The 5th Dimension Travelling Sunshine Show*. In a skit a member of the 5th Dimension delivers letters, one of which is intended for Merle Haggard. "Merle Haggard! Let *me* deliver *that*," another member of the group, Florence LaRue, swoons at the mention of the hunky star. Haggard then sings two numbers, "Someday We'll Look Back," his current single, and the proudly downscale "I've Done It All": he's hoboed, worn rummage-sale clothes, had holes in his shoes—and he's proud!

What? You were thinking Merle might take advantage of that setup—a beautiful Black woman expressing romantic desire for a white man—to pull "Irma Jackson" out of mothballs? Well, no, but Merle and Capitol did belatedly introduce Ms. Jackson to the world a few months later on 1972's *Let Me Tell You about a Song*. "Irma Jackson" was a song he'd written and recorded some time ago, Merle explained deep on the album's second side, but hadn't released.

"Possibly because the time wasn't right. But I feel it's right now. And the song is purely fiction, created solely from my imagination. It's just a love story of two people of two different races and a situation that their families and society wouldn't accept." Then he makes that claim about "Irma" being perhaps his favorite composition. Years later, Merle told Deke Dickerson that no one ever requested "Irma" at shows, surmising that the lack of interest was because of his *Let Me Tell You* admission that the song "really wasn't anything that happened to me." Maybe, but I lean toward a simpler explanation: fans tend not to request songs they've never heard.

Note, though, that Merle didn't attribute the lack of requests to the song's subject matter. "The real problem with country's racial politics during the sixties was that they pretended not to exist," writes Craig Werner in *A Change Is Gonna Come: Music, Race and the Soul of America*. "Blacks weren't attacked, they simply weren't anywhere to be seen," a neglect that's largely persisted into the twenty-first century. The music of Merle Haggard is a notable exception. Across the decades, he cut at least ten tracks that deal explicitly with race. Not that many, to be sure, but at least 1,000 percent more than every one of his contemporaries and every one of his musical descendants. Merle sang about race all through his Capitol years. Before "Irma," he'd cut "Go Home," a Tommy Collins song about a white man's friends terrorizing his Mexican bride to go back where she came from, and in 1976 the Cindy Walker–penned "Cherokee Maiden," where Merle pines for a Native American woman he calls his "sweet little chickadee," became his last #1 of the decade. In between those came "Brown-Skinned Gal" on the Wills tribute, and in '74 his own "Seashores of Old Mexico," in which a "young senorita" falls for Merle's "lingo" (rhymes with "gringo"). It wasn't all interracial romance, either. "Uncle Lem," for example, a Glenn Martin song Merle cut in 1973, features a man whose "mom was bought and sold" and had himself been "born a slave." At song's end, this "uncle" shames white elites with his forgiveness and generosity by leaving to them what little he has in his will.

Merle also wrote and recorded two songs in these years in which he goes out of his way to play the whiteness card. In 1974's "White Man Singin' the Blues," Merle uses a Black man to establish an authenticity claim for himself, telling us he feels validated to learn a Black man appreciates his music: "Old Joe said I was a soul brother from the things I'd been singing about." And in "I'm a White Boy," from 1977, he compiles a checklist of what makes him white in the first place. His father wasn't named "Willie Woodrow," for one thing; he "wasn't born and raised in no ghetto," either. "I ain't black and I ain't yellow," he attests. Then, in case you'd missed his point, he shouts it loud: "I'm proud! And white! And I got a song to sing!" He means he's got a song to sing, *too*. "I'm a White Boy" is an aggrieved-feeling white reply to James Brown's "Say It Loud—I'm Black and I'm Proud," a call-and-response rendered all the more conspicuous by the country-funkiest rhythm track of Merle's career.

"Okie from Muskogee" had been a kind of answer to Brown's record too. Okie, that Dust Bowl–days insult, was, after all, nothing but a time- and region-specific synonym for "white trash." Merle's song takes back the slur, asserting a contemporary pride in his audience's historical shame. Other stars followed Merle's example. Loretta Lynn declared she was proud to be a "Coal Miner's Daughter." Dolly Parton sang of a childhood "Coat of Many Colors" her mother had sewn from rags; her friends giggled and snickered but she "wore it so proudly." Merle had been called "Okie" all his life: *You could tell by the tone of their voices if it was the same as the N-word or not.* Now, his poverty behind him, it was easier to embrace the aspersion. Now he was proud of it.

The historian Peter La Chapelle notes a Depression-era sign in the lobby of at least one Bakersfield movie house: "Negroes and Okies Upstairs." A telling equation, and one that would have struck those southwestern newcomers hard. Back home, the privileges of whiteness had been nearly all Okies had going for them. You may have been living bottom of the barrel, cropping on the shares in a tumble-down shack, with your kids hungry, the store saying no credit, and Christmas coming. But, as Lillian Smith allegorizes the bargain made by the South's poor whites, at least you knew you were "a sight better than the black man....When you don't have meat to eat and milk for the young'uns, you can eat Jim Crow." Nixon had updated the bargain for the members of his Silent Majority, downplaying economic concerns while saluting, as historian Jefferson Cowie nimbly summarizes it, "their moral backbone, patriotic rectitude, whiteness, and machismo." There was potential cross-racial unity in shared poverty: as Merle sings in "White Man Singin' the Blues," he and Old Joe were from "the same side of the railroad track where people have nothing to lose"—except, of course, that "the same side" didn't mean "the same." Poor whites did have at least *one* thing to lose.

The Okies had a great deal to lose by the sixties and seventies. They'd worked hard, been assimilated—*become* "white," like the Irish and Italians before them—only to find their economic status in jeopardy. Haggard's white, blue-collar audience in the seventies faced material threats, via stagnant wages, inflation, and rising unemployment: "If We Make It through December" reflected the times, and a mood. The group felt political threats, too, resulting from newly empowered minorities whose gains were perceived by too many white working folks simply as loss of power for themselves. When white Americans had presumed that only they would see the benefits, for instance, they widely supported proposals for a national job guarantee and a federally funded minimum standard of living. But, as Heather C. McGhee notes, when the gains of the civil rights movement meant whites would have to share those nice things, white support for such ideas "nose-dived from around 70 to 35 percent from 1960 to 1964." Pushing from the other direction, there were psychological wounds, too, inflicted by a mainstream middle-class culture that continued to look down on white working folk, southerners and onetime southerners in particular, as racist and sexist and stupid by definition, no matter their advances and hard work. Trash was supposed to be Other People. But…*everybody'd been treating us like trash.*

Trash, white trash, poor white trash…these slurs need unpacking. Nowadays, "trash" is understood mostly in economic and aesthetic terms. It's shorthand for tacky, cheaply made consumer goods and for the people who lack the ambition, work ethic, and minimum intelligence to resist them. Such condescending snobbery might apply to anyone, but "poor *white* trash" makes a racist and classist accusation. Self-identified "native" Californians saw Okies like the Haggards as dirty, dumb, and dangerous breeders living so low-down they'd betrayed their race: they might as well have been Black and, therefore, deserved to be thrown away.

That line in "Workin' Man Blues" where Merle boasted he'd never been on welfare is easily read as a not-so-coded attack on poor Black Americans who did receive public assistance and, in stereotype, preferred it to getting a job. But Haggard's pride in keeping his nose close to the grindstone was also a self-defense, reinforcing his whiteness while reverse-engineering a justification for privilege. White people, *real* white people, the song suggests, work whether they would prefer to or not, and they do so without the privileged middle-class expectation that it will provide personal fulfillment in excess of cash payment. Merle in *Look*, 1968: "If you like your job, you're not doing it right."

Or, as Merle attests in "I'm a White Boy": "If you want to get ahead ya gotta hump 'n git it!" A few lines later, he slathers his voice with over-the-top twang and brays:

I'm a blue-eyed 'billy, kinda frail and ruddy,
So I'll have to work to be somebody…
I don't want no handout livin'…
I'm proud! And white!

Merle affects a cantankerous rural accent—he's country as all get out, dadburn it—and Roy Nichols and Bobby Wayne make sure to play their acoustics extry twangy: Hag and the Strangers are performing in hickface here, something akin to what Nadine Hubbs has termed "Jed-face," to underscore the song's title and to contrast it with who Merle's not. Jesse Jackson may have been encouraging underprivileged Black children in these years to proudly declare, "I am—Somebody!" Because he's a white boy, Merle reckons, he can only work if he wants to say the same.

Merle and the Strangers cut "I'm a White Boy" in May 1972, and it was included five years later as the closing track to *A Working Man Can't Get Nowhere Today*. "The title song is a blues," notes critic John Morthland, "as is most of the rest of the album. Appropriately, then, [the album] also includes 'I'm a White Boy,' in which Hag fights his racial confusion to a draw." I'm not sure about the draw part, but Merle's confusion abounds.

Deke Dickerson notes in his Bear Family liner notes that "I'm a White Boy" had actually been released as an early-summer single all the way back in 1972 but that it didn't so much as crack the *Billboard* Hot Country Singles chart. Such a complete commercial failure is remarkable, in part because the song is as catchy as any Merle had cut and, even more so, because at that point in his career Merle's releases didn't just make the charts; they routinely topped them. Haggard's "White Boy" single had been preceded by three straight #1's and would be succeeded by sixteen consecutive top-ten singles, including a dozen more chart-toppers. Dickerson: "Perhaps the title left the Capitol publicity department, or the record buying public, a little cold, but…[it] sold few copies and is rare to find today." The label's wariness of the song's racial theme—the backlash it might have received (or was it the possible enthusiasm it might have generated?)—does seem the likely explanation. But it was an odd move by the label, as well. If Capitol was looking to avoid controversy, why not nix the single altogether, the way they had convinced Merle to do with "Irma Jackson"? On the other hand, if "I'm a White Boy" was issued as a single because the label didn't want again to refuse Haggard, now a bigger star than ever, then releasing his latest record while notably failing to promote it does not seem like a good plan.

Perhaps it was Haggard himself who effectively pulled the plug? It had been only weeks earlier, after all, on March 21, when he'd received the letter containing his full and unconditional pardon from California governor Ronald Reagan. "I was no longer ex-convict Merle Haggard," he recalled of the moment in *House of Memories*. "I was Citizen Haggard. I had outlived my past." Then again, Merle turned to "I'm a White Boy" once more, three decades later, during sessions for *Chicago Wind*. That time, though, the song not only wasn't released as a single; it didn't even make the album.

Like "Okie" before it, "I'm a White Boy" may have been a satire gone wrong. Merle's play-acted hickface accent—he sounds like Ernest T. Bass, or maybe a *Hee Haw* extra—is plausibly poking fun at poor rural whites. He'll need "to hump 'n git it" to make it and avers he "don't want no part of no handout living"—but only after having already admitted he's on the prowl for a rich wife.

But even if the song was conceived as a joke, its punchlines don't land. And even if it may have meant to gently mock whites, it still reinforces whiteness. Haggard's white boy, after all, insists he likes "guitar...and fiddle" because "*that*'s the kind of soul," as opposed to soul music, that "it takes to light my flame." Drawing such allegedly rigid distinctions between Black and white musical tastes was one way, Charles Hughes notes, that "country musicians played a crucial role in structuring the larger perceived difference between black and white in the post–civil rights United States." Underline all of this with the not-at-all trivial detail that the song was performed by the Hag, and "I'm a White Boy" perpetuates the racist notion that country music is Whites Only.

The most interesting Merle Haggard album in his final years at Capitol is 1974's *I Love Dixie Blues...So I Recorded Live in New Orleans*. Like prior concert releases, the album climaxes with "Okie from Muskogee," the fourth time he'd released it in five years. Merle and his fans seized every opportunity to shout their pride to the world, or at least to themselves.

But "pride" is a tenuous state in Haggard's music. He worried it in his songs repeatedly through the years: "You always find a way to hurt my pride" and "I'd like to...be proud of who I am" and "I got to keep my reputation, I got to keep my pride." The word nears twenty-five more appearances in his lyrics and joins even more references to one shameful scar or another—that is, to the absence of pride or, as Hubbs calls it, by way of sociologists Richard Sennett and Jonathan Cobb, dignity. That is a lot of going on about pride.

Just as we can say that a person who makes a fetish of roots is a person who feels uprooted, and the fella who makes a big point of letting everyone know he doesn't give a shit what people think is a fella who gives a pretty big shit, we can add this rule of thumb: the man who won't stop talking about how he's proud to be this, takes a lot of pride in that, is either a man deeply ashamed of something or a man convinced that a lot of others believe he has nothing to be proud of. This doesn't mean he's lying to himself. But it's a precarious pride, perpetually identifying attacks on itself, some of which are real, and it's often a pride based less on what one's done than on what one couldn't help but be. Some of what Merle couldn't help but be was white and working-class, at a time and a place where the former was prized while the latter was paid only lip service, and that only intermittently. "I'm proud and white," Merle kept declaring in "I'm a White Boy." He was proud to be an Okie, too, and his audience boisterously sang along, in part because, even in our enlightened twenty-first century, the white southern working class is still routinely looked down on within ostensibly polite, middle-class society.

America's legacy of race and class looms over every note of Haggard's *I Love Dixie Blues*, though essential details of that history go mostly unspoken—frustratingly so, as Merle was uncharacteristically loquacious at the concert. Before singing a note, he explains that the show will be dedicated to "the music that originated in New Orleans over a half a century earlier," that he's especially interested in the origins of American music, and adds that "who knows, maybe it got started in the cotton fields of the south." Here he means the blues, of course. But because he's augmented the Strangers this evening with the Dixieland Express, a white horn trio, it's clear he also intends "Dixie Blues" to take in jazz, as well—specifically, hot jazz, the syncopated, improvisational style that emerged from Black New Orleans in the twenties but that by the seventies was better known by the nostalgic name of Dixieland.

Haggard loads the term "Dixie Blues" with at least one more meaning. When Merle sings "Big Bad Bill (Is Sweet William Now)" and "I Ain't Got

Nobody (And Nobody Cares for Me)," he introduces them as having been recorded "by a fella by the name of Emmett Miller." Not many people remember him, he admits. But when he explains that Miller inspired Hank Williams, Jimmie Rodgers, and Bob Wills (who'd introduced Merle to Miller's music a few years prior), the crowd cheers. What he doesn't explain is that Miller performed in blackface, a sin of omission on Merle's part that's a cousin once-removed of country music's neglect of race generally.

"What's better than blues?" he asks, then plays a lilting one of his own. Haggard's live "Everybody's Had the Blues," a country chart-topper in late summer 1973, pinpoints precisely that early twentieth-century intersection between jazz, big-city pop ("Love and hate, want and wait, till misery fills your mind," he sings in the Tin Pan Alley–ish bridge), what Merle later refers to as "the Negro blues," and go ahead and toss country in there, too. To put it another way, "Everybody's Had the Blues" is a song you could easily imagine Emmett Miller singing the hell out of because it fits so neatly into the tradition that preceded, and to varying degrees shaped, all those other American styles: minstrelsy.

America's original popular music, minstrelsy began in the early nineteenth century when white people began to mimic, inaccurately and stereotypically and with faces covered in burnt cork, the dance and music of Black people. Appreciative audiences—mostly working-class whites who competed against free Blacks in the urban labor markets of the North—used these mocking performances to reinforce their sense of relative superiority. Yet even while dehumanizing Blacks, minstrelsy performed humanizing labor as well, presenting "darkies" who got the blues (just like white people!) and who had a culture of improvisational resilience that Americans of all colors and classes have been using ever since. If Merle was looking for the origins of American music, then Miller isn't a half-bad place to *begin* the search—and I enter it as another credit to the Haggard legacy that he did: even his deeply problematic "I'm a White Boy" names the elephant in the room of country music rather than second the disingenuous "color blind" foolishness of his peers. If only he'd pursued matters much further. A celebration of the blues that showcases a blackface minstrel instead of actual Black people is nothing to be proud of.

I Love Dixie Blues was actually two albums, though only one of them was ever released. Merle had finished a new themed studio album called *I Love Dixie Blues*—test pressings were done, the cover art was set—when he called an audible and decided to rerecord some of that material live in New Orleans. Most of the abruptly shelved studio sides—a hot, bawdy "Stingeree"; Merle's own "Hag's Dixie Blues #2"; a number he titled "Combine Blues" because, presumably, it combines verses from W. C. Handy's "St. Louis Blues" with verses from Jimmie Rodgers's fourth blue yodel; and a few other tunes—would be dribbled out one and two at a time over the next few years on Haggard's remaining Capitol albums. Three of those studio sides, though—the pair of songs he introduced as Miller's and a version of "Lovesick Blues" he tells the crowd he learned from Hank Williams before copying Miller's version right down to the horns—wound up being replaced entirely by the live New Orleans versions.

It was another opportunity missed. If Merle had followed through with the studio version of *I Love Dixie Blues*, it would've been among his best albums, and perhaps even his most important. Still, the album he did release, *I Love Dixie Blues…So I Recorded Live in New Orleans*, is a thrilling document, loose and lively in a way Haggard rarely was, even at his finest. The addition of the Dixieland Express gives the songs drive and character without sounding quaint; the Strangers swing hard and free; and Merle, singing relaxed, is having a blast. Even the album's inevitable version of "Okie from Muskogee" has a bounding, playful quality his earlier versions lacked. But after all Merle's talk of minstrelsy, of "Dixie" and "Negro blues," the anthem manifests meanings that had always been its subtext. "Everybody sing one time," Merle coaxes his audience, and everybody does: *I'm proud to be an Okie…*Proud to be a worker, that is, not a moocher. A maker, not a taker. Proud to be white. Another prison, that. And one from which Merle too often did not attempt an escape.

CHAPTER 24

"A WORKING MAN CAN'T GET NOWHERE TODAY," 1977

T his is Merle "Workin' Man" Haggard at his working-his-ass-off best—all to a country funky groove right in line with records by Jerry Reed or Tony Joe White. In fact, the song posits Merle's ass as a kind of barometer of what all his labor has profited him, which, by his own estimation, ain't much. In the first verse, Merle gripes that "for years I've been bustin' my rear" to no account, save a growing pile of bills and an aching back, then elaborates on the theme in the chorus: "Today I'll work my fanny off—and leave it lay."

That's a joke, friend, though how funny you find it probably comes down to how much your own ass aches when you stare at your own stack of duns. If you feel like you're being pulled in a hundred directions and all of them down, if the only retirement community you can imagine for yourself is a cemetery, then this joke's for you. And it's nice to know a big star like Merle tries to do the right thing, just like you, and the right thing pays lousy for him, too. Merle sounds like a guy you could commiserate with over a couple of pitchers, especially when he shakes his head and bitches:

> I pay my income tax—and the government gives back
> What I got comin', but it ain't much

I pay my child support—'cause I'm a law-abidin' sort
And an easy touch

The album art makes the connection between artist and audience explicit. Merle's dressed in denim work clothes and schlepping a lunch pail with a hard hat cocked wearily on his head. He's playing a representative laborer and, as he's also waiting at a bus stop, he appears representatively hard put. It's a nice gesture on Merle's part, a touch of Carter-era, energy-crisis empathy to picture himself at a big-city bus stop when so many more of his fans than usual were doing the same. As always, though, this identification ran both ways for Merle. His entire life was built around catching the bus to work and pulling another shift on stage. No wonder that in the last chorus of "A Working Man Can't Get Nowhere," this working-class hero makes sure that "*today* I'll work my fanny off" becomes "*Tonight*." He's not just singing about the "Workin' Man Blues." As that earlier record's hammer clocks in here, too, it's clear he's got a chronic case.

CHAPTER 25

HIS COUNTRY GIRL WITH HOT PANTS ON

Merle Haggard and Leona Williams were married in October 1978, and "The Bull and the Beaver," a song Williams wrote to perform with Haggard, made the country chart before it was even Halloween. That doesn't mean the top-ten hit was like a musical wedding announcement—outtakes from the honeymoon is more like it. Ostensibly about two truckers arranging a hookup via citizen's band, its double entendres fly by like highline poles: her sleeper cab has a mirrored ceiling (perfect for the record's discotheque beat), and she goes by the name of "the Beaver," CB lingo for a, um, lady. His handle is "the Bull." Get it?

"The Bull and the Beaver" is by a wide margin the biggest hit Leona Williams ever had, which is really too bad. Throughout a career that was already fifteen years long before she met Merle, Williams proved an evocative singer as well as a successful songwriter and musician, an important overlooked figure from a time when country radio began its long, slow transition from a male-dominated format to a genre led, for a moment, by women.

Leona Helton was born in the northern Ozarks town of Vienna, Missouri, in 1943. The Heltons were a large musical family—Leona Belle was number nine of a dozen kids—but she distinguished herself as particularly talented and ambitious. At fifteen she convinced a radio station to give her a show if she signed up the necessary sponsors. Which she did, earning a weekly program, *Leona Sings*.

In 1959 she married and moved to St. Louis, studied for her beautician's license, and, a year later, had a son, but she was pushing toward music all the while, working as one half of a rhythm section for hire—her husband drummed; Leona slapped doghouse bass—for local acts and national up-and-comers passing through town. One of the latter was Loretta Lynn, who in 1966 tagged Leona to play bass in her first backing band, the Blue Kentuckians. "I used to have Leona Williams playing bass in my band and singing harmony," Lynn observes in her 1976 autobiography, *Coal Miner's Daughter*. "She's one of the best musicians in Nashville."

The Lynn gig didn't last even a year but led to things. For starters, Lynn included one of Leona's songs, "Get Whatcha Got and Go," on her chart-topping 1967 LP, *Don't Come Home a Drinkin' (With Lovin' on Your Mind)*. That exposure helped Leona get an Opry appearance, and she signed with Hickory Records in 1968. Results there were disappointing; a trio of basement-level chart entries dribbled over the next half decade. Williams's time at the label did produce, however, her indelible "Country Girl with Hot Pants On," a rousing what's-good-for-the-gander bit of not-quite-feminist rebellion. In addition to being a hip-cocking showcase for Williams's husky alto, "Hot Pants" documents sexy blue-collar femininity, circa 1971. From now on, Leona announces to her skirt-chasing better half, she's wearing embroidered short shorts—with tinted hose!—whether he likes it or not. Egged on by electric licks that whip about like a bunch of rubbernecking good old boys, she sounds confident he'll like it fine.

Early in 1974 Bonnie Owens requested a hiatus from the road and was replaced, briefly, by Louise Mandrell. Merle met a not-long-divorced Leona that September. He'd heard her on the radio, had liked her voice and filed away her name. Their mutual friend, Stranger guitarist Ronnie Reno, did the introductions while Haggard was recording in Nashville. Leona wound up, during a September session, providing backing vocals to "Where Have All the Hobos Gone?," later included on Haggard's *My Love Affair with Trains*. Merle was impressed with Williams from the start. He was smitten romantically ("I knew this wasn't just another 'girl singer' I could con into toeing the mark and warming the sheets" is how he describes his initial assessment of the situation in *Sing Me Back Home*) and wowed musically. "She had more talent…than any ten women I'd met," he writes. Quite a claim from a man only then surfacing from deep immersion in the hyper-talented charms of Dolly Parton.

Merle asked Leona to join him on the road as the show's harmony singer and featured vocalist. We can hear Leona to good effect in the latter role on her 1976 MCA album, *San Quentin's First Lady*. Cut live during a New Year's Day appearance at the prison (opening for Merle Haggard), *First Lady* comprises Leona's ten-song set backed by the Strangers and highlighted by Haggard songs, including one they wrote together, "Prisons Aren't Only for Men," and a brassy reading of "Workin' *Girl* Blues": "It's a big job gettin' by, *tryin' to be a wife!*" Her finale is "San Quentin," a number Merle wrote for the occasion. When she declares, "San Quentin prison, I learn to hate you more each visitin' day," her captive audience nearly whoops down the walls.

In the years running up to their marriage, Leona became a fixture of the Merle Haggard Show, while also experiencing a certain amount of hostility from Merle's audiences. They preferred Bonnie and viewed her, she felt, as a home wrecker. Never mind that Bonnie and Merle's romantic relationship was long over and that Bonnie famously stood as maid of honor at the Haggard-Williams nuptials. Rose Maddox sang "You Light Up My Life."

Williams also became during this time one of Merle's favorite cowriters. Except "After Loving You," however (a three-way cowrite with Reno from 1976's *It's All in the Movies*), none of their collaborations made it to vinyl until Merle moved on to MCA Records in early '77. He recorded a handful of Williams's solo compositions, too, notably a pair of chart-toppers from early in Merle's subsequent decade-long tenure at Epic: 1982's tellingly titled "You Take Me for Granted" and, from the following year and the very end of their time together, "Someday When Things Are Good." As in, "Someday, when things are good, I'm gonna leave you." Leona auditioned the song for Merle not long after filing for divorce.

Unwilling to forgo her ambitions in favor of her husband's, as Bonnie had, Leona continued to pursue a solo career. Merle seems to have alternated between supporting and undermining her efforts. For instance, on "I'm Gettin' High," a song Merle wrote for the B-side to "The Bull and the Beaver" single, Merle declares, "You don't have to roll me no reefer now," because he's plenty high on Leona's lovin', though not enough, apparently, to share the mic: she sings just two lines to his three verses. On the cover of a 1978 issue of *Country Music*, Merle did sport a Leona Williams t-shirt. He encouraged her to get her own band and hit the road, too, but he declined to perform with her in support of "The Bull and the Beaver," touring at the time with Bonnie behind him again, instead. (The couple did perform the number on an episode of *Hee Haw*, two years later.) In 1982 Merle got permission from Epic to team with Leona on a duet album for her label, Mercury. This was a move guaranteed to increase Leona's exposure but that had the additional effect of interrupting work on the solo LP she was just then in the process of completing. Mercury's excitement about landing a Haggard record led to Leona's album at first being delayed, then shelved altogether.

By the time *Heart to Heart* was released in summer 1983, Merle and Leona had been divorced for weeks, finishing their whirlwind decade of musical and romantic partnership. But, as the cliché goes, they sure did make beautiful music together while they lasted, and *Heart to Heart* tops the list. Though ostensibly a "duet" album, *Heart to Heart* sounds like a Merle Haggard record through and through, highlighting Merle and the band and, at times, downplaying his duet partner's contributions. Indeed, on some tracks Williams is allowed barely a supporting role—on the rollicking version of the Maddox Brothers & Rose–associated "Sally Let Your Bangs Hang Down," Leona sings exactly one line of lead vocal, while her fellow Strangers Roy, Don (on pennywhistle!), Norm, and Tiny are not only awarded significant solos, but also shout-outs. The country-pop standard "I'll Never Be Free" was originally a duet smash for Kay Starr and Tennessee Ernie Ford; here it is an exquisitely bluesy Merle Haggard special. Leona provides only way-in-the-back backup.

Given a chance, though, Leona more than holds her own on the title track and on "Don't Ever Let Your Love Sleep Alone," as well as on "Let's Pretend We're Not Married Tonight" and "Waltz across Texas," all worthy contributions to the country duet tradition. And on "It's Cold in California," a Freddy Powers song about former lovers who can't shake their exes even as they make their way back to separate worlds, Leona may actually upstage her ex, line for line and tear for gulped tear, recrimination for recrimination. She did it again in 2008. On the remarkable *Leona Williams Sings Merle*

Haggard, it's the singer at least as much as the songs, a couple of Hag hits she wrote included, that stands out.

The single off *Heart to Heart* was the doubly appropriate "We're Strangers Again," a pained, but blameless, farewell and the couple's final cowrite. It stiffed at radio, but I recommend it.

CHAPTER 26

HE'S ALWAYS ON A MOUNTAIN WHEN HE FALLS

By the latter half of the 1970s, Merle Haggard had come a very long way from Oildale and San Quentin. He'd placed forty-three singles on *Billboard*'s country charts, twenty-four of them #1's, and in 1970 he had won the industry's top prize, the Country Music Association's Entertainer of the Year. Even better, in 1972 he received a pardon from California governor Ronald Reagan: "Therefore, in view of indications...that the applicant is now a fully rehabilitated member of society..." Only a year later, he performed for President Nixon, and he appeared on the cover of *Time* a year after that. The Hag hadn't just made it. He'd made it to the top.

He ran. As the seventies wound to an end, Haggard was even more restless than usual. He felt overburdened by professional and personal obligations and hemmed in by expectations that he forever play a poet of the common man. After a long decade with Capitol, he signed with MCA, a move that meant he'd be recording in Nashville for the first extended period in his career. In 1976 he even moved to Nashville for a while, at the encouragement of then-girlfriend Leona Williams. "She loved Nashville. I hated it," Merle wrote in his autobiography just a few years later. "I love California. Leona hated it. She said it was too far from home. Hell, it was home."

"We had lots of arguments," Williams admitted to journalist Bob Allen. "He'd go back to Bonnie and then come back to me. I tried to get away from him, but when you really love somebody, you can't." In 1978 Merle and Bonnie were divorced, four years after she'd left the road and two after she'd first filed, and he married Leona.

The decision to sign with MCA came with great fanfare and ambition. A special twelve-page section of *Billboard* acknowledged the move and was dominated by ad-buy well-wishes from various promoters, bookers, labels, and publishing companies, from personal manager Fuzzy Owen, from Capitol Records and MCA, from the Custom Coach tour bus corporation, and Binion's Horseshoe Hotel and Casino in Las Vegas, and even "from your #1 touring band, the Strangers."

"In the next three or four years, I'd like to do what will someday be known as the cream of the crop as far as Merle Haggard is concerned," he told *Billboard*'s Todd Everett. "That's the goal. Everything else is secondary." A ridiculously high bar but also one that, in at least some respects, Merle's work for MCA would actually meet. It didn't look that way at first, though. "From about age 38 to 42 I was highly confused and depressed," Merle recalled to Bob Allen, citing a stretch that overlapped with his tenure at MCA. "I didn't have any desire. I couldn't make plans from one day to the next. I was so screwed up." In 1979, he announced, if mostly to himself, he was quitting the business entirely. "I thought, 'I'm sick of all this! I might as well retire and live off my song royalties.' " Merle headed back home and, for several months, lived mostly on a houseboat docked at Lake Shasta, near Redding, California. He "fished and did a lot of thinking," but felt trapped there too. "Male menopause," he later called it.

Merle struggled personally during his MCA years, and he fell off just a bit commercially as well. But country music was bigger than ever. The year 1978, for example, goes down as the commercial peak of the country-rockin' Outlaw movement. *I've Always Been Crazy*, by Waylon Jennings, which included another version of Merle's "The Bottle Let Me Down," became the first country album ever to ship gold, and duet album *Waylon & Willie*, behind the success of crossover single "Mammas, Don't Let Your Babies Grow Up to Be Cowboys," quickly went platinum.

What gets downplayed in most country histories, though, is that 1978 was just as notable for the sorts of pop-country typically portrayed as the Outlaws' mortal enemy. Kenny Rogers's *The Gambler* launched the process of turning the former First Edition singer into a superstar, while Dolly Parton's *Heartbreaker* was the most pure-pop effort she'd released to date. By 1980 both of these artists' singles would top the pop and country charts—Rogers with "Lady," a twinkling pillow-talk ballad written by Lionel Ritchie, and Parton with "9 to 5," a working-class workout perfect for dancefloors, exercise classes, and major motion pictures. All of these recordings anticipated the broadly popular country music moment dubbed Urban Cowboy, after the John Travolta film set amongst the Western wear and mechanical bulls of Gilley's Club, "the world's biggest honky tonk," in the Houston suburbs. The trend peaked a few years later around the time of Kenny and Dolly's "Islands in the Stream" and lured a host of new fans to the genre. Many of these converts came for the swooning strings and melodies of soft-shell crossover country but stayed for the hard-core stuff.

Not that it was always easy to tell the difference. Was George Jones's 1979 "He Stopped Loving Her Today"—its title playing tag team with "Today I Started Loving You Again"—a soft-shell hit, what with its soaring string section and angelic backing vocals, or was it an example of hard-core country at its hardest, thanks to its morbid story and Jones's twangy lead? Was Willie Nelson's 1978 pop smash *Stardust*, filled with Tin Pan Alley standards and produced by former-MG Booker T. Jones, a clear-as-day Urban Cowboy antecedent or the ballsiest Outlaw move of Nelson's career?

This is how it's always been in country music. Hard-core and soft-shell sounds compete: one style or the other may dominate at any given moment, but both are ever-present. Country radio during the long Urban Cowboy era was dominated by the countrypolitan likes of Crystal Gayle and Ronnie Milsap but also saw the emergence of tradition-minded stars like Reba McEntire and Ricky Skaggs as well as an innovative young star named Rosanne Cash, who included Merle's "You Don't Have Very Far to Go" on her breakthrough album in 1981. It saw the rise, too, of a pair of young country singers who made it a point going forward to carry torches for the Hag: George Strait, who covered Merle's "Our Paths May Never Cross" in 1983, and John Anderson, who duetted with him in 1982 on a version of the classic Lefty Frizzell hit "Long Black Veil." In '81 Johnny Paycheck went several steps further and released an entire Merle Haggard tribute album, *Mr. Hag Told My Story*, with Merle and the Strangers joining in. But old school and new weren't mutually exclusive, anyway. On 1981's

"Lefty," David Frizzell's tradition-minded but country-pollinated ode to carrying on his late brother's legacy, "Mighty Merle," as he is introduced, contributes one line: "But Dave, I had to learn it. You came by it naturally."

Haggard's MCA years, the waxing and waning of the Outlaw moment, and country's Urban Cowboy period were all overlapping sets, more or less. One takeaway is that when it came to choosing between hard-core or soft-shell sounds, Merle refused to choose.

Merle's first single for MCA, released in early 1977, was a country-soul-apolitan number written by Sonny Throckmorton and Glenn Martin, "If We're Not Back in Love by Monday." It became a #2 country hit, but Merle felt its melody was too close to his own "If We Make It through December" and quickly grew frustrated with it. "I'd start into 'Monday,'" he remembered in *House of Memories*, "and the band would mistake it for 'December' and play the wrong song."

Still, his first single at MCA foreshadowed more Urban Cowboy–styled records to come from Merle, a new country-pop sound for the Hag that only intensified across the next several years. The record's twin steels blended and bled until they could be mistaken for synthesizers. And its tune wasn't just reminiscent of any earlier hit; it was reminiscent of the biggest crossover success of his career. No wonder Throckmorton and Martin's country song transferred so easily to the R&B format, where inimitable soul singer Millie Jackson scored a slinky crossover hit with it that fall.

Merle's new hit was proto–Urban Cowboy in another, even more telling way: its point of view felt more bourgeois than blue collar. In Merle's version, the song is narrated by a man who suggests to his wife that a spur-of-the-moment flight to Florida for the weekend, "the way we used to do," might be just the thing to revive their dying marriage. "If we're not back in love by Monday, we can go our sep'rate ways," Merle croons, not sounding particularly optimistic. The song leaves it undecided if the cure takes or not, or if they even board the plane, but the couple apparently does have enough free time and disposable income to invest in such a romantic Hail Mary.

That same year Merle's second MCA single, also a #2 hit, was a modern-sounding bit of Music Row southern rock called "Ramblin' Fever." An anxious anthem to aimlessness, its lyric was powered by pull quotes: "My hat don't hang on the same nail too long." "If someone said I ever gave a damn, they damn sure told you wrong." "I wanna die along the highway and rot away like some ol' highline pole." And "Ain't no woman gonna tie me down." "I wrote it at Leona Williams' house in the seventies there one afternoon," Haggard remembers in the 1987 concert video *Poet of the Common Man*. "I don't recall what in the hell caused me to write it."

"Ramblin' Fever" was Merle in chugging, twin-guitar Outlaw mode, deploying a team of Nashville pros to second Waylon's bruising and boastful "I'm a Ramblin' Man" from 1974 and to predict Willie's own great, aimless anthem (albeit a far more amiable and community-spirited one), "On the Road Again." "I caught that ramblin' fever long ago," Merle sings, "when I first heard that lonesome whistle blow"—a callback to his own songbook that claimed "Mama Tried" for Outlaw bedrock. Nailing down Merle's Original Outlaw bona fides even more securely, "Ramblin' Fever" climbed the charts in the summer of 1977 alongside a likeminded hit that evoked the same connection to the Haggard catalogue: Johnny Paycheck's "I'm the Only Hell My Mama Ever Raised." Paycheck's follow-up single was close kin to Haggard as well: "Take This Job and Shove It," written by David Allan Coe, talks about quitting the whole blue-collar mess. It's just a fantasy, though, sung from the point of view of a stiff who knows he has to keep punching the clock if he wants to eat. All of these songs feel like they could be additional verses for "Workin' Man Blues."

"Ramblin' Fever" seemed to promise plenty of strong new songs to come. Both the quantity and quality of original Haggard material had slowed considerably over his last Capitol releases, leading some to guess he was saving the good stuff for MCA. But there doesn't appear to have been much good stuff coming from Merle at the moment, or much new stuff at all. On his first MCA album, 1977's *Ramblin' Fever*, he had a hand in writing just two of ten tracks. On the other hand, at least all the covers on *Ramblin' Fever* spotlighted Haggard in familiar modes: the great vocal interpreter and humble admirer of musical heroes. "When My Blue Moon Turns to Gold Again," a C&W chestnut in the dreamy, sentimental vein of Stuart Hamblen's "My Mary," was probably best known as an early album track from Elvis Presley by the time Merle cut it. Hag's lope through the song, though, sounds more indebted to Cliffie Stone, the beloved Southern California personality who'd scored a western hit with the song not long after Merle's dad died. "The Last Letter," meanwhile, a major hit for crooner Rex Griffin the year Merle was born (and a minor one for Willie as recently as 1976), found Merle choosing to end his first MCA album on a suicide note:

a beat pulses wearily, razor-sharp telecasters flicker in and out of hearing, and "I will be gone when you read this last letter from me."

The rate of Hag originals only doubled the following year for his third MCA LP, *I'm Always on a Mountain When I Fall*. More worrisome was how few of his new songs came within shouting distance of his best. "It's Been a Great Afternoon," a horny hangover remedy propelled by disco high hat and what sounds like someone slapping hambone, came close. It was another #2 country hit.

"The Immigrant" comes close, too, and is straightforwardly political in a manner Merle had mostly left behind since his Muskogee Moment as well as a rare MCA return to explicitly proletarian themes. Cowritten with Stranger guitarist Dave Kirby, "The Immigrant" premiered on an album by Tejano country star Johnny Rodriguez the year before. Rodriguez, who counted Haggard as one of his biggest influences, sings the song as a plaint, borderline embittered and beautiful because of it. But Merle turns his own version into an unaccountably jaunty sing-along, and the arrangement's generic signifiers—Tex-Mex-ish horns and other sort-of-south-of-the-border instrumentation—trivialize its lyrics.

Haggard and Kirby's song is deadly serious. "The Immigrant" lays into an American agricultural system that exploits the labor of "illegal immigrants" and notes that it was rich gringos who stole "land from the Indian man way back when." The politics Merle espouses here are hardly left-leaning, of course, or even particularly progressive. On the one hand, there's no "These immigrants are stealing our jobs" here, no us versus them. On the other, the song fails to argue for a path to citizenship. Merle doesn't proclaim that there's power in a union (though with the recent passage of the California Labor Relations Act, some may have heard the song that way) or demand a living wage, either—perpetual blind spots in Haggard's working-class point of view. Then again, if Merle had cheered, "Viva la Mexico! The Mexican immigrant is helping America grow," as he does here, on a recording released just before he died in 2016 instead of the late seventies, he'd have been demonized as un-American on FOX News. And he'd have been demonized there again for urging border patrols to look the other way. Like Woody Guthrie's far superior "Deportee (Plane Wreck at Los Gatos)" before it, Haggard's "The Immigrant" embraces a multiracial, mutually dependent view of America. Like his own Guthrie-esque "Hungry Eyes," it's on the side of working folks—and against that other class of people who keep them below. The song's intent is so humane that it makes you wish Merle's selection of Spanish rhymes and immigrant motivations ("Take home dinero and buy new sombrero") weren't as impoverished as the immigrants he's singing about.

The best cut on *I'm Always on a Mountain When I Fall* is the eggshell-fragile title track and first single, written by Chuck Howard. Merle teeters through his lines, bemoaning the way insult is always being added to his injuries, "the way losing's come to be a way of life for me." "I hate to say I've given up," Merle whines with real feeling. But why do the hardest falls always come "just when I thought I'd finally made it"? As if scripted, "I'm Always on a Mountain When I Fall" was only another #2 hit.

Merle had five of those at MCA, and another five top tens. All of those almost-but-not-quite chart-toppers were at least partly the result of MCA's Nashville releases being promoted by the label's Los Angeles office, with its bias toward rock and pop acts on the coasts. His MCA singles also fell just short because Merle was so often competing against himself for airplay and sales. Three Capitol singles charted during Merle's first two years at MCA: Capitol's "The Way It Was in '51," for example, debuted on the charts the same week as MCA's "The Bull and the Beaver." In the fall of 1977, Capitol's "A Working Man Can't Get Nowhere Today" and MCA's "From Graceland to the Promised Land" shared chart space with a third Haggard single, "I Haven't Learned a Thing," a duet with Porter Wagoner on RCA. And if anything, the album bins were more crowded with new Merle product. In 1977 and 1978, seven Merle Haggard albums charted—four of them on his *old* label. With so many options for fans to choose from, it was small wonder that only his much-hyped MCA debut, *Ramblin' Fever*, climbed even as high as #5.

Merle did have one #1 single during his first four years with MCA, though it came on a recording released by Elektra. In 1980 he teamed with Clint Eastwood for a sing-along-and-order-another-pitcher novelty called "Bar Room Buddies" ("That's the best kind!") from the soundtrack to Eastwood's *Bronco Billy*. Though "Buddies" became Haggard's twenty-fifth #1, it was not one of his better records, or even a middling one. That wasn't Merle's fault. Eastwood "shouldn't sell his camera, I'll put it that way," Haggard told *Newsweek*. "I told him before we started, 'I hope you're a better singer than I am an actor,' but I believe I'm a better actor than he is a singer." That sounds harsh, but Merle was being generous. Eastwood recites, rather than sings, his lines, delivering them in the same clenched growl he used to portray Dirty Harry Callahan. By contrast, Merle sings effortlessly, winningly, even gliding up to a lovely falsetto yodel just to rub it in to Clint who the singer is here.

During the Urban Cowboy years, country music was showing up on the big screen like it rarely had before, Hag's included. In 1978, in the CB flick *Convoy*, assorted cops and sheriffs listen to "Okie from Muskogee" on the radio while plotting their next move against our outlaw hero, played by an eighteen-wheeling Kris Kristofferson. Two years later, in June 1980, *Urban Cowboy* hit theaters, just days before the premiere of *Bronco Billy*; a month after that, *Honeysuckle Rose*, starring Willie Nelson, hit the screens. In that film Nelson's guitarist Jody Payne leads the Family Band through a delightfully loud and scruffy "Workin' Man Blues."

Outlaw Blues, another country music–related film of the era, didn't include any of Haggard's music but did seem inspired by his bio: the film begins with Peter Fonda, who plays a country-singing convict, attending the prison concert of a major country star—just as Merle had once seen Johnny Cash perform at San Quentin. In another little-noticed coincidence, the movie also shares a key plot point with one of Elvis Presley's first films, *Jailhouse Rock*: the established C&W star steals the young con's song. Another coincidence: *Outlaw Blues* hit theaters on August 15, 1977, and Presley, just two years older than Merle, died the next day. The object lesson for Haggard couldn't have been clearer. Mass adulation breeds social isolation and is just another trap.

Within the month Merle penned a tribute to Presley called "From Graceland to the Promised Land." It isn't much of a song, lyrically anyway: "It's a long way from Memphis to that mansion in the sky, but he kept his faith in Jesus all along" and "Millions screamed to see him do his thing" illuminate nothing new about Presley's legacy or Haggard's fandom. Launched dramatically with a bit of "Also Sprach Zarathustra," the recording, on the other hand, is right on point for a tribute, ricocheting easily between an acoustic version of Merle's Bakersfield Sound and Presley's dynamic rhythms and crescendos.

An entire album, *My Farewell to Elvis*, was out by October, sandwiched tightly between *Ramblin' Fever* and *I'm Always on a Mountain*. But unlike the earlier Rodgers and Wills tributes, which Merle had prepped for months, the rushed Presley project was banged out in days and felt generic in a faux-fifties sort of way: the players included some of Presley's old Nashville Sound–era sidemen—the Jordanaires, drummer Buddy Harman—but not the King's modern collaborators and Haggard friends Glen Hardin and James Burton. Merle's vocals on ballads like "Are You Lonesome Tonight?" and "Love Me Tender," which couldn't possibly have been more in his wheelhouse, are unaccountably thin and high and oddly restrained. The album whiffs, as well, on all the ways Merle's Burton-led sessions were a direct source of Presley's seventies sound. And the obvious thematic parallels between the Haggard and Presley catalogues aren't taken advantage of, either. "Jailhouse Rock" allows Merle the chance to sing another prison number but with comic relief. "In the Ghetto" is a poor-side-of-town neighbor to Merle's "Mama Tried," but without the comparatively happy ending of a life sentence. Interesting connections, potentially. Unfortunately, it's me making them, not the performances on *Farewell to Elvis.*

After three dispiriting efforts in a row, Merle's fourth MCA album, 1979's *Serving 190 Proof,* was a revelation. An unprecedented intersection in the Haggard catalogue of introspective songwriting and musical experimentation, *Serving 190 Proof* can still startle all these years later with its forthright examinations of alcoholism and depression and its jaded takes on the musician's life.

It doesn't even sound like a Merle Haggard record. Its themes, jazzy solos, and spare thumping rhythms are Outlaw at its most idiosyncratic. But, cut and tinkered with across months, the album's pristine acoustic picking and tinkling electric pianos are slick and studio clean. The brooding opener, "Footlights," is kicked off by an electric piano quote of fellow proletarian poet Bill Withers's "Lean on Me," but Haggard is by no means offering listeners a helping hand. Sounding beat-down but resolute (though resolute about what isn't clear) and plumbing the depths and cragged textures of his range like never before, Merle is the one who sounds in need of a lifeline. "I live the kind of life most men only dream of," the country superstar begins, acknowledging his privilege. But he's over forty now and feeling suffocated by it all. He's sick of having to put on his "old inst-o-matic grin" and play the badass every night, weary of having "to kick the footlights out again," even on nights when that's the last thing he feels like doing. The inspiration for the song came to him, Merle's said, when, just as he was preparing to take the stage one evening, he was informed that Lefty Frizzell had died. The music bristles with energy, but feels like it's dragging him down, too, holding him back, and Merle's craggy baritone is a long, weary sigh of duty and resentment: "Tonight I'll kick the footlights out and walk away without a curtain call."

Many hard-core Haggard fans will go to bat for *190 Proof* as his best, and they might be right. The album also gets cited as Merle's most personal, and there's no doubt that's true. Lines like "I'm 41 today, still going on 22," from "Red Bandana," or "I'll hide my age and make the stage," from "Footlights," are among the reasons why Haggard is so widely perceived not merely to write from, but about, his personal experiences, and from here on out Merle would write far more often from explicitly autobiographical points of view. Though lest we think that clarifies matters, consider that when "old Hag," as the song says, visits a "psychoed-out psychologist" in "Heaven Was a Drink of Wine," he's doing it in a song written by Sanger Shafer.

All through the album Haggard feels like he's just barely hanging on to his right mind. He's not just alone; he's lonely—and insistent that nothing can change on that score if he wants to stay free. To the hypnotically eddying melody of "Driftwood," he tells a lover goodbye: "Like the colors of the rainbow we blended well together," he tells her, "for a while." Then the current sweeps him away. In "I Can't Get Away," over a jazz-funk rhythm track you'd swear was yanked from Steely Dan's *Aja*, he confesses that he's going to keep trying to run, not simply from stardom or marriage or other responsibilities but from life itself—a terrifying, death wish of an admission, considering the alternative. "I Can't Get Away" is a country-jazz existential crisis, where "life" and "freedom" are perceived as mutually exclusive: "Life won't let us be free." Merle makes a run for it anyway.

With an allusion to Kris Kristofferson's most famous song ("You're never gonna be no Bobbie McGee, but you're trying to"), "Red Bandana" is frequently assumed to be inspired by tensions between Merle and new wife Leona Williams. But the song's "after thirty years and knowing me the way you do" sounds more like Merle is singing about new ex-wife Bonnie Owens. Maybe the song is about any romantic partner who dares domesticate him. "I wonder why you grew up, and why I never will?" Merle asks, getting down to the real issue. When he chases that honest assessment with "I can't change and live the way you want me to," though, his "can't" feels more and more like a "won't." Leona and Bonnie harmonize behind him.

"My Own Kind of Hat" is a remarkable assertion of idiosyncratic individualism, though notably it proclaims its individualism (not to be confused with individuality) in the same proud and not-a-little-adversarial terms used by millions of people threatened by diversity. There are two kinds of mothers, two kinds of cherries and of fairies, and so on, Merle sneers over brittle fiddle. Or so he's been told, he adds with mock innocence. There's just the one of Merle.

The album's closer, "Roses in Winter," has a melody that evokes the darkness of "Shelly's Winter Love" and the brightness of "The Day the Rains Came," and Merle's lyrics find the wisdom to split the difference. "We'll have roses in winter," he croons with great patience and greater need. "We'll have good times with the bad." That may not be the kind of life most men dream of, but for sure it's the most any of us are going to get.

Serving 190 Proof wasn't a big commercial success. It barely cracked the top 20 on *Billboard*'s Country Albums chart, and its singles, "Red Bandana" and "My Own Kind of Hat," both stalled at #4. It was well received critically, though, praised even in publications that deigned to cover country music only sporadically. "Merle Haggard is writing and singing as if these songs meant more to him than any he's done in years," John Morthland observed in *Rolling Stone*, while in the *Village Voice*, rock critic Robert Christgau awarded Merle's "fourth and best album for MCA" a stingy B+. "Forty and feeling it," the Hag had "written a batch of wise songs," Christgau concluded, "autumnal" in their "impeccable simplicity and sensitivity."

Well before he knew how *Serving 190 Proof* would be received—in fact, even before the album was released—Merle determined he was done with the music biz. He stared in the mirror, saw gray hairs and new wrinkles and a retreating hairline (the MCA years are when Merle committed to facial hair and hats), and said to hell with it: to hell with having to make a new album every other season; to hell with meet and greets and autographs and working your publishing; to hell with interviews and TV appearances and more interviews; to hell most of all with the Sisyphean toil of what he later described to writer Alanna Nash as "a twenty-year bus ride." He moved back to California, got himself a houseboat on Lake Shasta, and told people he was done. He may even have meant it. Notably, what had him looking for the exit was not "music but business," as Peter Guralnick summarized Merle's feelings in a 1980 cover profile for *Country Music*.

"Not song writing but self-promotion, not playing the guitar, his first and perhaps still his most consuming ambition, but selling himself as a product."

His ambivalence toward stardom and its many extra-musical bottom lines had been building for years. Merle admitted to country beat reporter Jack Hurst that he'd started dreaming of "semi-retirement" as far back as 1974 or '75. In the fall of 1976 Haggard briefly went missing, failing to make consecutive dates in Denver and Salt Lake City, then canceling a ten-day run in Reno. The Associated Press reported that "concern over [the singer's] whereabouts intensified when authorities received an anonymous telephone call saying Haggard's body could be found in a ditch in a Nevada gully." Fuzzy Owen vouched for his safety: "He's somewhere between Arizona and Los Angeles, resting up from too much stress and pressure on the road....He's with his bus driver and they're just taking a little vacation."

In early 1978 Merle wrestled again with conflicting emotions in the pages of the *Minneapolis Star*: "I could retire and go fishin'. But I have a moral obligation to do this for the people in my organization and for the people who want to see me. I just try to live up to my personal standards and my obligations." In January 1979, just a couple of weeks after cutting all but one of the tracks for *Serving 190 Proof*, Merle and the Strangers played a gig in Utah. Reviewing the show for the *Salt Lake City Tribune*, journalist Terry Orne wrote:

> Two years ago Merle Haggard was scheduled to play Salt Lake City and did not show up. One year ago Haggard did show, gave a lackluster performance, leaving many to believe he had better take a long rest and recoup from the life of one-nighters. Friday night...he played one song with the Strangers, promptly announced he was ill, "not drunk," and going back to bed.

Back in Nashville the next month, he cut a final *190 Proof* track, an in-the-wee-hours Red Lane song called "I Must Have Done Something Bad." The song doesn't say what that something was, exactly, but Merle knows he's been paying for it as far back as he can remember: "And the pain grows each day, ten times ten times ten," he sings, wincing. Then he took off for his California houseboat and a long rest.

As Merle told and retold the story through the decades, his decision to stay away lasted about six months. As he insisted on keeping the Strangers and other support staff on payroll for the duration, it turned out to be a particularly pricey vacation. And he couldn't get away in any case. "There ended up being about 50 people on my boat every day. I found that I couldn't escape," he told Bob Allen. "So I knocked on the door of my personal prison—the music business—and asked to be let back in." In August he played a few dates on the East Coast. By Labor Day, the never-ending bus ride was back in business.

"One day I thought, 'What if someone you really loved and admired decided to quit?'" Merle said, recalling his thinking a couple years later to Allen. "'What if Bob Wills had decided to go fishin' when he was about forty? Look what you would have missed!'"

Merle had reprised "From Graceland to the Promised Land," a top-five hit, for *Nashville Remembers Elvis on His Birthday*, a nationally televised tribute in January 1978, but as had long been his way, Haggard paid respects to ancestors and relatives all through his MCA years. The same month as the Elvis special, Merle honored hero Bob Wills on television, as well, when he fronted a lineup of former Texas Playboys on an NBC special, *50 Years of Country Gold*, and tore through western-swing classics "Roly Poly," "Ida Red," and "San Antonio Rose."

Another hero often on Merle's mind in these years was Ernest Tubb. In 1977 Merle and the Strangers had done some recording with that old country Crosby. Those sessions never saw the light of day. But he did join Tubb, Charlie Daniels, Chet Atkins, and others for a version of "Walking the Floor over You" that became a minor hit right around the time Merle returned from his hiatus. And in December, when he revisited Nashville to begin work on a new album, he cut a trio of the Texas Troubadour's honky-tonk hits from the early 1940s: "Take Me Back and Try Me One More Time," "I'll Always Be Glad to Take You Back," and "It's Been So Long Darlin'." Here and there, he even allows himself to imitate Tubb, nailing his phrasing and tone. But where Tubb's twang always quavered, like he was singing into an electric fan, Merle is a different sort of country Crosby, singing smooth and relaxed amidst a suite of violins.

The Way I Am, Haggard's fifth MCA LP in just three years, even with that long vacation, is half covers. It's an indication that, despite the time off, he hadn't returned to Nashville with a suitcase full of new songs; it also testifies to the way Haggard turned to his musical heroes for comfort and inspiration in a difficult time. If he had to promote himself, he could at least spend some of the cultural capital on helping out his friends and repaying musical debts. That spring, he played on *Music*, an instrumental album by Tiny Moore, the former electric mandolinist for the Texas Playboys and current Stranger. Merle contributed swinging fuzz guitar, playing sideman for his own sideman. And, besides those three Tubb songs, *The Way I Am* features two additional covers in honor of men who'd made him the way he was: a relaxed but still fiercely swinging rendition of Stuart Hamblen's "(Remember Me) I'm the One Who Loves You" and a version of Floyd Tillman's classic statement of romantic fatalism, "It Makes No Difference Now." Merle makes his voice sound so beaten down on that one, it's a tiny miracle he can even summon the strength to shrug his shoulders in resignation.

Merle's songwriting ran hot and cold during his MCA tenure, but his vocals were always nuanced and hauntingly melodic, gorgeous enough even to save his mediocre originals. "Wake Up" has a deadly opening line ("Don't just lay there like cold granite stone") but remains inert. Both Merle's "No One to Sing for (But the Band)" ("Once I had a girlfriend, she loved to hear me sing / But I left her in Nashville, flew west on a silver plane") and a new Leona Williams number, "Where Have You Been," feel true enough to Merle's recent crises, if perhaps a bit too on the nose. Not even Merle could salvage his silly "Sky-Bo": "That's a new kind of hobo for planes!"

When the songs were great, though, as with another #2 hit, the whatta-ya-gonna-do-but-yearn title track, Merle's MCA recordings were as good as they'd ever been. "The way I am don't fit my shackles," he sings, his voice flying powerfully to stretch out that "am," then collapsing into a moaning heap each time he feels those "shackles." That line would make a pretty good thesis statement for Haggard's entire career. "Wish I enjoyed what makes my living, did what I do with a willing hand," from the same song, is pretty apt, too. In hindsight, "The Way I Am" feels as if it couldn't possibly be more autobiographical—a recounting of Merle's decision to tell the music business to take their job and shove it, followed by his resignation at having to hire back on. But the song is actually by Sonny Throckmorton, the cowriter of "If We're Not Back in Love by Monday." With credits like "Middle Age Crazy" (a 1977 country hit for Jerry Lee Lewis) and "I Wish I Was Eighteen Again" (for Lewis, in '79, and in the following year for comedian George Burns), Throckmorton was something of a specialist in "male menopause." Once again Merle had discovered someone telling his story in a song.

But not just his story. "The Way I Am" marks a shift for Haggard, and for country music generally, that would slowly but surely intensify through the decades. Previously, even as he sang about staying put and supporting his family, putting in another day for another dollar for as long as his body held up, the Hag insisted his *real dream* was to bail on those responsibilities and hit the road. Even when pausing midflight, as in "Ramblin' Fever," he's eying an exit: "There's times I'd like to bed down on a sofa and let some pretty lady rub my back," he croons coyly, but the real thrill will come in the morning, "drinkin' coffee and talkin' about when I'll be comin' back."

In "The Way I Am," by contrast, Merle pines to be done with striving and with running both. "I can almost see that bobber dancing," he sighs, indulging a kind of restorative indolence that will make perfect sense to anyone who's ever just wanted to spend their day off doing exactly nothing. Its lazy lilt evoking warm breezes and drowsy afternoons, "The Way I Am" dreams of that most underappreciated but necessary element of freedom: free time. Merle just wants to rest. Retire. Maybe do some fishing.

His next album, *Back to the Barrooms*, includes the top-ten "Leonard," dedicated to friend and mentor Tommy Collins, and "Our Paths May Never Cross," which besides establishing the melodic template for a couple of dozen George Strait hits to come, finds Haggard both hopelessly romantic (there's someone out there he's meant to be with, he just knows there is) and hopelessly fatalistic (not that he'll ever find her). But as its title suggests, the album is built around Merle's strongest batch of drinking songs since he'd made his name with the genre back in the sixties. First up is "Misery and Gin," a Snuff Garrett composition that had originally appeared on the *Bronco Billy* soundtrack alongside his Eastwood duet and that cultivated a Great American Songbook classicism that suited Haggard's mature voice and phrasing. The record chimes in with piano, then Norman Hamlet makes his pedal steel mimic a violin. Or rather it sounds like that until the real violins and other strings, forty-eight pieces in all, show up.

The rest of the record is honky-tonk classicism at its finest, albeit all slicked up in shiny new Urban Cowboy duds. "Make Up and Faded Blue Jeans," about spying a flirty woman from the stage in "downtown Modesto…

working the Holiday Inn," digs an Outlaw-meets-disco groove. Merle wails "Back to the Barrooms Again" ("my shaky legs trying to stand") as if he'd known all along that the taverns were where he'd end up. He announces to whoever's buying that "I Don't Want to Sober Up Tonight" and, to that end, "I Think I'll Just Stay Here and Drink," which at the start of 1981 became his only MCA single to reach #1.

His woman, he bitches on that album-closer, doesn't care what he thinks; he mutters defensively, "Ain't no woman gonna change the way I think." That's a bald assertion of male chauvinism, but the song's subject is male impotence. Merle has lost the argument, maybe even lost the woman he loves, and has retreated to console himself with a bottle that's bound to let him down sooner or later. Until he works up the courage to head home and apologize, he can at least listen to the band. "I Think I'll Just Stay Here and Drink" is as close as Merle had come to capturing in the studio (albeit mostly with Nashville ringers, not the Strangers) the energy and abandon of his stage show. For nearly four minutes, an eternity on country radio, Merle sings a few lines then steps aside so Larry Muhobarec can pound the keys, so Don Markham can wail on sax, so guitarist Reggie Young can play the blues. "We're gone," Merle says at the fade, and for the most part that was true to life, too. Within a couple of months he'd moved on again, signing with Epic Records, though not before quickly delivering two albums he still owed to MCA.

Rainbow Stew, a live album released in 1981, finds Merle on home soil, running through a set of mostly recent hits at Anaheim Stadium and showing off his band to better effect than his three Capitol concert sets combined. The Strangers were as fierce as any band going in these years, and on *Rainbow Stew* steel player Norman Hamlet, horn man Don Markham, and pianist Mark Yeary all get room to stretch out and improvise. Here and there Merle joins in himself on jagged electric guitar, though it's Roy Nichols who keeps stealing the show with sprightly, jazzy solos. In the studio those recent drinking numbers had broken a sweat trying to maintain control, but live they don't even try to keep their cool, especially on fiddle breakdowns that run hot, then burst into flame. The show ends with "Sing Me Back Home," which after all the rocking and racing around that's come before seems to move at a crawl. A funereal crawl, I'm tempted to say, except that the slowed pacing gives the prisoners in Haggard's old song room to breathe free. As Hamlet's pedal steel flies away, the doomed men fly too, and at last "Sing Me Back Home" is revealed as the anthem it was all along.

Recorded in April 1981, *Songs for the Mama That Tried* was a gospel set dedicated to the seventy-nine-years-young Flossie Haggard, "the Mama that tried and is still trying." Stripped down to mostly acoustic arrangements, produced by Merle alone, graced by Merle's reverent, soulful singing and the harmonies of both Bonnie Owens and Leona Williams, the album is filled with old country gospel favorites ("Softly and Tenderly," "Keep on the Sunny Side") and new ones (Kris Kristofferson's "Why Me" and "One Day at a Time"). On the Mosie Lister altar-call standard "Where No One Stands Alone," Merle delivers one of the finer vocal performances of his life, his voice stretching single syllables into half a dozen, his voice cracking with humility and hope. *The Mama That Tried* included no hit singles and next to nobody bought it. It included no grand Haggardian thesis statements, and nobody today calls it his best album. It will just have to settle for being perfect.

CHAPTER 27

"RAINBOW STEW," 1981

In 1929, when Jim and Flossie Haggard moved west the first time, a popular song among the Okies was "Big Rock Candy Mountain." In that Harry McClintock number, a hobo encourages us to ride alongside him to utopia. He's headed "where you sleep out every night," where "the handouts grow on bushes" and "the boxcars all are empty," where there are lemonade streams and cigarette trees and "they hung the jerk that invented work." If this land exists anywhere, it's only somewhere over the rainbow, but at the time it reminded a lot of folks of California.

Fifty years on, Merle Haggard, that lifelong Californian, is having none of it. He'd told us a decade earlier that "Every Fool Has a Rainbow"—even him, placing empathetic emphasis on *fool*. Now, on the title track to his MCA live album, a #4 country hit, he says to hell with empathy and mocks outright what he considers over-the-rainbow dreams, sardonic emphasis on *rainbow*. Merle even recycles bits and pieces of McClintock's tune. Compare, for example, the melody of Hag's "eatin' rainbow stew with a silver spoon" to McClintock's "there's a lake of stew and of whiskey too." "Rainbow stew," country journalist Jack Hurst tells us, is "a hobo term denoting something too good to be true."

With Norman Hamlet's steel guitar snickering away, Haggard advises that we "don't need to get high to get happy," clue enough he's pulling our leg. Then, calling on piano ("Alright, Marky") and sax ("Here comes Don!") for exclamation-point solos, he lays out a series of presumably fever-dream scenarios. When we learn how to burn water for fuel and use the sun to heat our homes, when a president actually does what he promises and "people start doing what they oughta be doin'," why, then "we'll all be drinkin' that free Bubble Up and eatin' that Rainbow Stew."

Like any of that could ever happen.

CHAPTER 28

HE WISHES A BUCK WAS STILL SILVER (NOT REALLY) AND LIKES THE TASTE OF YESTERDAY'S WINE (REALLY)

In 1981 Ronald Reagan became president of the United States. Reagan's campaign slogan, "Let's Make America Great Again," trafficked in nostalgia for a 1950s America as yet unsullied by hippies, draft dodgers, civil rights, environmental protections, Great Society safety nets, and liberal kowtowing to special interests. "In the present crisis," Reagan warned in his inaugural address, "government is not the solution to our problem. Government *is* the problem."

Faced with nearly 10 percent unemployment, chronic energy shortages, the national humiliation of the Iranian hostage crisis, and more, Americans were desperate for less complicated times and eager to feel strong about themselves and their prospects for the future—anxieties paramount to a working class whose paychecks had been stagnant since the Nixon administration. And just as Nixon had earlier exploited country music, and Merle Haggard, to gain Silent Majority support, Reagan now used country music to woo that same bloc, now dubbed Reagan Democrats. Haggard, meanwhile, appeared willing once again to play along. Part of it was personal rather than political. Reagan had pardoned him in 1972, and Haggard returned the favor by performing several times at presidential events and, in a number of interviews in the early eighties, endorsed what he felt Reagan had done for the nation "in the area of morale" and displays of patriotism.

Once again, Haggard's music began to sing a tune a lot of Americans already were humming. A bustling modern shuffle, "Big City" was another #1 hit in 1982 and the title track for his Epic Records debut, an album that in its country music way sings the working-man blues, Reagan-era edition, no less than did contemporaneous releases such as Grandmaster Flash & the Furious Five's "The Message" or Bruce Springsteen's *Nebraska*. "Big City" found the Hag again longing to quit a life of "entirely too much work and never enough play." Except here, instead of lighting out for another town, Merle dreams, hippie-like, of dropping out entirely. "I'm tired of this dirty old city," he attests in a voice as weary as his audience felt. "Set me free," he demands, "somewhere in the middle of Montana." All he wants, he says, is just what pay he has coming, and "You can keep your retirement and your so-called Social Security." He pauses before "so-called," registers the economic desperation and *in*security plain as day all around, then curls his lip at the program's name like he's bitten into something rotten. "Big City! Turn me loose and set me free."

Country music's name rests on a contrast between the presumably old-fashioned country, where life's hardscrabble but honest, and the big city, where bright lights turn people into wage-slaving strivers or lazy welfare dependents. Merle's chapters of the country narrative tell a somewhat different story. For one thing, he doesn't sing much about country living, and the rare exceptions are almost never paeans to pastoral life. Merle's in-the-country country songs are more like manifestoes to the idiocy of rural life—not in the sense of stupid or foolish, but in precisely the sense of provincial, isolated, individualistic, and tethered-by-mere-animal-necessity that Marx and Engels had in mind in their version of the workingman blues. "Tulare Dust," "Kern River," "Hungry Eyes," "California Cottonfields," "One Row at a Time"…these Haggard songs are all literally "country," but they're hardly what you'd call Odes to an Agrarian Kern.

Is there a country artist who sings about big cities more than Merle Haggard? I count two Miami songs in his catalogue, two New Orleans songs, a minimum of four Chicago songs, and at least three L.A. songs (including "Big City," inspired by West Hollywood, where he was recording at the time). He also has "New York City Blues" and "What's New in New York City" and "Here in Frisco" and "Return to San Francisco." He cut live albums in Philadelphia and Anaheim and took musical road trips to places like Tulsa, Modesto, Muskogee, and Bakersfield, which aren't *big* cities, maybe, but are cities just the same. His many factory-floor-to-barstool laments usually don't cite any city in particular but clearly take place in one—or, maybe more to the point, take place in all of them, every day.

The density of urban settings in the Haggard catalogue reflects the reality of the country audience, which had been moving cityward for the bulk of the twentieth century. Merle's "Big City" recognizes common frustrations of that life and echoes, albeit rather ambiguously, familiar complaints. "There's folks who never work and they've got plenty," Haggard sings, but it's unclear if those freeloaders are the richest Americans, the poorest, or both. In any event, Merle's proposed escape from the clutches of urban living, fending for himself in the middle of Big Sky Country, was pure fantasy—a fantasy, as country music historian Bill C. Malone writes, that "many working people may have shared, but that only someone like a millionaire singer could realize." Indeed, as a description of how people live today, or could live or should, the *Survivorman* version of rugged individualism "Big City" offers would've been downright delusional if it were anything more than a daydreaming respite from the working-man blues. As so many other Haggard songs imply, you can run from wage slavery but you can't hide. Too bad if you don't love it, because you can't leave it—not in the world as it is and certainly not by yourself. To forge one's way, alone, in the middle of a wilderness, remains a potent ideal of American freedom, but in the main, Americans have long accepted that their chances of making a life for themselves are going to be much improved in town, where the jobs and people are. On this point, we might say an emphasis on rugged individualism within so-called free markets—everyone for themselves, everyone against everyone else—is not the solution to our problem. Individualism *is* the problem.

As for Merle himself, he's noted in interviews that he doesn't even enjoy touring in Montana: too cold.

The publication of Merle's autobiography, *Sing Me Back Home: My Story*, coincided with the release of the *Big City* album. The projects even shared the same cover art: Merle seated on the back of his bus, picking an electric guitar—and with whatever city he's leaving visible out the window behind him; the back cover of the album was a shot of "Big Sky Country," postcard-beautiful and unpopulated. The memoir is notable for how well written it is, thanks to coauthor Peggy Russell, and for how forthright Merle is regarding his criminal past as well as his bad behavior generally. Whether as a son, a friend, or a spouse, he more than once allows himself to come off as the asshole in his own tale. "I'm not sure it was the right thing, putting all my life down in this book," he confessed to *People Weekly*'s Dolly Carlisle that fall of 1981. "I can see it in people's faces."

The book recounts what one of the several Dolly Parton songs he'd cut identifies as "The Good Old Days (When Times Were Bad)." You might say *Big City* is one album-long daydream of dropping out of the modern present altogether. "Stop the World and Let Me Off," Merle insists in a version of the old Carl Belew song that keeps going 'round and 'round just the same, spun ever harder by Mark Yeary's dizzying electric piano. Cut in July 1981 and produced by Haggard and Lewis Talley, *Big City* finds Merle not only dreaming Big Sky dreams but longing to spend a few days riding the rails and living off the land in "Good Old American Guest." On a new version of "You Don't Have Very Far to Go," its third appearance on a Haggard album, he hits the brakes on the pace and turns it into a sniffly showcase for steel man Norman Hamlet. In "My Favorite Memory," the album's chart-topping first single, Merle scrunches his eyes tightly and loses himself in the past: "I guess everything changes," Merle sighs, "except what we choose to recall."

What Merle chooses to recall in the album's third hit single, "Are the Good Times Really Over (I Wish a Buck Was Still Silver)," seems to have him not only recalling the past but lobbying for its return. He wishes a buck was still silver, that Nixon had never lied to us, that the country was still strong—"back before Elvis and the Vietnam War…the Beatles and 'Yesterday'…when a man could still work and still would." The precise datelines for these historical destinations are moving targets, but they line up with the 1950s consistently enough—the preferred golden age of Reagan nostalgia, that is, those good old Jim Crow days when Merle was in prison and when women, themselves under a kind of house arrest, "could still cook," as Haggard grouses, "and still would."

It's hard to take Merle's wish for a pre-Elvis world too seriously, coming barely half a decade after his album-length tribute to the King, and considering the source, the same goes for Merle's wish in the song that "a joint" still meant merely a seedy dive. But the melody and music of "Are the Good Times Really Over" are as serious as a death march—Markham's horn suggests "Taps" without ever playing it—and Merle drags his voice through the lowest notes he can. Is American greatness gone for good? Merle keeps wondering. "Are we rolling downhill like a snowball headed for hell?"

And then something remarkable happens. In the record's final verse, his first-person switches to third, and he answers his own questions—let's *stop* rolling downhill, the good times *aren't* over, and so on—with an optimism unprecedented in his career. In the years following *Big City*, in concert patter he went even further. He often mocked some of his earlier complaints ("when a woman could still cook," he'd laugh, "and chop wood"), and he liked to repeat that final, optimistic verse—"the good times ain't over," sometimes several times—even going so far as to goose it with the exclamation point of a concluding key change. Did Haggard, temperamentally so downbeat and prone to expecting the worst, actually believe it? I think the point is that he very much wanted to believe it, and wanted us to believe it, too.

In August 1982, with *Big City* still high on the album charts, Merle Haggard released a duet album, *A Taste of Yesterday's Wine*, with George Jones, the singer most often cited as country music's greatest. Five months later he released *Pancho & Lefty* with Willie Nelson, a songwriter routinely short-listed as country music's greatest.

For these projects to emerge in such a rush and with such high-profile contemporaries is surprising. Haggard had no track record of sharing the artistic bill on recordings where he wasn't literally the Man of the House or at least headlined as a very special guest. George and Willie, however, were Merle's artistic equals. What's more, if we allow not only for career-spanning artistry but for country radio commercial clout, circa 1980, then the Possum and the Red-Headed Stranger were nearly the Hag's only artistic peers still standing.

Country may have played along with Reagan-era nostalgia, thematically speaking, but musically it was a new day. By the early 1980s the Nashville Sound was on its deathbed. It had fought off serial in-house coups—Bakersfield, country-soul-infused countrypolitan, the Outlaws—and one by one, each challenge was synthesized into the whole. Significant, even radical, changes were recorded as links rather than breaks in the chain of tradition (though not without persistent accusations of chain breaking). This process would be ongoing. But right around the time that Elvis died and Merle left

Capitol for MCA, the center of gravity in country music, steady for thirty or so years, began shifting; the Urban Cowboy years saw new sounds and sources and a fresh generation of stars, producers, and session personnel. By the time Merle moved to Epic, these changes had solidified for good. The old sounds persisted, to be sure—to varying degrees they persist yet—as would for a time the careers of many of the old stars. But they ceased to dominate the charts or define the music for new generations of fans.

For Haggard, Jones, and Nelson, the early 1980s was a period of transition, even as they were making some of the best and most popular music of their lives. Merle's *Big City* was his first nonconcert, nonanthology album ever to go gold. Willie's *Always on My Mind* was a chart-topping country album (his third in a year) and barely missed matching that feat on the pop chart; and George's last two LPs, *I Am What I Am* and *Still the Same Ole Me*, would go platinum and gold, respectively, the former including "He Stopped Loving Her Today," his signature recording. Now, though, and fairly or not (mostly not), these legends would no longer be considered state-of-the-art updaters but the last living links to a possibly dying tradition. Merle's recognition of his new status (with his first autobiography just out to make the case) accounts in part for why this notorious lone wolf was newly receptive to collaboration with Jones and Nelson, his friends, contemporaries, and fellow traditionalists.

George Jones and Willie Nelson have a great deal in common—they're Hall of Fame Texans of nearly identical vintage, for starters—but they're about as different as artists in the same genre can be. They're both country-as-can-be, but they occupy opposite poles of the aesthetic. There are various overstated-but-still-helpful binaries to sketch the differences: George the interpreter versus Willie the songwriter; Jones's honky-tonk and hard-core twang versus Nelson's country-jazz and Tin Pan pop; George's carefully sculpted do versus Willie's couldn't-be-bothered braids. But the overstated binary that resonates most helpfully for me is an emotional one: hot versus cool.

George sang hot. He was emotionally present in the lyric, a slave in a sense to the song's particular passion. He took the lyrics personally, or it sure seems that way. His melismas hurt us because we believe they hurt him even more. This isn't to suggest his vocals are absent any emotional distance, any cooling irony, but they *lean* hot. Jones's representative performances exhibit an earnest—some would say overwrought and, therefore, embarrassing—white, working-class brand of clenched-jaw desperation he appears all but powerless to control.

Willie sings cool, breezy. His brittle voice can bare his broken heart unreservedly, but Nelson tends to place himself not within the emotions of the song but just above them. Nelson's songs abound with wondrous, writerly conceits—angels flying too near the ground; men conversing with windows and walls—and he sings them with self-conscious self-possession. His more guarded onstage approach comes with its own class connotations. His adoption of middle-class restraint reads as bohemian, worldly, and keeps him from coming off unpolished or "trashy" to listeners who might otherwise claim they don't like country music.

The greatest singers, Haggard included, can touch both ends of this affective spectrum, even as they tend to rest most of their weight on one pole or the other. If Jones sang Nelson's "Crazy," he'd sound like it, just a little. When Nelson (or nearly anyone else, for that matter) sings "Crazy," he makes sure we know that "I'm crazy" is only a figure of speech. Merle sang like Jones and Nelson both, and differently than both, stuck once more somewhere in between. In his recordings Merle doesn't so much split the difference between emotional poles as he's split by them. What distinguishes his emotional territory from that of other great singers is the way we hear him straining for cool and failing. He aspires to a respect and acceptance that another class of people has placed beyond the reach of Oildale Okies. His tricks of poetic cool—silver wings, big cities—are as transparent and delightful as Nelson's, but somewhere along the road from conception to execution, from smooth Cali croon to hard Okie twang, his voice betrays him, turns defensive. This was perhaps Merle's singular power as a singer. The Hag mingled optimism with resignation, wanted to have it both ways because both ways was how he felt. He was eager to try on a swinging, middle-class nonchalance, but those same blues inevitably swung him back home to Oildale, running hot all the way.

The opening track for George and Merle's *A Taste of Yesterday's Wine* is the Willie Nelson–penned title track. George and Merle render it Willie cool, with lots of boozy, bluesy harmonies and on-the-road-again bonhomie: Merle (forty-five when the track was cut) runs into George (pushing fifty) somewhere out there on their never-ending tours, and invites him to sit down and talk over old times, to tell again the old stories. Looking back has always been a favorite activity of the middle-aged, and for middle-aged musical outlaws, rehearsals of one's misspent youth come with the added enjoyment of solidifying legends. "Come sit down here with us and tell us your story," Merle grins across the table at George, but the only story they ever get around to telling is the one about how they like the old stories, how they love getting high on memory. The album's first single, "Yesterday's Wine," topped the country charts in early October.

Other tracks on the album lean hard to the hot, sometimes to a fault, but revealingly even then. "Silver Eagle," a Freddy Powers song, gives Jones a chance to laud his singing partner, "this great American poet" of "the everyday working man's life." The song describes the life of a touring musician who's "loved by millions [but is] somehow...their prisoner," riding the highways in a "ten-wheeled aluminum cell." The tone is very serious. The song more than implies that his jailer is...us.

As self-referential star turns go, I usually prefer my woe-is-me in novelty form. The album's Haggard-penned second single, "C. C. Waterback," which peaked at #10 on the country charts a couple of weeks before Christmas, offers about the nosiest hangover cure you've ever heard, a recipe that includes, besides hair of the dog, a blaring Dixie blues trumpet and a lot of loud talk. Last night, during a party at Jones's place, Merle's woman drank so much "she couldn't find the door. She wound up in old Jonesy's bed and I wound up on the floor." Jonesy and the Hag crack up at that, so you can be pretty sure that "wound up" means nothing more scandalous than "passed out." That's their story, anyway, and in the song they're sticking to it. The record achieves a low-level riotousness—shouted asides; laughter louder than the jokes prompting it deserve; more Don Markham trumpet, too, brassier than before—and as the record fades, the party's on again.

All of the funny songs on *Yesterday's Wine*, and there are several, are hot enough to burn. The closing "No Show Jones" goes a long way to dismissing the self-seriousness of many earlier cuts by dancing all over Jones's early eighties notoriety for canceling performances and nearly killing himself with drink and drugs. Haggard was by all accounts doing his level best to keep up with Jones during these years. Leona Williams recalled that near the end of their marriage, Merle warned her: "Last year was Jones' time to fall apart. This year it's my turn." But even in the darkest periods of his life, Jones remained a master of the lighthearted novelty, skimming along the silly surface of "Old King Kong" or "White Lightning," willing to come off like a big ol' goof for the benefit of a big ol' goofy song.

Not Merle, who seemed incapable of sustaining a novelty mood. His jokes were usually at the expense of other people. On "Must've Been Drunk," the joke is on a woman from the Salvation Army who some night previous had tried to save George's and Merle's souls by getting them to promise they'd set down the bottle. "Well, we must've been drunk, Hag, when we said we'd stop drinking," Jones reminds him, yelling and slurring to let us know he's off on another bender. When Jones passes back the bottle, the Hag shares his part of the tale, which is to mock the woman who tried to change him. "I rolled a smoke as she read us the scripture. St. Peter! St. Luke! St. Paul!" He snorts the names of the apostles like belches or curses, like punch lines to the very idea of reinvention, never mind salvation.

The darkest cut on the album has a very different sort of punch line. Another of his own songs, "I Think I've Found a Way" finds Merle singing about some girl who's gone but is still banging around in his head. Now, he tells George, he's figured out how to make it without her: "I think I found a way I can be happy." "Tell me, Merle," George begs, because of course he has his own pain to deal with. "All I have to do-oo-oo-oo-ooh...," Merle explains—the record pauses a split second; wait for it—"...is die."

That's morbid even for country, and Merle eschews any hint of authorial distance. You want relief? Get a noose.

Funny shit.

Pancho & Lefty was released in January 1983, several months after *A Taste of Yesterday's Wine*, but the LP had actually been completed five months before the Jones album. Epic held it back because Willie already had so many other albums in the can or already in the racks.

Billy Sherrill, producer for *Yesterday's Wine*, must have struck Haggard as the antithesis of the hands-off Ken Nelson. Sherrill liked to be the boss of everything, from song selection to arrangements, sometimes even dictating specific licks or phrasing. So it's likely no coincidence that the equally head-strong Haggard worked with the producer only once more during his Epic tenure, when he sang a duet with Ray Charles for the Freddy Powers song "Little Hotel Room" in 1984. Working conditions were far more relaxed on the *Pancho & Lefty* sessions. Recording took place over five hazy nights at Nelson's Pedernales studio, with Merle living out of his tour bus. This duet album's producer, Chips Moman, had just served the same role during Nashville sessions for Willie's *Always on My Mind*. For the Haggard project he'd enlisted the same players, including Nashville A-Team guitar legend Grady Martin as well as several of the country-soul players—guitarist Reggie Young and drummer Gene Chrisman, among them—who Moman had relied on for late-sixties sessions at Memphis's American Studios, on hits by everyone from Elvis Presley and Dusty Springfield to James Carr and King Curtis. In fact, "Always on My Mind" itself was recorded by Moman in Texas when Nelson fell in love with it, suggested it to Merle for a duet, but couldn't sell him on the idea.

Nelson didn't give Merle a chance to pass on the song that became the duet project's title track. Near the end of the sessions, Willie's daughter played him a version of Emmylou Harris doing songwriter Townes Van Zandt's "Pancho and Lefty." Willie and Chips immediately set to recording it while Merle crashed on his bus, rousing him only when everything else was finished, at four A.M., to sing a single short verse. He tried to beg off until morning: "I'd been asleep about an hour, and I was completely bushed," he told journalist Tom Roland. "I couldn't get my bearings, and he had this song and it seemed like it was half a mile long. It had more words than any song I've ever seen in my life." Haggard did as he was told, figuring he'd rerecord his part later when he was more familiar with the song and more alert. But per Nelson biographer Joe Nick Patoski, when Merle mentioned that possibility during a round of golf the following day, Nelson just laughed: "Hell, the tape's already on the way to New York."

Pancho & Lefty isn't a duet album in the old-school sense of two singers trading verses and sharing choruses, singing to one another and sharing a story and an experience, à la a classic duet team like Jones and Tammy Wynette or, for that matter, George and Merle on *A Taste of Yesterday's Wine*. *Pancho* also isn't a duet album in the even older-school sense of two men singing together in close harmony, in the manner of brother teams like the Louvins or Everlys. Merle and Willie barely join their voices here at all, close or otherwise.

There are two duets on the album. Merle and Willie sing "All the Soft Places to Fall" to one another as a "we," and at each chorus they join in worn harmony to confess that while "most of our lives we've been Outlaws" (with a fondness for "women, smoking, and good al-kee-hol"), they've now overdosed on young men's fun and want to settle down. Or at least to settle—for a family, freshly laundered linens, "and all the soft places to fall." This sounds like wishful thinking, and not just on the part of songwriter Leona Williams. The problem for Merle and Willie, after all, was never an unwillingness to fall, as it were, into soft places: the trick was to stick around those soft places longer than sunup.

Pancho & Lefty's other duet repeats the poor, put-upon Outlaw theme: "We keep roaring down the fast lane, like two young men feeling no pain … laughing at the price tag that we've paid" is how Merle puts it in his own soft-places-seeking "Reasons to Quit." Reason #1: they've built up such a tolerance to "the smoke and booze" they have to stay high nearly all the time. Reason #5: it's tough to write decent songs while high. Not that any reason gains traction for long. "Reasons to Quit," the album's first single and a top-ten country hit, is chased on the album by "No Reason to Quit," a Dean Holloway song that finds Merle claiming he knows he's man enough to put aside the bottle; he just needs something to motivate him, though that seems unlikely. On "It's My Lazy Day," he and Willie can't even summon the willpower to make a trip to the old fishing hole.

They trade verses back and forth on that one, their indolence encouraged by a mandolin that can barely find the strength to sound like a ukulele, and they trade them again, though without as much narrative sense, on Willie's cool conceit, "Half a Man," and on Texas Playboy Jesse Ashlock's "My Life's Been a Pleasure." The division of labor is split more or less down the middle that way throughout. Each man gets two solo leads: Merle has "No Reason to Quit" and his lovely reading of Stuart Hamblen's "My Mary." Willie gets another Ashlock number, "Still Water Runs the Deepest," and a stunning piano-blues reading of "Opportunity to Cry," this duet album's Merle-less final word. That sequencing choice, coupled with the famously Merle-light title track—Nelson gets three verses there (plus four choruses) to Hag's one—makes *Pancho & Lefty* feel like a Willie Nelson solo effort, though Merle does get top billing.

Pancho & Lefty opens with "Pancho and Lefty," which itself opens with a manic ride cymbal and a cheesy synthesized piano intro that serves no discernible purpose, not even to establish mood, unless reminding us that "it's the early 1980s!" counts as mood. And maybe it does: "Pancho and Lefty" starts like a dead-on-arrival ringer for "Believe It or Not," the theme song to TV's *Greatest American Hero* and a #2 pop hit the previous summer.

Fifteen seconds in, though, producer Moman punches reset, and the song shifts with we-interrupt-this-program abruptness. The intro's synthy piano dribbles to dust, and Willie takes the reins, his tenor made all the chillier by the song's distancing-by-definition third-person narrative. Van Zandt's song offers up a Pancho who maybe is or maybe isn't Mexican revolutionary Pancho Villa, but whoever he is, this Pancho is a "bandit boy" who eludes capture until he doesn't. Eventually he's killed, probably by Lefty, who may or may not have been paid to do it by the Federales, but who in any event hightails it for a "cold" Cleveland the same day Pancho bites it in the "quiet" desert. Meanwhile, the few surviving Federales insist to anyone who'll listen (the lyric switches to first-person plural, twice, for the last line of the chorus, so apparently Willie is one of them?) that they could have laid Pancho low at will but let him hang around instead "out of kindness." Or maybe, as I prefer, that's just the story they tell to save face. Or maybe Pancho's hanging around at the end of a rope? The song isn't so much rich with poetic ambiguity as it is incoherent—and things become even more muddled if you think the songwriter might help. Van Zandt said that as far as he was concerned his Pancho wasn't *the* Pancho, yet his song drafts significance off the inevitable confusion: Why would "*the poets* tell how Pancho fell" if he wasn't *the* Pancho?

But that just means Van Zandt's famed story-song is less interested in relating a specific story, per se, than in establishing cinematic atmosphere and articulating a way of feeling a hard world. On that front, Merle and Willie's record is both a turnoff and a seduction. The tone of the song— macho, pretentious, admiring of rebellion for its own sake, siding with an impulse toward rugged individualism and against anything bigger than the self, damn the lonely consequences—is more than a little grating. That's doubly the case coming from Willie and Merle, who use Van Zandt's tale of one dead outlaw and of another dying to sing a self-aggrandizing ode to the outlaw life of the touring musician and to their own widely admired skills for eluding capture: "Livin' on the road, my friend, was gonna keep you free and clean," Willie begins. Of course, the song sequels that young man's rainbow with the older and wiser, "Now you wear your skin like iron, your breath as hard as kerosene," so I take critic Geoffrey Himes's point that this "push-and-pull of romantic notions and sobering reality" is a Van Zandt trademark. I'd only note that pushing and pulling through all that sobering reality—bravely, stoically, fatalistically—is many a romantic's idea of a pretty picture indeed. And never mind that Pancho (the famous historical one, I mean) remains a beloved folk hero in Mexico precisely because he faced those sobering realities in support of collective, not individual, freedom.

The record has undeniable power for all that. Once the sonics reboot and Willie settles into Van Zandt's elegiac melody, "Pancho and Lefty" laughs at my attempts at explication and just is. Each time I hear it, there comes a point, usually right about the time Moman's layered guitars start to mimic steel drums and just before Merle's dusty baritone comes sliding in, when the tune pulls from me a jumble of emotions, about diminished dreams and growing old and dying alone. Van Zandt's half a mile of mere words matters less with each syllable. Then "Pancho and Lefty" is like a siren's call to the universal human desire to "keep running from life," as Merle had put it a few years earlier—to be free by being free and clear. It's a reminder, too, for those who will hear, that you can never be free by yourself.

CHAPTER 29

"KERN RIVER," 1985

"**K**ern River" is a scary record, maybe the scariest I know, because its terror is just a synonym for the world. Country music has any number of scary songs that take place at river's edge, but unlike "Banks of the Ohio," say, where the singer plunges a knife into the chest of a woman who refuses to marry him, "Kern River" has neither a murderer nor a murder victim. No one takes his own life in the song, either; Merle doesn't sing as Hank Williams does in "Long Gone Lonesome Blues" of "going down in it three times but, Lord, I'm only coming up twice." The story Haggard tells in "Kern River" is so hopeless, its character so utterly powerless, that if its narrator did kill himself, it would feel like a perverse little victory for the human race. Spoiler alert: he doesn't kill himself.

At the dawn of what Ronald Reagan's reelection campaign only months before had called "Morning in America," Haggard's "Kern River" would come on the radio—it was a top-ten hit in the summer of 1985—and it would suddenly feel like the sun had been punched from the sky, like it might never come up again. In a noisy country radio mix that might include Exile declaring "She's a Miracle" without sounding miraculous, or the Oak Ridge Boys shrieking relentlessly through "Little Things," a heart song performed by what sounds like amusement-park automatons, Merle's record screamed quiet and startled you alive. "I'll never swim Kern River again," he almost whispers at the start, like someone or something might be eavesdropping. He's not singing a cappella but might as well be: what little music there is registers more like a barely beating heart than a band. "It was there that I met her," he sings, reviving the memory, trapped in images indistinguishable from every imprisoning moment since. "It was there that I lost my best friend."

She drowned in that river, he says, long ago, stolen by the Kern, a river "not deep nor wide but…a mean piece of water" and the real-world dividing line between Oildale and Bakersfield. Now, on the single, a woman's cold and bloated voice pursues him to the end of the record and beyond. "I may drown in still waters," he keeps saying in a way that lets us know he's considered it. "But I'll never swim Kern River again."

Listen long enough and you can even begin to believe that the song's most indelible line, a detail so small but that feels so enormous—"I may cross on the highway but I'll never swim Kern River again"—is expressing not an option Merle allows himself but a privilege that's somehow been granted to him. He *may* cross on the highway, but right-of-way can be revoked without notice. The Kern, Mt. Whitney, Lake Shasta, the San Joaquin Valley—Merle moves about them all, but only as a bird flits in a cage, and he can't feel at home even in nature anymore. His dreams ("I grew up in an oil town but my gusher it never came in"), his movements ("The river was a boundary where my darling and I used to swim"), his very agency ("I live in the mountains, I drifted up here with the wind") are beyond his control.

He did have this grim song to write and sing. But even his own craft—the alliteration and internal rhymes of "one night…moonlight…the swiftness swept her life"—can do nothing but slant inexorably toward doom.

CHAPTER 30

HE'S GOING WHERE THE LONELY GO

Merle was living in California again in the eighties, working obsessively, nose to grindstone, but dutifully doing his Nashville rounds. He recorded there, between long stints on the road, almost exclusively throughout the decade. In 1984 he informed *Music City News* he was planning a Johnny Cash tribute album. Like the music of World War II project and a possible Linda Ronstadt duet album he mentioned to Bob Allen around the same time, and like the novel he was writing that he'd sometimes mentioned to reporters in the early seventies, "The Sins of John Tom Mullen," and like the Ernest Tubb tribute he would continue to tease for decades—it never happened. He did work with Ray Charles that year, duetting on "Little Hotel Room," a song written by a new Haggard friend and collaborator, Freddy Powers. And a year earlier, Merle cut "Everybody's Had the Blues" with Dean Martin, the cool crooner he'd had in mind when writing the song a decade earlier. That year George Jones scored a major hit with "I Always Get Lucky with You," a *Big City* track Haggard and Powers had written together.

In just his first two years on Epic, Haggard released eight albums. In addition to the politically minded *Big City* and its follow-up, the romantically minded *Going Where the Lonely Go* (cut during the same forty-eight hours in July 1981), there were those three duet projects with George Jones, Willie

Nelson, and, on Elektra, Leona Williams. Another solo effort, *That's the Way Love Goes*, came in 1983: its lovely, gratitude-practicing title track was among Lefty Frizzell's final compositions and became Merle's thirty-second #1 country hit in what was now a twenty-year recording career. His second holiday release, *Goin' Home for Christmas*, was sprinkled in there, too, as was his fourth live album, *The Epic Collection (Recorded Live)*. Unpromisingly titled, that one, but it was his tightest and most wide-ranging concert set yet, opening with a wild medley of two Capitol-era carousers, "Honky Tonk Night Time Man" and "The Old Man from the Mountain." He was constantly working.

Or constantly partying. In 1969, in "Muskogee," folks may not have made "a party out of lovin'," but by the mid-1980s, on Merle's Lake Shasta houseboat, they'd grown more broad-minded. "A famous female country music star and I once spent five days nude on the boat," Merle writes in the opening chapter to *My House of Memories*. "We snorted drugs the entire time and didn't go to sleep once." That second autobiography is stuffed with similar tales of debauchery. Running-buddy Freddy Powers's book about their wild years at Silverthorne, the Lake Shasta resort Merle owned at the time, is packed with even more. "We bought cocaine and speed by the bags," Powers writes. "It seemed as if we were living every day as if it were our last." Merle was smarting from the end of his marriage to Williams, and Powers, an ace rhythm guitarist with a background in Dixieland who Merle met through Willie Nelson, had recently divorced as well. Powers's oral history of the period, with Haggard's significant contributions, was titled for what the pair dubbed their raging in real time: *The Spree of '83*.

Haggard's self-destructive Silverthorne adventures unspooled amidst serial crises. Some of them were rich man's problems, like fraudulent promoters, financially catastrophic investments, and meeting payroll. But most of Merle's troubles were of a more everyman variety. His mother, Flossie Haggard, passed in 1983. In 1986 Merle's dear friend, producer, and longtime manager, Lewis Talley, died unexpectedly (cardiac arrest while on the houseboat), and in 1987 Texas Playboy and Stranger alum Tiny Moore passed away, too. Roy Nichols, Merle's boyhood hero and his collaborator since the Wynn Stewart days, announced he was retiring from the road that same year, due to ill health. Somewhere in there, Merle married his fourth wife, Debbie Parret, his longtime road cook and housekeeper. "I knew about an hour after the wedding it was a mistake," he says in *House of Memories*.

246 THE RUNNING KIND

Then he began seeing Theresa Lane, who'd been the girlfriend of fleet-fingered young guitarist and new Stranger Clint Strong. Merle and Theresa lived together on the houseboat for five years or so and were married in 1993. Lane was "wife number five—the true love of my life—the last wife I'll ever have," he pledged in *House of Memories*. The Rev. Tommy Collins officiated.

The eighties were turbulent years for Merle. And, perhaps inevitably, the music suffered, though less in quality than significance. Often working with producer Ray Baker, Merle developed a new radio-friendly ballad style, built around electric keys, sax, and pulsating bass with room enough to live between each jazzy note—and with a string section lurking around often as not. Increasingly, his studio sound captured the "country jazz" that he played in concert with the Strangers. In 1980 the sound landed him on the cover of *Downbeat*. "I want you to come up to Lake Shasta and hear us when we get to play what we choose," he enthused to journalist Barry Robinson in 1984. "When they get going, they ain't playing nothin' different than what [jazz guitarist George] Benson's playin'."

Things in the studio may have swung a bit less fiercely than they did in concert halls or at the lake. But Merle's sound on record was also sharper and silkier, more dynamic, than it had ever been. One representative instance of the style is also the quietest record of his career: 1983's "It's All in the Game," a jazz-age leftover that had been a dreamy R&B-crossover smash for Tommy Edwards during Haggard's first months at San Quentin. Merle had actually recorded it in 1980, and his former label, MCA Records, noting Haggard's renewed popularity, released it as a single. Epic, not wanting to undermine its own Haggard releases, acquired the record (and several more previously unreleased MCA-era tracks) after what Dave Samuelson terms "considerable negotiations" and a check for $120,000. "It's All in the Game" became the title track to a new album in 1984.

That was possible because the old record sounded so much like his new ones. The first thirty seconds of "It's All in the Game" is nothing more than Merle's warm, "relaxed-American" voice cradling each note and accompanied just barely by a bass guitar. Then, for another thirty seconds, a keyboard considers joining but keeps deciding against it. Finally, it's on to the pitter-patter pulse of brushes on drum and jazzbo fills and solos from electric mandolin and guitar. Breathtaking.

* * *

As Haggard's sonic options grew, his themes contracted. By the middle of the decade, Merle had settled comfortably into a new role as a first-rate crooner of sometimes soaring and sexy, but more often sullen and sexy, love songs. There was "My Favorite Memory" (about that time they made love in the hall) and "Going Where the Lonely Go" (as opposed to "running in all directions trying to find you"). Also: "You Take Me for Granted" and "Someday When Things Are Good" (Leona Williams's finest songs); "What Am I Gonna Do (With the Rest of My Life)" (He can probably keep occupied till morning, but then what?); "That's the Way Love Goes," "Let's Chase Each Other around the Room," and "I Had a Wonderful Time"; and "A Place to Fall Apart" (a song Merle cowrote with Willie Nelson, who suggested the title, and with Powers, who encouraged Merle to write about the end of his marriage). Each of these, with Merle alternating between pillow talk and crying into his pillow, was a top-five hit or better between 1982 and 1986. The best of a strong bunch is another Powers song, "Natural High," on which Merle, embraced by backing vocals from Janie Fricke, fashions a Nashville equivalent to R&B's Quiet Storm. "You put me on a natural high," Merle purrs, sensual and feeling free. "And I can fly!"

This was all honorable, necessary work. Attending to affairs of the heart, after all, is job one for any sort of pop music, right up there with "It's got a good beat and you can dance to it." Set beside the music he'd made in the Nixon years, though, and what he'd done early in Reagan's first term—that work had been as big as history and had made it—most of what Haggard did in the mid-to-late 1980s felt small. It recognized a narrower range of human concerns—with class concerns absent most notably. Not that the country audience was encouraging him to widen it. In 1985, on "Forty Hour Week," the country band Alabama declared, "There are people in this country who work hard every day…the fruits of their labor are worth more than their pay." That was as close to a Marxist critique of capitalism as country radio had ever heard. But instead of rallying workers to unite, the rest of the song would dare only to cheerily salute the exploited. During Reagan's second term, that was as far as class consciousness on country radio went. More typically, in Haggard's catalogue, as on country radio at the time, blue-collar struggles didn't come up in the first place. "I'm proud to be an American, where at least I know I'm free," Lee Greenwood sings in 1984's "God Bless the USA." That "at least" was like a black box containing every American trouble that that "free" was determined to ignore.

White working-class vernacular hadn't disappeared from radio entirely, though. It had just moved over to top 40 and AOR stations and to the song-books of heartland rockers such as John Cougar Mellencamp and Bruce Springsteen. The family farmers losing their land and livelihoods in Mellen-camp's roots-rocking "Rain on the Scarecrow," for instance, sound like they were probably big "Hungry Eyes" and "Tulare Dust" fans. His "Small Town" is located in Indiana, presumably, but could have been Oildale or Checotah or even Muskogee. Mellencamp's "I can be myself here in this small town, and people let me be just what I want to be" certainly doesn't evoke "Muskogee," or any other small town you might care to name—ways of living right and being free there tend to be strictly monitored. But it does capture the ideal Merle was after in his great, tolerant fantasy, "Big Time Annie's Square."

There had always been a fair amount of Merle Haggard in Bruce Spring-steen, too. They were both "Born to Run," after all, though unlike Merle, Bruce tended to have a clear destination in mind. Bruce is bound, like Curtis Mayfield's train a-comin', for "That place where we really want to go" or, as he later named it, "The Land of Hopes and Dreams." Merle just ran. Still, Springsteen's opening to "Hungry Heart" in 1980—"Got a wife and kids in Baltimore, Jack / I went out for a ride and I never went back"—is an East Coast, industrial version of Haggard's country-to-the-core "It's a big job with nine kids and a wife.... Want to throw my bills out the window and catch a train to another town." And Springsteen's "Born in the U.S.A.," impossible to avoid in the middle of the decade, stars a vet who answers his country's patriotic call but can't get back on at the refinery when he returns home from war. It's like "Workin' Man Blues" and "The Fightin' Side of Me" rolled into one.

All of this seems to have rubbed off on Haggard. When Willie Nelson, Mellencamp, and Neil Young announced a Farm Aid benefit concert for that fall, raising awareness and funds for struggling family farmers, Merle signed right up. He also announced a project of his own: a USA for America train tour, traveling from Bakersfield to the concert site in Champaign, Illinois. The plan was for stars, including Tammy Wynette, Hank Snow, Lacy J. Dalton, Arlo Guthrie, the Judds, and Janie Fricke, to join him for a string of thirty-eight whistle-stop shows across eight states along the way. "It is my way of justifying my existence here," he told Robert Hilburn. "I'm an

American." But the three-thousand-mile trip was canceled almost as soon as it had been announced—they couldn't raise the quarter of a million dollars AMTRAK required up front to pull it off.

Merle did release *Amber Waves of Grain*, a live album cut at dates in Indiana and Nebraska, in support of the cause. A pair of new patriotic singles emerged from the project—the title track and "American Waltz." The latter is as clichéd as a campaign video and was as ignored. "Amber Waves" is punchier (without American farmers, "will an Idaho spud be stamped 'Made in Japan'?") as it criticizes, against mournful fiddle and trumpet, a US government that sends foreign aid overseas but won't help people here. The applause as the anthem closes on the album goes on for nearly a minute. But even with all the attention surrounding Farm Aid and with Epic's support, it was Merle's least successful single of the decade, stalling at #60.

Much better was the following year's "Out among the Stars," an Adam Mitchell song that returned Merle to twinned specialties—working-class desperation ("He can't find a job, but man, he's found a gun") and shame ("His father cries, 'We'll never live this down' "). But that wasn't what radio wanted from Merle Haggard anymore.

"Oh, how many travelers get weary, bearing both their burdens and their scars," Merle worries, his voice soaring, then cracking, in sympathy as E Street keyboards shimmer and soar behind him. "Don't you think they'd love to stop complaining and fly like eagles out among the stars?" In December 1986 it peaked at just #21.

That same month a new film about the Vietnam War used Haggard and his music in an old, familiar way, to signify a mighty wall between us. A young white solider hears "Okie from Muskogee" on the radio and salutes. "Listen to that," he enthuses. "That's a bad jam." His young Black platoon mate calls bullshit: "Redneck noise, dude. That's all it is.…Fuck that honky shit."

Excepting greatest-hits collections and live sets, *Big City* was the first Haggard album certified gold. Its follow-ups, *Going Where the Lonely Go* and *That's the Way Love Goes*, which concludes with the momentarily peaceful and against-type "I Think I'll Stay," weren't anywhere near that popular but were nearly as strong. *It's All in the Game*, in addition to its hits, included a version of "To All the Girls I've Loved Before" that bested Willie Nelson and Julio Iglesias's smash version. Merle sounds genuinely grateful where Julio and Willie sound full of themselves, and full of it.

Haggard's albums in the eighties were never great, but always solid, some more rewarding than others. A few highlights among many: *Out among the Stars* finds Merle riding lush strings and counting his blessings in "My Life's Been Grand," then momentarily indulging rainbow dreams in a brassy, hard-swinging, and smartly phrased "Pennies from Heaven." *Chill Factor*, released in 1987, includes the misery-accepting top-ten title track, the misery-rejecting "We Never Touch at All," and what turned out to be his final #1 hit, "Twinkle, Twinkle Lucky Star," which merges Haggard's mature '80s style with the 1950s doo-wop classicism of the Elegants' "Lucky Star."

That album served as a here's-how-to-do-it contribution to the era's "new traditionalist" movement. The Neo-Traditionalists, as they became known, were a group of singers who recalled twangy earlier stars like Hank and Lefty, though more so if you hadn't listened closely to many Hank and Lefty records. Merle Haggard was who they sounded most like. Proto-Neo-Traditionalists George Strait and John Anderson were joined in the decade's second half by Randy Travis, Ricky Van Shelton, and Keith Whitley, and by the early incarnations of Hat Acts Alan Jackson, Clint Black, and Garth Brooks. Another young singer-songwriter, Steve Earle, didn't sound like a new Haggard, but his songs were similarly, proudly working class. And star Dwight Yoakam was a Buck-and-Merle fiend. He'd emerged from a roots-minded Los Angeles punk scene that demonstrated just how broadly Merle's influence had spread. Lone Justice, for example, made its blistering race through "Workin' Man Blues" a staple of its live sets. The Knitters, a country-rock side project for members of X and the Blasters, recorded "Silver Wings" in 1985.

Merle's final Epic album, 1988's *5:01 Blues*, was perhaps too enamored of Jimmy Buffet–ish island rhythms, but it does include the searching "Someday We'll Know," maybe Merle's finest ballad since "Somewhere Between" twenty years earlier. Another new country star, Suzy Bogguss, had a minor hit with a marvelous "Somewhere Between" in 1989. That was just a few months before Merle scored with the sad-sack "A Better Love Next Time." No one knew it then, but hindsight would reveal it to be the final top-ten hit of his career.

In 1987, five years after *Pancho & Lefty*, Merle and Willie released a sequel, *Seashores of Old Mexico*, backed throughout by the Strangers. The title track reprises a number Merle had first cut in 1974, in which he gets a lift from peasants "in route to a town I can't say." (Not because he's being cagey; it's just his Spanish needs work.) There is also Willie and Merle's exquisitely lonesome take on an exquisitely lonesome song by Texas singer-songwriter Blaze Foley called "If I Could Only Fly," and the two joined for an ethereal reenvisioning of "Silver Wings," as well. Merle's solo flight through his own "Without You on My Side" seems to pack an entire worldview into a single preposition: Merle needs us not *at* or *by* his side, but *on* it.

And there's "Yesterday." I remember just staring at my speakers the first time I heard it, not long after *Seashores* was released. The first shock of "Yesterday" is that Merle's singing it. Hadn't he wished, only a few years ago, that we still lived "before the Beatles and 'Yesterday'"? But the second shock is bigger. Merle's voice is suddenly high and cracked and frail. His rich baritone, in especially fine form on *Seashores'* every other track, feels like it's been unexpectedly pumped with air and left out overnight in the chill and damp. His phrases, which normally snap off crisply or, more often, fade slowly like a sunset, here merely crumple. This thin thread of a voice didn't sound like Merle at all. Was he sick? Wasted, or wasting away? Like the grandpa character he played on *Goin' Home for Christmas* but stripped of all playfulness, Merle's voice on "Yesterday" is the voice of an old man.

Willie's here, too, doing his normal Willie thing, phrasing at sharp, unpredictable angles through each chorus and sounding ageless; Merle sings the verses. Zen master Willie observes each regret, feels its not unpleasant sting, releases it. Merle sounds like he's pacing a crowded cage, imprisoned by, and with, his past. Now, he *believes* in "Yesterday," because each regret's inseparable from who he's become. Mistakes and wrong turns pile up like bricks here in the present, burden upon burden, a barrier so high it places out of reach even the notes he's trying to hit.

Twenty years later, when the Hag really was an old man with an old man's voice—indeed, when he'd had a cancerous piece of lung removed and part of his range with it—Merle's "Yesterday" voice returned for keeps. But how could he have known that in 1987? Merle had always been a gifted mimic, but how could we have known that "Yesterday" would be the then-fifty-year-old Haggard's greatest impersonation yet? Ladies and gentlemen, his voice says, Merle Haggard...at seventy.

CHAPTER 31

"ME AND CRIPPLED SOLDIERS," 1990

In August 1990, at the Missouri State Fair in Sedalia, Merle Haggard and George Jones played a double bill. A small group of inmates from the Missouri State Penitentiary in nearby Jefferson City were bused in before state fair performances to set up rows of folding chairs between the stage and grandstand and to stack them up again when the concert was over. In between, they got to watch the show, staring down at the musicians from tall scaffolding on one side of the stage.

Former prisoner Haggard closed that show, the first time I'd seen him live. Beyond a general sense of feeling amazed by the strength of his singing and the Strangers' hard swing, what I remember most was what happened when he played "Me and Crippled Soldiers," the B-side to his latest single. An anti-flag-burning flag-waver, it was Merle's response to recent Supreme Court decisions affirming flag burning as constitutionally protected speech. Merle wasn't buying it, and neither was his audience. When the crowd discerned what this new Merle song was about, they rose as one to honor flag and country, holding aloft flickering, disposable Bic lighters in approval. My friends and I remained seated, our little protest in support of free speech.

One sign of vitality in a song or recording is that you want to talk back to it. When Merle complains that "now that it's all right to burn the Stars and Stripes...we might as well burn the Bill of Rights," you could complain, if you wanted, that he wasn't making sense: What good is a Bill of Rights if you can't practice the liberties it enshrines? Likewise, when Merle asks

> *Has the Holocaust been so long?*
> *Is Hitler really gone?*
> *As we burn our only cause for Vietnam?*

you could tell Merle his comparison's idiotic. Or, playing the record at home, you can hear Merle sing

> *I've been known to wave the flag before,*
> *And [been] saddened when we went to war,*
> *fighting for the symbol of our land . . .*

and you can patiently explain to Merle, or impatiently shout, that fighting to defend one's country and fighting to defend a *symbol* of one's country are very different things, only one of which is ever worth dying for. In the song Merle shakes his head at those Supreme Court decisions and wonders, "Is *this* the freedom that we won?" And you can answer him very simply: "Yes."

Or you could not answer him at all. Even Merle didn't sound terribly invested in his dudgeon. No matter how many times he sang "only me and crippled soldiers give a damn," the record never insisted we give a damn about it the way Merle's earlier anthems had. Lyrics aside, that was because "Me and Crippled Soldiers" wasn't a very good record. Children's voices (our future!) provide oddly creepy, metronomic harmonies throughout. A Salvation Army–sounding brass band (emphasis on "Army") blows briefly about the middle of the recording, suggesting "The Star Spangled Banner" and "Stars and Stripes Forever" and "Bringing in the Sheaves" and "Dixie," too, while failing to connect you to any of them. Merle's Bakersfield licks, normally switchblade sharp, have been processed into butter knives, and the riled-up rhythm of the like-minded "Fightin' Side of Me" has been beaten to a plod. Illogical, lifeless as a corpse, "Me and Crippled Soldiers" might be the nadir of the Haggard catalogue.

But that's the recording. In Sedalia, Missouri, that night, there was no denying the song's power, and there was no talking back, no conversation, only coercion. Throughout Jones's part of the show and into Haggard's set, I'd exchanged appreciative glances and a couple of high-fives with several large, happily drunken men behind us who were enjoying themselves at least as much as my friends and I. But when they noticed we hadn't stood with the rest of the crowd, they not so subtly made us understand that we should stand up, too, unless we wanted our asses kicked.

Well, you pick your battles.... When a few more gentlemen in the row in front of us, almost as large and nearly as drunk, allowed that ass-kicking sounded like a plan to them, we determined this was a battle we had no chance of winning. Outsized and outnumbered, we swallowed our pride and stood up. We did as we were told and celebrated our freedom.

It was dark by then, and as Merle finished his song, I caught sight of the prisoners' silhouettes above the stage. I remember watching them up there on their scaffolding and how the ends of their lit cigarettes dimmed and glowed and dimmed like stars.

CHAPTER 32

THE HAG VERSUS THE MAN IN BLACK

As the 1980s came to a close, Merle Haggard had been among country music's biggest stars, and arguably its major figure, for nearly a quarter of a century. In the 1990s, however, Haggard was, for all practical purposes, a no-show—and during a decade when country music was more popular and diverse than it had ever been.

The nineties will go down in country music history for two closely related developments. Most prominently, the decade saw the rise of a wildly successful radio format, and eponymous modern sound, called Hot New Country. Major performers of the style included the soft-rock-influenced Garth Brooks and the hard-rock-influenced Shania Twain, two country stars who moved units like the pop stars they also were. Representative Hot New Country records included Billy Ray Cyrus's "Achy Breaky Heart" and Brooks & Dunn's "Boot Scootin' Boogie," which together helped fuel a line-dancing craze. Hot New Country, or HNC, aka Young Country, as it was known, was studio-slick, cul-de-sac-identified, and arena-loud. HNC was for the millions of lifelong country fans seeking new sounds to navigate their new material conditions and was embraced, as well, by millions of Americans who'd never before thought of themselves as country fans but did now. As it had during the Muskogee Moment, and had again during the days of the Urban Cowboy, country became in the '90s part of the popular culture of a large portion of the white American middle class, increasing slightly the visibility of the music's working-class base in the process.

HNC wasn't loved by all country fans, however, which brings us to the decade's other significant country music development, the emergence of what became known as Alternative Country—another country-rock return, following the brief cowpunk moment several years earlier and expanding soon enough into the broad roots music scene we know today as Americana. Composed of a small, loose community of backward-glancing fans and musicians, the "alt.country movement," generally speaking, deemed vintage sounds to be raw and authentic, and it cursed as overproduced and suburban any country of the Hot and New type, which, it allowed, had destroyed "real" country music. Exemplars here include the Waco Brothers, one of the genre's smartest and hardest-rocking outfits, and their "The Death of Country Music," a besotted eulogy that summarizes the subgenre's sense of betrayal at what country music had become: "We spill some blood on the ashes / of the bones of the Joneses and the Cashes." That emotion was seconded by singer-songwriter Robbie Fulks, who flipped the bird at modern country's "moron market" in one exaggeratedly twangy record called "F—k This Town": "This ain't country-western / It's just soft-rock feminist crap." Hot New Country, loved most dearly by contemporary white, working-class folks who'd only recently shoved their way into the middle class, walked on the fightin' side of Alternative Country, predominantly a music of middle-class college rockers who'd begun to slum, however sincerely, in the blue-collar back catalogues of people like Johnny Cash and Merle Haggard.

In 1994 Johnny Cash used Alternative Country's brief cachet to rise from the dead. During the Muskogee Moment, Cash had been about the only country act to outshine Haggard, but his star had dimmed considerably in the years since—in 1987 Columbia had dropped Cash outright after twenty-eight years on the label, causing Merle to protest loudly (Epic, still his label at the time, was a Columbia subsidiary) and to begin fearing for his own career.

Released in the spring of 1994, *American Recordings* gave Cash his career back. Not because it included any big singles or was a monster seller. Rather, Cash's new work provoked immediate critical acclaim like he'd never seen. *American Recordings* was "a milestone work" (*Los Angeles Times*), "a breathtaking blend of the confessional and the self-mythologising" (*Mojo*), "an instant classic" (*Rolling Stone*).

The album is sweet and scary—bracing. Then again, pop music is littered with great albums that have gone mostly unappreciated, so the all-but-unanimous enthusiasm that greeted *American* had at least as much to do with fortuitous timing (and sound marketing) as with the music itself. Cash made *American Recordings* alongside rap/metal producer Rick Rubin, a collaboration that won the project rebel cred before anyone ever heard a note. The disc's savvy cover (Cash looming like a backwoods version of Bergman's Death), as well as its several savvy covers (Cash sings Waits! Cohen! Danzig!), intensified that effect, and the album's lo-fi sound and minimalist settings sealed the deal. The project's much-repeated backstory—this was just the Man in Black singing songs of violence and self-immolation, strumming simple guitar on Rick Rubin's couch—mattered greatly to listeners predisposed to believe that sparser arrangements were more authentic arrangements, that darker emotions and subjects were self-evidently the best, most real emotions and subjects. Cash's realness was the album's primary draw: Johnny Cash, punk rocker! Johnny Cash, Original Gangsta! The comparisons were facile, but the enthusiasm was undeniable. Cash's old-school moves were received with an of-this-very-moment urgency.

Like a detail from an epic landscape painting, *American* offered a revealing, though only partial, view of Cash's art. Nonetheless, a Cash renaissance was a welcome development. The album, along with the several name-brand sequels it inspired, was particularly important within the Alternative Country scene. *American*'s dark and stormy themes reinforced the movement's preexisting one-dimensional appreciation for both Cash and the country tradition. Its troubadourish approach expanded what would pass for cool going forward, and the bare-bones arrangements flattered the burgeoning community's own rejection of glossy Nashville.

As Cash was being reborn, Haggard was slipping away.

A couple of weeks before the release of *American Recordings*, Merle Haggard released an album of his own. Not that anyone noticed. The new album, *1994*, announced itself as literally up-to-date, but its music sounded merely dated. With several songs written by Nashville ringer Max D. Barnes, and all of it recorded with cavernous-sounding blues-rock guitar and big drums, *1994* found Merle trying very hard, in a Hot New sort of way, to land a hit. But country radio no longer had any use for an old-timer like Haggard, no matter how contemporary his records sounded. Younger rock fans, meanwhile, who were just discovering Cash and other alternative countries and who might have been inclined to check out a similarly craggy legend like Merle Haggard, would've likely been deaf to 1994's contemporary sounds even if they'd heard them.

This is just the way it would go for Haggard in the nineties, by any measure the low point of his career. For one thing, he was facing major financial difficulties. As he told journalist Robert Price, "I had earned maybe a hundred million dollars in 25 years. By 1990, I was practically broke." For another, he'd grown dissatisfied with his longtime label. He left Epic Records in 1989 because he was angry about the way Cash had been treated, because he felt increasingly anonymous there, and because the label had shown little enthusiasm for "Me and Crippled Soldiers." He signed to Curb Records the following year, yet that was disappointing from the start. "Crippled Soldiers" was promptly released, but only as the B-side to "When It Rains It Pours," a generic ballad that straight out of the gate became the lowest-charting Merle Haggard single ever.

His subsequent debut album for Curb sold as poorly, and got what it deserved. In addition to "Crippled Soldiers," 1990's *Blue Jungle* includes two more songs pulled from Reagan-Bush era headlines—specifically, news reports of a homelessness epidemic. Yet beside earlier masterpieces on the subject, these new songs looked like Merle Haggard forgeries. Next to "Hungry Eyes," "Under the Bridge" is pure fantasy, its version of homelessness scrubbed clean of pain and dirt, want and death, while "My Home Is in the Street" gives up on the hard-knock lessons of "I Take a Lot of Pride" to channel Little Orphan Annie optimism. The rest of *Blue Jungle* isn't much better. The album's relative standouts—"Sometimes I Dream," "A Bar in Bakersfield" (what if, the song imagines, Merle had never made it big), a glossy new version of "Driftwood"—stand out mainly because everything else sounds so dreary and, occasional topicality notwithstanding, so old.

Merle continued to write and record, but it would be four long years before he had a new record—and this from an artist who'd once shoe-horned seven albums into twenty-three months. Haggard took to bitching in interviews that Curb was happy enough to use his name for bait, luring future stars like Tim McGraw to the label, but that it wouldn't release his music. When it finally showed up, 1994 improved considerably on *Blue*

Jungle. "Set My Chickens Free" is agreeably funky in both the odd and the on-the-one senses, while a remake of "Ramblin' Fever," solo-crammed and stretched to four minutes, challenges HNC on its own rocking terms and wins, if only aesthetically. But the album was nowhere near strong enough to overcome another dud of a first single: Barnes's slushy "In My Next Life," about a man who works until his hands are no longer fit to use but is apparently eager to get back to working his ass off up in heaven. Then again, not much could have withstood the album's afterthought title, Curb's scant promotion, and undercooked cover art—just "Merle Haggard" and, smaller, "1994," in gray type against an all-black background.

1994 entered the country charts the first week of April, inched its way to #60 (lowest-charting Merle Haggard album, ever), and was gone by the first week of May. That commercial failure carried over to the road, where venues got smaller—"honky tonks and army bases," as he puts it in one *1994* cut, "Troubadour." Merle could no longer count even on headlining. His two hands were still fit to use, though, so he kept at it, singing "everybody's favorite song...warming up the crowd for some big star...trying to keep my name up there in lights."

For just a second there, things turned back Haggard's way. On October 5, during the nationally televised Country Music Awards, Haggard was inducted into the Country Music Hall of Fame. Emmylou Harris led the celebration, singing the opening to "Hungry Eyes" and narrating a brief bio that included a priceless clip: Merle rising to accept the Country Music Association's Entertainer of the Year honors, in 1970, his shoulders being squeezed from behind by a beaming Johnny Cash. Harris next introduced a group of current Nashville stars who offered a "Workin' Man Blues" that was described as "a good old country jam"—workmanlike, that is, and proud of its apprenticeship. Finally, Harris presented the award: "In some ways his life sounds like fiction, but if it were fiction no one would believe it." Cue standing "O."

Merle's acceptance speech was perfectly in character. Rather than thanking a Young Country music industry that applauded him tonight but wouldn't play his records come morning, he made a point of recognizing first "my plumber out in Palo Cedro...for doing a wonderful job on my toilet." It wasn't "f—k this town," but it was pretty close.

The week following his Hall of Fame induction saw the release of

Mama's Hungry Eyes: A Tribute to Merle Haggard. The various-artists collection gave several of Merle's biggest hits the mainstream Nashville treatment, with mostly solid results from the likes of Alan Jackson, Vince Gill, Alabama, and Randy Travis. Brooks & Dunn contributed a version of "The Bottle Let Me Down" that seems to have nothing at all to do with the failures of self-medication, but that has everything to do with helping folks achieve an equally worthy end, scooting their boots. Radney Foster's version of "The Running Kind," chosen as the single for the project, didn't really sound like it had done much running, but its blend of Buckaroo beats and Desert Rose Band guitar jangle was positively beautiful.

Only a couple of weeks later, a second collection was released, *Tulare Dust: A Songwriters' Tribute to Merle Haggard.* It features a lineup of like-minded Americana cohorts—Peter Case, Lucinda Williams, Marshall Crenshaw, John Doe, and so on—most of them traveling light, guitar and voice only. The spare approach fit skimpy indie recording budgets but did aesthetic work, too: less-is-more signified less is more *real.* On that score, the *Tulare* acts were of a piece with Cash's *American Recordings* and in line with alt.country sensibilities generally, favoring a closer-to-deep catalogue version of Haggard's songbook. *Mama's Hungry Eyes* has the obvious classics—"Mama Tried," "Sing Me Back Home," "Workin' Man Blues," "Today I Started Loving You Again," and the title cut, among others—just as you'd figure it would. *Tulare Dust* skips those, choosing away from the charts instead (Joe Ely, for instance, sounding sick to death but getting used to it on "White Line Fever" and Barrence Whitefield declaring his love for a white woman named "Irma Jackson"); or at least it chooses less frequently anthologized hits like "My Own Kind of Hat" or "Kern River."

Indeed, *Mama's Hungry Eyes* and *Tulare Dust* testify to the sheer quantity of quality material in the Haggard songbook. Together the discs comprise an impressive thirty songs, with only "Silver Wings" redundant—and, notably, with "Okie from Muskogee" and "The Fightin' Side of Me" ignored altogether. But the discs also argue for competing conceptions of what the country music tradition still meant to people at century's end, of the ways it might continue to matter, and to whom, in the coming millennium. On *Mama's Hungry Eyes* Haggard is an esteemed forefather whose past contributions can be honored and appreciated, though fleetingly and with perhaps more duty than devotion. It climbed to #52 on the country album chart, a nice showing for a project raising money for Second Harvest Food

Bank. *Tulare Dust*, meanwhile, intended for an audience all but invisible to country radio (and whose creators liked it that way), didn't chart at all. That was bad news for Haggard, long accustomed to chart dominance and the cultural impact and more lucrative bookings that accompany it. The good news was that the acts on *Tulare Dust* thought Haggard still had something to say: his songs were old tools with plenty of use left in them.

At the same time, the Americana community understood that Merle Haggard would be, for many in its audience, an iffy reclamation project—and, just as it had been for earlier generations of country-infatuated rockers, the barriers to be overcome were named "Okie" and "Fightin' Side." In liner notes to *Tulare Dust*, contributing artists (and executive producers) Tom Russell and Dave Alvin are effusive in their praise but a little defensive: "De-tractors often dredge up 'Okie from Muskogee' or 'Fightin' Side of Me' as evidence of exaggerated patriotism, but they've missed the point." The point being, apparently, that they hated those songs, too, but liked his other ones a lot. For any Hag-appreciating rocker with political and cultural affinities to the left of, say, Hank Williams Jr., redirection was just a rule of the road.

Much less common were alt.country acts willing to engage Merle while also talking back to him. Like the Bottle Rockets, for example. In 1993 they fixed Merle's "I'm a White Boy" by swapping out his lyrics for love lines that were full-on fun and goofily sly ("I'm stuck on you like Elmer's white glue") in a new song called "Every Kinda Everything." Or like the Stark-weathers, who, in the final verse of their "Burn the Flag," back-sass Merle directly in a way that's tough to miss: "If you don't love it, *change* it!" That was in 1994, and Haggard just kept coming up like that all year long—as inheritance, sounding board, inspiration, both out on the alternative fringes and smack in the HNC mainstream. A week after *Tulare Dust* arrived in stores, Nashville hit maker Ricky Van Shelton released *Love and Honor*, its title track on loan from Merle's 1974 *If We Make It through December*. Also that fall, Clint Black, whose "I Take a Lot of Pride" had been a *Mama's Hungry Eyes* standout, enjoyed a top-five country hit with "Untanglin' My Mind," a song he and Merle had written together. In November the Old '97s, soon-to-be alt.country stars, put "Mama Tried" on their debut album, while a country star–studded documentary called *Merle Haggard: An American Story* aired on the Nashville Network. As 1994 came to a close, it seemed everything was pointing to a Haggard renaissance in 1995 of the sort Johnny Cash was already enjoying.

But if Merle had any shot at a Johnny Cash–style comeback, he missed out for the simple reason that he was never allowed to show up for the party. After the tributes, it was almost two years before Haggard released another album—and even fans on the lookout for a new record likely missed it. "The DJs in the world lost track of me," he wrote a few years later in *House of Memories*. Thanks to Curb, he might as well have gone in to hiding. "Patty Hearst could've been on Curb," he joked. "For that matter, Amelia Earhart may be there now. And Jesse James could've hid out there for a hundred years." Consequently, Merle's third album for Curb did worse than the first two, neither charting nor producing a charting single. Country music critic, journalist, and historian Michael McCall summarized the situation this way:

> His record company didn't send promotional copies to reviewers until the album had been out for nearly a month, and no advertising or promotion has been devoted to the music. The album artwork and cover reflect this lack of care: the title, *1996*, is boxed on the cover like a tomb, exactly like Hag's last set, *1994*.

In fact, the only difference between this cover and the preceding one was that the color scheme had been reversed from gray on black to black on gray—ashy and dull either way. Merle was enraged by the lack of support. He called out label chief Mike Curb in interviews ("He tried to kill my career any way he could") and even told journalist Dave Hoekstra, "I'd like to publicly challenge him to a boxing match." To be a singer and a writer with next to zero chance of being heard was maddening enough. That *1996* boasted several strong new originals only compounded the frustration. A pair of updated Singing Brakeman–styled numbers, "Truck Driver's Blues" and "Sin City Blues," sing rueful call-and-response with the road, while "Beer Can Hill," about growing up drunk and disorderly in Bakersfield, finds Merle joyriding through Oildale with Buck Owens, Dwight Yoakam, and the Cajun accordion of Merle's coproducer, Abe Manuel Jr.

Best of all is Merle's take on a ballad by Iris DeMent. Wowed by her keening version of "Big City" on *Tulare Dust*, Merle had sought her out ("the best singer I've ever heard," he told Edvin Beitiks) and fallen for her song "No Time to Cry." Cutting it himself let Merle wave from a distance to the off-the-charts country scene where DeMent was much beloved, but Merle's attraction to the song was personal. DeMent had written "No Time to Cry" about the death of her father—"There beside my mother in the living room I stood, with my brother and my sister knowing Dad was gone for good"—and about the busy numbness of her road life after his funeral. Merle recognized that pain and made it his own, ticking off commitments and responsibilities, a world of toil and tragedy ("The baby that was missing was found dead in a ditch today"), of another show to do and no time even to weep. "Now I'm walkin' and I'm talkin' doing what I'm s'posed to do-oo," he croons, barely in control. "Working overtime to make sure I don't come unglued." He changes what DeMent remembers from "when I was a girl" to "before there was a Merle," then snorts at his joke. Or grunts in agony, it's hard to say. Once again, someone had told Merle's story in a song. DeMent toured with Haggard briefly, and they cowrote a song, "This Kind of Happy," that appeared on her next album, 1996's *The Way I Should*. That title and its theme evoke Haggard's earlier *The Way I Am* just as the album's righteous "Wasteland of the Free" channels a progressive "Fightin' Side of Me."

1996 was Merle's best work since leaving Epic nearly a decade before, but almost no one heard it. After the tributes and Hall of Fame announcement, it had seemed Haggard, with the right song and a bit of promotion, might yet find the footing to climb back onto the radio or at least to catch a ride on Cash's train to Americana glory. There was even a four-disc, career-spanning box set to build on: 1996's essential *Down Every Road: 1962–1994*. But there would be no renaissance for Haggard as long as he was on Curb. Those tombstone-like covers to *1994* and *1996* felt like markers for a career that was dead and buried.

"The Hall of Fame thing, bless their hearts, is almost like the iron door shutting on the box I'm in," he told Jack Hurst as 1994 came to its end. "I don't know if I'll ever get out of there now."

Johnny Cash had been inducted into the Country Music Hall of Fame all the way back at the beginning of his own career downturn, in 1980, and had joined the Rock and Roll Hall of Fame in 1992, two years before his Rick Rubin–assisted comeback elevated him to a level of pop culture immortality few artists have attained. Though his sensibility is country to the core, Cash came through that slender 1950s window when boom-chuck country boogie overlapped with rockabilly rebellion, and that fortuitously timed entrance, succeeded by an appreciation for rock songwriters like Bob

Dylan and Bruce Springsteen, helped put him on the short list of country acts embraced by the larger pop audience. As *Rolling Stone* asked in the summer of 1994, "Can you name anyone in this day and age who is as cool as Johnny Cash?"

In an alternative universe, the answer might have been, "Well, there's Merle Haggard." The two had much in common. The San Quentin–incarcerated Haggard had considered Cash a role model ever since he saw the star perform at the prison on New Year's Day 1959, though it wasn't until 1964 or thereabouts that they'd met face-to-face. They were in the basement bathroom of a Chicago television station when, as Haggard told *Vanity Fair*'s Eric Spitznagel, Cash offered the kid a Dexedrine pill and a drink of wine. From there, Johnny became Merle's friend, advisor, and booster: Cash booked him twice for his TV show and encouraged Merle to come out of the ex-con closet; the pair were chart contemporaries at a time when the charts amplified national conversations by speaking in the more-or-less common language of pop and country radio hits. The Man in Black and the Hag were kindred artistic personas, too, "outlaws" long before that term became a highly remunerative pop-country marketing category.

But Haggard was never going to be cool like Cash. At heart, Cash was a latter-day American romantic—like Mark Twain, he was into local color mostly for the tall tales—and over the breadth of his career, he presented himself as a somber prophet who was, simultaneously and without contradiction, a corn-loving cutup. People allowed Cash his moral gravitas, sought it out, even, because his judgments felt forgiving and because his righteousness came sugarcoated with backslapping laughter. The Man in Black was always edging toward symbol and myth, and his story-songs hint, optimistically, at the possibility of a more moral, more intense and adventure-filled, more consequential life for us all. The Man in Black starts down-to-earth but soars.

The Hag looked to fly, but he remained earthbound in the end. He was life-sized, circumscribed, life as it is, a realist—and like a character out of Crane or Dreiser, the Hag was most often not part of something bigger than himself so much as swept away by forces beyond his control. In the 1990s Cash's life story spoke directly, inspiringly, to alt.country fans like me who'd been raised up blue collar, had maybe gone and gotten ourselves college-educated but were on the lookout for ways to stay connected to the best part of roots we'd otherwise fled. Cash's catholic taste, in sounds and songs and collaborators, flattered those of us who liked to think wide-ranging record collections were proof of an evolved broad-mindedness generally. By evoking a past presented as folklore, Cash seemed living proof that even if you got above your raising, you could look back without looking down—and move ahead without too much of the shame and other hard feelings associated with a wrong-side-of-the-tracks youth. The Man in Black promised both the acceptance and the transcendence of one's roots.

Merle Haggard had risen, too, but because his music and image worked overtime not to let on, the Hag seemed a less likely role model for reconciliation. Glancing over his shoulder at a still-touchable past from a point of view grounded unmistakably in right now, Haggard warned that the old stories of class division and prejudice weren't old in the least. His themes and Okie accent were relentless, merciless reminders—for those of us, that is, who had the memories and didn't appreciate their revival—of rigid kinfolk and "white trash" humiliation, of prayers for change unanswered, of ditch-digging dads whose hands were no longer fit to use but who had to get up for work in the morning just the same. Haggard, the man or the persona, wasn't more real than Cash any more than his music was more authentic. But for some alt.country types who'd been born and bred blue collar, had gotten away and wanted to stay gone—and, too, for many Hot New Country fans who hadn't gone to college but knew in present tense the sting of redneck stereotypes—Merle Haggard's brand of country music hit just a little too close to the old home place. Cash's southern trash exoticism had been tamed—by his for-the-whole-family television series, his comparatively liberal politics, the totality of his iconic persona. But for those without a life history rooted in the white working class, Haggard remained threatening and a little scary. It is not a coincidence that the class divide of nineties country—working-class HNC versus middle-class alt—is exactly the divide replicated in the audiences of the Hag and the Man in Black.

In 2000, on Cash's third American album, *Solitary Man*, Merle joined his old friend on a song called "I'm Leavin' Now." They trade verses to begin with, each announcing with exaggerated bravado that he's had it and will be hitting the road just as soon as he finishes this song. "Get out of my face, get out of my space, I'm leavin' now," they sing at the end, together, though they sound headed in different directions: Cash, taking off because there are still so many places to see, pop-culture immortality at the top of the list; and Haggard not bound anywhere in particular, but running, always running.

CHAPTER 33

HE'LL NEVER BE GONE?

MERLE HAGGARD IN THE TWENTY-FIRST CENTURY

Watching while some old friends do a line
Holding back the want-to in my own addicted mind…

T he nineties had been a lost decade for Haggard, but with these opening lines to 2000's *If I Could Only Fly*, his first album of new material in four years, Haggard seems instantly to have found himself. And to have been found. *If I Could Only Fly* came out on the independent Anti- label, a fit that was just odd enough (a country Hall of Famer on a punk label?) and just right enough (Isn't a drug-using musical outlaw a kind of a rocker, after all?) that it was bound to pique the interest of the rock press, college radio, and other Americana-friendly outlets. Hag's comeback prompted comparisons to Johnny Cash's ongoing collaboration with Rick Rubin, the most relevant similarity being that Haggard was making the music he wanted to make and country radio could go to hell. There were no hit singles on the album and no attempts at one.

As it turned out, that anticommercial approach paid commercial results. In fact, *If I Could Only Fly* did approximately as well on the Hot Country Album chart (making it as high as #26, lasting twenty-seven weeks) as Cash's *American Recordings* had done (#23, for twenty-two). It was a big comedown for an act with fifteen #1 country albums to his credit (second only to Haggard-fanatic George Strait) and more top-ten entries than any country act ever. But after those underperforming Curb albums—*1996* had been such a nonevent it hadn't charted at all—*If I Could Only Fly* was an honest-to-God success.

It was also Haggard's best work in years, since at least 1987's *Chill Factor* and maybe even since *Big City* all the way back in '81. Those arresting first lines were to "Wishing All These Old Things Were New," a Haggard original that finds him fighting the urge to sniff coke with pals. Not running from the urge but standing his ground, facing and fighting it. "I had a difficult time kicking one drug, a stimulant, and Theresa had an even harder time," he'd confided in *House of Memories* a year earlier, then humble-bragged that they kicked their habits without the aid of professionals. The song also has him massaging old wounds reopened when watching young men do a perp walk: "and they show it all on TV, just to see somebody fail." Haggard's craggy, strained voice makes certain we understand how glad he is to see those days gone, but also hints that he half wishes that they weren't, maybe more than half. Other old things he misses in the song include some he'd never known, such as "good times like the Roaring Twenties," when Jimmie Rodgers walked the earth, and others he most definitely had experienced out on his houseboat: "The Roaring Eighties, too!"

"That was before it all fell through," he groans, invoking his not-so-roaring nineties. Not that the decade had been all bad. He'd remarried in 1993, to longtime girlfriend Theresa Lane, and he'd become a father twice more, to daughter Jenessa in 1990 and to son Binion, known as Ben, in 1992. This fresh crop of good old days was harvested elsewhere on the album. He'd been using—amending, exaggerating, reorganizing, inventing—details from his own life in his songs all along, but on *If I Could Only Fly*, Haggard at last embraced the kind of autobiographical songwriting people had been pegging him with all along. On "Thanks to Uncle John," he paid respect to an old family friend who taught him how to play a G chord and helped him after his dad died: "Now John Burke was really not my uncle, but we were kin, 'cause he shared his home and family and he took me in." Another original, "I'm Still Your Daddy," begins brooding and hard: "I knew some-day you'd find out about San Quentin...," Merle says, in a voice sounding a little like the Man in Black's. But when he finishes the thought, singing, "...And your heart would break and your faith would go away," his voice becomes instantly high and fluttery, a scared little boy's. He's singing to

Ben and Jenessa, telling them he's ashamed of what he did back then and hoping they will love him anyway: "Daddy needs some family love today."

The rest of the album mixes the playfully sweet and the sexually playful to extremes unprecedented in his catalogue. "Crazy Moon," a comely, timeless-sounding ballad of fanciful heartache, abuts "Bareback," a galloping western-swinger that begrudgingly advocates safe sex ("Ain't no taking chances like before!"), though from its locked-in groove, it seems to be adjusting just fine. That randy romp is followed by a whimsical children's song, "Think about a Lullaby," with a dreamy concluding harp glissando. Haggard pictures himself throughout the album as nestled within a family life he adores. But it's still something of a shock when, on "Leavin's Getting Harder," this inveterate escape artist wishes for once he could just stay put. His two hands remained fit to use, though, and as music journalist Chris Richards reports in a piece smartly titled "For Merle Haggard, Music Is a Life Sentence," he has "a monthly $80,000 payroll he feels duty-bound to pay the musicians, managers, and helping hands who have served him so faithfully through the years." "If I don't travel," he moans wearily in each chorus of the song, "I don't make a dime!"

In the first decade of the new century, Haggard was putting out new music almost as rapidly as he had in his most productive years for Capitol. He followed 2000's *If I Could Only Fly* on Anti- with *Roots, Volume 1*, in 2001. That album found him once again honoring old influences like Hank Thompson, Hank Williams, and, of course, ol' Lefty, even enlisting Norm Stephens, a vintage Frizzell sideman, to play guitar on the album and tour with him for a time. ("This man played *on the record*," he liked to gush in concerts while Stephens soloed during "If You've Got the Money.") The album's highlight comes on a blasphemous original: a grinning Merle declares not only that he loves his wife "More Than My Old Guitar," but more than "God loves the poor." That's a lot.

Haggard's twenty-first-century revival actually began in the final years of the twentieth. Though not released on Audium until 2002, *The Peer Sessions*—a collection of old pop and country standards drawn from the Ralph Peer publishing catalogue, cut in intimate, small-combo settings— was actually recorded between 1996 and '98 when he was ostensibly working for Curb. Merle's uptown pop rendition of Jimmie Rodgers's "Miss the Mississippi and You" is just lovely, his "Shackles and Chains" pure lonesome. Then, in 1999, no longer Curbed, he rushed out *For the Record: 43 Legendary Hits*, faithful if mostly uninspired versions of his biggest hits with a few surprises. The new "Silver Wings" and "That's the Way Love Goes" are duets with breathy-voiced pop star Jewel, for example, and the new "Daddy Frank" builds to Don Markham punching out trumpet lines while Merle scats giddily through the fade. The two-disc set was additionally part of an entire Merle-is-back media blitz: "For the Record" was the subtitle of his second autobiography, *House of Memories,* out around the same time, and it was also the name of a new pay-per-view special.

He was just getting started. The year 1999 also saw the release of *Cabin in the Hills,* an excellent country gospel set that includes a cover of Iris DeMent's "Shores of Jordan," harmonies by Bonnie Owens, and a solemn-to-sanctified "This World Is Not My Home," with Albert E. Brumley Jr. That last led to *Two Old Friends,* an entire album with Brumley (son of country-gospel legend Albert Brumley, brother of pedal steel player and former Buckaroo Tom Brumley), released in 2002, and which for stripped-down spiritual perfection is the equal of Merle's earlier *Songs for the Mama That Tried.*

In 2003 Merle released an album that claimed he was *Haggard Like Never Before.* "Haggard," as in he'd never been this beat-to-the-bone exhausted, his ragged voice yelping on the title line to prove it. But also "Like Never Before," as in tackling topics and sounds unprecedented in his catalogue. On "Garbage Man," he sings atop a percussive groove led by what sounds like someone banging on a trashcan lid, then leads the group in nonsense call-and-response like he's a dusty Cab Calloway. "Because of Your Eyes" is a not-quite-coy but ever-so-tender seduction ("When I look at you, I double in size"), while the title track earnestly counts the ways that, at last, "living on the road today don't have the same appeal."

He proved he was a new man again that year when he came out in support of the vilified Dixie Chicks after they'd run down their country, seemingly, by griping about President George W. Bush during the buildup to the Iraq War. "It was like a verbal witch-hunt and lynching," the way country music had treated those women, Merle wrote on his website in June 2003. "I think the Dixie Chicks are probably the most unique artists allowed to be on the radio," he told Nashville music journalist Peter Cooper that fall, "and now we've kicked 'em off the radio because of an opinion." The Chicks admired him too. The trio's rollicking hit from the year before, the Darrell Scott song "Long Time Gone," is about fleeing a life as a future farmer, a subject after Merle's heart, and even posits the Hag as an exemplar of what had been lost by the mainstream version of the genre: country radio "ain't got no soul / They sound tired but they don't sound Haggard."

"I don't agree with what they said," Merle made certain to clarify to Cooper, once again respecting the college dean. "But I certainly agree with their right to say it."

And he agreed with his own right, it seemed, to change his mind and criticize the president perpetually. Merle's single off *Haggard Like Never Before*, "That's the News," complains about the president's so-called Mission Accomplished speech, even as US soldiers still fought in Iraq, and points out the media's willing regurgitation of Bush's spin. "Politicians do all the talking, soldiers pay the dues," Merle griped. "Suddenly the war is over, that's the news."

He released two more albums the following year. *Chicago Wind* features "Some of Us Fly" (but "all of us fall"), a duet with country star Toby Keith that sighs an acceptance of universal limits, and a new, Chicago-bluesier version of "White Man Singin' the Blues." *Unforgettable*, meanwhile, produced by old friend Freddy Powers, made good on the hints of Tin Pan Alley he'd been trailing behind him for decades: the album sways to jazzy fiddle, guitar, and piano and favors pop songwriters ranging from Ira Gershwin ("I Can't Get Started") and Hoagy Carmichael ("Stardust") to Cindy Walker ("Goin' Away Party"). Merle's reading of "Cry Me a River" is announced with a mixture of longing, heartache, and "fuck you" that is uncomfortable to hear—"Nooooo-oow you say you're lonely"—and irresistible.

He wasn't done yet. Over the next couple of years Haggard released three more themed albums or collaborations: a second duet album with George Jones, *Kickin' Out the Footlights…Again: Jones Sings Haggard, Haggard Sings Jones*; the majestic *Last of the Breed* with Willie Nelson and country crooner nonpareil Ray Price; and the self-explanatory *The Bluegrass Sessions*, produced by former Stranger Ronnie Reno. Throw in his third career holiday album, *I Wish I Was Santa Claus* in 2004, a collection called *Working Man's Journey* in 2007, and a pair of *Live at Billy Bob's* sets from 1999 and '04, respectively, and Haggard released sixteen albums in the time it had taken him to release three on Curb. Clearly, he had it in mind to make up for lost time while he still had the time to do it. "These two old friends enter the studio 25 years after their first album together," read the notes to *Kickin' Out the Footlights…Again*, "to pay tribute to each other one last time." That "one last time" recognized one last limit: so much life but only so much living.

The pick of the run is *Working Man's Journey*. Little known, let alone heard—it was released by the Cracker Barrel restaurant chain for sale in its "Old Country Store" gift shops—*Journey* collects a dozen previously unreleased twenty-first-century studio sides, cut in spare, relaxed settings and featuring a rotating all-star lineup of late-in-the-game Strangers, including lifers Norman Hamlet on pedal steel, of course, and Don Markham on horns, plus Doug Colosio on piano, Abe and Joe Manuel on a variety of color instruments, and Clint Strong, Norm Stephens, or Red Volkaert on electric lead guitar. Half of the album revisits singles across his career, from "Shade Tree Fix-It Man" to "Rainbow Stew" to "Kern River."

But it's the album's other half, comprised of new Haggard songs worthy of standing beside his best, that makes *Working Man's Journey* deserving of greater exposure. There's "Like a Train Left the Tramp," where it's Merle who gets rambled on, and "Poor Boy Mansion," where Merle rules his domain from his "front-porch…family throne." "Stormy New Orleans" is a post-Katrina blues about the town "down where the black and the white folk meet." On "In the Mountains to Forget," the world has so wearied old Hag ("I don't wanna hear about Bin Laden or Saddam Hussein. I'm tired of wars 'n rumors of war. Don't care which one's to blame") that he determines, yet again, to run away and call it quits.

On a stunning artistic summing-up called "Songman," Haggard offers his wares—"a song about me and one about you," "a song about wrong and one about right," not to mention "some good stories to tell"—but he wonders if anyone needs those anymore. On "C'mon 65," he voices an all-too-common lament, his fingers crossed grimly in hopes he can just make it long enough to retire: "The name of the game is to survive, past 65." He sings another version of "Workin' Man Blues," then, Merle and the band digging an easy groove, unhurried but steady as they go. From nine to five is a long day, after all, and the task isn't going anywhere. No need to break a sweat.

Haggard slowed down considerably after that, though only by comparison. In early 2008 he was diagnosed with lung cancer and by the end of that year had had a hunk of a lung removed. But he was soon back to performing a hundred-plus shows a year. His voice was airier after that, his range newly circumscribed, more haggard—his old man voice from "Yesterday" was now his voice for real. But it was still vibrant and mostly intact, and he was still recording. *I Am What I Am*, featuring masterful minor-key originals like "Bad Actor," "Down at the End of the Road" (his children are born, grown, and gone—all in barely three minutes), and a scary gospel song called "How Did You Find Me Here," appeared in 2010. *Working in Tennessee*, released in 2011, includes rousing covers of two Johnny Cash–associated songs, "Cocaine Blues" and, with love-of-his-life Theresa taking June Carter's part, "Jackson."

In 2015 the seventy-eight-year-old Merle released two more duet projects, the final albums of his career. *Timeless*, another Cracker Barrel volume, teamed Haggard with Mac Wiseman, the masterful bluegrass and country-pop vocalist, age ninety himself, on a collection of songs that have stood that title's test. "If Teardrops Were Pennies," "Keep on the Sunny Side," "I'll Be All Smiles Tonight"—Merle's and Mac's voices, solo or in harmony, steadied by lap-steel or mandolin or Autoharp, crackle and crack, tear up, throughout the disc. They strain for high notes now out of reach, fall flat here or there, trace melodies worn into their souls. They embrace each precious imperfection.

Merle teamed with Willie Nelson one last time on *Django and Jimmie*, the pair's third duet album together and their first since 1987's *Seashores of Old Mexico*. The longtime friends sing several new songs and a clutch of old ones. They extol long-gone musicians who inspired them early on (the title track refers to gypsy-jazz guitarist Django Reinhardt and, of course, to the Father of Country Music, Jimmie Rodgers). Nelson and Haggard enlisted the aid of another country patriarch, eighty-year-old Bobby Bare, to mourn a departed contemporary in one new Merle song, "Missing Johnny Cash," and they covered a song by another generational cohort, Bob Dylan's "Don't Think Twice, It's All Right." Straight along, they look back. Nothing new there: for Merle and Willie, as for country singers historically, counting the miles and adding up the years has long been part of the gig.

"Time flies by in the blink of an eye," Nelson sings on a song by Shawn Camp and Marv Green. What elevates that cliché to wisdom is Willie's diminished-yet-still-distinctive voice, always a bit brittle but now chipped and worn, particularly at the bottom of his range. Merle's magnificent voice had more power and range to begin with but now sounds even more ravaged, compromised up top, raspy rather than crisp. "Can't look back, we might turn to stone," he says too earnestly, like a wink. Then, contradicting himself, he looks back and determines they'd have both taken better care of themselves if only they'd known they were going to "Live This Long."

"We'll keep rockin' along," Merle predicts. "Till we're gone."

Haggard had once more been writing political songs through this stretch. On *Chicago Wind* his "America First" insists we "get out of Iraq" and start rebuilding our highways and bridges, a subject this road warrior, who just then was coheadlining in theater shows around the country with Bob Dylan, knew something about: "I make twenty trips a year from coast to coast." "What I Hate," from *Working in Tennessee*, gathers what most got on his fightin' side in 2011, including "chemtrails in a clear blue sky" and "the war still going on down South."

Haggard returned momentarily to country radio in 2005, featured with Gretchen Wilson on a sharp, and delightfully titled, rabble-rouser, "Politically Uncorrect." Wilson and "Ol' Hag" declare their mutual allegiance to the Bible and the flag, hardly unpopular positions. More to the point, they are also "for the low man on the totem pole," "the guys still pulling third shift," "the farmer," and "the working man." They are for "the single Mama raisin' her kids," too. "I'm just one of many that can't get no respect," Wilson snarls, and Merle seconds the emotion: "None!"

In 2007 he briefly included a song in his sets, "Hillary," that seemed to endorse Hillary Clinton for president: "This country needs to be honest. Our changes need to be large. / What we need is a big switch of gender. Let's put a woman in charge." "It hurt my feelings," Merle revealed later to Heather Svokos, claiming the Clinton campaign had told him they liked the song even as they were placing calls with an eye to finding a Clinton-endorsing country song they liked better. "I thought they might use it, or respect it, but they didn't do either." When Barack Obama beat Clinton for the Democratic nomination, Haggard told journalist Steve Wildsmith he was glad Obama won the election. "Some have referred to me as America's poet of the common man. And I have written something that may be just right for the occasion," Merle posted to his website that January, preface to a new poem called "Hopes Are High":

> We've got bad times behind us
> and good time up ahead

bet your money on the promise land
and the good things that he said
We got a new style with sincere smile
and a new song to sing along
and we got sunshine and a new guy
and hope's are high

"I think we're probably guilty of living up to our constitution for the first time in the history of America," he told music journalist Randy Lewis a few months later. "In my lifetime, they were still lynching Blacks without a court, without a trial. To see it come all the way to (an African American) being elected president is really something."

These statements surprised a lot of people and pissed off some of his fans. But after several years of hearing Merle running down George W. Bush, the war in Iraq, and the Patriot Act, they shouldn't have. At least once in concert, he'd slammed Bush, via Harry McClintock's "Big Rock Candy Mountain," as "the jerk who invented work." Music journalist Chris Willman wrote that in 2005 Merle reckoned the "top three assholes of all time" would "have to be Hitler and Nixon, and then G.W. would be in there right under 'em." By the latter stages of his career, Merle's latest social commentary in interviews was more likely to gain attention than any of his new politically minded music. (Just before his death, Haggard told Patrick Doyle of *Rolling Stone* that he also didn't trust then–presidential candidate Donald Trump: "I think he's dealing from a strange deck.") Without radio play, and after three decades of the desensitizing Culture War, new songs like "That's the News" and "What I Hate" weren't going to have the impact of "Okie from Muskogee" and "Fightin' Side of Me" anyway, even if they'd been as sharp.

Haggard was more and more out of lockstep with the red-state consensus and out of sync with the current country mindset. Country radio increasingly favored the identity politics he'd introduced to the music back in his glory days, and though he'd been revising or rejecting that stance ever since, the way he was in his Muskogee Moment would continue to be a dominant part of Haggard's legacy: Toby Keith's "Angry American" is the "Fightin' Side" of the post-9/11 era, and major hits like Montgomery Gentry's "My Town," Rodney Atkins's "These Are My People," Alan Jackson's "Where I Come From," Gretchen Wilson's "Redneck Woman," Blake Shelton's "Hillbilly Bone," and Randy Houser's "How Country Feels" (among many,

many others) were all fresh, and very earnest, declarations of "I'm proud to be an Okie from Muskogee." At times in the twenty-first century, country radio has sounded like an entire format determined to "Pledge Allegiance to the Hag," as Eric Church phrases it in a 2006 track featuring a guest vocal from the Hag himself.

The trouble is that these pledges of allegiance sound as if the only Hag the writers were familiar with was the lyric to that one damned song. Twenty-first-century country music doesn't *sound* like Merle's old music, of course, but that's not a problem. Sounds change, inevitably. Not even Merle's own Jimmie Rodgers tribute sounded like Jimmie Rodgers, though it did sound connected. Changes, connected—that's the country tradition. Sounds aside, what had gone missing from mainstream country was everything else that had defined Haggard's body of work, all of the grown-up subject matter that kept country music connected to itself, change after change. Like Rodgers and Frizzell, Cash and Parton, Merle sang about marriage and kids, divorce and death, jobs you needed and ones you hated (often one and the same), love and its many lingering losses, growing old—a whole world of limits, human-made and built-in. These topics were no more or less up-to-date than they'd ever been, but as the twenty-first century progressed, mainstream country audiences were, for the moment, less interested in hearing about any of them on the radio.

Over the last several years of Haggard's life, mainstream country radio became an almost exclusively youth-fixated format and—with women receiving less and less airplay and promotion and with Black country acts mostly never signed at all—an all but entirely white male one. So-called Bro-Country, originally defined by critic Jody Rosen as "by and of the tatted, gym-toned, party-hearty young American white dude," is a relentlessly in-this-very-moment music, by and for middle-class university types who, like their metaphorical "Muskogee" elders, enjoy college football and respect the dean and who maybe run a little wild on spring break.

The Bros added hip-hop-influenced rhymes and rhythms to country music but whittled its lyrical interests to drinking and hooking up. Near the end of his life, Haggard complained about this to Emily Yahr:

> They're talking about screwing on a pickup tailgate and things of that nature. I don't find no substance. I don't find anything you can whistle and nobody even attempts to write a melody. It's more of that kids' stuff.

Focusing on melody without also crediting the new-to-country rhythms, one more mostly unacknowledged adoption of Black sounds for white audiences, mainly just marked Merle as an old white man no longer keeping up with what the kids were into. And, coming from the man behind "Living with the Shades Pulled Down," "Shade Tree Fix-It Man," and "Let's Chase Each Other around the Room," any beefs about "screwing" as a subject matter are classic pot-calling-kettle hypocrisy. But Merle was on to something. Nothing wrong with country hits about making love in trucks or anywhere else. But complaints that radio now seemed *only* about that were more on point. Haggard and his forebears had understood life as tragic: you can't always get what you want; things don't always work out for the best; everybody dies. Life hadn't changed, but the working-class concerns that mattered so much to Haggard and his audience were now mostly limited on the radio to the expression of down-market recreational tastes, breezily signified by location, location, location: the suburbs and the lake, small towns, back roads and the bench seats of Ford F-150s. If the characters in Bro-Country hits by Florida Georgia Line and Luke Bryan ever had to get up and go to work in the morning, they were careful not to mention it.

What I suspect will continue to draw future listeners to Haggard's twenty-first-century work will be his singing. His voice betrays the miles and years, but he takes his time with his phrasing and tackles high notes head on—and the work it clearly takes him to do it complicates his songs, piles up layers of meaning. You can hear him having fun on these late-in-life records, too, at his ease and acting the fool, playing in ways he'd previously only allowed himself around Christmastime.

He added many more smart cover songs to his catalogue in these years. Many of those saw him returning to musicians he'd been loving and living with all his life—Frizzell and Rodgers, first on the list as ever—but there were surprises too. On a 2003 various-artists tribute to classic duo the Louvin Brothers, he joined Carl Jackson on a version of "Must You Throw Dirt in My Face" that is queasy with shame. He duetted with the Eagles' Don Henley on "The Cost of Living" ("everybody pays"), and he performed "Workin' Man Blues" and "Memphis" at a 2012 concert honoring Chuck Berry at the Rock and Roll Hall of Fame. He duetted twice on record with Jerry Lee Lewis. He contributed two tracks to a Buddy Holly tribute album.

He filled in a few glaring blanks on his résumé, as well. On 2003's

Haggard Like Never Before, he finally covered a Woody Guthrie song, du-etting with Willie Nelson on "Reno Blues (Philadelphia Lawyer)." He sang Woody again in 2009, delivering "Jesus Christ" over the closing credits to the Michael Moore film *Capitalism: A Love Story*. Guthrie's song presents Christ as a working man himself, crucified precisely because he dared instruct rich men and women to give their money to the poor. Notably, Merle tinkers with the lyrics to create an even angrier version than Woody's original. "When the patience of the workers give a-way, would be better for the rich if they'd never been born," Merle snarls with real conviction, envisioning a future when that class of people who'd put him and his fellow Okies somewhere just below would themselves be buried.

In 2012 he told journalist Jason Fine about plans to cut a new tribute album, this time celebrating Bob Dylan, but it wasn't until *Django and Jim-mie*, Willie again at his side, that he released his first recording of a Dylan song, "Don't Think Twice, It's All Right." I know of no recording of the song that captures so effectively the irony of Dylan's title. Thinking twice, and many more times besides, is what the song is about—and, historically, has been a big part of the job description for country singers old and young alike. Their voices broken-in but far from broken, Merle and Willie revel for a moment in the song's hitting-the-road-again, never-gonna-let-it-go bitterness. Then—the old friends have so much to do and the hour glass is just about empty—they let it go after all.

"I ain't sayin' that you treated me unkind," Willie sings near the end, citing what at this point in their lives was a far greater offense: "You just sort of wasted my precious time."

"Look out your window," Merle predicts. "I'll be gone."

In December 2015 Merle had a second lung surgery, a follow-up, as re-ported by *Billboard*'s Tom Roland, to the 2008 procedure that had removed "a lemon-sized cancerous tumor." He returned home but developed double pneumonia, spent some more time in the hospital, and canceled shows while he recovered. He attempted to play a date in early February 2016 but called it off at the very last minute. He apologized to fans from the stage: "Sadly I'm just not strong enough."

He canceled his remaining February dates, then quickly announced he'd be back on stage sooner than planned. On February 6 he made a date in Las Vegas, a big payday for the band but, needing to perform while using portable oxygen, couldn't finish the show. Friend Toby Keith, there as a fan but on-call if needed, took the ball and finished the set. Merle canceled his March dates not long afterward. Then he canceled his April dates.

On February 9, at his home studio outside of Redding, California, Merle made his final recording, "Kern River Blues," accompanied by his son Ben on guitar. The song, as later explained on his website, is about "his memories of leaving Bakersfield in the late seventies." But Merle's voice, weak and broken but phrased elegantly, evokes larger meanings. In retrospect, it sounds like a farewell.

> *I'm leavin' town tomorrow, I'll get my breakfast in the sky...*
> *I'm leavin' town forever, kiss an old boxcar goodbye.*

Merle Haggard died on his seventy-ninth birthday, April 6, 2016, surrounded by friends and family on his tour bus. Ben posted a black-and-white photo to social media: the son's hand clasping the father's, a faded "PSI" brand on Merle's forearm.

Willie Nelson, at the close of his 2017 album *God's Problem Child*, makes a prediction about his late friend in a song written by Gary Nicholson: "He Won't Ever Be Gone." "When it comes to country music, he's the world," Nelson sings. "And it wouldn't be all it is without Merle....His songs live on." It was a nice song and a nicer thought. Was it wishful thinking?

A few weeks before the release of *God's Problem Child*, on what would have been Merle's eightieth birthday, eighteen thousand people gathered for an event called "Sing Me Back Home: The Music of Merle Haggard," at Bridgestone Arena in Nashville. The several generations of fans present already knew both the words to Haggard's songs and his roles in country history: blue-collar poet and proto-Outlaw, devotee of idiosyncrasy, a brooding and brokenhearted balladeer, a repeat offender at maintaining and transforming tradition. They well understood how often what appeared to be a chip on his shoulder had turned out to be his heart on his sleeve.

A few contemporary radio stars showed up to pay their respects at the "Sing Me Back Home" concert (released in 2020 on DVD and compact disc). Dierks Bentley sang Haggard's Nixon-era Christmas song, and biggest pop hit, "If We Make It through December"; Kacey Musgraves was an ideal match for Haggard's whimsical "Rainbow Stew"; the Avett Brothers did a spry take on "Mama Tried." Honky-tonk bros Chris Jansen and Jake Owen palled around to "Footlights," a bitter midlife-crisis anthem, and Miranda Lambert performed "Misery and Gin," a Haggard-identified weeper she'd often turned to onstage through the years. But most of the thirty or so performers on hand were of an older vintage, either just past their hit-making prime, like Toby Keith and Ronnie Dunn, or well past it, like Bobby Bare, ZZ Top's Billy Gibbons, Loretta Lynn, John Mellencamp, Connie Smith, Tanya Tucker, and Hank Williams Jr.

Lynn, who concluded the first half of the program, needed assistance to make it to the microphone, then delivered a devastating version of Haggard's most recorded number, "Today I Started Loving You Again." Willie Nelson closed the show. He sounded a bit frail himself at first but gained power as he traded vocal and guitar lines with Keith Richards on "Reasons to Quit." Climaxing with Lynn and Nelson, ages eighty-five and eighty-four at the time, respectively, was as it should be. But it also underscored a generational gap apparent all evening. The lineup argued that the case for Haggard's continued relevance would be made, at least initially, by old-school country acts (reportedly Nelson has a Merle tribute in the can), by Americana artists, and by roots-favoring rockers, not by any of today's mainstream country stars.

Merle Haggard won't be forgotten anytime soon. When he died, Haggard appeared, finally, on the cover of *Rolling Stone*, and a year later the magazine placed him atop its list of the "100 Greatest Country Artists of All Time." The US House of Representatives voted to rededicate a Bakersfield, California, post office in his name, and there have been other similar honors. But such gestures won't translate to continued influence. For Haggard to enjoy a musical legacy, he will need to be more than remembered and admired in interviews or at the occasional tribute concert. His music will need to be used, his songs performed and recorded. A bit of retro-minded Hag mimicry might be welcome now and again, but the more urgent question will be whether or not any current or future star will mimic Merle's methods: he made old music sound up to date; he made other people's music sound like his music.

Only a handful of artists lately have attempted anything of the kind. In 2014 Suzy Bogguss released *Lucky*, an exceptionally smart Merle tribute. She perfectly updated Nashville Sound sensibilities for our world—acoustic, less-is-more arrangements shaded by jazzy guitar and sultry organ. In 2017, on *Best Troubador*, the singer-songwriter Will Oldham, working in a rag-gedly self-aware old-time style and under his stage name, Bonnie "Prince" Billy, performed versions of Merle songs selected mostly beyond the great-est hits. His readings of cult favorites "The Day the Rains Came," "Roses in Winter," and "If I Could Only Fly" are so delicate and mysterious that you fear a stiff breeze might blow them away forever. Far less successful was *Working Man's Poet: A Tribute to Merle Haggard*, from 2014. Prom-isingly, it featured a lineup of contemporary country stars: Jason Aldean, Luke Bryan, Randy Houser, and Jake Owen, among them. But it mostly just sounded old-fashioned, as if for some reason they decided to aim for airplay twenty years ago. Aldean and company treated Haggard's songs like beloved keepsakes and not, as Bogguss and Oldham had done, like tools they could use. It felt like the difference between hanging onto a late grandparent's cookbook merely as a sentimental memento or also keeping it because you know you can tweak some of its best recipes for dinner next week—or maybe as encores on your next tour.

Popular music rarely lasts, even when its creators build it for that purpose—as Haggard typically did, with one eye on the past, the other on the ages. Endurance through the decades depends on external factors. It helps considerably when a body of work finds evangelists among younger generations of stars: the legacies of Lefty Frizzell, Jimmie Rodgers, and Bob Wills, among others, were reignited when Merle Haggard committed himself to carrying their torches. It also helps if a star's children become stars themselves. A key to the continued relevance of Johnny Cash is that, like Hank Williams before him, he had a music-making kid, Rosanne Cash, who became not only an innovative hit-maker but a popular ambassador for the family's traditions.

At the "Sing Me Back Home" concert, Ben Haggard opened the show with one of his dad's songs from the 1980s called "What Am I Gonna Do (With the Rest of My Life)." He was only twenty-four at the time but had been a Stranger since around the time he could drive. He was already a better guitarist than his father ever was (he backed Nelson on "He Won't Ever Be Gone"), and his voice, pitched somewhat higher than his father's, quivers evocatively in a relaxed, modern style: "I got whiskey I could drink, that would help me not to think, about you leaving," Ben sang at the tribute show, repurposing a song that his dad had recorded before he was born.

When he was just nineteen, Ben Haggard appeared with his father and

Willie Nelson on a new version of Merle's onetime signature anthem, "Workin' Man Blues," from 2011's *Working in Tennessee*. "I've been a working man, damn near all my life," Merle declares, coming up just then on his seventy-fifth birthday. And he will keep working, "as long as my two hands are fit to use." You picture him examining those hands, turning them over, shaking his head, hoping against hope. "I might get a little *high* on the weekend," Willie says, updating the old line, and Merle, very much out of character, approves at the top of his lungs: "Weeeee-eeell! Hey! Hey!" Then Ben, in a high Cali tenor, gets to sing a verse with his elders. Outsings them actually, and on a bounding Telecaster solo, Ben outplays Willie, too. I like that.

This new version of the song keeps suggesting the old one straight along, but this "Workin' Man Blues" isn't riding a rocking Elvis Presley rhythm any longer. The new groove still rocks—it's slower but just as steady—and it swings harder. I like that, too, the way the record is new and old at once, the way sameness butts up against difference, and how each has something helpful to say to the other across the gap between generations. It's one more reminder that even a backward cast of mind as finely honed as Merle Haggard's was always bound to look ahead.

"Don't look back," Satchel Paige famously cautioned, with good reason. "Something might be gaining on you." Over a career that spanned a half century, Merle Haggard offered different advice. Look back, his music instructs. Look back often. Because life is precious and because memories savored add context, intensity, and flavor to the present. Because looking back is our best measuring stick for the inevitable gains and losses of life, because it keeps us in conversation with our ancestors and allows us to engage the influences that made us who we are—connecting us to stories bigger than our own. Because it's the *only* tool we have for judging how far we've come and how far we have to go. Look back for another reason too: *Because something might be gaining on you.* Merle Haggard's music and career taught that, moving forward, it's always wise to check the rearview.

CHAPTER 34

"IF I COULD ONLY FLY," 2001

A Blaze Foley song, "If I Could Only Fly," goes down with Liz Anderson's "The Fugitive," Dallas Frazier's "California Cottonfields" and "Too Many Bridges to Cross Over," and Sonny Throckmorton's "The Way I Am," not to mention about a dozen Merle Haggard compositions, as essential statements of the Haggard aesthetic. Merle had been singing "If I Could Only Fly" in concert for years, ever since his friend Lewis Talley introduced it to him on the houseboat in 1985: "That's the best damn song I've heard in 15 years," Talley told him. When Talley died not long afterward, Merle explained the next year on an episode of *Pop! Goes the Country*, he sang the song at the funeral of the man he called "my first fan."

In 1998 he sang it at another funeral, via a prerecorded performance: Tammy Wynette's memorial service at the Ryman Auditorium, which was broadcast live on CNN. He accompanied himself on acoustic guitar and barely made it through the performance. Merle's final jumbled guitar notes were heavy, noisy sobs beyond his control. "That's the best I could do," he said. He removed his black hat, stared at the floor, sniffled. "It's not very good…"

Merle first recorded the song with Willie Nelson in 1987. But where that recording is wistful and almost sweet, his 2001 reading of the song, on *If I*

Could Only Fly, is stark and harrowing, its sweetness a little bitter, like life. "I almost felt you touching me just now" is how Merle begins, but there's no one to touch. "I feel so good," he sings, quite carefully, "and then I feel so bad. I wonder what I ought to do." Merle's voice has an eye to the sky, threatens to take wing, but Foley's melody keeps turning flat and halting, and there Merle is, grounded again, and alone. The music's so minimal, just the chords really, that it almost feels like even his old friends the Strangers aren't with him. "If I could only fly," Merle imagines. He would soar to his lover then, and there would be no more lonely nights. But in the song he can barely stand up.

There's the Hag character in all its poignancy. He can't fly but he can't stop dreaming about how amazing, how freeing, it would be if he could. "If I could only fly," he sings, his baritone cracking, tumbling backward, then lifting. "If *I* could only fly...if *we* could only fly...if *you* could only fly..." Then we wouldn't need to run anymore.

EPILOGUE

CUBA, MISSOURI

JULY 15, 2010

I n late December 2010 Merle Haggard became a Kennedy Center Honoree. He'd hobnobbed with presidents before, of course, and when this particular president, Barack Obama, was about to be inaugurated two years earlier, Merle had written a poem, "Hopes Are High," and posted it on his website. But Merle Haggard as a Kennedy Center Honoree was something else again. Here was that old Oildale Okie, San Quentin's own, being feted by the president and first lady, recognized as a Great American Artist and seated between Broadway composer Jerry "Hello, Dolly" Herman and jillionaire talk show host Oprah Winfrey—a seating chart that read on television like a middle-class seal of approval. As he told music journalist Chris Richards at the time, "It's gotta be the most prestigious award not usually given to someone from the dirt."

For Hag watchers, it was a moving sight—the seventy-three-year-old Merle looked grizzled but fine, a gold medal hung about his neck by rainbow ribbon and wearing a silver-and-gray beard of a decidedly Lincolnesque cut. He got teary and sang along quietly to himself when "Silver Wings" was performed in his honor. A Kris Kristofferson–narrated biography film was smartly done: it got to "Okie from Muskogee" soon enough but kicked off with "Footlights," a Merle favorite; the inevitable Willie Nelson–led all-star

284

jam skipped "Workin' Man Blues" in favor of "Ramblin' Fever." When it was over, Haggard stood, removed his black hat, and nodded thank you.

A few months earlier Merle had been in a more familiar setting when he played the Crawford County Fair in Cuba, Missouri, along historic Route 66, Ghost Road of the Okies. A lot of the old folks who'd never left these hills in the first place got to the show early to set up their lawn chairs in the good spots, under tall shade trees that lined the grass-and-dirt concert area. Middle-aged men nursed their beers, younger parents shooed away kids playing grab-ass across their picnic blankets, and everyone fought the July heat as best they could with complimentary "It's Cool to Be a Republican" cardboard fans. Every five minutes or so, a prerecorded message suggested we visit the Hag Store for CDs, autographed photos, and "cropped-top baby-tees."

Noel Haggard, Merle's boy from his first marriage, wandered out and played a few songs. Then came the Malpass Brothers, a North Carolina duo signed to Hag Records, who sang classics like "Walking the Floor over You" and "Are You Sure Hank Done It This Way" ("We're all about keeping traditional country music alive!"), and then Merle came out. He was dressed in black, from boots to Stetson, and he moved very slowly.

It took him a few numbers to get his voice going. Merle in his later years wasn't afraid to deploy the spoken phrase when he needed it to catch his breath, but he did so sparingly, artfully, and he also played a lot more electric guitar—it became like a second voice. He launched "I Think I'll Just Stay Here and Drink" with jagged power chords, and when he took a solo, his notes were delicate and jazzy, then turned abruptly violent, almost pure noise.

Once his voice was warmed up, he sang ballads—"Twinkle, Twinkle Lucky Star," "Today I Started Loving You Again." On "If We Make It through December," a big guy to my right, silent and still for the last half hour, heard Merle croon, "Got laid off down at the factory," pumped his fist in the air, and shouted, "God DAMN it!"

People cheered, hard, for "Workin' Man Blues," though when Merle boasted about never being on welfare, normally an assured-applause line of the "Hell, yeah!" variety, it passed by in this county (45 percent of the locals are on food stamps) without so much as a clap. "I'm tired of this dirty old city," however, earned a half dozen enthusiastic whoops in the Missouri Ozarks.

Across the way, another man kept hounding Merle to play "Mama Tried." "Maaaaaa-maaaaaa," he bellowed between songs, each time louder and longer than before. "I'll play it," Merle finally snapped, "but I ain't gonna play it *now*." Then he thought about it: "Well, now wait a minute.... Would it *fit* now? Yeah, I think it would. All right, this one goes out to this ol' loud fella over here." The crowd roared, a thousand people singing together—"Mama tried. Mama Tried. MAMA TRIED"—and very nearly a thousand people missing that final highest note, Merle included, and it was beautiful.

A young woman behind me, late twenties, said to no one in particular: "It's like every song he sings is the most amazing song ever. *Every song.*"

Merle played "Fightin' Side of Me," dedicating it to the soldiers fighting overseas, solemnizing the moment and quelling the "U-S-A" chant that had arisen instantly at his mentioning of the song's title. He played "Okie from Muskogee," introducing it as "A song I wrote for my father. He was from Oklahoma and he did not smoke marijuana. He. Did. Not." The applause seemed like it would never stop after that, and Haggard stood stock still, smiling broadly, and let it come. Then he was gone.

After a while I headed over to where his Silver Eagle was parked by the side of the stage to check out the autograph line. Merle was already onboard, though, the bus just beginning to lumber its way across the fairgrounds. It took a left onto the main road, old Route 66, and I watched until the taillights disappeared in the distance, Merle Haggard heading toward Oklahoma and points west, looking for home.

SELECTED DISCOGRAPHY

Merle Haggard released more than eighty albums over half a century, and that's not counting a quartet of mostly instrumental albums by the Strangers or greatest hits and other anthology releases, both pricey and cheapo, that at this rate will sooner than later outpace official releases. It can be daunting even figuring out where to start.

The best place to begin exploring the Haggard catalogue—the way to get the most essential Haggard music all in one place—remains *Down Every Road: 1962–1994* (Capitol, 1996). That four-disc set encompasses a body of work as foundational to modern country music (as well as to all varieties of country rock) as the sides on James Brown's *Star Time* set have been to R&B, soul, and hip-hop. For a less pricey first step, however, go with *The Complete '60s Capitol Singles* (Omnivore, 2013), which collects on a single disc all of Haggard's 45s (B-sides included) from the first half decade of his career, everything up to "Okie from Muskogee," when he was establishing the sound and persona he in one way or another pursued ever after.

Something along those same lines needs doing for Merle's short half decade at MCA Records, as well. Though most of Haggard's individual MCA albums are in print, the only collection currently available for that era is the four-disc import set from Bear Family, *Troubadour*—marvelous but expensive. Efficient single-disc options are even scarcer for anyone looking to understand Haggard's decade at Epic Records. The least bad choice, *The Essential Merle Haggard: The Epic Years*, clocks in at a miserly fourteen tracks—not including "Kern River" and "Natural High," which is to say the disc doesn't even meet the limited criteria of its title. As for the time Merle served at Curb in the 1990s, no current anthology covers this period of his career nor is one particularly desired.

What serious Haggard fans will want to do, eventually, is venture beyond anthologies to the man's individual albums. Of those four score albums, almost all are worth your time in one way or another. Even culling from the herd only the very best of his albums would still have us choosing from among dozens. For recommendations nearer to complete, see *The Running Kind: Listening to Merle Haggard* itself, but what follows is this selected discography's attempt to be extremely selective: a list of only a dozen Merle Haggard albums, taking in the masterpieces (well, the bulk of them anyway), but also attempting to capture the scope of his sounds, styles, themes, and interests.

Merle Haggard and the Strangers
Mama Tried (Capitol, 1968)
A theme album about prison as both place and state of mind. Its bookends are key: the regretful-but-defiant "Mama Tried" and Dallas Frazier's "Too Many Bridges to Cross Over." "Like an eagle, I'm a prisoner of the wind." His first masterpiece.

Merle Haggard and the Strangers
Pride in What I Am (Capitol, 1969)
From the boastful humility of the title track to the beautiful strangeness of "The Day the Rains Came" to the hounded "I Can't Hold Myself in Line" to the kiss-my-ass celebration of "I'm Bringing Home Good News," this brooding, low-key, and mostly acoustic album gets my nomination for greatest country-rock album ever.

Merle Haggard
Same Train, a Different Time (Capitol, 1969)
The country music tradition's finest tribute album is, not at all coincidentally, an exemplar of how the country tradition works: yesterday's songs done up so they sound like today. Changes, connected.

Merle Haggard and the Strangers
Hag (Capitol, 1970)
The most consistently political album of Hag's career and, bonus, one of his best, thanks especially to "Shelly's Winter Love," "Jesus, Take a Hold," "I Can't Be Myself," "I'm a Good Loser," and "The Farmer's Daughter."

Merle Haggard and the Strangers
Someday We'll Look Back (Capitol, 1971)
Read 'em and weep: "Someday We'll Look Back," "Train of Life," "One Sweet Hello," "One Row at a Time," "Big Time Annie's Square," "I'd Rather Be Gone," "California Cottonfields," "Carolyn," "Tulare Dust," "Huntsville," and "The Only Trouble with Me." If this country-soul effort isn't Merle Haggard's best album...

Merle Haggard
Serving 190 Proof (MCA, 1979)
...then this country-jazz one is. A low and lonesome testament to rugged individualism ("My Own Kind of Hat") running smack into a wall ("Red Bandana") and the disillusionment and depression ("Footlights," "I Can't Get Away") that follow. Self-medication included ("Heaven Was a Drink of Wine"), along with hard-won wisdom ("Roses in Winter").

Merle Haggard
Songs for the Mama That Tried (MCA, 1981)
The most reverent and soulful, the sparest and most beautiful, of his four gospel sets. "Swing Low Sweet Chariot" finds Merle's baritone hitching a ride with a choir all the way to glory.

Merle Haggard
Big City (Epic, 1981)
The definitive statement of backward-glancing Reagan-era country, thanks to the title track, "Are the Good Times Really Over (I Wish a Buck Was Still Silver)," and a swell cover of "Stop the World and Let Me Off."

Merle Haggard and George Jones
A Taste of Yesterday's Wine (Epic, 1982)
In which Merle Haggard joins Tammy Wynette as the only human being

ever to outsing George Jones. Also, humor doesn't get any darker than "Must've Been Drunk" or "I Think I've Found a Way."

Merle Haggard and Leona Williams
Heart to Heart (Mercury, 1983)
Probably the most underrated album in Merle's catalogue. Leona is at her best here. Roy Nichols is very near to his.

Merle Haggard
The Epic Collection (Recorded Live) (Epic, 1983)
Okie from Muskogee and *The Fightin' Side of Me* were more culturally significant concert albums, and *I Love Dixie Blues* a more historically minded one, but for capturing Merle's emotive and musical range as a singer, as well as showcasing the improvisational skills of his Strangers, this is the live album to get. (An alternate concert pick: the inexpensive *I Think I'll Just Stay Here and Drink*, a sixteen-track disc released by One Media Publishing in 2009, clearly reorders the evening's performances and includes zero information about where or even when it was recorded—I'm guessing late 1980s or very early 1990s, based on the set list and its more rocking than country-jazz approach. It's swell.)

Merle Haggard
If I Could Only Fly (Anti-, 2000)
The first and still the best of his twenty-first-century releases. The alternately harrowing and heart-swelling personal ballads ("Wishing All These Old Things Were New," "I'm Still Your Daddy") will grab you first. But it's the loosest, hottest western swing of his life ("Bareback," "Honky Tonk Mama") that will keep you coming back.

A HALF DOZEN NEXT STEPS...

Merle Haggard and the Strangers
A Portrait of Merle Haggard (Capitol, 1970)

Merle Haggard and the Strangers
Merle Haggard Presents His 30th Album (Capitol, 1974)

Merle Haggard
Back to the Barrooms (MCA, 1980)

Merle Haggard
That's the Way Love Goes (Epic, 1984)

Merle Haggard
Unforgettable (Capitol, 2004)

Merle Haggard
Working Man's Journey (Cracker Barrel, 2007)

ACKNOWLEDGMENTS

O f course, I must first thank Merle Haggard. Listening again, and so intensely, to his body of work was fun, challenging, and inspiring—and not a little humbling.

Those who influenced my thinking about Haggard, class, and country music as I worked on the first edition of *The Running Kind* were many. In varying ways—I know some of them personally, even well, but others only through their work—they together formed a kind of critical chorus of voices in my head: Dave A. Cantwell, Cheryl Cline, Julie Criner, Chuck Eddy, Howard Eisberg, John Floyd, Bill Friskics-Warren, the late Paul Hemphill, Charles Hughes, Mike Ireland, C. J. Janovy, Roy Kasten, Bill C. Malone, Greil Marcus, Dave Marsh, Barry Mazor, the late John Morthland, Diane Pecknold, the late Richard Peterson, Tex Sample, Ed Scanlon, Alan Scherstuhl, Mike Warren, Jon Weisberger, Carl Wilson, Gary Wilson, and Don Yates.

Several others not only influenced my work but helped me directly. Craig Werner and Danny Alexander read behind me and provided invaluable feedback and support. I owe a great debt to Deke Dickerson and to all the other liner notes writers and sessionographers of Bear Family Records' several Merle Haggard box sets. Important parts of my work would be impossible without their work.

I am indebted to Casey Kittrell at the University of Texas Press for helping this book become a reality and for taking me seriously as I pestered him about doing a second edition. I must thank Victoria Davis, Lynne Ferguson, Lindsay Starr, Wendy Moore, and Allison Faust at the University of Texas Press for their commitment and their patience, and Paul Spragens and Leslie Tingle, copyeditors extraordinaire. Peter Blackstock approached me about contributing a volume to the American Music Series, for which I am beyond grateful. Many others—including the late Liz Anderson, Cary Baker, Don Cusic, Todd Everett, the late Chet Flippo, Dallas Frazier, Michael Gray, Peter La Chapelle, Michael McCall, Patrick Milligan, Bryan Murray, the late Bill Osment, Robert Price, and several of the good folks at Johnson County Community College's Billington Library—were generous with their time and expertise when I had questions or otherwise needed assistance.

During the years when I was mulling, and then writing, the second edition of *The Running Kind*, my editor at the *New Yorker*, David Haglund, gave me the space there to work out ideas I was able to use here (elements of chapter 33 first appeared in a piece he edited, "The Uneasy Legacy of Merle Haggard"). My editors at *Rolling Stone Country*, Joseph Hudak, and at *Engine 145*, Juli Thanki, did the same. I owe a thank you, as well, to the many people who answered questions and shared leads, provided resources and insights and otherwise helped, supported, or inspired me as I plugged away: Shepherd Alligood, Eric Banister, Jonathan Bernstein, Scott Bomar, Kathleen Campbell, Brenda Colladay, Iris DeMent, Steacy Easton, Shannon Erb, Stephen Thomas Erlewine, Jon Freeman, Bill Glahn, Thomas Alan Holmes, Nadine Hubbs, Amanda Martinez, Chris Molanphy, Betsy Phillips, Tresa Redburn, Alexander Shashko, John Shaw, Elaine Schock, RJ Smith, Alfred Soto, Rob Tannenbaum, the late John Walker Ross, Andrea Williams, John Yuelkenbeck, Annie Zaleski, and Andy Zax. I also owe a very special thank you, for so many reasons, to Jewly Hight and to Charles Hughes.

Finally, thank you to Doris Saltkill for her bottomless support, practical and emotional and otherwise: every word I write is for you. Someday, as Merle Haggard sang, we'll look back and say, "This was fun."

SELECTED BIBLIOGRAPHY

Allen, Bob, ed. *The Blackwell Guide to Recorded Country Music*. Blackwell Reference, 1994.

———. "A Good Ol' Boy Lets His Hair Hang Down." *Esquire*, Sept. 1981: 76–78.

———. "Merle Haggard: An American Spokesman." *Cashbox,* July 28, 1984.

———. "Merle Haggard: Everything Else You Want to Know." *Country Song Roundup*, Sept. 1982: 14–17, 46.

———. "Merle Haggard: From Convict to Country King." *Hustler*, July 1982: 34–38, 50, 54, 132–134.

———. "Merle Haggard: Looking Forward into the Past." *Country Song Roundup*, Dec. 1981: 15–17, 26.

Anderson, Liz. Telephone interview by author, 2011.

Aronowitz, Alfred G. "New Country Twang Hits Town: The Merle Haggard Scene." *Life*, May 3, 1968: 10.

Auchmutey, Jim. "Country's Final Outlaw." *Atlanta Journal Constitution*, Nov. 8, 1980.

Banister, C. Eric. *Johnny Cash FAQ: All That's Left to Know about the Man in Black*. Backbeat Books, 2014.

Beitiks, Edvins. "Songwriter Iris DeMent Takes a New Step." *Chicago Tribune*, Sept. 5, 1997.

Betts, Stephen. "Flashback: Merle Haggard Sings an Emotional 'If I Could Only Fly.' " *Rolling Stone Country* online, Apr. 6, 2019.

"Beyond Nashville." *Lost Highway: The History of American Country*. Season 1, episode 3. BBC, 2003.

Bomar, Scott B. Liner notes to *The Bakersfield Sound: Country Music Capital of the West, 1940–1974*. Bear Family Records, 2019.

Bowen, Jimmy, and Jim Jerome. *Rough Mix: An Unapologetic Look at the Music Business and How It Got that Way*. Simon & Schuster, 1997.

Bronson, Barry. "Merle Haggard Speaks: 'I'm Laid Back in My Mind.'" *Music City News*, Oct. 1984.

Bufwack, Mary A., and Robert K. Oerman. *Finding Her Voice: The Illustrated History of Women in Country Music*. Henry Holt, 1993.

Burton, Charlie. "We Don't Smoke Marijuana in Muskogee. We Steal." *Rolling Stone*, Mar. 18, 1971.

Cantwell, David. "Blowin' in the Wind." *No Depression*, Mar./Apr. 2006: 109.

———. *George Strait: An Illustrated Musical History*. Boulevard Books, 1996.

———. Liner notes to *From Elvis in Nashville*. RCA/Legacy Recordings, 2020.

———. "The Merle Haggard Songbook: A 1968 Playlist." Guest post, *The '68 Comeback Special* edited by Charles Hughes, Apr. 8, 2018. Blog.

———. "No More Country for Old Men." *New Yorker* online, June 9, 2015.

———. "Pledge of Allegiance: Merle Haggard Salutes His Greatest Influence, the Legendary Lefty Frizzell." *Country Music*, Feb. 2002: 22–25.

———. "Reality Check: A Legend in His Own Right, Merle Haggard Still Pays Tribute to His Inspirations." *The Pitch*, Sept. 13, 2001.

———. Review of *If I Could Only Fly* by Merle Haggard. *Miami New Times*, Oct. 5, 2000.

———. Review of *Unforgettable* by Merle Haggard. *No Depression,* Mar./Apr. 2005: 119–120.

———. "The Uncertain Musical Legacy of Merle Haggard." *New Yorker* online, July 24, 2017.

———. "What Sturgill Simpson's Viral Rant about Merle Haggard Misses about Merle Haggard." *Slate* online, Sept. 2, 2016.

Cantwell, David, and Bill Friskics-Warren. *Heartaches by the Number: Country Music's 500 Greatest Singles*. Country Music Foundation Press/Vanderbilt University Press, 2003.

Carlisle, Dolly. "What Are Merle Haggard's Favorite Memories? Not San Quentin, but His Crush on Dolly Parton." *People Weekly*, Nov. 23, 1981.

Carr, Patrick. "Merle: That's the Way It Goes." *Country Music*, Jan./Feb. 1986: 26–31.

Cash, Johnny, with Patrick Carr. *Cash: The Autobiography*. Harper Collins, 1997.

Christgau, Robert. "In Search of Jim Crow: Why Postmodern Minstrelsy Studies Matter." In *Book Reports: A Music Critic on His First Love, Which Was Reading*, 23–40. Duke University Press, 2019.

———. *Rock Albums of the '70s: A Critical Guide*. Da Capo Press, 1981.

Cocks, Jay. "Down to Old Dixie and Back." *Time*, Jan. 12, 1970.

Coe, Tyler Mahan. "Breaking Down Merle Haggard's 'Okie from Muskogee.'" *Cocaine & Rhinestones*, Nov. 21, 2017. Audio blog.

Cooper, Daniel. *Lefty Frizzell: The Honky-Tonk Life of Country Music's Greatest Singer*. Little, Brown, 1995.

———. Liner notes to *Down Every Road: 1962–1994*. Capitol Records, 1996.

Copper, Peter. "Down and Dirty with the Hag: Legendary Songwriter Angry about Nation's Eroding Freedoms." *Nashville Tennessean*, Oct. 11, 2003.

———. "50 Country Songs Every Songwriter Should Know." *American Songwriter*, May/June 2010: 48–51.

———. "Merle Haggard as He Is." *American Songwriter*, May/June 2010: 58–65.

Cowie, Jefferson. *Stayin' Alive: The 1970s and the Last Days of the Working Class*. New Press, 2010.

Dawidoff, Nicholas. *In the Country of Country: People and Places in American Music.* Pantheon, 1997.

DeParle, Jason. "Merle Haggard: Workin' Man Blues." *Journal of Country Music* 16.1 (1993): 11–15.

DeVoss, David. "Lord, They've Done It All." *Time,* May 6, 1974: 51–55.

Dickerson, Deke. Liner notes to *Bonnie Owens: Queen of the Coast.* Bear Family Records, 2007.

———. Liner notes to *Concepts, Live & the Strangers: Hag, the Capitol Recordings 1968–1976.* Bear Family Records, 2008.

———. Liner notes to *Hag: The Studio Recordings 1969–1976.* Bear Family Records, 2007.

DiSalvatore, Bryan. "Ornery." *New Yorker,* Feb. 12, 1990: 39–44, 48–49, 52–77.

Doggett, Peter. *Are You Ready for the Country: Elvis, Dylan, Parsons and the Roots of Country Rock.* Penguin Books, 2001.

Doyle, Patrick. "Merle Haggard Returns to Road after Health Scare: 'I'm Lucky to Be Alive.'" *Rolling Stone* online, Feb. 21, 2016.

Dufour, Jeff. "Woodstock Producer: Roy Rogers, Not Hendrix, Could Have Closed." *Washington Examiner,* Aug. 8, 2009.

Durkee, Cutler. "Merle Haggard Plays Musical Wives, and His Ex Now Sings Backup." *People Weekly,* June 25, 1979: 80–82.

Ehrenreich, Barbara. *Fear of Falling: The Inner Life of the Middle Class.* Pantheon, 1989.

Einarson, John. *Desperados: The Roots of Country Rock.* Cooper Square Press, 2001.

Escott, Colin. Liner notes to *Wynn Stewart: California Country—The Best of the Challenge Masters.* AVI Recordings, 1995.

Eskow, Gary. "Classic Tracks: Merle Haggard's 'Mama Tried.'" *Mix: Professional Audio and Music Production* online, May 1, 2009.

Eubanks, Bob. "Merle Speaks His Mind." *Billboard,* Feb. 19, 1977: H4, H8, H11.

Everett, Todd. "Interview by Todd Everett." *Billboard,* Feb. 19, 1977: H1–H2, H10.

Farris, Mark. "Merle Haggard Recalls Jail to Fame." *Wisconsin State Journal,* Jan. 22, 1982.

Fine, Jason. "The Fighter: The Life and Times of Merle Haggard." *Rolling Stone* online, Oct. 1, 2009.

———. "The Running Kind: In the Last Decade, Merle Haggard Found Solace on His Ranch, but He Stayed Restless to the End." *Rolling Stone,* May 5, 2016: 52–53.

Flippo, Chet. "Merle Haggard: 'Let's Get Out of Iraq.'" *Counterpunch* online, Oct. 18, 2005.

Fong-Torres, Ben. *Hickory Wind: The Life and Times of Gram Parsons.* Pocket Books, 1991.

Foster, Alice. "Merle Haggard: I Take a lot of Pride in What I Am." *Sing Out! The Folk Song Magazine,* Mar./Apr. 1970: 11–17.

Fox, Randy. Liner notes to *Leona Williams: Yes, Ma'm, He Found Me in a Honky Tonk.* Bear Family Records, 2013.

Frazier, Dallas. Telephone interview by author, 2010.

Gerome, John. "New Merle Haggard Tune Blasts US Media Coverage of Iraq War." Associated Press, July 25, 2003.

Giddins, Gary. *Bing Crosby: A Pocketful of Dreams, the Early Years 1903–1940.* Little, Brown, 2001.

Gillette, Charlie. *The Sound of the City: The Rise of Rock 'n' Roll*. Dell, 1972.

Gilmore, Mikal. "The Outlaw: Merle Haggard, 1937–2016." *Rolling Stone*, May 5, 2016: 44–51, 68.

Gottschalk, Earl C. "Love It or Leave It: New Patriotic Music Wins Fans, Enemies." *Wall Street Journal*, Aug. 18, 1970.

Green, Douglas B. "The Mountain Sound Revived." In *The Illustrated History of Country Music*, edited by Patrick Carr, 201–216. Country Music Magazine Press/Doubleday, 1979.

Gregory, James N. *American Exodus: The Dust Bowl Migration and Okie Culture in California*. Oxford University Press, 1989.

Grein, Ted. "Merle Haggard: He's Everything He Sings About." *Country Song Roundup*, Apr. 1969: 30–31.

Griffis, Ken. "I've Got So Many Million Years: The Story of Stuart Hamblen." *JEMF Quarterly* 14.49 (1978): 4–22.

Grissim, John. *Country Music: White Man's Blues*. Paperback Library, 1970.

———. "I'm Still Not Sure It Wasn't Planned." *Rolling Stone*, May 28, 1970.

Guralnick, Peter. "Haggard at the Crossroads: A Portrait of the Artist in Mid-Life." *Country Music*, Jan./Feb. 1981: 42–46.

———. "Merle Haggard: In the Good Old Days (When Times Were Bad)." In *Lost Highway: Journeys and Arrivals of American Musicians*, 232–247. Back Bay Books, 1979.

Haggard, Merle. "A New Song." *Merle Haggard* online, Jan. 21, 2009.

———. "Songs I Wish I'd Written." *Rolling Stone*, Oct. 27, 2011: 72.

Haggard, Merle, with Tom Carter. *Merle Haggard's My House of Memories: For the Record*. Cliff Street Books, 1999.

Haggard, Merle, and Peggy Russell. *Sing Me Back Home: My Story*. Pocket Books, 1981.

Halberstadt, Alex. "Merle Haggard." *Salon* online, Nov. 14, 2000.

Hamill, Peter. "The Revolt of the White Lower Middle Class." *New York* magazine online, Apr. 14, 1969.

Hansen, Liane. "Buck Owens Stayed True to His Bakersfield Sound." *Weekend Edition*. NPR, Mar. 26, 2006.

Haslam, Gerald. "Back off, Bakersfield." *Los Angeles Times*, Apr. 2, 2006.

———. *Workin' Man Blues: Country Music in California*, University of California Press, 1999.

Heath, Chris. "The Last Outlaw." *GQ*, Nov. 2005.

Hedgepeth, William. "Merle Haggard: He Sings for the Folks Who Fought World War II." *Look*, July 13, 1971: 36–41.

Hedy, Judy. "Merle Haggard: You Can't Buy His Respect…and He Puts No Price Tag on Pride." *Country Song Roundup*, Feb. 1978: 14–15, 40.

Hemphill, Paul. *The Nashville Sound: Bright Lights and Country Music*. Simon & Schuster, 1970.

———. "Okie from Muskogee." In *The Good Old Boys*, 123–127. Simon & Schuster, 1974.

———. "A Restless Aries Loses His Devils." *Country Music*, Nov. 1972: 24–30.

Hentoff, Nat. "White Line Fever." In *Listen to the Stories: Nat Hentoff on Jazz and Country Music*, 153–164. Harper Collins, 1995.

Hicks, Dan. Review of *A Tribute to the Best Damn Fiddle Player in the World (or My Salute to Bob Wills)*. *Rolling Stone*, Oct. 27, 1972.

Hilburn, Robert. *Johnny Cash: The Life*. Little, Brown, 2013.

———. "Merle Haggard Will Voice Patriotism on Train Route to Farm-Aid Concert." *Los Angeles Times*, Sept. 6, 1985.

Hillman, Chris. *Time Between: My Life as a Byrd, Burrito Brother, and Beyond*. BMG Books, 2020.

Himes, Geoffrey. "Alternative Country." In *The Blackwell Guide to Recorded Country Music*, edited by Bob Allen, 249–286. Blackwell Reference, 1994.

Hoekstra, Dave. "Legendary Merle Haggard's Life Goes Full Circle." *Chicago Sun-Times*, Apr. 6, 2016. Blog.

———. "Merle Haggard's America." Davehoekstra.com, Apr. 6, 2016. Blog.

———. "When push comes to shove, there may be no better expert on American Wanderlust than Merle Haggard." Davehoekstra.com, Nov. 16, 2003. Blog.

Hubbs, Nadine. *Rednecks, Queers, and Country Music*. University of California Press, 2014.

Hughes, Charles. *Country Soul: Making Music and Making Race in the American South*. University of North Carolina Press, 2015.

Hughes, Kye. "An Okie from Muskogee and a Wild and Crazy Guy." *Bennington [VT] Banner*, Aug. 7, 1979.

Hurst, Jack. "Country Singin' Man Blues: Everyone's Saluting Merle Haggard—So Why Can't He Get on the Radio?" *Chicago Tribune*, Nov. 13, 1994.

———. "Haggard Keeps Going His Own Way Right to the Top." *Chicago Tribune*, June 7, 1977.

———. "Terri Gibbs Takes to the Road." *Indianapolis [IN] News*, Dec. 16, 1981.

Jarrett, Michael. *Producing Country: The Inside Story of the Great Recordings*. Wesleyan University Press, 2014.

Kingsolver, Barbara. "A Pure, High Note of Anguish." *Los Angeles Times*, Sept. 23, 2001.

Kitsinger, Otto, et al. "Merle Haggard: The Tally & Capitol Discography 1962–1968." *Untamed Hawk: The Early Recordings of Merle Haggard*. Bear Family Records, 1995.

Kitsinger, Otto, and Richard Weize. "Merle Haggard: The Capitol Discography 1968–1976." *Merle Haggard: The Studio Recordings 1969–1976*. Bear Family Records, 2007.

La Chapelle, Peter. *Proud to Be an Okie: Cultural Politics, Country Music, and Migration to Southern California*. University of California Press, 2007.

Lanham, Tom. "Hag at 70: Country Legend and Working Man's Hero Still Breaking a Sweat." *Paste*, Apr. 2007.

Lewis, Randy. "An Appreciation: Merle Haggard, a Voice of the People." *Los Angeles Times*, Apr. 6, 2016.

Linderman, Lawrence. "Penthouse Interview: Merle Haggard." *Penthouse*, Nov. 1976: 126–128, 178–182.

Logan, Andy. "Around City Hall." *New Yorker*, June 6, 1970: 104–108.

Luvollo, Sam, and Marc Eliot. *Life in the Kornfield: My 25 Years at Hee Haw*. Boulevard Books, 1996.

Malone, Bill C. *Country Music, U.S.A.* 2nd ed. University of Texas Press, 2002.

———. *Don't Get above Your Raisin': Country Music and the Southern Working Class*. University of Illinois Press, 2002.

Marsh, Dave. *The Heart of Rock & Soul: The 1,001 Greatest Singles Ever Made.* Plume, 1989.

———. "The Lonesome Death of Florence Thompson." In *Fortunate Son: The Best of Dave Marsh.* Random House, 1985.

Marsh, Dave, with John Swenson, eds. *The Rolling Stone Record Guide.* Random House/Rolling Stone Press, 1979.

Maslin, Janet. "Down-Home Fare and Police Shows." *New York Times,* Jan. 16, 1981.

Mazor, Barry. *Meeting Jimmie Rodgers: How America's Original Roots Music Hero Changed the Pop Sounds of a Century.* Oxford University Press, 2009.

McCabe, Peter. "A Candid Conversation with Merle Haggard." *Country Music,* Feb. 1974: 90–95.

McCall, Michael. Review of *1996* by Merle Haggard. In *All Music Guide to Country: The Definitive Guide to Country Music,* 2nd ed., 312–313. Backbeat Books, 2003.

McGhee, Heather C. "The Way Out of America's Zero-Sum Thinking on Race and Wealth." *New York Times,* Feb. 13, 2021.

McLenon, Andy, and Grant Alden. "Branded Man." *No Depression,* Nov./Dec. 2003: 99–109.

"Merle Haggard Resting out West." *Kansas City Times,* Nov. 3, 1976.

"Merle Haggard's Farm Aid Train to Cancel." *Tyrone [PA] Herald,* Sept. 14, 1985.

"Merle Haggard Tried Springfield First." *Springfield [MO] Leader and Press,* May 2, 1971.

Millard, Bob. *Country Music: 70 Years of America's Favorite Music.* Harper Perennial, 1993.

Morthland, John. *The Best of Country Music.* Doubleday Dolphin, 1984.

———. Review of *Serving 190 Proof* by Merle Haggard. *Rolling Stone,* Sept. 6, 1979.

———. "Wills Power." *Texas Monthly,* May 2000.

Nash, Alanna. "Merle Haggard." In *Behind Closed Doors: Talking with the Legends of Country Music,* 155–171. Knopf, 1988.

Nelson, Ken. *My First 90 Years Plus 3.* Dorrance Publishing, 2007.

Ochs, Michael. "Merle Haggard: America's Proletarian Poet." *Coast FM & Fine Arts,* June 1970: 22–26.

O'Connor, John. "ABC Huckleberry Finn Marred by Coyness." *New York Times,* Mar. 25, 1975.

"Okie from Muskogee." *Controversy.* Season 1, episode 9. Country Music Television, Sept. 26, 2003.

Oppenheimer, Peer J. "Country Star Merle Haggard: 'Peace of Mind—I Still Haven't Found It!'" *Austin American-Statesman,* May 28, 1972.

Orne, Terry. "Marty Robbins Carries the Ball for Haggard." *Salt Lake Tribune,* Jan. 28, 1979.

Owen, Fuzzy, with Phil Neighbors. *Merle Haggard, Bonnie Owens & Me: Stories from Merle's Best Friend and Manager.* Owen Publications, 2019.

Palmer, Robert. "Riding the Country's Wave of Patriotism?" *New York Times,* May 13, 1981.

Parton, Chris. "Merle Haggard's Last Song Set for Release." *Rolling Stone* online, May 11, 2016.

Patoski, Joe Nick. *Willie Nelson: An Epic Life.* Little, Brown, 2008.

Pearce, Donn. "The Improbable Ballad of Merle Haggard." *Penthouse,* Jan. 1973: 42–44, 125–128, 133.

Perlstein, Rick. *Nixonland: The Rise of a President and the Fracturing of America.* Scribner, 2008.

Peterson, Richard. "Soft Shell vs. Hard Core." In *Creating Country Music: Fabricating Authenticity*, 137–155. University of Chicago Press, 1997.

Pew, Thomas W., Jr. "Route 66: Ghost Road of the Okies." *American Heritage*, Aug. 1977.

Phelan, Nellie. "Merle Who? An Interview with Merle Haggard." *Country Music*, Feb. 1978: 23–24, 27.

Phillips, Kevin. "Revolutionary Music." *Washington Post*, May 6, 1971.

Pikula, Joan. "Haggard's C&W Fame Is Rapidly Spreading." *Asbury Park [NJ] Evening Press*, Sept. 15, 1969.

Powers, Freddy, and Catherine Powers, with Jake Brown. *The Spree of '83*. Waldorf Publishing, 2017.

Price, Robert. *The Bakersfield Sound: How a Generation of Displaced Okies Revolutionized American Music*. Heyday Books, 2018.

———. Liner notes to *Merle Haggard, Original Outlaw*. Time Life/EMI, 2007.

Pugh, Ronnie. *Ernest Tubb: The Texas Troubadour*. Duke University Press, 1996.

Randolph, Ann. "Country Music World Interviews: Merle Haggard." *Country Music World*, Mar./Apr. 1973: 25–29, 44.

Richards, Chris. "For Merle Haggard, Music Is a Life Sentence." *Washington Post*, Dec. 3, 2010.

Roberts, Jeremy. "Inside Merle Haggard's Long-Gestating 'Tribute to the Troubadour' Album." Medium.com, Apr. 5, 2018. Blog.

Rockwell, John. "Haggard's Country Songs Celebrate Common Man." *New York Times*, Apr. 7, 1974.

———. "The Pop Life." *New York Times*, Apr. 5, 1974.

———. "Strong Country Bill Sung at Felt Forum by Merle Haggard." *New York Times*, May 4, 1975.

Roland, Tom. *The Billboard Book of Number One Country Hits: Country Music's Chart-Topping Records, Artists and Songwriters*. Billboard Books, 1991.

———. "Country Icon Merle Haggard Is in a California Hospital for Treatment of a Recurring Bout of Double Pneumonia." *Billboard* online, Mar. 2, 2016.

———. "Merle Haggard Talks Health Scare, Young Fans and Sturgill Simpson: 'He's Got Something.'" *Billboard* online, Aug. 4, 2015.

Rose, Mark. "Merle Haggard: Big Wheels Keep Rollin'." *BAM: The California Music Magazine*, Oct. 24, 1980: 22–25.

Rosen, Jody. "Jody Rosen on the Rise of Bro-Country." *Vulture* online, Aug. 11, 2013.

Rubin, Rachel Lee. *Okie from Muskogee*. Bloomsbury, 2018.

Ruggles, Brock. "Branded Man." *Phoenix New Times*, May 9, 2002.

Russell, Peggy. "A Glimpse of Merle Haggard." *Country Song Roundup*, July 1973.

Sample, Tex. *White Soul: Country Music, the Church, and Working Americans*. Abingdon Press, 1996.

Samuelson, Dave. Liner notes to *Merle Haggard: The Troubadour*. Bear Family Records, 2012.

———. Liner notes to *Old Loves Never Die*. Bear Family Records, 2001.

Samuelson, Dave, and Richard Weize. "Merle Haggard: The MCA Discography." *Merle Haggard: The Troubadour*. Bear Family Records, 2012.

Scherman, Tony. "The Last Roundup." *Atlantic*, Aug. 1996.

Schneckloth, Tim. "Merle Haggard: Country Jazz Messiah." *Downbeat*, May 1980: 16–19.

Scott, Susan. "Merle Haggard: Headin' up the Road…" *Country Song Roundup*, Jan. 1976: 15–19.

Sisk, Eileen. *Buck Owens: The Biography*. Chicago Review Press, 2010.

Small, Christopher. *Music of the Common Tongue: Survival and Celebration in African American Music*. Wesleyan University Press, 1998.

Smith, Lillian. *Killers of the Dream*. Anchor Books, 1963.

Smith, RJ. "Working Man Blues." *Spin*, Nov. 2000: 130–133.

Smucker, Tom. *Why the Beach Boys Matter*. University of Texas Press, 2018.

Spitznagel, Eric. "Merle Haggard Has Some Helpful Prison Advice for Lindsay Lohan." *Vanity Fair* online, July 30, 2010.

Stokes, Geoffrey. "The Counter-Counterculture." In *Rock of Ages: The Rolling Stone History of Rock & Roll*, by Ed Ward, Geoffrey Stokes, and Ken Tucker, 388–402. Rolling Stone Press, 1986.

Svokos, Heather. "Merle Haggard May Have Mellowed a Bit, but Continues to Speak His Mind." *Pop Matters* online, Apr. 28, 2008.

Taylor, Paul S. "What Shall We Do with Them? Address before the Commonwealth Club of California." In *On the Ground in the Thirties*. Peregrine Smith Books, 1983.

Trombley, William. "Admitted Red Fired from UCLA Faculty." *Los Angeles Times*, Sept. 20, 1969.

Troy, Tevi. "When Merle Haggard Played at the Nixon White House." *Observer*, Apr. 7, 2016.

United Press International. "People." *Sandusky [OH] Register*, June 2, 1983.

Vincent, K. Liner notes to *Okie from Muskogee: Recorded "Live" in Muskogee, Oklahoma*. Capitol Records, 1969.

Vinicur, Dale. Liner notes to *Untamed Hawk: The Early Recordings of Merle Haggard*. Bear Family Records, 1995.

Warren, Mike. Review of *It's Christmas, Man!* by Brave Combo. *[Kansas City] New Times*, Dec. 10, 1992.

Weize, Richard. "Bonnie Owens: The Discography, 1953–1971." *Bonnie Owens: Queen of the Coast*. Bear Family Recordings, 2007.

Weize, Richard, et al. "Merle Haggard: The Capitol Discography 1968–1976." *Concepts, Live & the Strangers: Hag, the Capitol Recordings 1968–1976*. Bear Family Records, 2008.

Werner, Craig. *A Change Is Gonna Come: Music, Race & the Soul of America*. University of Michigan Press, 2006.

Whitburn, Joel. *Hot Country Albums, 1964 to 2007*. Record Research Inc., 2008.

———. *Top Country Singles, 1944–2017*. Record Research Inc., 2018.

———. *Top Pop Singles, 1955–2015*. Record Research Inc., 2016.

Whiteside, Jonny. "Merle Haggard's Twin Oracles." *L.A. Weekly*, Oct. 15, 1999.

———. *Ramblin' Rose: The Life and Career of Rose Maddox*. Country Music Foundation Press/Vanderbilt University Press, 1997.

Wildsmith, Steve. "Remembering the Notable, Quotable Merle Haggard." *[TN] Daily Times* online, July 19, 2018.

Williams, Raymond. "Individuals and Societies." In *The Raymond Williams Reader*, edited by John Higgins, 65–83. Blackwell, 2001.

Willis, Ellen. "On the Barricades." *New York Times*, Nov. 8, 1998.

———. "Records, Rock, Etc." *New Yorker*, Feb. 22, 1969: 116–118.

Willman, Chris. *Rednecks and Bluenecks: The Politics of Country Music*. New Press, 2005.

Wolfe, Charles K. Liner notes to *Same Train, a Different Time: A Tribute to Jimmie Rodgers*. Bear Family Records, 1993.

Wolff, Kurt. "Stay a Little Longer." *No Depression*, Nov./Dec. 2000: 74–85.

Wren, Christopher S. "Country Music: The Great White Soul Sound." *Look*, July 13, 1971: 11–13.

———. "Merle Haggard: He Sings for the Folks Who Fought World War II." *Look*, July 13, 1971: 36–41.

Yahr, Emily. "Merle Haggard May Have Hated Modern Country Music, but the Singers Loved Him." *Washington Post*, Apr. 8, 2016.

Zollo, Paul. *Songwriters on Songwriting*. 4th ed. Da Capo Press, 2003.

———. "Story Behind the Song: 'Mama Tried.'" *American Songwriter* online, Jan. 24, 2020.

INDEX

working class, 6, 8, 16, 18, 21, 26, 52, 76, 134–135, 144, 145–146, 158, 182–184, 187, 196, 200, 201, 202, 203, 215–216, 229, 230, 231, 235, 247–248, 249, 250, 256, 264–265, 273, 276–277

Haggard, Merle, albums of: *Amber Waves of Grain*, 249; *Back to the Barrooms*, 224–225; *The Best of Merle Haggard*, 117; *Big City*, 231–233, 234, 244, 249, 262, 267; *The Bluegrass Sessions*, 270; *Blue Jungle*, 258–259; *Branded Man*, 107, 110, 111; *Cabin in the Hills*, 269; *Chicago Wind*, 48, 199, 270, 273; *Chill Factor*, 250, 267; *Christmas Present*, 176, 177–178; *Django and Jimmie* (with Willie Nelson) 272, 277; *Down Every Road: 1962–1994*, 263; *The Epic Collection (Recorded Live)*, 245; *The Fightin' Side of Me*, 63, 64, 141, 154, 159, 165; *5:01 Blues*, 250; *For the Record: 43 Legendary Hits*, 269; *Going Where the Lonely Go*, 244, 249; *Goin' Home for Christmas*, 175, 176–177, 245, 251; *Hag*, 168–171; *Haggard Like Never Before*, 269–270, 277; *Heart to Heart* (with Leon Williams), 208; *I Am What I Am*, 272; *If I Could Only Fly*, 266–268; *If We Make It through December*, 191, 261; *I Love Dixie Blues . . . So I Recorded Live in New Orleans*, 199–202; *I'm a Lonesome Fugitive*, 52, 90–91, 107, 121, 122; *I'm Always on a Mountain When I Fall*, 215–216, 217; *It's All in the Game*, 249; *It's All in the Movies*, 181, 191, 207; *It's Not Love (But It's Not Bad)*, 191; *I Wish I Was Santa Claus*, 175, 176, 178, 270; *Just Between the Two of Us* (with Bonnie Owens), 99; *Keep Movin' On*, 190–191; *Kickin' Out the Footlights . . . Again: Jones Sings Haggard, Haggard Sings Jones* (with George Jones), 27, 270–271; *The Land of Many Churches*, 151,

189–190, 192; *Last of the Breed* (with Willie Nelson and Ray Price), 270; *The Legend of Bonnie and Clyde*, 107, 114, 129; *Let Me Tell You about a Song*, 70, 183, 191, 194–195; *Live at Billy Bob's*, 270; *Mama Tried*, 105, 107, 108, 115; *Merle Haggard Presents His 30th Album*, 48, 190; *Merle Haggard's Christmas Present (Something Old, Something New)*, 174, 176; *My Farewell to Elvis*, 217–218; *My Love Affair with Trains*, 33–34, 181, 191, 206; *1994*, 257–259, 263; *1996*, 262, 263; *Okie from Muskogee: Recorded "Live" in Muskogee, Oklahoma*, 12, 141, 143, 147, 154, 180; *Out among the Stars*, 250; *Pancho & Lefty* (with Willie Nelson), 55, 57, 233, 237–241, 250; *The Peer Sessions*, 268; *A Portrait of Merle Haggard*, 107, 130–131; *Pride in What I Am*, 107, 121, 122, 124; *Rainbow Stew*, 225–226; *Ramblin' Fever*, 216, 217; *Roots, Volume 1*, 45, 46, 268; *The Roots of My Raising*, 27, 191; *Same Train, a Different Time*, 53, 107–108, 117, 121, 123, 124, 151, 165–166, 218, 275; *Seashores of Old Mexico* (with Willie Nelson), 250–251, 272; *Serving 190 Proof*, 218–221; *Sing Me Back Home*, 45, 107, 111, 114, 120, 121; *Someday We'll Look Back*, 24, 171, 190; *Songs for the Mama That Tried*, 28, 226, 269; *Songs I'll Always Sing*, 192–193; *Strangers*, 85, 86, 89, 98; *Swinging Doors and the Bottle Let Me Down*, 86, 121; *A Taste of Yesterday's Wine* (with George Jones), 233, 235–237, 238; *That's the Way Love Goes*, 245, 249; *Timeless* (with Mac Wiseman), 272; *A Tribute to the Best Damn Fiddle Player in the World (Or My Salute to Bob Wills)*, 57, 60, 151, 165–167, 195, 218; *Two Old Friends* (with Alfred E. Brumley Jr.), 269; *Unforgettable*, 270; *Untamed*

Wallace, George, 139, 147, 158, 163

Waltons, The (TV series), 188

Wanted: The Outlaws (album by various artists), 186

Ward, Jerry, 90, 122

Watson, Gene, 94

Waylors, the, 77

Wayne, Bobby, 198

Wayne, John, 120

Weathermen, 143

Webb, Jimmy, 119

welfare, 18, 76, 134, 145–146, 159, 197, 230, 285

Wells, Junior, 94

Wells, Kitty, 97

West, Speedy, 62

West Coast Playboys, 77, 80, 84

western swing, 59, 60, 78, 79, 187

Wheeler, Onie, 115

White, Artie (Blues Boy), 94

White, Clarence, 62

White, Lavelle, 94

White, Tony Joe, 203

Whitefield, Barrence, "Irma Jackson," 260

Whiteside, Jonny, 62

white trash, 21, 22, 265

white working class. *See* working class

Whitley, Keith, 250

Wilco, 67

Wildsmith, Steve, 273

Williams, Hank, 49, 58, 69, 99, 201, 202, 250, 268, 280; Haggard tribute album to, 192; "Long Gone Lonesome Blues," 242

Williams, Hank, Jr., 261, 279; "I'd Rather Be Gone," 120

Williams, Leona Belle Helton, 63, 205–209, 210–211, 214, 219, 223, 236, 239, 245, 247; "The Bull and Beaver," 205; "Country Girl with Hot Pants On," 206; "Get Whatcha Got and Go," 206; *Leona Williams Sings Merle Haggard*, 208–209; "Prisons Aren't Only for Men," 207; "San Quentin," 207; *San Quentin's First Lady*, 207; "Workin' Girl Blues," 207

Williams, Lucinda, 260

Williams, Raymond, 6

Willis, Ellen, 6, 127–128

Willman, Chris, 274

Wills, Bob, 24, 57–60, 62, 126, 151, 165–168, 190, 195, 201, 217, 222, 280; *For the Last Time*, 168; Haggard tribute album to, 57, 60, 165–168; "San Antonio Rose," 57, 59; "Stars and Stripes on Iwo Jima," 159

Wilson, Gretchen, "Politically Uncorrect," 273; "Redneck Woman," 274

Winchell, Walter, 157

Winfrey, Oprah, 284

Wise, Chubby, 165

Wiseman, Mac, 272

Withers, Bill, "Leon on Me," 218

Wizard of Oz, The (film), 32–33

Wonder, Stevie, 186

Woods, Bill, 67, 126

Woodstock, 128

working class, 8, 16, 18, 21, 26, 52, 76, 134–135, 158, 182–184, 187, 196, 200, 201, 202, 203, 215–216, 230, 231, 235, 247–248, 249, 256, 273, 276–277; and Haggard, 6, 182–184, 250; and politics, 35, 144–146, 229; and whites, 144–148, 184, 265

Working Man's Poet: A Tribute to Merle Haggard (album by various artists), 280

World Tomorrow, The (radio show), 140

World Trade Center, 158

World War II, 71, 157, 159, 160, 169, 175

Wren, Christopher, 41, 158, 163

Wright, Johnny, 161; "Hello, Vietnam," 160

Wynette, Tammy, 99, 118, 187, 238, 248, 282; "Stand by Your Man," 123; "(We're Not) The Jet Set," 187

X (band), 250

X Records, 97

Yahr, Emily, 275

Yeary, Mark, 225, 232